Machine Learning for Decision Sciences with Case Studies in Python

Machine Learning for Decision Sciences with Case Studies in Python

S. Sumathi

Suresh V. Rajappa

L. Ashok Kumar

Surekha Paneerselvam

CRC Press
Taylor & Francis Group
Boca Raton London New York

CRC Press is an imprint of the
Taylor & Francis Group, an **informa** business

First edition published 2022
by CRC Press
6000 Broken Sound Parkway NW, Suite 300, Boca Raton, FL 33487-2742

and by CRC Press
2 Park Square, Milton Park, Abingdon, Oxon, OX14 4RN

© 2022 S. Sumathi, Suresh V. Rajappa, L Ashok Kumar and Surekha Paneerselvam

CRC Press is an imprint of Taylor & Francis Group, LLC

ISBN: 978-1-032-19356-4 (hbk)
ISBN: 978-1-032-19357-1 (pbk)
ISBN: 978-1-003-25880-3 (ebk)

DOI: 10.1201/9781003258803

Typeset in Times
by codeMantra

Contents

Preface

Decision science is a set of quantitative tools for informing individual- and population-level decision-making. It includes decision analysis, cost-effectiveness analysis, constrained optimization, risk analysis, and behavioral decision theory. Decision science provides a unique framework for understanding and designing strategies to address such problems by focusing on decisions as the unit of study. Machine learning generates usable models by evaluating a large number of solutions against the given data and selecting the one that best fits the situation. As a result, machine learning can be useful for solving problems that require a lot of human effort. It can efficiently and accurately inform judgments and generate predictions about challenging topics. Insurers may predict likely results of crucial decisions using the Data Science Life Cycle and Decision Science platform, which is powered by machine learning, to achieve optimal decision outcomes. After decisions have been made, the results can be used to inform future decisions. As a result, high-value decision-making is streamlined and repeatable, which benefits both shareholders and policyholders.

Acknowledgment

The authors are always thankful to the Almighty for perseverance and achievements.

The authors owe their gratitude to Shri L. Gopalakrishnan, Managing Trustee, PSG Institutions, and to Dr K. Prakasan, Principal-In-Charge, PSG College of Technology, Coimbatore, India, for their wholehearted cooperation and great encouragement in this successful endeavor.

Dr. Sumathi owes much to her daughter S. Priyanka, who has helped a lot in monopolizing her time on bookwork and substantially realized the responsibility. She feels happy and proud of the steel frame support rendered by her husband, Mr. Sai Vadivel. Dr. Sumathi would like to extend wholehearted thanks to her parents who have reduced the family commitments and their constant support. She is greatly thankful to her brother Mr. M.S. Karthikeyan who has always been a "stimulator" for her progress. She is thankful to her parents-in-law for their great moral support.

Dr. Suresh V. Rajappa would like to thank his wife, Mrs. Padmini Govindarajan, for her unconditional support and time whenever needed during the writing of the book. Dr. Suresh also thanks his twin daughters Ms. Dharshini Suresh and Ms. Varshini Suresh for their continued encouragement for the book. He would also like to extend his gratitude to his present and former colleagues at KPMG, especially Mr. Vimal Kumar Mehta for his advice. Dr. Suresh also thanks Juan José Chacón-Quirós, CEO, Establishment Labs and Pratip Dastidar, Global Head of Operations, Establishment Labs for continuous encouragement. Finally, Dr. Suresh thanks Mr. Srihari Govindarajan, Principal at Kloudlogic Inc., for helping him to proofread the materials for this book and keeping his sanity.

Dr. L. Ashok Kumar would like to take this opportunity to acknowledge those people who helped me in completing this book. I am thankful to all my research scholars and students who are doing their projects and research work with me. But the writing of this book is possible mainly because of the support of my family members, parents, and sisters. Most importantly, I am very grateful to my wife, Y. Uma Maheswari, for her constant support during the writing. Without her, all these things would not be possible. I would like to express my special gratitude to my daughter, A.K. Sangamithra, for her smiling face and support. I would like to dedicate this work to her.

Dr. Surekha Paneerselvam would like to thank her parents, husband Mr. S. Srinivasan, and daughter Saisusritha who shouldered a lot of extra responsibilities during the months and years spent in writing this book. They did this with a long-term vision, depth of character, and positive outlook that are truly befitting of their name. Dr. Surekha offers her humble pranams at the lotus feet of Amma, Mata *Amritanandamayi.*

The authors wish to thank all their friends, colleagues, and research assistants who have been with them in all their endeavors with their excellent, unforgettable help and assistance in the successful execution of the work.

About the Authors

Dr. S. Sumathi is working as a Professor in the Department of Electrical and Electronics Engineering, PSG College of Technology, Coimbatore, with teaching and research experience of 30 years. Her research interests include neural networks, fuzzy systems and genetic algorithms, pattern recognition and classification, data warehousing and data mining, operating systems, and parallel computing. She is the author of more than 40 papers in refereed journals and international conferences. She has authored books with reputed publishers such as Springer and CRC Press.

Dr. L. Ashok Kumar was a Postdoctoral Research Fellow from San Diego State University, California. He is a recipient of the BHAVAN Fellowship from the Indo-US Science and Technology Forum and SYST Fellowship from DST, Govt. of India. His current research focuses on integration of renewable energy systems in the smart grid and wearable electronics. He has 3 years of industrial experience and 19 years of academic and research experience. He has published 167 technical papers in international and national journals and presented 157 papers in national and international conferences. He has authored ten books with leading publishers such as CRC, Springer, and Elsevier. He has completed 26 Government-of-India-funded projects, and currently, 7 projects are in progress.

Dr. Suresh V. Rajappa, PhD, PMP, MBA, is seasoned senior IT management consulting professional with 25 years' experience leading large global IT programs and projects in IT strategy, finance IT (Fintech) transformation strategy, BI, and data warehousing/data analytics and management for multiple Fortune 100 clients across diverse industries, generating millions of dollars to top and bottom lines. Successful professional in recruiting and leading onshore/offshore cross-cultural teams to deliver complex enterprise-wide solutions within tight deadlines and budgets. Highly effective in breaking down strategic program/project initiatives into tactical plans and processes to achieve aggressive customer goals. Excelled at leveraging strategic partnerships, global resources, process improvements, and best practices to maximize project delivery performance and ROI. He is an inspirational, solution-focused leader with exceptional ability managing multimillion-dollar P&Ls/budgets and change management initiatives. As an adjunct professor, Dr. Suresh V. Rajappa teaches data science for graduate and doctoral students at PSG College of Technology. His industry specializations include utility, finance (banking and insurance), and hi-tech manufacturing. He is a frequent speaker at Microsoft PASS conferences and SAP Financials and SAP TechEd conferences on data analytics-related topics. He also teaches data analytics and IT project management for undergraduate- and graduate-level students. He is also keynote speaker in the International Conference on Artificial Intelligence, Smart Grid and Smart City Applications.

Dr. Surekha Paneerselvam is an Assistant Professor (Sr. Gr) in the Department of Electrical and Electronics Engineering, Amrita School of Engineering, Amrita Vishwa Vidyapeetham, Bengaluru, India, with 20 years of experience in teaching, industry, and research. She has published 35 papers in international and national journals and conferences. She has authored seven books with leading publishers such as CRC Press and Springer. Her research interests include control systems, computational intelligence, machine learning, signal and image processing, embedded systems, real-time operating systems, and virtual instrumentation.

Introduction

Chapter 1 describes the basic concepts of data science, and structural patterns involved in decision sciences. The relation between machine learning and statistics is highlighted with an introduction to data science life cycle. The key role of a data scientist is briefed, and the real-world applications in these areas are emphasized.

In Chapter 2, the need for Python programming in machine learning, basics of Python programming, and data structures and their implementation using Python are presented. In addition, we introduce the readers to NumPy basics, Matplotlib basics, Pandas basics, and the computational complexity involved in programming using Python. The chapter also provides programming examples for beginners using Python. A few real-world examples are also programmed so that the reader will understand implementation in Python with NumPy, Pandas, and Matplotlib libraries.

Chapter 3 focuses on the phases involved in the data analytics life cycle for machine learning. The aspects involved in data discovery, data preparation and exploratory data analysis, model planning, and model building are delineated. The reader is also exposed to the process of communicating results and optimizing and operationalizing the models. The roles and responsibilities of the members involved throughout the phases of data analytics life cycle are explained in detail.

Chapter 4 gives an insight into the basics of unsupervised learning, distance measures, the concept of clustering, the most commonly used clustering algorithms, their applications to solve problems in real time, and their limitations.

In Chapter 5, the essential ideas behind all supervised algorithms in machine learning are discussed. The mathematical concept behind supervised algorithm with worked examples and implementation using Python is given in detail. Supervised algorithm for regression problem is well explained in this chapter with Python implementation.

The supervised learning method learns from the labeled data. Logistic regression, decision tree, and support vector machine are the various supervised learning classification algorithms widely used. In Chapter 6, a detailed description of these algorithms, their mathematical modeling, merits and demerits, solved examples, and real-world applications are provided with step-by-step implementation in Python.

Chapter 7 enlightens an analysis on feature engineering and reviews the basic requirements for features selection, wrapper models, and factor analysis with relevant Python examples.

In Chapter 8, we discuss the goal-oriented learning based on reinforcement learning, and how reinforcement learning (RL) varies when compared with other machine learning algorithms. The elements of RL such as agent, policy function, and value function are explained in detail, followed by the RL algorithms the Markov decision process (MDP) and dynamic programming (DP). The value functions, policy evaluation, and improvements are covered along with implementation of MDP and DP in Python.

Chapter 9 highlights a few applications of machine learning in various industries to solve problems where traditional programming cannot accommodate the reasoning for many combinations. The first use case, Retail Price Optimization Using the Price Elasticity of Demand Method, identifies the exact price at which the most profit may be made. We present the application based on a customer dataset in a supermarket in use case 2 – Market Basket Analysis – highlighting association rule mining. Use case 3 – Sales Prediction of a Retailer – shows how to create a machine learning model and determine the sales of each product at a certain store. In use case 4, the cost of insurance claims is predicted for a property and casualty (P&C) insurance company. This case study shows how to clean data, preprocess data, and deal with outliers.

1 Introduction

LEARNING OBJECTIVES

At the end of this chapter, the reader will be able to

- Understand the need for data science and machine learning (ML) in a real-world scenario.
- Appreciate the fundamentals of ML and deep learning.
- Describe structural patterns and understand their variants.
- Know the key roles of a data scientist for solving practical problems.
- Identify the real-world application areas of ML models.

1.1 INTRODUCTION TO DATA SCIENCE

The process of considering the algorithm and coding it with the help of a programming language can be executed by the computer. IT world has made people's life easier by providing helpful software. A design pattern provides a general refusal solution to the common problems that usually occur in software design. The patterns identify the connections between classes and objects. The primary purpose of patterns is to boost the performance of the development process. This chapter will understand the need for data science and machine learning (ML) in real-world scenarios, highlight the basics of ML and deep learning (DL), know how to describe structural patterns, and understand their variants. In addition, a detailed description of the key role of a data scientist in solving real-world applications is highlighted. Several areas in which ML algorithms are applied are also illustrated.

Data science is a part of software engineering in which we study where the information comes from and its organization. It represents how we can turn the valuable resources in the initialization of any business and the information technology strategies. Data science allows mining a large amount of data that helps to identify the patterns for any organization's efficiencies. There are some fields of data science: statistics, disciplines of computer science, data visualization, and data mining. Data scientists possess a combination of ML and analytic and statistical skills and experience in coding and algorithms. Data science is everywhere in today's world. Let's imagine that you are traveling to a new city. The user can search for some tourist places, restaurants, parks, hotels, etc., with just one click. How is this possible? It's the data science that saves and displays the results on your phone screen in a few seconds.

1.1.1 MATHEMATICS

Mathematics is everywhere around us, from counting money, temperature calculation, shapes, etc. Data science and mathematics have a strong relation in all the decision-making processes like predicting the routes and searching for the best possible answer. All these tasks are incomplete without mathematics. Data science uses ML algorithms for decision-making processes.

1.1.2 STATISTICS

Data science is nothing without statistics, and data scientists require a graphical representation of the data with less theory. Business providers prefer data visualization like a bar chart as it becomes easier to evaluate the data and gain more information.

1.2   DESCRIBING STRUCTURAL PATTERNS

Creating an application or software is a complex task. It becomes more difficult if not created with proper flow or patterns – software engineers use some patterns to symbolize their application patterns to solve many problems. The selection of patterns depends upon the application requirements. Design patterns boost the development process; structural patterns are all about the classes and their instances creation. For example, to create a website that stores student records, the class will be Student and will have attributes like student name, age, father's name, and address.

1.2.1   Uses of Structural Patterns

Structural patterns play an essential role in effectively solving the problems, as it covers the central concept of object-oriented programming, i.e., classes and their inheritance. These patterns allow classes to work together as a group. With the help of structural patterns, software engineers write less source code as most of the functions are extracted from inherited classes. Some of the commonly used design patterns are listed below:

- **Adapter design pattern**

    Adapter patterns create a connection between interfaces of different classes; let's take the real-life example; we have two applications created with two different programming languages. Now, you want to compile both applications on a single platform. The adapter works here as it changes the interface of one instance so that other instances can easily understand it. The adapter hides all the complex conversions.
- **Bridge design pattern**

    The bridge design pattern splits the abstraction from its implementation. Let's take the example of the main socket, which controls the lights, fan, TV, and AC of the house. This main socket acts as a bridge between the house's sub-switches that control turning ON/ OFF of the utilities.
- **Composite design pattern**

    Composite design patterns are used where a group of identical instances is considered as one instance. This pattern creates a hierarchal structure of similar objects. For example, the composite pattern creates a class that includes the faction of its objects.

    Let's understand the pattern with an example of grouping the teachers into different departments, classes will contain all the details of a teacher like a name, salary, address, and department, and *composite teacher* class will use teacher class to add teachers in a different department and print the teachers.
- **Decorator design pattern**

    Decorator design patterns are used whenever new functions are needed to be added to existing objects without changing the entire structure of the class. Decorator design pattern creates a new class that abstracts the original class and provides the newly added functionalities. Let's discuss an example of a decorator design pattern for a clearer understanding. Suppose we need to develop an online ordering system of a well-known burger restaurant that takes all requirements from a customer like what kind of bun, patty, and cheese they need in the burger and according to the requirement estimate the burger price.

    Since customer customization may vary from customer to customer, creating classes for each type of customization will be a difficult task. Here we can create a decorator pattern class, which will contain all the information to customize the burger, like adding extra cheese, extra patty etc. The main class will be the burger with the regular base price. By using a decorator class, the burger class can be extended and the price can be added according to the customization.

- **Façade design pattern**

  Façade design patterns act like abstraction, which conceals all the inner complex details of the application and provides a simple interface to the client to access the applications. Let us consider an example of a grocery shop, which is equipped with loads of items. When a customer visits the shop for the first time, he is unable to search and find the items he wishes to purchase. So he gives a list to the shopkeeper and the shopkeeper gives the customer all the required items. This is an example of Facade design pattern.

- **Flyweight design pattern**

  Flyweight design patterns, as the name implies, are patterns that fly away from the weight, i.e., a memory from the application. It reduces the objects from the source code to release the memory and boosts the performance. Flyweight design can be called code optimization. Flyweight searches the objects that are similar and use them. In case no match is found, it creates a new object. Improving system performance is a non-functional and essential requirement of software as it affects its appearance. Suppose we have an application running too slow due to lines and lines of code written and wastage of cache; now, flyweight design patterns work here. It will eliminate all the similar objects that are created and waste memory.

- **Private class**

  This type of pattern is used for security purposes where data are crucial. Create a private class and store the data, which will be in the same state throughout the code. All variables defined in the private class are only accessible within its class. To access the private class attributes, you need to create their getters and setters. The private class is used where information needs to be hidden from the outside world and only displayed to you.

- **Proxy**

  Proxy is all about providing access. In proxy design patterns, a class is created, which represents the functionality of other classes. Let's take the example of a credit card that acts as a proxy and contains all your bank account amounts.

1.3   MACHINE LEARNING AND STATISTICS

ML can forecast better and more accurate output. It builds the algorithms that use the input data statistics to predict the output. All social media websites use ML to display the data on the feed. The procedure of ML involves searching through data to look for patterns and program them accordingly. Some ML examples include ads displayed as a suggestion and fraud detection. Some of the ML methods are as follows:

Supervised machine learning algorithm

Supervised learning deals with the known and categorizes data. It can classify uncategorized data also. In supervised learning, a sample set contains input data with desired output data. Based on this new test, data can easily be categorized. For example, an application identifies the animal that is either an herbivore, a carnivore, or an omnivore animal. Using supervised learning, it already knew the classification of the animal. Now, whenever a new animal is entered into the system as an input, the system will automatically predict its category.

Unsupervised machine learning algorithm

In the unsupervised learning sample set, data are unknown and unlabeled. The data cannot be implemented directly as we are unaware of the outputs. It simply works on finding the similarities between the data and categorizes them as one. For example, categorize the customer based on which product they purchase, and based on a similar product, we can categorize customers.

Semi-supervised machine learning algorithm

Semi-supervised learning is the mixture of supervised and unsupervised learning as its dataset contains categorized and uncategorized data. The aim is to predict the new data that are more effective and accurate than the output data given by the user. For example, you wish to buy a product and watch ads related to the product, and suddenly, you want to review the same product. Though the product is from a different company, the categorized data would be the basic ad released by the company.

Reinforcement machine learning algorithm

In reinforcement learning, the machine does not learn from classified data; instead it learns from its experience and prediction, an agent takes all the actions (robotic avatar), finds all possible scenarios and fits in the best solution. Games such as hangman is the best example of reinforcement learning algorithm. Statistics is a representation of data, hypothesis, etc. It's the correlation between the points, invariable and multivariable.

Statistics types are as follows:

Forecasting continuous variable: If a variable can adapt value between minimum and maximum, then it is called continuous variable, for example, weight and age. It may be deterministic or probabilistic. A deterministic result can be compared and evaluated with respective observations. Probabilistic results are in the form of distribution.

Regression: It deals with the relationship between predictor and outcome variables. It analyzes the results based on predictive analysis and modeling. Let's take the example of dieting apps that predict the diet schedule based on your daily food routine, weight, and height.

Classification: It's the process of grouping the data on the basis of similar categories. For example, classify animals based on their habitats.

ML and statistics are two different methodologies, but how are they similar? The similarity between both of them is the prediction from the data. The primary difference between ML and statistics is manipulating the data; ML is simply working out the data using algorithms, whereas statistics is just mathematics in finding the patterns from the data.

1.4 RELATION BETWEEN ARTIFICIAL INTELLIGENCE, MACHINE LEARNING, NEURAL NETWORKS, AND DEEP LEARNING

There is always a debate among researchers and beginners about artificial intelligence (AI), ML, neural networks (NNs), and DL. Some of the popular Google search questions are "Are AI and ML different?", "Are ML and DL the same?", "How is NN related to ML and DL?", etc. Data scientists have come up with a clear definition for these terms:

Artificial intelligence (AI), like mathematics and biology, is a science. It researches how to create intelligent programs and machines that can solve issues creatively, which has historically been considered a human right.

Machine learning (ML) is a subcategory of AI that allows systems to learn and improve independently without being explicitly programmed. Different learning algorithms based on different architectures (e.g., **NNs**) are used in ML to address problems.

Deep learning (DL), also known as deep neural learning, is a type of ML that employs NNs to assess various elements with a structure similar to that of the human nervous system.

IBM data scientists illustrate the relation between AI, ML, NN, and DL through simple nesting dolls. An illustration is given in the figure to represent how each paradigm is a subset of the previous paradigm. In other words, ML is a subset of AI. For example, the foundation of DL techniques is NN, which is a subset of ML. In practice, the number of hidden layers in a NN determines the architecture of a DL algorithm (Figure 1.1).

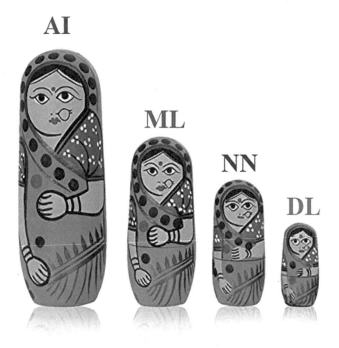

FIGURE 1.1   AI vs. ML vs. NN vs. DL analogous to a nesting doll.

AI is a discipline of computer science that teaches machines to think and function in the same way that people do. DL is a branch of AI that processes and manipulates data by mimicking the human brain's working pattern. For example, the NN is used in DL to predict output patterns. Let's look at the shortest route computation application as an illustration of how DL works. When we hurry and want to get to our end destination as soon as possible, we look for a shorter path.

The user will be asked to provide the following system input:

* Place to begin
* Destination

As previously said, DL is based on NNs, which have nodes similar to interconnected neurons. The input, hidden, and output layers are the three layers that make up a neuron. The input layer contains the records entered by the user, such as the beginning place and destination. The hidden layer contains all the calculations and implementation, such as calculating the shortest path that covers the least amount of time and kilometers based on the user's starting location and destination. There can be one or several hidden layers. Here are some DL implementations that feature more than one hidden layer. The final user output is contained in the output layer. In other words, it will show the user the optimized shortest route.

AI, DL, and ML all have one thing in common: They all use massive data and modern computer languages to anticipate outcomes. DL is the interrelationship between the three. ML is a subset of AI, and AI is a subset of ML.

So, as the figure suggests, AI is a broad concept that first exploded in the late 1950s, causing a significant shift in the data science industry. Later, in the late 1980s, ML was introduced, which improved AI features. Finally, in the late 1990s, DL was introduced, which combines AI and ML (Figure 1.2).

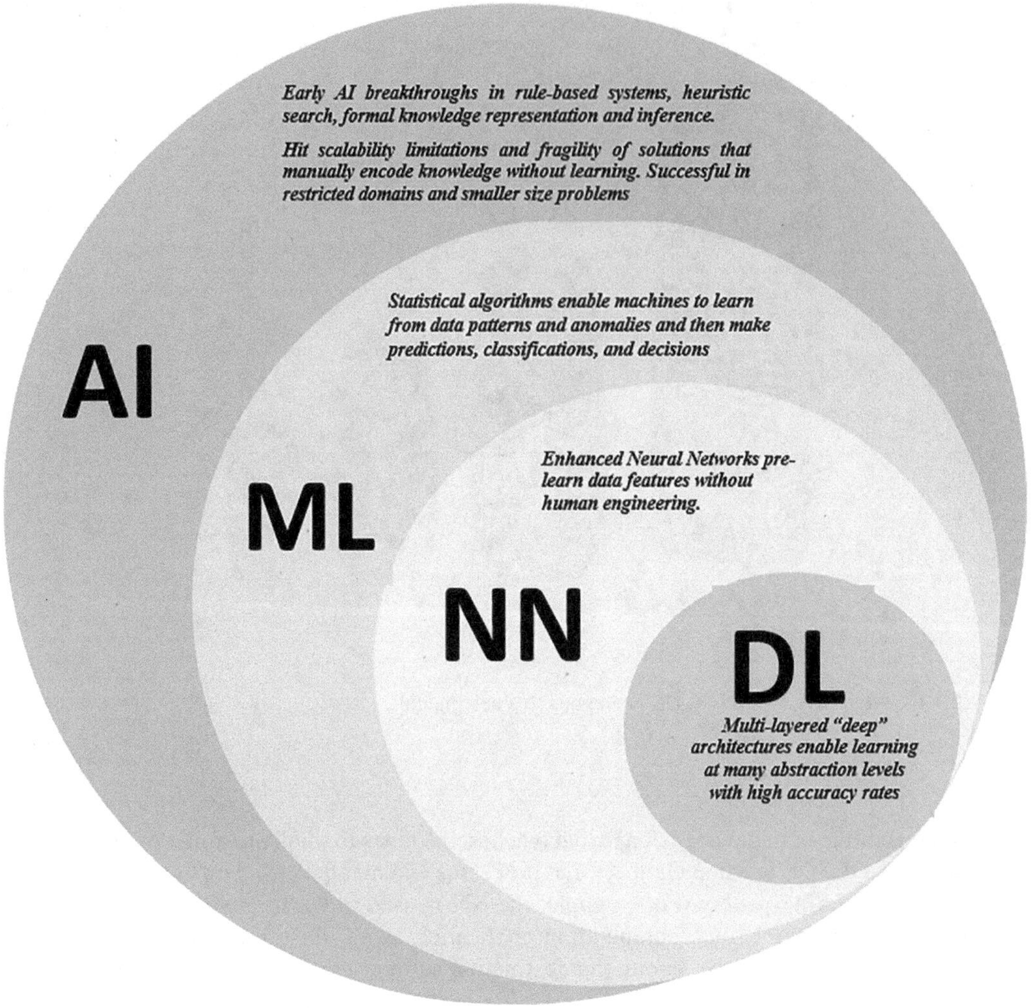

Early AI breakthroughs in rule-based systems, heuristic search, formal knowledge representation and inference.

Hit scalability limitations and fragility of solutions that manually encode knowledge without learning. Successful in restricted domains and smaller size problems

Statistical algorithms enable machines to learn from data patterns and anomalies and then make predictions, classifications, and decisions

Enhanced Neural Networks pre-learn data features without human engineering.

AI

ML

NN

DL

Multi-layered "deep" architectures enable learning at many abstraction levels with high accuracy rates

FIGURE 1.2   AI vs ML vs NN vs DL.

1.5   DATA SCIENCE LIFE CYCLE

Collection of data manipulates and analyzes the data and shows a meaningful result. All these processes are complex and lengthy. The Data scientists require a proper flow or cycle to perform the data science life cycle tasks. On the other hand, working with big data is an easy task; data scientist uses a proper workflow for the result. The data science life cycle consists of six phases (Figure 1.3):

- Discovery
- Data preparation
- Model planning
- Model building
- Communicate results
- Operationalize

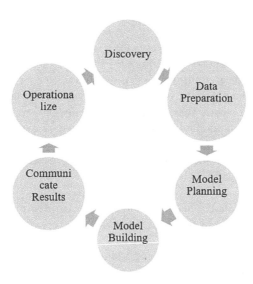

FIGURE 1.3   Phases of data science life cycle.

- **Discovery**

    Before starting the project, having a strong command of the background of the project is essential. It's essential to have all the questions clear at the start. Gather all the requirements needed during the project. A data scientist must have a question/answer session with clients for a better understanding of requirements. Quick review on the history of company and project whether the similar project has been done in the past for reference.

- **Data preparation**

    This step plays a critical and time-consuming role in the life cycle; this phase acts as a filtration process of data. In this step, all the cleaning and elimination of missing attributes are done. Why is the phase time-consuming? When we talk about big data, it can be in terabytes or more than that. Cleaning a large amount of data requires hundreds of scenarios. Let's take the example of variable "area," which has the data type integer. All the records are in integer except one record, which is in decimal. The integer data type cannot contain a decimal value; here, you need to eliminate that particular record.

- **Model planning**

    In this phase, you need to select the ML model for your project, which algorithm needs to be applied, and select the mathematical approach which will give the best possible outcome.

- **Model building**

    Once the model is finalized and created just codes, the most commonly used language is Python. As soon as the project is ready, we deploy the system and share it with a customer. In this way, QA is done by the client itself. Any changes at the client end are urgently taken up and resolved.

- **Communicate results**

    The client should have a clearer understanding of the model and result, which is very difficult as the client has no understanding of data science. Therefore, model interfaces should be transparent and interpretable as it will become easier for the client to absorb them.

- **Operationalize**

    The final step is where documentation and maintenance of the project are done. Documentation will help the client to understand the project and run it efficiently.

1.6   KEY ROLE OF DATA SCIENTIST

The activities the data scientists do are arranging the appropriate data and selecting models to meet the application needs. Data scientists are responsible for managing and presenting accurate data. Data scientist plays a vital role as all the business is depending on data analysis and data modeling.

The primary role of a data scientist is to investigate and manipulate the data in meaningful aspects and solve diverse problems. They have core knowledge of computer science, ML, big data, statistics, and mathematics. In addition, data scientists have core expertise in different programming languages like Java and Python. A data scientist's work starts with collecting, analyzing, and concluding a final result based on the decision-making process. Scientists also work on big data.

There are two types of big data:

- **Saturated data:** The data are mainly in an organized, sorted manner, for example, data gathered from devices like biometric devices, face detection devices, and longitudes and latitudes of different locations.
- **Unsaturated data:** The data are scattered and unorganized, which need to be organized before further processing. E.g., social media adds data, client feedback data, emails, letters, posts all are unsaturated data.

Data scientists manage these types of data. Below are some application examples on which data scientists work:

- Fraud detection applications
- Predictable applications
- Cost estimation applications
- Search engines

1.6.1   DIFFERENCE BETWEEN DATA SCIENTIST AND MACHINE LEARNING ENGINEER

A data scientist is responsible for the evaluation and classification of the data according to the business requirements. Whenever a problem needs to be solved based on data, at this point, data scientist plays their role. Data scientists analyze the data using statistical methods and create charts and graphs to understand the result better. On the other hand, ML engineers use algorithms to solve their problems. They develop programs that control robots and computer machines. They implement or create new models for better predictive results.

1.7   REAL-WORLD EXAMPLES

There is a wide range of application areas where AI, ML, and DL are gaining popularity. Some of the common areas that find the vast application of these domains are illustrated below:

Check deposit apps

Whether the business is small or large, AI is present in every field. AI helps in all cash management processes. People feel odium going to the bank and standing in the enormous queue for check deposits. AI had solved this problem. Check deposit applications allow the customer to automate the entire transaction process. AI observed the transaction patterns and saved them in the database now if any unusual step is identified in a transaction. It is considered fraud.

Google translator

Google translator uses an artificial neural network. It converts a sentence of one language into another language in just a few seconds. It works on the same pattern identification.

Patterns are saved in the database whenever a new word system matches the patterns from the history and concludes the translation.

Google Maps

Google Maps use AI tools for the navigation and calculation of the shortest route. So whenever you are lost or at some new place, you google the location, and it displays the navigation in just a few seconds. How this is possible? It's just because of AI.

Online shopping recommendation

Whenever you search for an item on a search engine, it is saved as a history. As per your search, next time, you will be displayed recommended ads. How is this possible? It's because of AI. Same with online shopping, whenever you purchase an item from an online store, you start getting suggestions related to the same product and your interests.

Rideshare applications

The rideshare application uses a ML technique to predict the ride fare. So whenever you book a ride, all the rides close to your current location are displayed on the screen and associated estimated costs for your destination. How is this possible? It's because of ML.

1.8 USE CASES

Following are the use cases of industries that use ML:

1.8.1 FINANCIAL AND INSURANCE INDUSTRIES

1.8.1.1 Fraud Mitigation

Many organizations give less importance to fraud detection; as a result, they experience significant losses.

1.8.1.1.1 How Can We Identify Fraud?

There are various frauds and threats taking place in almost every industry. The primary and most challenging step is to identify how fraud took place. Fraud can occur inside or outside the company. Fraud inside the company can occur like a company employee changing bank information without the permission of an authorized person. In the same manner, outside fraud can be like hacking websites or credit card fraud. In either case, to get rid of such kinds of fraud, data science helps here. Using predictive data science methodology, this issue can be overcome.

1.8.1.1.2 Machine Learning for Fraud Detection

Nowadays, ML is used in every field. ML algorithms identify the patterns with the help of data. It combines the data, relate them together, and concludes the fraud before something big happens. ML algorithms find the connection relation between locations and products and map them to people connected to that particular field. This approach of ML is convenient as it connects the data with all the individuals related to the fields.

1.8.1.1.3 Fraud Detection in Insurance Industries

Insurance industries are all about making a relationship with clients. However, it is next to impossible to keep the authenticity and verify each customer's information, which leads to data privacy issues.

These problems can be overcome by implementing a data analysis and ingestion platform, which makes data collaboration possible, checks transactions, and claims inappropriate information across insurance products. This solution identifies the unusual information about the insurer.

1.8.1.1.4 Fraud Detection in Financial Industries

The banking industry relies on data that need to be captured and preserved.. 14ike customer service calls, transactions etc. This is nearly impossible to keep the record, keep track, and analyze the data.

Fraud detections may occur in many forms including credit / debit card fraud, application fraud, and account take overs. To overcome this banking frauds, business providers use pattern analysis, which helps to analyze the data and build fraud prevention systems that identify unusual transactions taking place.

1.8.1.2   Personalized Pricing

1.8.1.2.1   What Is Personalized Pricing?

Personalized pricing is where retailers already know about customers, and prices vary from customer to customer, which depends on characteristics and behavior. Let's take the example of a shop market where retailers sell the same item at different prices to different customers. The customers who stay long-term, keep purchasing the items that retailers offer a special discount..

1.8.1.2.2   How Personalized Pricing Works?

As defined earlier, the pricing varies from customer to customer. This is because customers are categorized into different groups, and each group has a different price. Whenever a new or old customer arrives, the purchase system matches the customer with the most suitable group depending on their specifications and past visits. Accordingly, the prices are offered.

Let's take a hotel management system, for example, and their prices depend on the weather conditions and vacations. Whenever there are winters with snowfall, hotels' pricing is high due to the season. In the same off-season, hotels offer a special discount to their customers.

1.8.1.2.3   Client Response on Customized Pricing

No one agrees on paying more when someone is paying less. When a customer came to knew about customized pricing, majority of customers were loud and not satisfied. Even people who paid less for the product raised the objection. As per their understanding, companies are offering fewer prices to customers who don't want the product to attract them. The customer did not know it's legal to charge different prices to different customers.

1.8.1.3   AML – Anti-Money Laundering

Anti-money laundering refers to the laws and procedures that identify the criminals who show illegally obtained money as legal income.

1.8.1.3.1   How AML Works?

AML targets unlawful activities, including business activities, bank details, trading goods, drug smuggling, and taking money in large amounts to other countries.

All these activities are inspected by police officers who are hired for these works. They need to keep records of all the suspicious activities going around.

1.8.1.3.2   Machine Learning in Anti-money Laundering

To detect the criminal, it's essential to keep a record of every step taken. Manually, it's next to impossible. ML helps here; many models can be implemented to catch the criminal.

Anti-laundering software is built using ML and AI, and this software can learn and gain information from historical data. For example, discover hidden patterns, and identify the connection and relationship between the data. On the other hand, detect and predict the auspicious event taking place. The software decreases the risk of false alarms and predictions.

AI-based **analytical engine** helps to discover money laundering activities. It monitors all the banking activities like transferring money, payments, purchases, and investments; social media activities are also monitored to keep track of the extracurricular activities performed by the suspect.

The engine uses supervised and unsupervised learning techniques to discover irregularity taken place.

1.8.2 Utility Industries

1.8.2.1 Smart Meter and Smart Grid

Smart grid is the digital technology that allows communication between the utility and its customers; it controls energy consumption. Some of the smart grids are smart meters, smart appliances, etc.

Smart meters are advanced meters that give statistical information about the electricity that has been used; it tells the cost monthly/daily/hourly as per the usage. All the information is displayed on the digital screen.

1.8.2.1.1 Machine Learning in Smart Meters and Grid

The ML technique cuts the cost, decreases wastage, and improves convenience. Energy optimization is done based on preferences like the necessary appliances that need to be ON (AC, TV, washing machine, etc.). Based on historical data and preferences, smart meters work using analytical models.

It analyzes the house's resident profile and energy profile; then, as per the collected data, resident profile and energy consumptions are predicted. Now, based on the forecasted energy consumption, solar energy is fitted on an additional electricity power grid to reduce the main electricity power grid demand.

1.8.2.2 Manage disaster and Outages

Electricity utility companies find it a difficult job to manage and plan natural disasters. In addition, restoration of power in a disaster is a hazardous job. Let's take the example of the thunderstorm that destroys the trees and power lines that affect the electricity supply in the affected areas.

Due to significant storms/hurricanes in a city, people face 10–15 days of an electricity outage, and it becomes challenging to survive. AI cuts the duration to approx 4 days by using a prediction tool that detects the areas that will be affected after the disaster.

A predictive and data-driven approach will allow operational power to communicate with emergency service for instant recovery quickly. It can also control and analyze the historical data to improve its effectiveness.

AI had taken control over the disaster like earthquakes. It stores the information about the building constructions like soil and bricks used to identify which building will be effective in case of an earthquake.

1.8.2.3 Compliance

Utility companies' business flow differs from normal ones, as they do not buy the product and sell it to customers at a higher price. In utilities, prices are fixed by the government (or related public utility commissions – PUCs), which everyone has followed.

The utility industry is under extraordinary pressure from aging infrastructure and rapidly shifting customers and fulfilling their demands.

A utility can meet changing dynamics by applying AI; the first step is to improve utility programs and increase customer engagement and then enhance the customer experience using an AI-enabled digital experience that delivers real-time and secure information on mobile.

1.8.3 Oil and Gas Industries

1.8.3.1 Manage Exponential Growth

Oil has been one of the most demanding resources for decades. Oil providers cover half of the world's energy. Oil has been used everywhere, from vehicles to industries.

Since the business is vast, it needs to be controlled and managed correctly. The oil and gas industry is divided into different sectors, and AI technology can be applied differently. AI can help in lowering the cost and making the appropriate decision.

Using AI, the industry is applying new technology to gain more profit with a low margin. With the help of AI sensors, companies can keep a record of failures.

The companies that locate and extract oil and natural gas require a large amount of machinery and workers, increasing cost. We can reduce the cost by using AI sensors to control a real-time system and monitor data collection.

The companies that store, process, and deliver the oil and gas to providers also use AI for forecasting and measuring the optimization for better decision-making, which enhances the performance.

AI is growing day by day and increasing the efficiency and cost-effectiveness in the oil and gas industries.

1.8.3.2 3D Seismic Imaging and Kirchhoff

3D seismic is a tool that identifies crude oil and natural gas with the help of sound waves of rock underground. Seismologist uses ultrasensitive devices to record the sound of rock.

1.8.3.2.1 How Are the Seismic Data Collected?

There are two types of data recordings:

Passive source: They are generated by the movement of the earth. Humans are unable to feel as they produce significantly less vibration.
Active source: The data are gained by sending vibrations to the earth.

1.8.3.2.2 How Do AI and Machine Learning Work Here?

Using ML algorithms, the company can group oil and gas fields, which are implemented to predict and implement the preservation of pumps, trackers, turbines, etc. In addition, DL and ML techniques like image processing, forecasting methods, and analytical tools are implemented.

1.8.3.3 Rapidly Process and Display Seismic Data

ML systems automatically collect the data and identify the relation between them. Firstly, ML identifies all the data patterns, which may include some missing traces. It analyzes the data and identifies the hidden relationship between them. Now, using the known data, it will identify the missing traces for another set of input data.

This method only relies on its experience, i.e., learned and concluded from the identified dataset. It reduces the cost and time wasted in identifying the missing traces.

1.8.4 E-COMMERCE AND HI-TECH INDUSTRIES

1.8.4.1 Association and Complementary Products

Nowadays, everything is associated with the Internet, whether the purchase of items, selling, or studying. Most of the e-commerce business providers are looking for doing business and selling goods online. These companies try selling their products by promotion, displaying ads, and marketing. AI plays its role by creating a recommendation system that uses complementarity and similarity among goods and offers the best deal per customer needs and wants.

Recommendation systems are designed based on association. Therefore, they give importance to user interests and recommend only the products users are interested in.

Another critical factor is complementary association; it is applied in almost every field of e-commerce, where complementary products are offered to the customer. To increase the system's accuracy, users are offered suggestions.

1.8.4.2 Cross-Channel Analytics

Cross-channel analytics is a marketing intelligence technique that allows data from different platforms, including ads, promotion, and presenting it on a single platform.

It understands users' behavior to narrow downwhat sort of ads, products are popular among them. In an e-commerce website, data analysts investigate and find the paths and links created. These paths will help in making it possible for future marketing.

1.8.4.3 Event analytics

AI and ML are everywhere and have become popular due to their approach to solving problems, algorithms, and predictive models.

Analytics plays a vital role in a powerful AI system. The organization that uses a large amount of data collection and integrations and has mature model analytics plays its part here.

It has been identified that the business providers who are willing to opt for AI techniques integrate the data and functionality into their core system. An enterprise-wide strategy on data standards can help in analytics and ML practice.

SUMMARY

Design patterns: In computer science, it's a generalized solution to the most commonly faced problems. It's like a dummy template that develops. Then, based on the template code, the whole source code is written. There are three types of design patterns, creational, structural, and behavioral design patterns.

Data science: It's the study of data and its manipulation, analyzing the data, sorting the raw data into a meaningful manner. Data science includes mathematics, computer study, economics, and statistics.

Computer science: It is the branch of science that deals with computers and their study, how a computer works, and how to operate it. The person who studies computers is called a computer scientist.

Economics: It deals with the study of construction, expenditure, and distribution.

Machine learning: It's all about the representation of data, algorithms, and patterns. Nowadays, data scientist uses ML techniques and patterns to build an application.

Artificial intelligence: It is the process where a machine acts like a human. For example, human-like robots are created. This is possible because of AI.

Statistics: The branch of mathematics deals with gathering, arranging, organizing, and representing the data in graphical forms. It works excellent in concluding the results in the form of sets, charts, and graphs.

Data scientist: Data scientists are responsible for managing and presenting accurate data. Data scientist plays a vital role as all the business is depending on data analysis and data modeling.

Object-oriented programming: Explain its types, and object-oriented programming is all about creating classes and their instances. Data are converted into objects, and all the behavior of the data is performed in classes. It's an excellent aspect of writing code.

Object: The instance of a class is called an object; if we need to access the attributes and functions of class, it's compulsory to create its object.

Supervised machine learning algorithm: In this type of learning, data are in a meaningful format, and machines have some knowledge about the data and can predict the output.

Unsupervised machine learning algorithm: This type of data machine is unaware of the data and its output. It models the structure and classifies it to know much about the data.

Semi-supervised machine learning algorithm: In this type of data, both classified and unclassified data are present; machines learn from unclassified data without using the labeled data; in this manner, machines can learn some new information that was not present in human entered label data.

Reinforcement machine learning algorithm: In this type, no classified data machine learns from its experience and prediction. There is an agent who takes all the actions (robotic avatar), finds all the possible scenarios, and fits in the best.

REVIEW QUESTIONS

1. Is it necessary to use design patterns?
2. How many design patterns are there?
3. How are the proxy design patterns helpful?
4. Give an example of a private class.
5. Are mathematics and statistics the same?
6. How important is it to follow the data science life cycle?
7. What is the final step of the data science life cycle?
8. Give real-life examples where ML is used.
9. What is DL?
10. What are the advantages of a NN?
11. Which is the best suitable programming language to implement ML?
12. Give a real-life example of data science.
13. Explain the data science life cycle with an example.

2 Overview of Python for Machine Learning

LEARNING OBJECTIVES

At the end of this chapter, the reader will be able to:

- Understand the need for Python in machine learning (ML),
- Rejuvenate the basic Python programming concepts with simple examples,
- Refresh the basics of Numpy, MatplotLib, and Pandas libraries relevant to ML,
- Understand the computational complexity, and
- Implement Python-based simple examples using Pandas, Numpy, and MatplotLib.

2.1 INTRODUCTION

Python is a high-level, object-oriented programming language that is easy to learn; its syntax is easy to be remembered. Its effectiveness makes it the best language for applications. The language had made success in data sciences and ML. Python is an interpreted language; it uses compatible modules instead of a single long list of instructions standard for functional programming. Python does not convert its code into machine code. Instead, it converts the code into byte code which is not understandable by the CPU. So, we need an interpreter which executes the byte code, as shown in Figure 2.1. This interpreter is called a virtual machine. This chapter presents the need for Python programming in ML, the basics of Python programming, and data structures and their implementation using Python. In addition, we introduce the readers to Numpy basics, MatplotLib basics, Pandas basics, and the computational complexity involved in programming using Python. The chapter also provides programming examples for beginners using Python. A few real-world examples are also programmed so that the reader will understand implementation in Python with Numpy, Pandas, and MatplotLib libraries.

2.1.1 THE FLOW OF PROGRAM EXECUTION IN PYTHON

Steps were taken by the interpreter to execute a program:

1. The interpreter reads each line of the code and checks if any syntax error is found. In case of error, it halts the translation and displays an error message.
2. If no error is found, the interpreter translates the code into the equivalent language called byte code.
3. Byte code is sent to Python virtual machine, the byte code is again executed on the virtual machine, and if any error is found in this execution, an error message is displayed.

2.2 PYTHON FOR MACHINE LEARNING

Python is the fastest growing and multi-purpose programming language, because it is easily programmable and is less complex. Programmers can easily understand it. Python is open source, which has many advantages like maintainability, compatibility, and ease to learn and understand. Programmers can quickly code and update it without any complexity. Apart from this, it is an object-oriented, interpreted, and interactive programming language. It contains classes, objects, functions, and error-handling features. ML concepts are difficult to adapt to quick implementation.

DOI: 10.1201/9781003258803-2

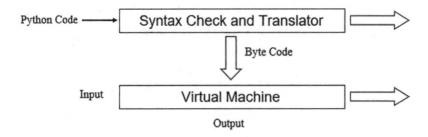

FIGURE 2.1 Python code with its interpreter.

Most ML models and concepts are built using Python because it is easy to understand, and the syntax is less complex.

2.2.1 WHY IS PYTHON GOOD FOR ML?

There has been a growing popularity of the Python language in ML, deep learning, and artificial intelligence in the last decade because of the following:

- Python is a platform-independent language.
- Python has concise and readable code, promotes rapid testing of complex algorithms, and makes the language accessible to non-programmers.
- While complex algorithms and versatile workflows stand behind ML, Python's simplicity allows developers to write reliable code.
- Developers get to focus on solving an ML problem instead of focusing on the technical nuances of the language.
- It can do a set of complex ML tasks and enable you to build prototypes quickly that allow you to test your product for ML purposes.
- Python comes with multiple frameworks and libraries to reduce developers' development time, and these libraries can be easily configurable. A software library is a pre-written code that developers use to solve everyday programming tasks.
- Python, with its rich technology stack, has an extensive set of libraries for ML.
- Python contains statistical libraries for statistical operation. It makes data visualizations easier.
- A larger user community works toward updating and sharing the libraries continuously.
- If the organization uses Python for other development activities, such as desktop development, those skills can be easily transferred to ML projects.

This chapter discusses how to set up Python Integrated Development Environment (IDE), Python frameworks, and libraries useful for ML and deep learning.

2.3 SETTING UP PYTHON

To enjoy the fast-growing programming language, the user will need to install a Python interpreter as per the operating system like Windows, macOS, and Linux.

2.3.1 PYTHON ON WINDOWS

- Download the latest Python installation package from https://www.python.org/downloads/ and run the executable file
- Choose the optional installation options; the user can add additional features or adjust the location as per the need.
- To access Python from any command prompt, kindly check on the second option, "Add Python 3.7 to PATH," as shown in Figure 2.2.
- The user can now verify the installation from the command prompt.

FIGURE 2.2 Screenshot of the installable window.

2.3.2 PYTHON ON LINUX

Linux distribution already has Python installed in the system; to verify, use the below-mentioned command:

$$
\begin{array}{l}
\text{Python} - \text{version} \\
\text{Python2} - \text{version}
\end{array}
\rightarrow
\begin{array}{l}
\textit{Shell Response} \\
\text{\$Python3} - \text{version}
\end{array}
$$

If Python installed is not the latest version and the user wants the latest version, then the steps depend on Linux distribution.

2.3.2.1 Ubuntu

If the users are using Ubuntu 16.10 or latest, then write the following command :

```
$ sudoapt-get update
$ sudoapt-get install python3.6
```

If the users are using Ubuntu 14.0, then they need to get personal package active, then write the following:

```
$ sudo add-apt-repository ppa: deadsnakes/ppa
$ sudoapt-get update
$ sudoapt-get install python3.6
```

2.4 PYTHON BASICS

Python is a high-level programming language with straightforward syntax. As a prerequisite, the user can learn Python faster if he appreciates the concepts of classes, objects, interface, etc. This section would directly deal with the Python operators, flow control, data structures, functions, exception handling, and debugging issues related to Python programming.

2.4.1   Python Operators

Operators manipulate the value of operands, and it performs operations on variables and values. In addition, it carries out all the arithmetic and logic operations.

Example: Consider the expression, $3+4=7$, where 3 and 4 are operands and $+$ is the operator.

A variety of operations are supported by Python, namely arithmetic, comparison, assignment, and logical operations. A detailed discussion of these operations is presented in this section with relevant Python examples.

2.4.1.1   Arithmetic Operators

Arithmetic operators perform all the arithmetic operations like addition, subtraction, multiplication, and division. Table 2.1 shows a list of all arithmetic operations supported by Python.

2.4.1.2   Comparison Operators

Comparison operators compare the variables and identify the relationship between them; it returns either True or False. Table 2.2 presents the comparison operators supported by Python.

2.4.1.3   Assignment Operators

Similar to other programming languages, a group of Python operators assign values to the variable, as shown in Table 2.3.

2.4.1.4   Logical Operators

Logical operators are used in Python to combine conditional statements. The list of Python logical operators is shown in Table 2.4.

TABLE 2.1
Arithmetic Operators in Python

Operator	Details	Example	Syntax
+	Add two operands	$X+Y$	$X=3; Y=2; \text{print}(X+Y)$
−	Sub two operands	$X-Y$	$X=3; Y=2; \text{print}(X-Y)$
*	Multiply two operands	$X*Y$	$X=3; Y=2; \text{print}(X*Y)$
/	Divide two operands	X/Y	$X=2; Y=2; \text{print}(X/Y)$
%	Divides left hand operand with right hand operand and returns remainder	$X\%Y$	$X=2; Y=2; \text{print}(X\%Y)$
**	Exponent calculates power	$X**Y$	$X=2; Y=2; \text{print}(X**Y)$
//	Floor division	$X//Y$	$X=2; Y=2; \text{print}(X//Y)$

TABLE 2.2
Comparison Operators in Python

Operator	Details	Example
==	Values of two operands are equal; it returns True	$X==Y$
!=	The values of two operands are not equal; it returns True	$X != Y$
<>	The values of two operands are not equal; it returns True same like (! =)	$X <> Y$
>	Greater than	$X>Y$
<	Less than	$X<Y$
>=	Greater than or equal to	$X>=Y$
<=	Less than or equal to	$X<=Y$

TABLE 2.3
Assignment Operators in Python

Operator	Details	Example
=	Assign a value to the variable	$X=5$
+ =	Add right operand to left operand and assign value to left operand	$X+=Y$
-=	Subtract right operand to left operand and assign value to left operand	$X-=Y$
*=	Multiply right operand to left operand and assign value to left operand	$X*=Y$
/=	Divide left operand to right operand and assign value to the right operand	$X/=Y$
%=	Find the modulus of two variables and assign the value to the left operand	$X\%=Y$
**=	Calculate the power and assign value to left operand	$X**=Y$
//=	It calculates floor division and assigns value to the left operand	$X//=Y$

TABLE 2.4
Logical Operators in Python

Operator	Details	Syntax
AND	True when both conditions are True	$X<5$ and $X<6$
OR	True when any one of the condition is True	$X<5$ or $X<6$
NOT	Reverse the result if the condition is True; it will return False	not $(x<5$ and $x<10)$

2.4.1.5 Membership Operators

These operators test for membership in a sequence such as lists, strings, or tuples. Two membership operators are used in Python (in, not in). It gives the result based on the variable present in a specified sequence or string.

2.4.2 PYTHON CODE SAMPLES ON BASIC OPERATORS

Operators are special symbols in Python that carry out arithmetic or logical computation. The value that the operator operates on is called the operand. This section provides the user with Python code snippets using the operators discussed in the above sections.

2.4.2.1 Arithmetic Operators

```
In [33]: 5+7 #adding integers
Out[33]:12

In [34]: 2+3+4+87
Out[34]:96

In [35]: 2*4+4+87 #Operators precedence(/,*,+,-)
Out[35]:99

In [36]: 2+10/2*5+20
         #order of operator precedence
         # 10/2 = 5
         # 5*5 = 25
         # 2+25+20=47
Out[36]:47.0
```

```
In [37]: 2+3*15%2+3*2
         # 3*15 = 45
         # 45%2 = 1
         # 3*2=6
         # 2+1+6=9
Out[37]:9

In [38]: x = 5 #variable declaration and initialization

In [39]: x#prints value of variable x
Out[39]:5

In [40]: type(x) #type is single argument built-in function and it returns
Data-type of the variable
Out[40]:int

In [41]: a = 2 #declaring a variable

In [42]: a
Out[42]:2

In [43]: type(a)
Out[43]:int

In [44]: a = 4

In [45]: atype(a)
Out[45]:int

In [46]: y = 5.67
         ytype(y)
Out[46]:float

In [47]: x = 2.5/2 #Dividing float value by integer
                   #result will float since integer is upcasted.

In [48]: X #prints value of variable x
Out[48]:1.25

In [49]: type(x) #data-type of variable x
Out[49]:float

In [50]: #String varible declaration and initialization
         string_one= 'first string'
         string_two= "second string"
         string_three= "'third string'"

In [51]: string_one
Out[51]: 'firststring'

In [52]: print(string_two) #prints value stored in the variable stirng_two
         second string

In [53]: type(string_one) #type is single argument built-in function and it
returns type of the variable
Out[53]:str
```

```
In [54]: type(string_three)
Out[54]:str

In [55]: #everything after # will be considered as a comment

In [56]: x = 4

In [57]: x
Out[57]:4

In [58]: type(x)
Out[58]:int

In [59]: #this is comment
         #this is second comment

In [60]: x = 15
         y = 4

In [61]: print('x + y =',x+y)
         x + y = 19

In [62]: print('x - y =',x-y) # Subtraction operation
         x - y = 11

In [63]: print(10-20) # NOTE:-lower is subtracted by higher value then result
is negative. """
         -10

In [64]: print('x * y =',x*y) # Multiplication operation
         x * y = 60

In [65]: print('x / y =',x/y) #Division- Result is accurate division value
         x / y = 3.75

In [66]: print('x // y =',x//y) # Floor division - division that results
into whole number adjusted to the left in the number line
         x // y = 3

In [67]: print('x **y=',x**y) # Exponent - left operand raised to the
power of right
         x ** y = 50625

In [68]: 25*25
Out[68]:625
```

2.4.2.2 Comparison Operators

These operators compare the values on either side of the operand and determine the relation between them. It is also referred to as a relational operator. Various comparison operators are (==,!=, >,<=, etc.)

```
In [69]: x = 20
         y = 35

In [70]: print('x>y is',x>y) # Operator Greater than - Left hand operand is
greaterthenre turns TRUE
         x > y is False
```

```
In [71]: print('x<y is',x<y) # Operator Less than - Left hand operand is
Lesserthenreturn s TRUE
         x < y is True

In [72]: print('x == y is',x==y) # Operator Equal - Left hand operand is
equal to the right ha nd operand then returns TRUE
         x == y is False

In [73]: print('x!= y is',x!=y) # Operator Not Equal - Left hand operand
is not equal then re turns TRUE
         x!= y is True

In [74]: print('x >= y is',x>=y) # Operator Greaterthan or Equal to - If left
hand operator is greater than or equal to then returns true
         x >= y is False

In [75]: print('x <= y is',x<=y) # Operator Less than or Equal to -If left
hand operand is les s than or equal to then returns true
         x <= y is True

In [80]: x = 4
         y = 5

In [81]: print(('x>y is',x>y))# Operator Greater than - left-hand operand is
greater than then returns true
         ('x > y is', False)

In [82]: print(x==y) # Operator Equals - BOth the operands are equal by
values then returns true
         False

In [83]: print(x!=y) # Operator Not equal to - Both operands are not
equal by values then returns true
         True
```

2.4.2.3   Logical Operators

Logical operators are the and, or, not operators.

```
In [76]: x = True
         y = False

In [77]: print('x and y is',x and y) # Operator Logical AND - True if both are
true or same
         x and y is False

In [78]: print('x or y is',x or y) # Operator Logical OR - True if Either one
is true
         x or y is True

In [79]: print('not x is',not x) # Operator Logical NOT -If true then returns
false
         not x is False
```

2.4.2.4   Membership Operators

The examples of in and not in operators used in Python are discussed in this section. For instance, we check whether the value of $x=4$ and $y=8$ is available in the list or not by using in and not in operators.

```
In [84]: x = 4
         y = 8
   list= [1, 2, 3, 4, 5 ] #List is a collection which is ordered and
changeable and als o allows Duplication
         if(x in list):
             print("Line 1 - x is available in the given list")
         else:
             print("Line 1 - x is not available in the given list")
         if(y not in list):
             print("Line 2 - y is not available in the given list")
         else:
             print("Line 2 - y is available in the given list")

         Line 1 - x is available in the given list
         Line 2 - y is not available in the given list

In [85]: s = "sakshi"

In [86]: 'a' in s # IN operator is to validate or evaluate the s of value
Out[86]:True

In [87]: 'b' in s
Out[87]:False

In [88]: "a" not in s # NOT IN operator is
Out[88]:False

In [89]: "b" not in s
Out[89]:True

In [90]: import keyword

In [91]: print(keyword.kwlist)
         ['False', 'None', 'True', 'and', 'as', 'assert', 'async',
'await', 'break', 'class',
         'continue', 'def', 'del', 'elif', 'else', 'except', 'finally',
'for', 'from', 'globa
         l', 'if', 'import', 'in', 'is', 'lambda', 'nonlocal', 'not',
'or', 'pass', 'raise', 'return', 'try', 'while', 'with', 'yield']

In [92]: print(keyword.kwlist)
         ['False', 'None', 'True', 'and', 'as', 'assert', 'async',
'await', 'break', 'class',
         'continue', 'def', 'del', 'elif', 'else', 'except', 'finally',
'for', 'from', 'globa
         l', 'if', 'import', 'in', 'is', 'lambda', 'nonlocal', 'not',
'or', 'pass', 'raise', 'return', 'try', 'while', 'with', 'yield']
```

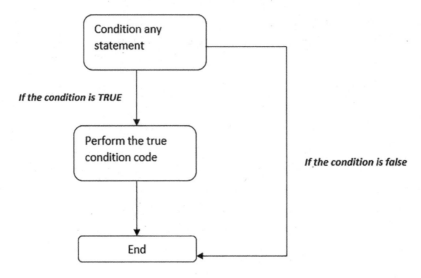

FIGURE 2.3   Control flow statement.

2.4.3   Flow Control

The flow of the program is sequential. One by one, each statement is executed. There is a condition when the user needs to repeat the statement again and again. In this case, the control flow statement works. Control flow statement includes if condition, for condition, else, if-else, and while loop. The computer program understands True and False's language; let's explain this with a flow diagram as shown in Figure 2.3.

2.4.3.1   If & elif Statement

Sometimes the user needs to execute statements depending on some conditions; for multiple conditions, we use elif.

```
If expression :
        Statement
Elifexpression :
        Statement
Elifexpression :
        Statement
Else expression :
        Statement
```

Let's explain this with an example, suppose create a program that identifies if the number is negative, else if the number is positive and even number else consider the number as a positive odd number

```
If y<0 :
        print "y is negative"
elif
        y/2 = 0:
        print "y is even number"
else :
        print "y is a negative number."
```

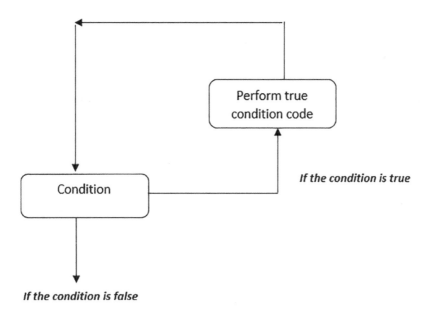

FIGURE 2.4   Flow diagram of the loop statement.

2.4.3.2   Loop Statement

A loop statement allows us to execute a statement multiple times. For example, if the user wants to print his/her name ten times, this care loop will help; instead of writing the name ten times, use the loop function and define its range. The flow diagram shown in Figure 2.4 explains the loop statement.

As discussed in the following sections, there are different types of loop statements, namely for, while, nested loops, etc.

For loop: The loop executes the statement repeatedly using the iterator variable that increments each execution. Let's take the same example of printing fruits name. Let "fruits" be the list that contains the names of three fruits. When the program executes, each fruit is saved in variable "I" and then printed one by one.

```
Fruits = ["apple", "mango", "banana"];
For I in fruits :
Print (i);
```

While loop: Repeats the group of a statement if the given condition is True. For example, add the first five natural numbers.

```
I = 0;
While y<6:
y = y+y
I++;
```

Nested loop: To use the loop inside another loop is called a nested loop. Let's take an example of distributing four chocolates to each student of the class. The nested loop will work here, as we have to use two loops, that is, for chocolate and students.

```
chocolate = ["Cadbury", "kitkat" " mars", " galaxy"];
students = ["Alice", " Jhon", " Nick" ];
```

```
For students in students :
For chocolate in chocolate :
Print (students + "got" + chocolate);
```

2.4.3.3 Loop Control Statements

To change the sequence of executing a code, Python provides multiple control statements. Following are the loop control statements:

Break statement: To exit from a loop, break statements are used. Let's take the example of 20 enrollment numbers, and the user wants to print only ten enrollment numbers.

```
x=1;
While x< = 20:
Ifx ==10:
break
Print (x)
x++;
```

> As soon as loop reaches the 10thenrollement the beak statement will exit the loop and will display 10 enrollements only

Continue statement: It is similar to the break statement, it exits the loop, but the loop itself is not exited. Let's consider the same previous example and replace the break with continue.

```
x=1;
While x < = 20:
if x ==10:
continue
Print (x)
x++;
```

> As soon as loop reaches the 10thenrollement the continue statement will exit the loop and will display all the enrollement from 1 till 20 except the enrollement 10

Pass statement: It is also called a null operator. Nothing happens when it is executed. Consider a project that two programmers complete; one falls sick and cannot come on a specific day. The problem is that another programmer cannot hold the work. In this case, all the functions that the sick programmer wrote will be left empty using the pass statement. Let's consider the same previous example with a pass statement.

```
x=1;
While x < = 20:
if x ==10:
pass
print "10 not included"
Print (x)
x++;
```

> As soon as loop reaches the 10thenrollement the pass statement will work and display all the enrollement from 1 till 20 except the enrollement 10 as we had passed it and will print 10 not included with it

2.4.4 Python Code Samples on Flow Control Statements

2.4.4.1 Conditional Statements

Decision-making is required when we want to execute code only if a specific condition is satisfied. The if…elif…else statement is used in Python for decision-making.

syntax:if test expression: statement(s)

The program evaluates the test expression and will execute statement(s) only if the text expression is True. If the text expression is False, the statement(s) is not executed. In Python, the body of the if statement is indicated by the indentation. The body starts with an indentation, and the first unindented line marks the end.

```
In [1]:
a = 5 #Declaration and assignment.
If a== 7: #Condition is false.
        print("True")
        print("True123") #Both these statements are not executed.
print("false") #Executed whenever it is encountered.
false


In [2]:
num= 3
ifnum>0:   #Condition is true then body of the statement is executed
        print(num, "is a positive number.")
print("This is always printed.")#Executed whenever it is encountered.
num= -1
ifnum> 0:
        print(num, "is a positive number.")
        #print("abc")
        print("This is also always printed.")
        #print("xyz")
print("xyz") #Executed whenever it is encountered.
3 is a positive number.
This is always printed.
xyz
```

2.4.4.2   Python if...else Statement

Syntax of if...else

    if test expression: Body of if-else: Body of else

    The if..else statement evaluates test expression and will execute the body of if only when the test condition is True. If the condition is False, the body of else is executed. Indentation is used to separate the blocks.

```
In [3]:
a = 5
if   a== 4: #condition is true body of the conditional statement is executed.
    print("True")
else:
    print("False") #Whenever condition fails this statement will be executed.

#print ("in else")#first unindentend line
False


In [4]:
# Program checks if the number is positive or negative
# And displays an appropriate message

num= -8

# Try these two variations as well.
# num = -5
# num = 0

if num>= -5:
        print("Positive or Zero")
        print("this no positive")
```

```
else: #Condition fails, Else part is executed.
    print("Negative number")
Negative number
```

2.4.4.3 Python if...elif...else Statement

```
Syntax of if...elif...else
```

if test expression: Body of if elif test expression: Body of elif else: Body of else. The elif is short for else if. It allows us to check for multiple expressions.

If the condition for if is False, it checks the condition of the next elif block and so on. If all the conditions are False, the body of else is executed. Only one block among the several if...elif...else blocks is executed according to the condition. The if block can have only one else block. But it can have multiple elif blocks.

```
In [5]:
  var= 150
  if(var< 200 and var> 50): #Condition with logical "and", means both
must be true onl y then its body gets executed.
    print("Expression value is less than 200")
    ifvar== 150: #Nested if condition
      print("Which is 150")
    elifvar== 100: #inner else if part
      print("Which is 100")
    elifvar==50: #inner else if part
      print("Which is 50")
  elifvar<50: #outer else if part
    print("Expression value is less than 50")
  else: #outer else part
    print("Could not find true expression")
  print ("Good bye!")
Expression value is less than 200
Which is 150
Good bye!

In [6]:
  # In this program,
  # we check if the number is positive or
  # negative or zero and
  # display an appropriate message

num= -8

  # Try these two variations as well:
  # num = 0
  # num = -4.5

ifnum> 0:
    print("Positive number")
elifnum==0: #else if conditional statement.
    print("Zero")
else:
    print("Negative number")
Negative number
```

2.4.4.4 The For Loop

The for loop in Python is used to iterate over a sequence (list, tuple, string) or other iterable objects. Iterating over a sequence is called traversal.

Syntax of for Loop

For Val in sequence: Body of for

Here, Val is the variable that takes the item's value inside the sequence on each iteration.

Loop continues until we reach the last item in the sequence. The body of for loop is separated from the rest of the code using indentation.

```
In [7]:
  # Program to find the sum of all numbers stored in a list

  # List of numbers
  numbers= [6, 5, 3, 8, 4, 2, 5, 4, 11] #list

  # variable to store the sum
  sum= 0

  # iterate over the list
  # val takes values in the list and increments till the list range.
  for val in numbers:
      sum = sum+val

  # Output: The sum is 48
  print("The sum is", sum)
The sum is 48


n = 6
# iterates from 0 to range of n
# range() returns sequence of numbers from 0(by default) to N, Increment by
1(default)
for i in range(n):
    print(i)
print('DDD')
0
1
2
3
4
5
DDD

In [9]:
a
Out[9]:
5
```

2.4.4.5 The range() Function

We can generate a sequence of numbers using the range() function. range(10) will generate numbers from 0 to 9 (10 numbers). We can also define the start, stop, and step size as range(start, stop, step size). Step size defaults to 1 if not provided. This function does not store all the values in memory; it would be inefficient. So it remembers the start, stop, step size, and generates the next number on the go. To force this function to output all the items, we can use the function list(). The following example will illustrate this.

```
In [10]:
  # creating a list by start from 2 end by 20 increment by 2 using
range() function.
  print(list(range(2, 20, 2)))
[2, 4, 6, 8, 10, 12, 14, 16, 18]

In [11]:
  a = range(10) # assigning range for variable.

In [8]:
a# prints starting and ending range.
Out[12]:

range(0, 10)
In [13]:
  # prints starting and ending range.
  print(range(10))
range(0, 10)

In [14]:
  # create list and assign it to variable.
  a = (list(range(10)))

In [15]:
  a# By default range starts from 0 and increments by 1.
Out[15]:
[0, 1, 2, 3, 4, 5, 6, 7, 8, 9]

In [16]:
  type(a) # returns the type of the argument
Out[16]:
List

In [17]:
  len(a) # returns the length of the argument
Out[17]:
10
In [18]:
  # Defining range,with start and end position
  print(list(range(2, 8))) #creates list.
[2, 3, 4, 5, 6, 7]

In [19]:
  # Defining range, with starting, ending position and increment value.
  print(list(range(2,20,2)))  # stepsize=2
[2, 4, 6, 8, 10, 12, 14, 16, 18]
```

We can use the range() function for loops to iterate through a sequence of numbers. It can be combined with the len() function to iterate through a sequence using indexing. Here is an example to
illustrate the usage of the range function.

```
In [20]:
  # Program to iterate through a list using indexing

  genre= ['pop', 'rock', 'jazz'] # List
```

```
  # iterate over the list using index
  foriinrange(len(genre)): # defining the range as list length
    print("I like", genre[i]) # Iterates through the list using
indexing
  print("z")
I like pop
I like rock
I like jazz z
```

2.4.4.6   For Loop with else

A for loop can have an optional else block as well. The else part is executed if the items in the sequence are used in for loop exhausts. The break statement can be used to stop a for loop. In such a case, the else part is ignored. Hence, a for loop's else part runs if no break occurs. Here is an example to illustrate this.

```
In [21]:
  digits= [1,2,3]

  foriindigits:
      print(i)
  #else:
  print("No items left.")
1
2
3
No items left.
```

2.4.4.7   While Loop

A while loop statement in Python programming language repeatedly executes a target statement as long as a given condition is True. The syntax of a while loop in the Python programming language is –
    while expression: statement(s)
    Here, statement(s) may be a single statement or a block of statements. The condition may be any expression, and True is any non-zero value. The loop iterates while the condition is True. When the condition becomes False, program control passes to the line immediately following the loop. The following example illustrates an application of the while loop:

```
In [22]:
  # Program to add natural
  # numbersupto
  # sum = 1+2+3+...+n

  # To take input from the user,
  # n = int(input("Enter n: "))

  n = 10

  # initialize sum and counter
  sum= 0
  i = 1

  whilei<= n:
    sum = sum + i
    i=i+1 # update counter
```

```
  # print the sum
  print("The sum is", sum)
The sum is 55

In [23]:
  n = 5
  i = 1
  while(i <= n):
    if(i==3):
      print(i)
  i = i + 1 # Each iteration i get incremented
3
```

In the above program, the test expression will be True as long as our counter variable *i* is less than or equal to *n* (10 in our program). Therefore, we need to increase the value of the counter variable in the body of the loop. This is very important (and mostly forgotten). Failing to do so will result in an infinite loop (never-ending loop).

2.4.4.8   While Loop with else

Same as for loop, we can have an optional block with while loop as well. The else part is executed if the condition in the while loop evaluates to False. The while loop can be terminated with a break statement. In such a case, the else part is ignored. Hence, a while loop's else part runs if no break occurs and the condition is False. Here is an example to illustrate the *while loop with else*.

```
In [24]:
  # Example to illustrate
  # the use of else statement
  # with the while loop

  counter= 0

  whilecounter< 0: #condtion fails and its body doesn't gets executed
    print("Inside loop")
    counter = counter + 1
  else:
    print("Inside else")
Inside else
```

2.4.4.9   Python Break and Continue

In Python, break and continue statements can alter the flow of a normal loop. For example, loops iterate over a code block until the test expression is False. Still, sometimes we wish to terminate the current iteration or even the whole loop without checking the test expression. The break and continue statements are used in these cases.

2.4.4.10   Python Break Statement

The break statement terminates the loop containing it. Control of the program flows to the statement immediately after the body of the loop. If the break statement is inside a nested loop (loop inside another loop), the break will terminate the innermost loop.

    Syntax

    break

    The working of break statement in Python with *for* loop and *while* loop is shown in the following example:

```
forval in"string":
    ifval== "i": # if condition true break the loop and exit.
        break
    print(val)
print("The end")
s t r
The end


In [26]:
  forletterin'Python': # First Example
    ifletter== 'h':
        break
    print('Current Letter :', letter)
  print('Out of For')

Current Letter : P
Current Letter : y
Current Letter : t Out of For
```

2.4.4.11   Python Continue Statement

The continue statement is used to skip the rest of the code inside a loop for the current iteration. Loop does not terminate but continues on with the next iteration.

Syntax of Continue
continue

```
In [27]:
  forletterin'Django':  # First Example
      ifletter== 'D': # condition true then continue by going back to the
for loop statement.
      continue
    print('Current Letter:', letter)

Current Letter: j
Current Letter: a
Current Letter: n
Current Letter: g
Current Letter: o

# Program to show the use of continue statement inside loops

forval in"string":
  ifval== "i": # condition true then continue by going back to the for
loop statement.
    continue
print(val)

#print("The end")
s t r
n g
```

This program is the same as the above example, except the break statement has been replaced with continue. We continue with the loop if the string is "i," not executing the rest of the block. Hence, we see in our output that all the letters except "i" get printed.

```
In [36]:
          sequence=[1,2,3,4,5]
          forvarinsequence:
            #codes inside the loop
            ifvar==3:
            continue
            print(var)
              #codes inside for loop
          #codes outside for loop
```

1
2
4
5

2.4.5   Review of Basic Data Structures and Implementation in Python

When we handle a huge amount of data, it is challenging to organize the data and use it efficiently. In recent years, applications are getting more complex with a large amount of data, which has led to issues in terms of data search, processor speed, and handling multiple requests. Thus, data structures have proved their efficiency to solve such complicated situations in the information technology world. Data structures are a systematic way to organize such data, thus enabling efficient use of data. A data structure has an *interface*, which corresponds to a set of operations and parameter types supported by the data structure. The internal representation and definition of the algorithms used in data structure operations are provided by the *implementation*. The three basic characteristics of a data structure are appropriateness, time efficiency, and space efficiency.

- **Appropriateness:** The data structure implementation should be able to employ its interface in the right way.
- **Time efficiency:** The operations executed by a data structure should consume as little time as possible.
- **Space efficiency:** The operations about data structures should be capable of occupying as little memory as possible.

In this section, we will review the following data structures with relevant Python examples:

- Array Data Structure
- Linked List
- Stacks and Queue
- Searching
- Sorting
- Recursion

2.4.5.1   Array Data Structure

Data structures use arrays to perform operations. Arrays, as we know, are an entity to hold a collection of similar items which belong to the same data type. The items stored in an array are called *elements,* and the location of each element is assigned with an *index* to access or operate on it.

In general, arrays are declared as **data_typearray_name [array_size].** For instance,
Int matrixA [5] = {1, 2, 3, 4, 5};

In the above example, the following points are to be considered:

- Array index starts from 0 and not 1.
- Array length is 5 – it can store five elements.
- Its index value accesses each element; for example, element three can be accessed as martixA[2].

```
#Commonly Used Codes
# Code    C Type                 Python Type    Min bytes
# 'b'     signed char            int `          1
# 'B'     unsigned char          int            1
# 'u'     Py_UNICODE             Unicode        2
# 'h'     signed short           int            2
# 'H'     unsigned short         int            2
# 'i'     signed int             int            2
# 'I'     unsigned int           int            2
# 'l'     signed long            int            4
# 'L'     unsigned long          int            4
# 'f'     float                  float          4
# 'd'     double                 float          8
```

2.4.5.2   Implementation of Arrays in Python

```
import array as arr
myArray = arr.array('d', [3.14, 3.5, 4.99])
print(myArray)  # Output is shown as -->  array('d', [3.14, 3.5, 4.99])


import array as arr
myArray2 = arr.array('i', [1, 2, 3, 5, 7, 11, 13, 17, 19])
print("First element:", myArray2[0]) # output is shown as --> First element:
1
print("Second element:", myArray2[1]) # output is shown as --> Second
element: 2
print("Last element:", myArray2[-1])  # output is shown as -->  Last element:
19


# Slicing the Array
print(myArray2[2:5]) # 3rd to 5th; The output is shown as --> array('i', [3,
5, 7])
print(myArray2[:-5]) # beginning to 4th ; The output is shown as  -->
array('i', [1, 2, 3, 5])
print(myArray2[5:])  # 6th to end; The output is shown as --> array('i', [11,
13, 17, 19])
print(myArray2[:])   # beginning to end; The output is shown as  -->
array('i', [1, 2, 3, 5, 7, 11, 13, 17, 19])


# Changing the values in the array
# changing first element
myArray2[0] = 99
print(myArray2) # the first value of the array is changed to 99; The
output is shown as --> array('i', [99, 2, 3, 5, 7, 11, 13, 17, 19])


# changing 3rd and 4th element
myArray2[2:3]= arr.array('i', [88,77])
print(myArray2) # the third and forth value of the array is changed to 88
and 77 respectively; The output is shown as --> array('i', [99, 2, 88, 77, 5, 7,
11, 13, 17, 19])
```

FIGURE 2.5 Singly linked list.

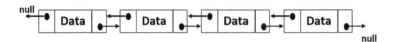

FIGURE 2.6 Doubly linked list.

2.4.5.3   Linked List

While storing data as arrays, the size cannot be extended or reduced to fit a certain set of data, since they are static structures. It becomes expensive to update arrays with new insertions and deletions. These limitations are overcome to an extent using Linked lists.

A sequence of data structures connected through links is called a linked list or simply a singly linked list, as shown in Figure 2.5. This sequence of links contains items that include the data and link element. The link element provides a link to the next link. Each *link* of a linked list stores a set of data called the data elements. Every link in a linked list has a link to the next link through the element called ***next***. Every linked list has an element called *first*. Overall, each element has a list consisting of the data and a reference to the next list. The last list consists of a reference with a null. Due to its dynamic property, the number of lists can expand or shrink based on the demand.

The disadvantage of a linked list is that we cannot access individual elements in a list. To access a single item, we need to start from the first list and travel down until access to the item is required. Another disadvantage of a linked list is the memory usage. In addition to storing elements in the memory, each reference element will also occupy nearly 4 bytes of memory on a 32-bit processor.

The variants of a linked list are doubly linked lists and circular linked lists. The lists can be navigated bidirectionally in a doubly linked list, that is, forward and backward, as shown in Figure 2.6. In contrast, the last list contains a link to the first link in the circular linked list, and the traversing happens circularly. The operations supported by a linked list are insertion, deletion, display, and search.

2.4.5.4   Implementation of Linked List in Python

```
class Node:  #Creating the Node Class
def __init__(mySelf, data):
mySelf.item = data
mySelf.ref = None

classmyLinkedList:  #Creating the Single Linked List Class
def __init__(mySelf):
mySelf.start_node = None  # First Node of the List

deftraverse_list(mySelf): # to go through the List
ifmySelf.start_node is None: # if the list is empty
print("List has no element")
return
else:  # If the List is not empty
        n = mySelf.start_node
while n is not None:
```

```
print(n.item , " ")
            n = n.ref

# MANUPULATING THE LIST

definsert_start(mySelf, data): # Inserting the value at the begining of the
list
new_node = Node(data)
new_node.ref = mySelf.start_node
mySelf.start_node= new_node

definsert_end(mySelf, data):  # Inserting the value at the end of the list
new_node = Node(data)
ifmySelf.start_node is None:
mySelf.start_node = new_node
return
    n = mySelf.start_node
whilen.ref is not None:
        n= n.ref
n.ref = new_node;


definsert_specific(mySelf, x, data): # Inserting after another specific item
    n = mySelf.start_node
print(n.ref)
while n is not None:
ifn.item == x:
break
        n = n.ref
if n is None:
print("item not in the list")
else:
new_node = Node(data)
new_node.ref = n.ref
n.ref = new_node

definsert_index (mySelf, index, data): # Inserting after Specific Index
if index == 1:
new_node = Node(data)
new_node.ref = mySelf.start_node
mySelf.start_node = new_node
        i = 1
        n = mySelf.start_node
while i < index-1 and n is not None:
            n = n.ref
            i = i+1
if n is None:
print("Index out of bound")
else:
new_node = Node(data)
new_node.ref = n.ref
n.ref = new_node
```

Testing the Results

```
myLIST = myLinkedList()# Creating "myLIST" as an object of the class
"myLinkedList"
myLIST = [1, 2, 3]
myLIST.insert_end(1) # Inserting at the end
myLIST.insert_end(3)
myLIST.insert_end(5)
myLIST.traverse_list()
myLIST.get_count()

myLIST.insert_start(7) # Inserting at the begining
myLIST.insert_start(9)
myLIST.insert_start(11)
```

2.4.5.5 Stacks and Queues

Consider a real-world example of a stack – a pile of books or a stack of plates. We will be able to place or remove a book from the top of the stack only. This implies that the stack operations can be performed from one end only, the top of the stack. Such a data structure is commonly referred to as a Last-In First-Out data structure. The element placed first will be accessed last, and the element placed last will be accessed first. The process of inserting an element into the stack is called PUSH operation, and removing an element from the stack is called POP operation.

In data structures, stacks can be implemented using arrays and linked lists. The size of the stack can either be static or dynamic (stack grows).

The primary operations of the stack involve push and pop, as illustrated in Figure 2.7. To check the efficiency of the stack, the user has to keep track of the data on the stack. To track the stack, functions such as peek(), isFull(), and isEmpty() are available. Peek() is used to access the element on top of the stack without getting it removed, while isFull() is used to check whether the stack is full and isEmpty() is used to check whether the stack is empty.

The series of steps involved in the PUSH operation is illustrated through a flowchart in Figure 2.8. The first step to initialize the PUSH operation is to check whether the stack is full. If the stack is empty, the PUSH operation will progress; otherwise, exit the PUSH operation with an error. The stack pointer (top of stack) increments and points to the next available space in memory to insert data. The data element is added to the location, and a success message is returned.

The steps involved in the POP operation are illustrated with a flowchart, as shown in Figure 2.9. In the POP operation, data are accessed from the top of the stack, and the top of the stack is decremented to the next lower address. Finally, the memory location is deallocated.

Implementing Stack in Python Using list and collections. deque

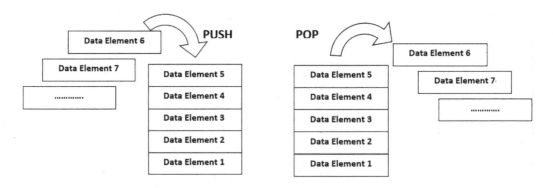

FIGURE 2.7   Stack operation.

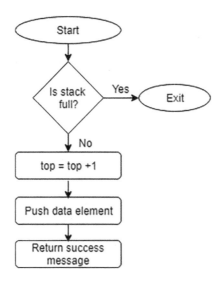

FIGURE 2.8 Flowchart for PUSH operation.

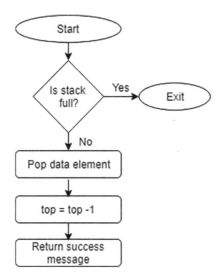

FIGURE 2.9 Flowchart for POP operation.

```
myLIST = []
myLIST.append('I')
myLIST.append('Love')
myLIST.append('Python')
myLIST.append('Coding')

myLIST # Returns the valuses -->['I', 'Love', 'Python', 'Coding']

myLIST.pop#  myLIST Returns the valuses -->['I', 'Love', 'Python']
'Coding'
myLIST.pop() #  myLIST Returns the valuses -->['I', 'Love']
'Python'
myLIST.pop() #  myLIST Returns the valuses -->['I']
'Love'
```

```
myLIST.pop()
'I'
# when the lis is empty
myLIST.pop() # We get the Error -->IndexError: "pop from empty list"

# USING collections.deque AS STACK
from collections import deque
myQUEUE = deque()
myQUEUE.append('I')
myQUEUE.append('Love')
myQUEUE.append('Python')
myQUEUE.append('Coding')

myQUEUE # Returns the valuses -->deque(['I', 'Love', 'Python', 'Coding'])

myQUEUE.pop#  myQUEUE Returns the valuses -->['I', 'Love', 'Python']
'Coding'
myQUEUE.pop() #  myQUEUE Returns the valuses -->['I', 'Love']
'Python'
myQUEUE.pop() #  myQUEUE Returns the valuses -->['I']
'Love'
myQUEUE.pop()
'I'

# when the lis is empty
myQUEUE.pop() # We get the Error -->IndexError: "pop from empty list"
```

2.4.5.6 Queues

Though similar in appearance to stacks, queues are accessed from both ends. Data are usually inserted from one end and removed from the other end. The process of inserting elements into the queue is called enqueue, and removing elements from the queue is called dequeue. Therefore, the queue is based on the concept of First-In First-Out, as shown in Figure 2.10. Unfortunately, queues use two separate data pointers – front and rear – making it difficult for the programmer to implement the algorithm.

The primary operations of the queue are enqueue and dequeue. To track the queue, functions such as peek(), isFull(), and isEmpty() are available. Peek() is used to access the element from the front of the queue without getting it removed, while isFull() is used to check whether the queue is full and isEmpty() is used to check whether the queue is empty.

The series of steps involved in the enqueue operation is illustrated in the flowchart as shown in Figure 2.11. The first step to initialize the enqueue operation is to check whether the queue is full. If the queue is empty, the insert operation will progress; otherwise, exit the process with an overflow error – next, the rear pointer increments and points to the next available space in memory to insert data. Finally, the data element is added to the location, and a success message is returned.

The series of steps involved in the dequeue operation is illustrated with a flowchart in Figure 2.12. In the remove operation, data are accessed from the front pointer. The front pointer is incremented to the point to the next available data element.

FIGURE 2.10 Queue operation.

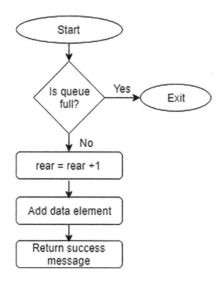

FIGURE 2.11   Enqueue operation.

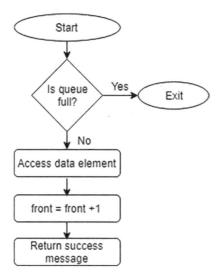

FIGURE 2.12   Dequeue operation.

2.4.5.7   Implementation of Queue in Python

```
class Queue:

    #Constructor
def __init__(mySelf):
mySelf.queue = list()
mySelf.maxSize = 5
mySelf.head = 0
mySelf.tail = 0

    #Adding elements
defenqueue(MySelf,data):
```

```
        #Checking if the queue is full
ifMySelf.size() >= MySelf.maxSize:
return ("Queue Full")
MySelf.queue.append(data)
MySelf.tail += 1
return True

    #Deleting elements
defdequeue(MySelf):
        #Checking if the queue is empty
ifMySelf.size() <= 0:
MySelf.resetQueue()
return ("Queue Empty")
data = MySelf.queue[MySelf.head]
MySelf.head+=1
return data

    #Calculate size
def size(MySelf):
returnMySelf.tail - MySelf.head

    #Reset queue
defresetQueue(MySelf):
MySelf.tail = 0
MySelf.head = 0
MySelf.queue = list()
Testing the results
myQueue = Queue()
print(myQueue.enqueue(1))#prints True
print(myQueue.enqueue(2))#prints True
print(myQueue.enqueue(3))#prints True
print(myQueue.enqueue(4))#prints True
print(myQueue.enqueue(5))#prints True
print(myQueue.enqueue(6))#prints Queue Full!; Since we have defiend the
size as 5


print(myQueue.size())#prints 5
print(myQueue.dequeue())#prints 5
print(myQueue.dequeue())#prints 4
print(myQueue.dequeue())#prints 3
print(myQueue.dequeue())#prints 2
print(myQueue.dequeue())#prints 1
print(myQueue.dequeue())#prints Queue Empty; Queue is reset here

print(myQueue.enqueue(1))#prints True
print(myQueue.enqueue(2))#prints True
print(myQueue.enqueue(3))#prints True
print(myQueue.enqueue(4))#prints True
```

2.4.5.8 Searching

Searching is one of the common tasks we do in our day-to-day life, for example, we search for a book in the library, we search for a phone number from our contacts list, and we search for a misplaced key, etc. The simplest form of searching for a key element in a data structure is tracing a path from the root of the data structure. As each node or list is visited, the algorithm compares the data element in a node or list with the key element to be searched. If a match is found, then the success message has to be returned. Otherwise, the search continues with the next successive nodes or lists. If the search has been completed without a match, then the algorithm returns a null, indicating that the key element has not been found in the list.

The search algorithms can handle two scenarios before searching:

- Algorithms that search irrespective of the order of the list.
- Algorithms that have a clear assumption about the order of the list.

Based on these scenarios, we have the following search algorithms in data structures:

- Linear Search
- Binary Search
- Interpolation Search
- Hash Table

2.4.5.8.1 Linear Search

One of the simplest search algorithms is the linear search algorithm. In this algorithm, a search is performed on all items in the list, one after the other. Each item is compared with the item to be searched; once the search item is found, the algorithm quits and returns the index at which the search item was found. Otherwise, it searches for the item up to the end of the list, and if no match is found, it returns a null. The process is explained through a flowchart as shown in Figure 2.13. Consider an array arr with length n. Let x be the element to be searched. Initially, the index of the array is set to 1 to ensure that the array consists of at least one element. If $i>n$, then the search

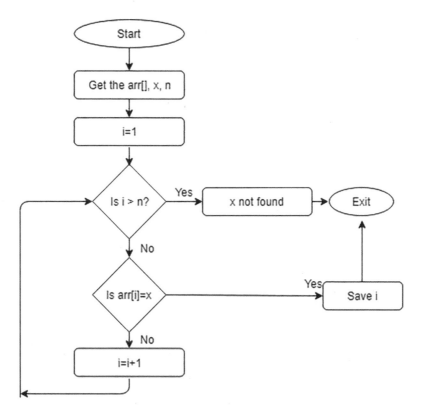

FIGURE 2.13 Linear search.

process terminates. If arr[i]=x, then search process terminates with i as the return value. If the match has not been found, then the search process continues until $i=n$.

2.4.5.8.2 Binary search

Linear search has been performing well on the unordered list of data elements. Linear search algorithm suffers when the number of elements in the unordered search list is too big. The algorithm takes a long time to find the match or search for the element. But if the list of data elements is arranged in order before the search is performed, then the task of searching is made simpler. For example, think about searching for a person's phone number in our contact list. The names in the contact list are ordered alphabetically. So it makes sense to confine the search based on the starting alphabet of the search element. A binary search algorithm can exploit such a situation.

In this algorithm, a comparison is made every time we make a search. Based on the comparison results, some part of the list (that does not contain the search element) is eliminated from the search process. Generally, the search is performed by comparing the middle item in a list. The search item can lie either in the upper half or in the lower half of the list. The algorithm eliminates one half of the list that does not contain the search element and the other half that contains the search element is again compared with the middle item. The search process continues by eliminating one-half of the list every time until the match is found. It can be concluded that the binary search algorithm halves the searchable list, thus reducing the number of comparisons.

The procedure of binary search is well explained through a flowchart as shown in Figure 2.14. Consider an ordered array arr with length n. Let x be the element to be searched. Initially, the lower bound (LB) of the array is set to 1, and the upper bound (UB) is set to the length of the array n. If UB is greater than LB, then the algorithm terminates. Otherwise, the algorithm continues by first computing the midpoint based on the UB and LB values. Next, if the element indexed by the midpoint in the array is greater than the search element, then the UB is set to midpoint-1; if the element indexed by the midpoint in the array is lesser than the search element, then the LB is set to midpoint+1. Finally, the index midpoint is saved if the element indexed by the midpoint in the array is equal to the search element. This indicates the location of the searched item x.

2.4.5.8.3 Interpolation Search

The interpolation search algorithm is a variant of the binary search algorithm. The algorithm searches based on the probe position. Initially, the probe position is in the middle of the search list and then gets modified as the algorithm progresses. The algorithm is explained through a flowchart, as shown in Figure 2.15. The algorithm works similarly to binary search, except for the calculation of the midpoint value.

2.4.5.9 Implementation of Searching in Python

```
mylist = [1, 2, 3, 5, 7, 11, 13, 17, 19, 23, 29, 31, 37, 41, 47] # Defineing
the list with Prime numbers
print('List has the items: ', mylist)
searchItem = int(input('Enter a number to search for: '))
found = False
for i in range(len(mylist)):
ifmylist[i] == searchItem:
found = True
print(searchItem, ' was found in the list at index ', i, '. So the number
given is a prime number')
break
if found == False:
print(search item, ' was not found in the list!. So the given number is not a
prime number')
```

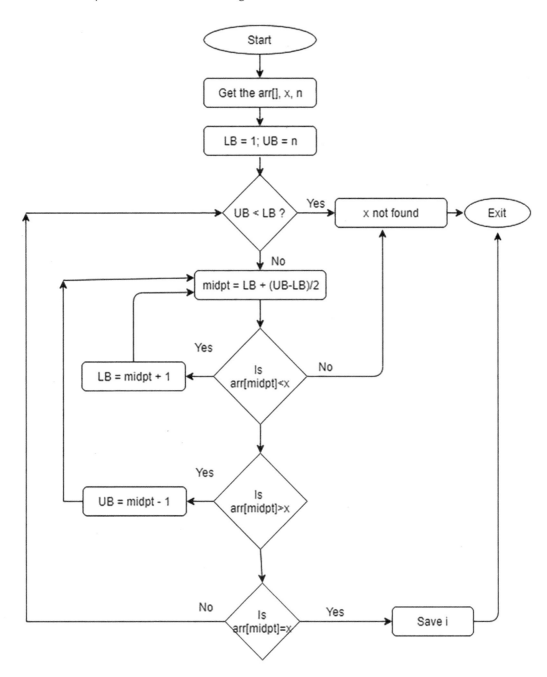

FIGURE 2.14 Binary search.

```
Testing the results:
List has the items:  [1, 2, 3, 5, 7, 11, 13, 17, 19, 23, 29, 31, 37, 41, 47]
Enter a number to search for: 31
31  was found in the list at index  11. So the number given is a prime number
********************
Enter a number to search for: 45
45  was not found in the list!. So the given number is not a prime number
********************
```

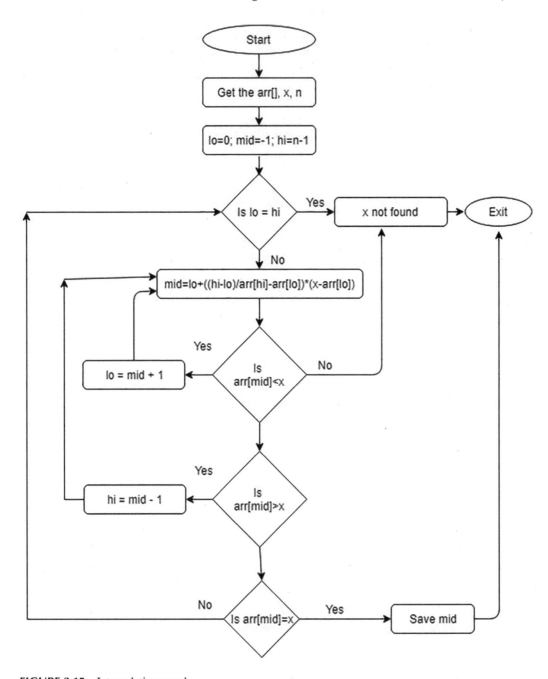

FIGURE 2.15   Interpolation search.

2.4.5.10   Sorting

In data structures, one has to understand how to arrange a set of elements in order. There are several ways or methods in which elements can be arranged. Sorting refers to these methods of arranging data in a specific format. Sorting algorithms provide a set of procedures to arrange the data. The process of searching can be optimized to an efficient level if the sorting is organized. Data can be represented in a simple, readable form once sorted. The most common sorting orders are lexicographical order or numerical order.

The sorting algorithms in data structures are bubble sort, insertion sort, selection sort, merge sort, shell sort, and quicksort. These algorithms can fall under two broad categories based on the additional memory requirement – in-place sorting and not-in-place sorting. When the sorting algorithm works in-place (within the array itself) without consuming extra space, it is called in-place sorting. The best example of an in-place sorting algorithm is bubble sort. On the other hand, certain sorting algorithms require additional space (memory) apart from the array size. This space is generally more than the elements being sorted. Hence, this group of algorithms is called not-in-place sorting, and one of the best examples would be the merge sort.

2.4.5.10.1 Bubble Sort

One of the simplest sorting algorithms is the bubble sort, also known as the exchange sort. The algorithm is based on a comparison between adjacent elements. If the elements are in the right order, they are left in their place and if the elements are in the wrong order, they are swapped (interchange their positions). The process is repeated until all the elements are compared and sorted. The algorithm is found suitable for sorting fewer data elements.

The procedure for bubble sort is illustrated in the flowchart as shown in Figure 2.16. Consider an array arr[] with n elements. Let i be the index pointing to the elements in the array. For each element in the array, a comparison is made between arr[i] and arr[i+1]. If arr[i] is greater than arr[i+1], then the elements are swapped, else kept in place. The process is repeated, and each pair of the array arr is compared until the whole array is completely sorted.

2.4.5.11   Implementation of Bubble Sort in Python

```
defbubbleSort(mylist):
forpassnum in range(len(mylist)-1,0,-1):
for i in range(passnum):
ifmylist[i]>mylist[i+1]:
temp = mylist[i]
mylist[i] = mylist[i+1]
mylist[i+1] = temp

mylist = [1, 2, 3, 5, 47, 31, 13, 17, 19, 23, 29, 11, 37, 31, 47] # sameple
list to get it bubble sorted
print('the original list:', mylist) # Before sort
bubbleSort(mylist)
print('the sorted list:', mylist) # After sort
```

Testing the results

```
the original list: [1, 2, 3, 5, 47, 31, 13, 17, 19, 23, 29, 11, 37, 31, 47]
the sorted list: [1, 2, 3, 5, 11, 13, 17, 19, 23, 29, 31, 31, 37, 47, 47]
```

2.4.5.12   Insertion Sort

The insertion sort algorithm is a type of in-place sorting algorithm, which in turn is based on the comparison. In this algorithm, a sub-array is maintained, and this sub-array is sorted continuously. Successive elements of the array are added or inserted into this sub-array and sorted within the sub-array. Hence, the name insertion sort. Sometimes, the algorithm is referred to as an online algorithm since the values are sorted and added into the sub-array.

The insertion sort algorithm is simple to implement, and it is efficient on small datasets. This comparison sort builds a sorted array by adding one element at a time. The algorithms are explained with a flowchart, as shown in Figure 2.17. Consider an array arr[] whose length is n. The first element of the array is used to form the sub-array, and its position is noted. The next element is chosen

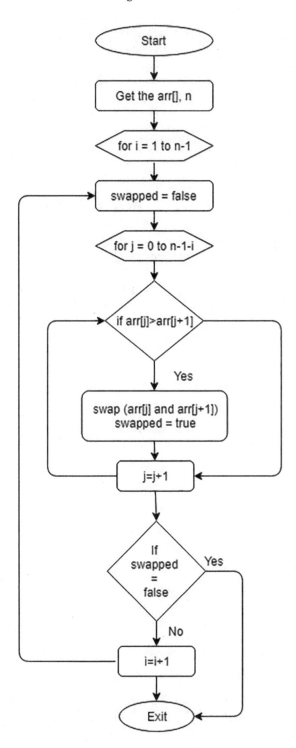

FIGURE 2.16 Bubble sort.

for comparison with the first element. If the first element is less than the second element, then the algorithm leaves the elements in their place and continues to compare the next value. If the first element is greater than the second element, then the elements are sorted, and this forms the sub-array to which the third element would be added. The process repeats until all the elements are sorted.

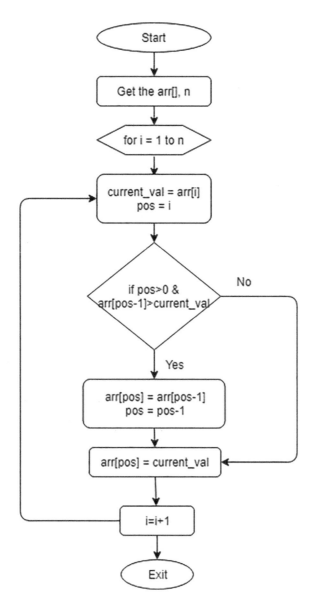

FIGURE 2.17   Insertion sort.

2.4.5.13   Implementation of Insertion Sort in Python

```
defmyinsertionSort(mylist):
# for every element in our array
for index in range(1, len(mylist)):
current = mylist[index]
position = index

while position > 0 and mylist[position-1] > current:
print("Swapped {} for {}".format(mylist[position], mylist[position-1]))
mylist[position] = mylist[position-1]
print(mylist)
position -= 1
```

```
mylist[position] = current

return mylist

mylist = [1, 2, 3, 5, 47, 31, 13, 17, 19, 23, 29, 11, 37, 31, 47]

print(myinsertionSort(mylist))
```

Testing the results

```
print(myinsertionSort(mylist))
Swapped 31 for 47
[1, 2, 3, 5, 47, 47, 13, 17, 19, 23, 29, 11, 37, 31, 47]
Swapped 13 for 47
[1, 2, 3, 5, 31, 47, 47, 17, 19, 23, 29, 11, 37, 31, 47]
Swapped 47 for 31
[1, 2, 3, 5, 31, 31, 47, 17, 19, 23, 29, 11, 37, 31, 47]
Swapped 17 for 47
[1, 2, 3, 5, 13, 31, 47, 47, 19, 23, 29, 11, 37, 31, 47]
Swapped 47 for 31
[1, 2, 3, 5, 13, 31, 31, 47, 19, 23, 29, 11, 37, 31, 47]
Swapped 19 for 47
[1, 2, 3, 5, 13, 17, 31, 47, 47, 23, 29, 11, 37, 31, 47]
Swapped 47 for 31
[1, 2, 3, 5, 13, 17, 31, 31, 47, 23, 29, 11, 37, 31, 47]
Swapped 23 for 47
[1, 2, 3, 5, 13, 17, 19, 31, 47, 47, 29, 11, 37, 31, 47]
Swapped 47 for 31
[1, 2, 3, 5, 13, 17, 19, 31, 31, 47, 29, 11, 37, 31, 47]
Swapped 29 for 47
[1, 2, 3, 5, 13, 17, 19, 23, 31, 47, 47, 11, 37, 31, 47]
Swapped 47 for 31
[1, 2, 3, 5, 13, 17, 19, 23, 31, 31, 47, 11, 37, 31, 47]
Swapped 11 for 47
[1, 2, 3, 5, 13, 17, 19, 23, 29, 31, 47, 47, 37, 31, 47]
Swapped 47 for 31
[1, 2, 3, 5, 13, 17, 19, 23, 29, 31, 31, 47, 37, 31, 47]
Swapped 31 for 29
[1, 2, 3, 5, 13, 17, 19, 23, 29, 29, 31, 47, 37, 31, 47]
Swapped 29 for 23
[1, 2, 3, 5, 13, 17, 19, 23, 23, 29, 31, 47, 37, 31, 47]
Swapped 23 for 19
[1, 2, 3, 5, 13, 17, 19, 19, 23, 29, 31, 47, 37, 31, 47]
Swapped 19 for 17
[1, 2, 3, 5, 13, 17, 17, 19, 23, 29, 31, 47, 37, 31, 47]
Swapped 17 for 13
[1, 2, 3, 5, 13, 13, 17, 19, 23, 29, 31, 47, 37, 31, 47]
Swapped 37 for 47
[1, 2, 3, 5, 11, 13, 17, 19, 23, 29, 31, 47, 47, 31, 47]
Swapped 31 for 47
[1, 2, 3, 5, 11, 13, 17, 19, 23, 29, 31, 37, 47, 47, 47]
Swapped 47 for 37
[1, 2, 3, 5, 11, 13, 17, 19, 23, 29, 31, 37, 37, 47, 47]
[1, 2, 3, 5, 11, 13, 17, 19, 23, 29, 31, 31, 37, 47, 47]
```

2.4.5.14 Selection Sort

Selection sort is yet another in-place sort algorithm based on the comparison. The entire array is divided into two groups, one sorted part and the other unsorted part. The sorted portion of the array is kept empty initially, and the unsorted part contains all the elements of the array. The element that has the smallest value is selected from the unsorted portion and added as the first element to the sorted portion. The element that was located already in the sorted portion swaps position with the smallest element. The comparison process continues with the next smallest element from the unsorted portion. The algorithm continues until all the elements of the unsorted portion are compared. The algorithm is explained with a flowchart as shown in Figure 2.18.

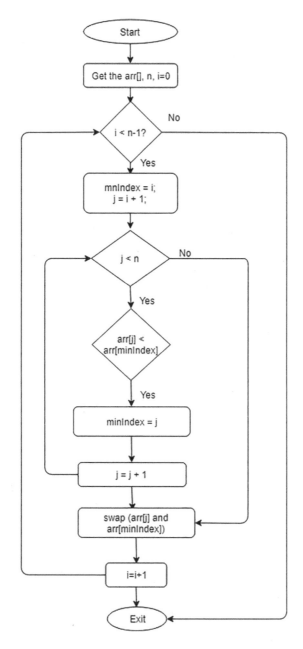

FIGURE 2.18 Selection sort.

2.4.5.15   Implementation of Selection Sort in Python

```
defselectionSort(myLIST):
forfillslot in range(len(myLIST)-1,0,-1):
mp=0  # Max Position
for location in range(1,fillslot+1):
ifmyLIST[location]>myLIST[mp]:
mp = location

temp = myLIST[fillslot]
myLIST[fillslot] = myLIST[mp]
myLIST[mp] = temp

myLIST = [1, 2, 3, 5, 47, 31, 13, 17, 19, 23, 29, 11, 37, 31, 47]
print('Before SELECTIONSORT:',myLIST)
selectionSort(myLIST)
print('After SELECTIONSORT:',myLIST)
```

Testing the results

```
Before SELECTIONSORT: [1, 2, 3, 5, 47, 31, 13, 17, 19, 23, 29, 11, 37, 31,
47]

After SELECTIONSORT: [1, 2, 3, 5, 11, 13, 17, 19, 23, 29, 31, 31, 37, 47, 47]
```

2.4.5.16   Merge Sort

The merge sort algorithm works based on the divide and conquer mechanism. The array is first divided into two halves; then, each half portion is divided into equal halves. The dividing process continues until each divided portion consists of only one element of the array (the array cannot be further divided). Then, the elements are combined (merged) in the order of their division. During the combination of elements, a comparison is made, and sorting happens in successive halved arrays. Finally, the merged array results in a sorted array. An example for merge sort is shown in Figure 2.19. The algorithm is explained with a flowchart, as shown in Figure 2.20.

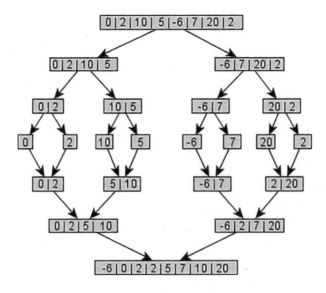

FIGURE 2.19 Working of the merge sort algorithm.

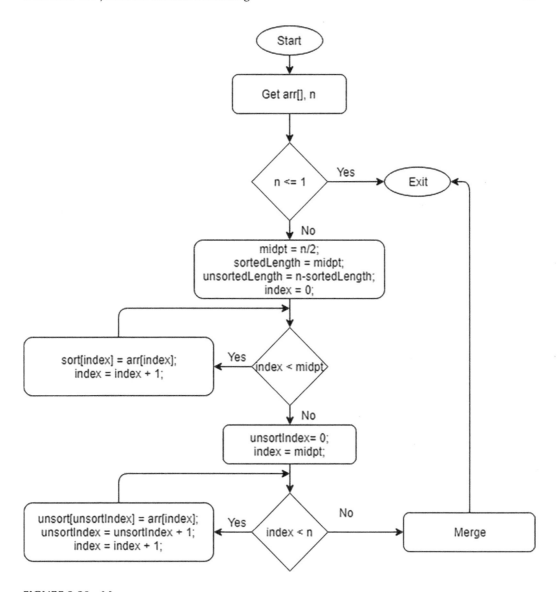

FIGURE 2.20   Merge sort.

2.4.5.17   Implementation of Merge Sort in Python

```
defmergeSort(myLIST):
print("Splitting ",myLIST)
iflen(myLIST)>1:
mid = len(myLIST)//2
lefthalf = myLIST[:mid]
righthalf = myLIST[mid:]

mergeSort(lefthalf)
mergeSort(righthalf)
        i=j=k=0
while i <len(lefthalf) and j <len(righthalf):
iflefthalf[i] <righthalf[j]:
```

```
myLIST[k]=lefthalf[i]
                i=i+1
else:
myLIST[k]=righthalf[j]
                j=j+1
          k=k+1

while i <len(lefthalf):
myLIST[k]=lefthalf[i]
          i=i+1
          k=k+1

while j <len(righthalf):
myLIST[k]=righthalf[j]
          j=j+1
          k=k+1
print("Merging ",myLIST)

myLIST = [1,6,7,8,3,2,8]
mergeSort(myLIST)
print(myLIST)

Testing the results

Splitting  [1, 6, 7, 8, 3, 2, 8]
Splitting  [1, 6, 7]
Splitting  [1]
Merging  [1]
Splitting  [6, 7]
Splitting  [6]
Merging  [6]
Splitting  [7]
Merging  [7]
Merging  [6, 7]
Merging  [1, 6, 7]
Splitting  [8, 3, 2, 8]
Splitting  [8, 3]
Splitting  [8]
Merging  [8]
Splitting  [3]
Merging  [3]
Merging  [3, 8]
Splitting  [2, 8]
Splitting  [2]
Merging  [2]
Splitting  [8]
Merging  [8]
Merging  [2, 8]
Merging  [2, 3, 8, 8]
Merging  [1, 2, 3, 6, 7, 8, 8]
 [1, 2, 3, 6, 7, 8, 8]
```

2.4.5.18 Shell Sort

The shell sort algorithm is a variant of the insertion sort algorithm. It varies with insertion algorithm in terms of the following features:

- The insertion sort algorithm is more efficient for an array that is almost sorted.
- The insertion algorithm is not optimal since it moves an element only by one position at a time, thus consuming more time.

The insertion sort is improved in shell sort by comparing elements separated by a gap of several positions. This algorithm uses insertion sort on the large interval of elements to sort. Further, the interval keeps on decreasing until the value becomes 1. These intervals are referred to as the gap sequences. Thus, the algorithm allows sorting different combinations of smaller gap sizes through multiple passes. The array is almost sorted by the time the algorithm reaches its termination, so a normal insertion sort would be sufficient to get the sorted list. The algorithm of shell sort is explained with a flowchart as shown in Figure 2.21.

2.4.5.19   Quicksort

Quicksort is one of the efficient data structure algorithms based on partitioning the array into smaller sub-arrays. First, a pivot value is chosen, and the partitioning of a large array is done based on this value. Each sub-group of the array will be holding values based on the pivot value. Once the array is partitioned, the quicksort algorithm recursively calls itself to sort the sub-arrays. This algorithm is efficient on large-sized data. Indices start from both ends of the array, with one index starting from the left and the other starting from the right. The left index selects the element smaller than the pivot, while the right index selects the element larger than the pivot value. Then, these two selected elements are compared and exchanged based on the caparison results. The process repeats until all the elements to the left of the pivot and right of the pivot are compared. Finally, the pivot value is also moved if required to maintain the sorted order. The procedure of the algorithm is explained using a flowchart, as shown in Figure 2.22.

2.4.5.20   Data Structures in Python with Sample Codes

The purpose of data structures is to hold some data together. It is used to store a collection of data. There are four built-in data structures in Python – list, tuple, dictionary, and set.

2.4.5.20.1   List

A list is a data structure that holds an ordered and similar collection of items, that is, one can store a sequence of members in a given list. In Python, the list is initialized with square brackets, and each item is comma-separated. Items in a list are stored with an index. Once the items are stored in the list, they are changeable in the future. This is easy to imagine if the user wants to store the student's name of a class; the student's name can be similar and is ordered.

Example:
StudentName ["Alice", "Luna", "Alice", "Mack", "Jhon"]
Output: ["Alice", "Luna", "Alice", "Mack", "Jhon"]
If the user wants to access the 1 st element of a list: print (StudentName[0])

2.4.5.20.2   Tuple

The main purpose of the tuple is to hold multiple objects. They are very similar to lists but lack the extensive functionality that list offers, that is, items not changeable once stored. To create a tuple, specific items need to be defined separated by commas within an optional pair of parenthesis. If the user wants to store final marks scored by students in different subjects,

Mack=("Science", 20, "English" 30)
Output : (Science", 20, "English" 30)

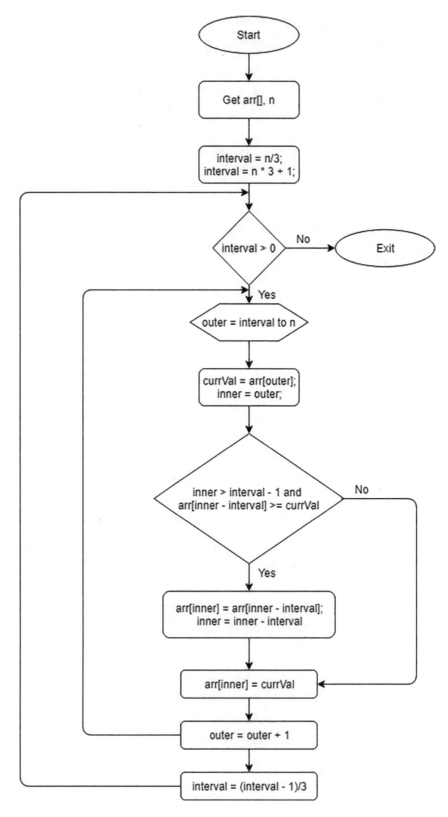

FIGURE 2.21　Shell sort.

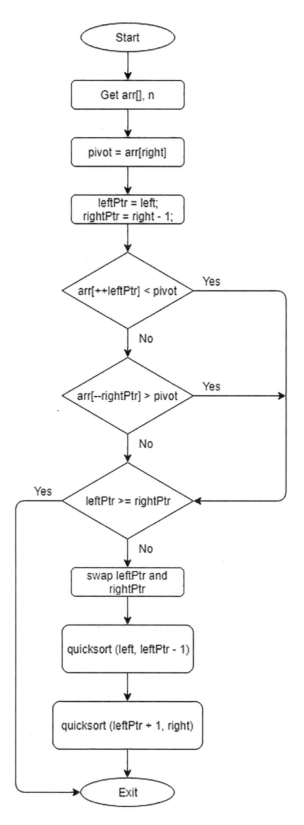

FIGURE 2.22 Quicksort.

2.4.5.20.3   *Dictionary*

Dictionary is like a box of an unordered set of objects. It acts like a telephone dictionary that saves the telephone numbers based on a person's name, the dictionary's key, and phone numbers will be its details. In the dictionary, the key should always be unique.

Dictionary is initialized with curly braces; the key is separated from its value by a colon ":" and commas separate items. Items can be of any data type, but the key should be an immutable data type.

Example: Saving students record based on enrollment numbers which will be the key, and it is always unique.

Dict = {'enroll' : '121', 'name' : 'adam', 'class' : 'first'}

Print dict['enroll']

Print dict['name']

To access the value with the help key, Python uses the following code:

Dict[enroll];

2.4.5.20.4   *Set*

The concept of sets is same as sets we study in mathematics. An unordered group of items is known assets, and the user can find union, intersection, and set difference. Their usage is primarily when the existence of an object in a collection is more important than the order or how many times it occurs.

Set can be initialized by using brackets. Let's take the example of an equal set.

Input:

A= {1, 2, 3};

B = {3,2, 1};

Print (A==B);

Output: *true*

2.4.5.21   Python Code Samples for Data Structures in Python

2.4.5.21.1   *List*

A list is a sequence of values, and these values can be of any type. Values in the list are called elements. There are several ways to create a new list, and the simplest is to enclose the elements in a square bracket. A few examples are illustrated below for better understanding.

```
In [8]: list= ['a',2,3,'xyz',True]

In [9]: list
Out[9]: ['a', 2, 3, 'xyz',True]

In [10]: x = [-10,-20,-30,-40] #from left to right index starts from 0 in
python and for right to left it starts from -1
In [11]: x[1]
Out[11]:-20

In [12]: x[-2]
Out[12]:-30

In [13]: x[-1]
Out[13]:-40

In [14]: type(x)
Out[14]:list
```

```
In [15]: car= ['Merceedes','audi','bmw']
         print(car)

         ['Merceedes', 'audi', 'bmw']
```

2.4.5.21.2 Nested List

A nested list is a list contained in another list.

```
In [16]: a = [10,20,30,['abc','xyz']]

In [17]: a
Out[17]: [10, 20, 30, ['abc','xyz']]

In [18]: a[2]
Out[18]:30

In [19]: a[1]
Out[19]:20

In [20]: alist= [ [4, [True, False], 6, 8], [888, 999],[1,[2,3],3]]
         ifalist[0][1][0]:
             print(alist[1][0])
         else:
             print(alist[1][1])
         888
In [21]: alist[0][1][0]
Out[21]:True

In [22]: alist[2][1][1]
Out[22]:3

In [23]: alist[1][1]
Out[23]:999

In [24]: alist[0]
Out[24]: [4, [True, False], 6,8]

In [25]: alist[1]
Out[25]: [888,999]

In [26]: alist[0][3]
Out[26]:8

In [27]: alist[0][1]
Out[27]: [True,False]

In [28]: alist[0][0:2]
Out[28]: [4, [True,False]]

In [29]: x = []

In [30]: type(x)
Out[30]:list

In [31]: s = 'hello python'
```

```
In [32]: message= "Welcome to Python Class"

In [33]: message_list= message.split()

In [34]: message_list
Out[34]: ['Welcome', 'to', 'Python','Class']

In [35]: words = ['apple','mango','banana','fig','strawberry']

In [36]: words[1:7]
Out[36]: ['mango', 'banana', 'fig','strawberry']

In [37]: words[-2:4]
Out[37]:['fig']

In [38]: words[:]
Out[38]: ['apple', 'mango', 'banana', 'fig','strawberry']

In [39]: words[:2]
Out[39]: ['apple','mango']

In [40]: words[1:-1]
Out[40]: ['mango', 'banana','fig']

In [41]: words[-1]
Out[41]:'strawberry'

In [42]: len(words)
Out[42]:5

In [43]: words[3]
Out[43]:'fig'

In [44]: words.index('fig')
Out[44]:3

In [45]: words[1:3] #upper end is always exclusive
Out[45]: ['mango','banana']

In [46]: words[2:]
Out[46]: ['banana', 'fig','strawberry']

In [47]: words[-1]
Out[47]: 'strawberry'

In [48]: words[0:-1]
Out[48]: ['apple', 'mango', 'banana','fig']

In [49]: words[-2:5]
Out[49]: ['fig','strawberry']

In [50]: words[1:-1]
Out[50]: ['mango', 'banana','fig']

In [51]: words[:]
Out[51]: ['apple', 'mango', 'banana', 'fig','strawberry']
```

```
In [52]: words[1:-1]
Out[52]: ['mango', 'banana','fig']

In [53]: words[2:4]
Out[53]: ['banana','fig']

In [54]: 'guava' in words
Out[54]: False

In [55]: animals = ['cat','dog','snake','fish','elephant','fish']

In [56]: animals.index('fish')
Out[56]:3

In [57]:len(animals) #To check no of elements in a list
Out[57]:6

In [58]: x = words + animals x
Out[58]:['apple',
        'mango',
        'banana',
        'fig',
        'strawberry',
        'cat',
        'dog',
        'snake',
        'fish',
        'elephant',
        'fish']

In [59]: words.append('cherry')

In [60]: words
Out[60]: ['apple', 'mango', 'banana', 'fig', 'strawberry','cherry']

In [61]: words.extend(['Gua','vaGrapes','berries','pineapple'])

In [62]: words
Out[62]:['apple',
        'mango',
        'banana',
        'fig',
        'strawberry',
        'cherry',
        'Gua',
        'vaGrapes',
        'berries',
        'pineapple']

In [63]: words.remove('berries')

In [64]: #remove first 4 elements from list x?

In [65]: words
Out[65]:['apple',
        'mango',
```

```
          'banana',
          'fig',
          'strawberry',
          'cherry',
          'Gua',
          'vaGrapes',
          'pineapple']
In [66]: words.remove(words[1])

In [67]: words
Out[67]:['apple',
          'banana',
          'fig',
          'strawberry',
          'cherry',
          'Gua',
          'vaGrapes',
          'pineapple']
In [68]: words.append('cherry')

In [69]: words
Out[69]:['apple',
          'banana',
          'fig',
          'strawberry',
          'cherry',
          'Gua',
          'vaGrapes',
          'pineapple',
          'cherry']
In [70]: words.count('cherry')
Out[70]:2

In [71]: words.remove('cherry')

In [72]: words
Out[72]:['apple',
          'banana',
          'fig',
          'strawberry',
          'Gua',
          'vaGrapes',
          'pineapple',
          'cherry']
In [73]: my_list= [1,67,84,98,34,90,76,56]

In [74]: a = ['a','g','f']
          a.sort()
          a
Out[74]: ['a', 'f','g']

In [75]: my_list.sort()

In [76]: my_list
Out[76]: [1, 34, 56, 67, 76, 84, 90,98]
```

```
In [77]: my_list= [1,67,22,9,77,13,78,48]
         print(my_list.sort())
         None
In [78]: my_list
Out[78]: [1, 9, 13, 22, 48, 67, 77,78]

In [79]: print(my_list)
         [1, 9, 13, 22, 48, 67, 77, 78]

In [80]: word=["apple","mango","banana","fig","strawberry"]
         word
         #word[0]
Out[80]: ['apple', 'mango', 'banana', 'fig','strawberry']

In [81]: word[1:5:3]
Out[81]: ['mango','strawberry']

In [82]: word[1:5:2]
Out[82]: ['mango','fig']

In [83]: word[0]
Out[83]:'apple'

In [84]: my_list.sort(reverse = True) # Sort the list in descending
order,reverse is true

In [85]: my_list
Out[85]: [78, 77, 67, 48, 22, 13, 9,1]

In [104]: my_list.sort(reverse = False)# Sort the list, Reverse is false
which means make the list in ascending order
         my_list
Out[104]: [1, 9, 13, 22, 48, 67, 77, 78]

In [87]: my_list*3
Out[87]: [1,
         9,
         13,
         22,
         48,
         67,
         77,
         78,
         1,
         9,
         13,
         22,
         48,
         67,
         77,
         78,
         1,
         9,
         13,
         22,
         48,
         67,
```

```
                77,
                78]
In [88]: my_list[1:7] #list[firstindex:lastindex:step]
Out[88]: [9, 13, 22, 48, 67,77]

In [89]: my_list[1:2]
Out[89]:[9]
```

2.4.5.21.3 Tuples

A tuple is a sequence of values much like a list. The values stored in a tuple can be any type, and integers index them. The important difference is that tuples are immutable.

```
In [90]: #To create a tuple with a single element, you have to include
the final comma:
         t1 = ('a',)
         type(t1)
Out[90]:tuple

In [91]: t1 = ('a')
         type(t1)
Out[91]:str

In [92]: #Another way to construct a tuple is the built-in function tuple.
         #With no argument, it creates an empty tuple:
         t = tuple() print (t)
          ()
In [93]: #If the argument is a sequence (string, list or tuple),
         #the result of the call to tuple is a tuple with the elements of the
sequence:
         t = tuple('123')
         print (t)
          ('1', '2', '3')

In [94]: t1 = tuple("helloworld") print(t1)
('h', 'e', 'l', 'l', 'o', 'w', 'o', 'r', 'l', 'd')

In [95]: l = (1,2,2,3,'xyz',(3,4))

In [96]: l
Out[96]: (1, 2, 2, 3, 'xyz', (3, 4))

In [97]: l[1]
Out[97]: 2

In [98]: type(l)
Out[98]: tuple

In [99]: l.index(1)
Out[99]: 0

In [100]: l.count(2) #no of times that elemnt is occuring
Out[100]: 2

In [101]: b = l*5
```

```
In [102]: b
Out[102]:(1,
          2,
          2,
          3,
          'xyz',
          (3, 4),
          1,
          2,
          2,
          3,
          'xyz',
          (3, 4),
          1,
          2,
          2,
          3,
          'xyz',
          (3, 4),
          1,
          2,
          2,
          3,
          'xyz',
          (3, 4),
          1,
          2,
          2,
          3,
          'xyz',
          (3, 4))

In [103]: len(b)
Out[103]:30
```

A good rule of thumb is as follows: Use lists when the items are similar and tuples when the items are non-similar. A sequence of 50 first names? That's a list. A sequence consisting of a first name, last name, age, and address? That's a tuple.

2.4.5.21.4 Dictionary

Python dictionary is an unordered collection of items. While other compound data types have only value as an element, a dictionary has a key: value pair.

Dictionaries are optimized to retrieve values when the key is known.

```
In [4]: #Declaration and definition of dictionary variable
        ab= { 'Suresh' : 'Suresh@Sureshch.com', 'Ashok' : 'Ashok@wall.org',
             'Sumathi' :'Sumathi@rubylang.org', 'Surekha' :
'Surekha@hotmail.com'
        }
        print(ab) #Prints in single line

        #Whereas here it prints as it is defined.
        ab
        {'Suresh': 'Suresh@Sureshch.com', 'Ashok': 'Ashok@wall.org',
'Sumathi': 'Sumathi@ruby
```

```
            -lang.org', 'Surekha': 'Surekha@hotmail.com'}
Out[4]: {'Suresh': 'Suresh@Sureshch.com', 'Ashok': 'Ashok@wall.org',
            'Sumathi': 'Sumathi@rubylang.org', 'Surekha': 'Surkha@hotmail.com'}

In [5]: mydict= {1:['python',"2019-01-03"],2.5:'java',3:'C',4:'Machine
Learning'}

In [6]: mydict
Out[6]: {1: ['python', '2019-01-03'], 2.5: 'java', 3: 'C', 4:
'MachineLearning'}

In [7]: type(mydict) #Checking type of the variable
Out[7]:dict

In [8]: print(ab)
        print(type(ab))
        {'Suresh': 'Suresh@Sureshch.com', 'Ashok': 'Ashok@wall.org',
'Sumathi': 'Sumathi@ruby
        -lang.org', 'Surekha': 'Surekha@hotmail.com'}
        <class 'dict'>

In [9]: print("Suresh's e-address is", ab['Suresh'])
        Suresh's e-address is Suresh@Sureshch.com

In [10]: # Deleting a key-value pair
         Del ab[Surekha]

In [11]: ab
Out[11]: {'Suresh': 'Suresh@Sureshch.com', 'Ashok': 'Ashok@wall.org',
           'Sumathi': 'Sumathi@ruby-lang.org'}

In [12]: # Adding a key-value pair ab['Chinmay'] =
         'Chinmay@python.org' ab

Out[12]: {'Suresh': 'Suresh@Sureshch.com', 'Ashok': 'Ashok@wall.org',
           'Sumathi': 'Sumathi@ruby-lang.org', 'Chinmay':
'Chinmay@python.org'}

In [13]: mydict= {1:2,3:4,5:6}

In [14]: mydict
Out[14]: {1: 2, 3: 4, 5:6}

In [15]: dict1 = {1:'carrots', 'two':[1,2,3], 6.4:2,9:8}

In [16]: dict1
Out[16]: {1: 'carrots', 'two': [1, 2, 3], 6.4: 2, 9:8}

In [17]: len(dict1)
Out[17]:4

In [18]: 'two' in dict1 #check whether the value is present or not.
Out[18]:True

In [19]: 'carrots' in dict1
Out[19]:False
```

```
In [20]: dict1['two'] = 'radish' #adding new value for key.

In [21]: dict1
Out[21]: {1: 'carrots', 'two': 'radish', 6.4: 2, 9:8}

In [22]: words= {'house': "haus",'cat ':" katze"}

In [23]: words["dog"] = "dogiee" #adding new value to the dictionary
variable.

In [24]: words
Out[24]: {'house': 'haus', 'cat ': ' katze', 'dog':'dogiee'}

In [25]: #copy the value to another variable
         w = words.copy()
         #words["dog"] = "dogiee"
         print(w)
         {'house': 'haus', 'cat ': ' katze', 'dog': 'dogiee'}

In [26]: #check the result
         W
Out[26]: {'house': 'haus', 'cat ': ' katze', 'dog':'dogiee'}

In [27]: #clear the value
         w.clear()
         #now check out the result
         w
Out[27]:{}

In [28]: words1 = {"red": "rounge", "blue":"bleu"}

In [29]: words2 = {"red": "round", "blue":"bluue"}

In [30]: words1.update(words2) #update the key values

In [31]: words1
Out[31]: {'red': 'round', 'blue':'bluue'}

In [32]: #list down the items like keys and data
         words1.items()
Out[32]: dict_items([('red', 'round'), ('blue','bluue')])

In [33]: #list down only the keys
         words1.keys()
Out[33]: dict_keys(['red','blue'])

In [34]: #list down only the values
         words1.values()
Out[34]: dict_values(['round','bluue'])

In [35]: #list the keys
         for key in words1:
          print(key)
         red
         blue
```

```
In [36]:  #combine keys respective values from to dictionary variable.
          A={'a':72,'b':17,'c':8}
          B={'a':1308,'b':1,'c':12}
          combinedDict={}
          for key in A.keys():

                    if key in B.keys():

                                combinedDict[key]=[]
                                combinedDict[key].append
                                (A[key])
                                combinedDict[key].append
                                (B[key])
In [37]:  combinedDict
Out[37]:  {'a': [72, 1308], 'b': [17, 1], 'c': [8,12]}
```

2.4.6 FUNCTIONS IN PYTHON

To perform a task that will be used throughout the project, we code such a task as a function that will be reusable in the future. Thus, functions provide better modularity for the project. In addition, it becomes easy for programmers to manage code using functions.

The function can be initialized using the keyword "def" followed by the function name and brackets; input data are positioned within these brackets, *and docstring describes the function's performance*. It is an optional documentation string. Colon (:) signifies the end of function header.

Let's take an example of writing a function of adding two numbers.

```
inta,b;
Def add (a, b) :
sum = a + b
Print ('the sum is ', sum)
Return
```

We can call the function using its name and parameters:

```
add(1,2);
```

2.4.6.1 Python Code Samples for Functions

A function is a block of organized, reusable code used to perform a single, related action. As a result, functions provide better modularity for the application and a high degree of code reusing.

```
SYNTAX: def functionname(parameters): "function_docstring" function_suite
return [expression]
In [1]:  def my_first_function(name): #Function declaration with parameters.
              return(name)
         print(my_first_function('suresh')) # Arguments has to be passed.
         suresh
```

2.4.6.2 Returning Values from Functions

The user can use a function to return a single value or multiple values.

```
In [2]:  def add_two_numbers(num1=6,num2=5): #Default assignment for
parameters in function definition.
```

```
        return(num1+num2)
    #number1 = 34
    #number2 = 44.6
    result= add_two_numbers() #No vales are passed, so default value is
```
used.
```
    print(result)

    11
```

In [3]: **def** print_max(a, b): # Fucntion with parameters and must pass
value.
```
        if a>b:
            print(a, 'is maximum')
        elif a== b:
            print(a, 'is equal to', b)
        else:
            print(b, 'is maximum')
    # directly pass literal values
    #print_max(3, 4)

    x = 5
    y = 7
    #pass variables as arguments
    print_max(x, y) #Arguments must be passed else error may return.
    7 is maximum
```

2.4.6.3 Scope of Variables

All variables in a program may not be accessible at all locations in that program. This depends on where the user has declared a variable. The scope of a variable determines the portion of the program where the user can access a particular identifier. There are two basic scopes of variables in Python:

   i. Global variables
  ii. Local variables

The following example shows the use of a global and local variable in functions:

In [4]: total= 10 # This is global variable.
```
    # Function definition is here
    def sum(arg1, arg2):
        # Add both the parameters and return them. "
        total1 = arg1 + arg2
        a = total + 2
        total; # Here total is local variable.
        print("Inside the function local total : ", total1)
        print(total)
        return total1

    # Now you can call sum function
    sum(10, 20)
    #print ("Outside the function global total : ", total)

    Inside the function local total : 30 10
```
Out[4]:30

2.4.6.4   Function Arguments

The user can call a function by using the following types of formal arguments:

Keyword arguments
Default arguments
Variable-length arguments

2.4.6.4.1   Keyword Arguments

Keyword arguments are related to the function calls. When the user uses keyword arguments in a function call, the caller identifies the arguments by the parameter name. This allows the user to skip arguments or place them out of order because the Python interpreter can use the keywords provided to match the values with parameters. The user can also make keyword calls to the printme() function in the following ways:

```
In [1]: def printme(str):
            #"This prints a passed string into this function"
            print(str)
            return

        # Now you can call printme function
        printme(str= "My string")

        My string

In [3]: def func(a, b=5, c=10): # value assignment to function varible
must be from right to left.
            print('a is', a, 'and b is', b, 'and c is', c)

        func(2) # In this case, Default value of b&c are taken as its value.

        func(25, c=24) # In this case, Default value of b laone is taken,
since other two values are passed.

        func(c=50, a=100)

        a is 2 and b is 5 and c is 10
        a is 25 and b is 5 and c is 24
        a is 100 and b is 5 and c is 50
```

2.4.6.4.2   Default Arguments

A default argument is an argument that assumes a default value if a value is not provided in the function call for that argument. The following example gives an idea of default arguments; it prints the default age if not passed.

```
In [9]: def say(message, times=3):
            print (message * times)

        say('Hello ')

        say('World ', 5)

        Hello Hello Hello
        World WorldWorldWorldWorld
```

```
In [10]: # Function definition is here
        def printinfo(name, age = 35):
          #"This prints a passed info into this function"
          print("Name: ", name)
          print("Age ", age)
          return

        # Now you can call printinfo function
        printinfo( age = 50, name = "miki" )
        printinfo( name = "miki")

        Name: miki
        Age 50
        Name: miki
        Age 35
```

2.4.6.4.3 Variable-Length Arguments

The user may need to process a function for more arguments than those specified while defining the function. Unlike required and default arguments, these arguments are variable-length arguments and are not named in the function definition.

Syntax for a function with non-keyword variable arguments is given below:

deffunctionname([formal_args,] *var_args_tuple): "function_docstring" function_suite return [expression]

An asterisk (*) is placed before the variable name that holds the values of all non-keyword variable arguments. This tuple remains empty if no additional arguments are specified during the function call.

```
In [24]:# Function definition is here
        def printinfo(arg1, *vartuple):
            #This prints a variable passed arguments
            print("Output is: ")
            print (arg1)
            forvarinvartuple:
                print (var)
            return
        # Now you can call printinfo function

        printinfo(10)
        printinfo(70, 60, 50)

Output is:
10

Output is:
70
60
50
In [12]: def multiply(*nums): #*arg is the variabl length list of the
argument
            z  = 1
            fornuminnums:
                z*=num
            print(z)

In [13]: multiply(2,3)
        6
```

```
In [14]: multiply(2,3,5)
         30
```

2.4.6.4.4 The Return Statement

The return statement [expression] exits a function, optionally passing back an expression to the caller. A return statement with no arguments is the same as a return None.

```
In [15]: # Function definition is here
         def sum(arg1, arg2):
             # Add both the parameters and return them."
             total= arg1 + arg2
             print("Inside the function : ", total)
             return total

         # Now you can call sum function
         total= sum(10, 20)
         print("Outside the function : ", total)

         Inside the function : 30
         Outside the function : 30
In [32]: #Function to Find the biggest number.
         def maximum(x, y):
             ifx>y:
                 returnx
             elifx== y:
                 return'The numbers are equal'
             else:
                 return y

         c = maximum(2,3) print(c)

3
In [33]: #Function to find its squares of a number.
         def square(x,y):
             return x*x,y*y
         t = square(2,3)
         print(t)
         (4, 9)
```

2.4.6.4.5 Lambda Function

The syntax of lambda functions contains only a single statement, which is given as follows:

```
lambda [arg1 [,arg2,.....argn]]:expression
In [35]: double= lambda x: x**2
         print(double(10))

         100
In [36]: my_list= [1,5,4,6,11,34,12]
         new_list= list(filter(lambda x : (x%2 == 0),
         my_list)) print(new_list)

         [4, 6, 34, 12]
```

Most of the programming languages like C, C++, Java use braces { } to define a block of code. Python uses indentation. A code block (body of a function, loop, etc.) starts with indentation and ends with the first unindented line. The amount of indentation is up to the user, but it must be consistent throughout that block. Generally, four white spaces are used for indentation and are preferred over tabs. The following example describes such a scenario:

```
In [4]: for I inrange(0,11): print(i)
             if i== 5:
                     break #Break and Exit the loop
        print("a")

        0
        1
        2
        3
        4
        5
        a
```

The enforcement of indentation in Python makes the code look neat and clean. This results in Python programs that look similar and consistent.

```
In [5]: a = 'apple'

        if a== 'apple': # Indented, If condition is true body of the if
is executed
             print('Logging on...')
             print("True....")
        else:
             print('Incorrect password.')
             print('All done!')
             print("unindent line")

        print("Always print")

        Logging on...
        True....
        Always print

In [6]: """"learning about indentations learning about indentations"""""
        If  i =='apple':
             print('Logging on....')
        else:
             print('Incorrect password')
        print('All done!')

        Incorrect password
        All done!

In [7]:
#Anything after # is ignored by python
#comments in python
```

2.4.7 File Handling

File handling allows the application to access the files available on the computer. Therefore, it plays an important role in web applications.

The generic function of working with files is *open()* function. The file can be in four different states:

- **Read:** Opens the file for reading only, and the keyword used is "*r*."
- **Append:** Opens to add a file, and the keyword used is "*a*."
- **Write:** Opens the file for writing, creates a new file if the file doesn't exist, and the keyword used is "*w*."
- **Create:** It creates a new file, identifies errors if the file already exists, and the keyword used is "*x*."
- **Text:** it is the text mode by default, and the keyword used is "*t*."

Example: Suppose we have an application that uploads the documents present on the computer and allows the user to update and create the documents.

Read Files

```
q = open ("myfile.txt", "r")
print(q.read())
```

Write/Create Files

```
q = open ("myfile.txt", "r")
q.write("hi")
q.close()
```

> Open function is a default function which will return the file and as we had print the read function, as a result it will print the data present in file

Delete Files

```
import os
Os.remove("myfile.txt")
```

2.4.8 Exception Handling

It is the process of handling all the unexpected errors which occur during the execution of code. Exception handling helps to handle the errors so that the program does not stop working.

There are many exceptions like arithmetic errors, system errors, standard errors, index errors, and import errors.

The syntax of handling an exception is by defining a try, and except block, a try statement can have multiple exception blocks

try :
//perform your action

exceptException1:
//if error occurs perform this action

The index error is the most common error that occurs during the execution; it occurs when a list contains ten elements and the user accesses the index not present in the list. Let's take the example of the list of fruits.

p= [apple, banana, orange, peach]
    try :

print "the fruit is " %(p[1])
print "the fruit is " %(p[4]) //this will throw exception as there are only 3 elements

except for Index Error :
print "no fruit found"

2.4.9 DEBUGGING IN PYTHON

The process of identifying errors from the source code is called debugging. It helps the programmer dry run each step and identifies the exact line of code due to which error occurred. The software which allows the programmer to debug the code is called a debugger.

There are many ways to debug the code and identify errors. For example, some of the developers print all the lines, which may execute errors. The print statement will help show the output on each step; preserving the log is another way to debug the code. Besides all this, many debugging tools assist developers in automating the debugging.

Python has a debugger, which is known as PDB (Python Debugger). The user can configure it to explore all the debugging features included in it. Thus, the user can easily look into their code while debugging and identify the error-affected lines.

PDB can easily be configured using below-mentioned code:

```
import pdb;
Pdb.set_trace()
```

> While execution, as soon as compiler reaches this line, command prompt opens in the terminal which displays all the debugging information

Following are the built-in commands used during debugging:

1. **List:** Allow the user to view the line which is currently executed.
2. **Up and Down:** The user can change the position of execution with this command.
3. **Step and Next:** Both commands allow the sequential execution of the code. Next, it will go to the next line of the code, ignoring the call to another function. The step will not ignore the call to other functions and goes deeper.
4. **Break:** Allow the user to add break points at different points. It stops the debugging.

2.4.9.1 Packages

Let's take the example, suppose the user is creating an application that includes many modules, it becomes very difficult to manage the code if all are placed into one location. Packages help in creating a hierarchical structuring of the module name using dot notation.

Packages are the namespace that holds many packages and modules themselves. They are the directories that are imported into the projects. The directory should contain a file called "init.py". It indicates that it is a Python library and is imported into the program.

Example: Suppose we have a package that contains two modules name "a.py" and "b.py"

Now the user can import the modules using the following package:

import package.a, package.b

2.5 NUMPY BASICS

Numpy stands for numerical Python, which deals with the multi-dimensional array and contains functions and objects to process and access it. Numpy allows performing all the logical and mathematical operations on the array.

2.5.1 INTRODUCTION TO NUMPY

Numpy is the library for multi-dimensional arrays and their operations. It is also used as a useful multi-dimensional container of generic data. Besides, Numpy also has a built-in function for linear algebra.

The array of Numpy is called ndarray because of its multi-dimension nature. It contains a collection of data with the same data type. The data inside the ndarray can be accessed using an index that starts from zero. In Numpy, the dimensions of the array are called ranks.

2.5.1.1 Array Creation

The array can be initialized in multiple ways by defining several ranks and defining the array's size. Let's initialize a multi-dimensional array:

```
import Numpy  as ns

a = ns.array([1, 2, 3])     # Create a rank 1 array
print(type(a))              # Prints "<class 'numpy.ndarray'>"
print(a.shape)             # Prints "(3,)"
print(a[0], a[1], a[2])    # Prints "1 2 3"
a[0] = 5                   # Change an element of the array
print(a)                   # Prints "[5, 2, 3]"

b = ns.array([[1,2,3],[4,5,6]])    # Create a rank 2 array
print(b.shape)                     # Prints "(2, 3)"
print(b[0, 0], b[0, 1], b[1, 0])   # Prints "1 2 4"

## The out put shown as below
##<class 'numpy.ndarray'>
## (3,)
## 1 2 3
## [5 2 3]
##   (2, 3)
##   b1 2 4

import Numpy  as ns

a = ns.zeros((3,3))     # Create an array of all zeros
print(a)                # Prints "[[0. 0. 0.]
                        #          [0. 0. 0.]
                        #          [0. 0. 0.]]


b = ns.ones((1,2))      # Create an array of all ones
print(b)                # Prints "[[ 1.  1.]]"

c = ns.full((2,2), 7)   # Create a constant array
print(c)                # Prints "[[ 7.  7.]
                        #          [ 7.  7.]]"

d = ns.eye(2)           # Create a 2x2 identity matrix
print(d)                # Prints "[[ 1.  0.]
                        #          [ 0.  1.]]"

e = ns.random.random((2,2))  # Create an array filled with random values
print(e)                     # Might print "[[ 0.91940167  0.08143941]
                             #               [ 0.68744134  0.87236687]]"
```

2.5.1.2 Array Slicing

Array slicing is creating a duplicate of the original array, which contains an index of elements of the original array. It is the most powerful technique used in various ML algorithms.

Slicing is initiated using a colon ":" with a "start" and "end" index before and after the colon. The slicing extends from the "start" index and ends on 1 item before the "end" index.

```
slice[start : end]

 import Numpy  as ns

 # Create the following rank 2 array with shape (3, 4)
 # [[1,3,5,7]
 #  [2,4,6,8]
 #  [3,6,9,12]]
a = ns.array([[1,3,5,7], [2,4,6,8], [3,6,9,12]])

# Use slicing to pull out the subarray consisting of the first two rows
# and columns 1 and 2; b is the following array of shape (2, 2):
# [[2 3]
#  [6 7]]
b = a[:2, 1:3]

# A slice of an array is a view into the same data, so modifying it
# will modify the original array.
print(a[0, 1])   # Prints "3"
b[0, 0] = 99     # b[0, 0] is the same piece of data as a[0, 1]
print(a[0, 1])   # Prints "99"
```

2.5.2 NUMERICAL OPERATIONS

Once the array is created, the user can do arithmetic operations on it. Numpy provides a large number of arithmetic operations which include arithmetic operations and trigonometric functions. An example of arithmetic operations in Numpy is shown below.

```
import Numpy  as ns

x = ns.array([[1,2],[3,4]], dtype=np.float64)
y = ns.array([[5,6],[7,8]], dtype=np.float64)

# Element wise sum; both produce the array
# [[ 6.0  8.0]
#  [10.0 12.0]]
print(x + y)
print(ns.add(x, y))

# Element wise difference; both produce the array
# [[-4.0 -4.0]
#  [-4.0 -4.0]]
print(x - y)
print(ns.subtract(x, y))

# Element wise product; both produce the array
# [[ 5.0 12.0]
#  [21.0 32.0]]
print(x * y)
print(ns.multiply(x, y))
```

TABLE 2.5

Additional Functions in Numpy

Function	Use	Syntax
Real	Returns the real part from complex number	Numpy.real()
Imaginary	Returns the imaginary part from complex number	Numpy.imag()
Mode	Returns the remainder of the division	Numpy.mod()
Conjugate	Returns the conjugate part of a complex number	Numpy.conj()

```
# Element wise division; both produce the array
# [[ 0.2        0.33333333]
#  [ 0.42857143  0.5        ]]
print(x / y)
print(ns.divide(x, y))

# Element wise square root; produces the array
# [[ 1.        1.41421356]
#  [ 1.73205081  2.        ]]
print(ns.sqrt(x))
```

A set of additional Numpy functions are presented in Table 2.5.

Numpy solves linear algebra operations; some of the functions are mentioned below.

- **Dot:** It solves the dot product between two arrays.
- **Determinant:** Solves the determinant of two arrays.
- **Multi Variate INVerse of the matrix (INV):** Solves the multiplicative inverse of the matrix.

2.5.3 PYTHON CODE SAMPLES FOR NUMPY PACKAGE

The example given in this section illustrates the declaration of an array using Numpy and the array variable type.

2.5.3.1 Array Creation

There are several ways to create arrays. For example, a user can create an array from a regular Python list or tuple using the array function. The type of the resulting array is deduced from the type of the elements in the sequences.

```
import numpy  as np # Array-processing package – The user had to import
the package to create and use the array

x = np.array([1,2,3]) # 1-D Array
x
## OURPUT --> array([1, 2, 3])

x1 = np.array([1,2,3])
a = (1,3,5)
b = np.array(a) # Assigning array-a to new variable
print(b)
## OUTPUT --> [1 3 5]

type(b) # Type of the variable
##OUTPUT --> numpy.ndarray
```

```
distance = [12,44,54,70,50]
time = [0.27,0.54,0.77,0.55,0.29]
distance1 = np.array(distance)
time1 = np.array(time)

type(distance)
##OUTPUT --> list
type(distance1)
##OUTPUT --> numpy.ndarray
## ARRAY CREATION
import numpy  as np
arr1 = np.array([2,3,4])
arr1

##OUTPUT --> array([2, 3, 4])

import numpy  as np
x = np.array([1,2,3])
arr2 = np.array([1.2, 3.5, 5.1])
arr2
##OUTPUT --> array([1.2, 3.5, 5.1])

arr3 = np.array(["abc","def"])
arr3
##OUTPUT --> rray(['abc', 'def'], dtype='<U3')
arr3.dtype
##OUTPUT --> dtype('<U3')

arr4 = np.array(["xyz","ijk"])

#A frequent error consists in calling array with multiple numeric arguments,
rather than #providing a single list of numbers as an argument.
#a = np.array(1,2,3,4)    # WRONG
#a = np.array([1,2,3,4])  # RIGHT
```

Array transforms sequences into two-dimensional arrays, sequences of sequences into three-dimensional arrays, and so on.

```
b = np.array([[[(1.5,2,3), (4,5,6),(7,8,9)]]])
b
##OUTPUT --> array([[[[1.5, 2., 3. ],
##OUTPUT -->        [4., 5., 6. ],
##OUTPUT -->        [7., 8., 9. ]]]])

b.ndim # Number of array dimensions.
##OUTPUT --> 4

b.shape # Current shape of an array
##OUTPUT -->  (1, 1, 3, 3)

c = np.array([ [1,2], [3,4] ], dtype=complex)
c

##OUTPUT --> array([[1.+0.j, 2.+0.j],
##OUTPUT -->        [3.+0.j, 4.+0.j]])
```

```
d = np.ones((3,3,4), dtype=np.int16)  #2=no.of arrays
d

##OUTPUT --> array([[[1, 1, 1, 1],
##OUTPUT -->          [1, 1, 1, 1],
##OUTPUT -->          [1, 1, 1, 1]],
##OUTPUT -->
##OUTPUT -->        [[1, 1, 1, 1],
##OUTPUT -->          [1, 1, 1, 1],
##OUTPUT -->          [1, 1, 1, 1]],
##OUTPUT -->
##OUTPUT -->         [[1, 1, 1, 1],
##OUTPUT -->          [1, 1, 1, 1],
##OUTPUT -->          [1, 1, 1, 1]]], dtype=int16)

d.ndim
##OUTPUT -->3

d.shape
##OUTPUT -->(3,3,4)

e= np.array([[[1,2],[3,4,5],[6,7,8,9]]])
e

##OUTPUT --> array([[list([1, 2]), list([3, 4, 5]), list([6, 7, 8, 9])]],
dtype=object)


import numpy  as np
a = np.arange(10,21,3)
print(a)
##OUTPUT --> [10 13 16 19] - Array sttarting from 10 and ends in 21 with the
increments in value of 3
s = slice(2,7)
s
print(a[s])
print(s)
##OUTPUT --> slice(2, 7, None)
a[2] = 3
print(a)
##OUTPUT -->[10 13  3 19] - Changed the thrid value (index value 2 from 16 to
3)

s = slice(1)
print(a[s])
##OUTPUT --> [10]

a = ("a","b","c","d","e","f","g","h")
x = slice(4,6)
print(a[x])
##OUTPUT --> ('e', 'f')

b = np.arange(2.5,6.5)
b
##OUTPUT --> array([2.5, 3.5, 4.5, 5.5])
```

```
# slice single item
a = np.arange(10)
b = a[5]
print (b)
##OUTPUT --> 5

x = np.arange(10,21)
print(x)
##OUTPUT --> [10 11 12 13 14 15 16 17 18 19 20]

a = np.arange(10)**2 # Square of number from zero to Nine
a
##OUTPUT --> array([ 0,  1,  4,  9, 16, 25, 36, 49, 64, 81], dtype=int32)

a[0:6:2] = -1000  ## Please note the elements starting from index 0 and
till index 5 in the increments of 2 will be changed to -1000
a
##OUTPUT --> array([-1000,    1, -1000,    9, -1000,   25,   36,
49,    64, 81], dtype=int32)
```

The array can be created from scratch, as shown above, or from another array. The below code examples show how an array can be created from an existing array.

```
#creating an array from existing array
import numpy  as np

x = [1,2,3]
a = np.asarray(x)
print (a)
##OUTPUT --> [1,2,3]

# dtype is set
a = np.asarray(x, dtype = float)
print (a)
##OUTPUT --> [1. 2. 3.]

# ndarray from a tuple

x = (1,2,3)
a = np.asarray(x)
print (a)
##OUTPUT --> [1,2,3]

type(a)
##OUTPUT --> numpy.ndarray

# ndarray from list of tuples

x = [(1,2,3),(4,5)]
a = np.asarray(x)
print (a)
##OUTPUT -->[(1, 2, 3) (4, 5)]

import numpy  as np
x = np.arange(5)
print (x)
##OUTPUT --> [0 1 2 3 4]
```

```
# dtype set
x = np.arange(5, dtype = float)
print (x)
##OUTPUT --> [0. 1. 2. 3. 4.]

# start and stop parameters set
x = np.arange(10,20)
print (x)
##OUTPUT --> [10 11 12 13 14 15 16 17 18 19]

import numpy  as np
#numpy.linspace(start, stop, num=50, endpoint=True, retstep=False,
dtype=None, axis=0)
x = np.linspace(10,20,4) # returns evenly spaced numbers over a specified
interval.
#Start from 10 and End at 20
print (x)
##OUTPUT --> [10.        13.33333333 16.66666667 20.        ]
#PLEASE NOTE THE NUMBER OF ELEMENTS

import numpy  as np
x = np.linspace(10,20,10)
print (x)
##OUTPUT --> [10.          11.11111111 12.22222222 13.33333333 14.44444444
15.55555556
##OUTPUT -->  16.66666667 17.77777778 18.88888889 20.        ]
```

2.5.3.2   Class and Attributes of ndarray—.ndim

Numpy's array class is "ndarray," also referred to as "numpy.ndarray." This refers to the number of axes (dimensions) of the array. It is also called the rank of the array.

```
f = np.array([[[(1.5,2,3), (4,5,6),(7,8,9)]]])
f.ndim
##OUTPUT -->2

#Describes how the bytes in the fixed-size block of memory corresponding to
an array item should be interpreted
f.dtype
##OUTPUT --> dtype('int32')

f.itemsize
##OUTPUT --> 4   ## The array is 32 bit length; 8 bytes ; 32/8 = 4

np_first_trial_cyclist = np.array([10,12,15,16]) #Create an array with data
np_second_trial_cyclist = np.array([20,25,30,45])
np_first_trial_cyclist + np_second_trial_cyclist # addition of two arrays
##OUTPUT -->  array([30, 37, 45, 61])
```

2.5.3.3   Class and Attributes of ndarray—.shape

This consists of a tuple of integers showing the size of the array in each dimension. The length of the "shape tuple" is the rank or ndim.

```
b = np.array([[[(1.5,2,3), (4,5,6),(7,8,9)]]])
b
##OUTPUT --> array([[[[1.5, 2., 3. ],
```

```
##OUTPUT -->        [4., 5., 6. ],
##OUTPUT -->        [7., 8., 9. ]]]])

b.ndim # Number of array dimensions.
##OUTPUT --> 4

b.shape # Current shape of an array
##OUTPUT -->  (1, 1, 3, 3)
```

2.5.3.4 Class and Attributes of ndarray—ndarray.size, ndarray.Itemsize, ndarray.resize

It gives the total number of elements in the array. It is equal to the product of the elements of the shape tuple. Itemsize describes how the bytes in the fixed-size block of memory corresponding to an array item should be interpreted.

```
import  numpy  as np
f = np.array([[1, 2,5], [3, 4,7]])
print (f)
##OUTPUT -->[[1 2 5]
##OUTPUT -->  [3 4 7]]

f.size
##OUTPUT -->6 - 6 elements

#Describes how the bytes in the fixed-size block of memory corresponding to
an array item should be interpreted
f.dtype
##OUTPUT --> dtype('int32')

f.itemsize
##OUTPUT --> 4  ## The array is 32 bit length; 8 bytes ; 32/8 = 4

f.resize (3,3)
f
##output -->array([[1, 2, 5],
##output -->        [3, 4, 7],
##output -->        [0, 0, 0]]) - note the last elements are zeros
```

2.5.3.5 Class and Attributes of ndarray—.dtype

It is an object that describes the type of elements in the array. It can be created or specified using Python.

```
import numpy  as np
x = np.array([1,2,3])
arr2 = np.array([1.2, 3.5, 5.1])
arr2
##OUTPUT --> array([1.2, 3.5, 5.1])

arr3 = np.array(["abc","def"])
arr3
##OUTPUT --> rray(['abc', 'def'], dtype='<U3')
arr3.dtype
##OUTPUT --> dtype('<U3')

c = np.array([ [1,2], [3,4] ], dtype=complex)
c
```

```
##OUTPUT --> array([[1.+0.j, 2.+0.j],
##OUTPUT -->          [3.+0.j, 4.+0.j]])

d = np.ones((3,3,4), dtype=np.int16) #2=no.of arrays
d

##OUTPUT --> array([[[1, 1, 1, 1],
##OUTPUT -->          [1, 1, 1, 1],
##OUTPUT -->          [1, 1, 1, 1]],
##OUTPUT -->
##OUTPUT -->        [[1, 1, 1, 1],
##OUTPUT -->          [1, 1, 1, 1],
##OUTPUT -->          [1, 1, 1, 1]],
##OUTPUT -->
##OUTPUT -->         [[1, 1, 1, 1],
##OUTPUT -->          [1, 1, 1, 1],
##OUTPUT -->          [1, 1, 1, 1]]], dtype=int16)

d.ndim
##OUTPUT -->3

d.shape
##OUTPUT -->(3,3,4)

e= np.array([[[1,2],[3,4,5],[6,7,8,9]]])
e

##OUTPUT --> array([[list([1, 2]), list([3, 4, 5]), list([6, 7, 8, 9])]],
dtype=object)
```

2.5.3.6 Basic Operations

Numpy uses the indices of the elements in each array to carry out basic operations. In this case, where we are looking at a dataset of four cyclists during two trials, vector addition of the arrays gives the required output.

```
import numpy  as np
cyclist_trial = np.array([[10,12,15,16],[20,25,30,45]])
cyclist_trial

##OUTPUT --> array([[10, 12, 15, 16],
##OUTPUT -->          [20, 25, 30, 45]])

first_trial = cyclist_trial[0] # Assign value at row-index(0) of all column
first_trial # Prints the data assigned to it.
##OUTPUT --> array([10, 12, 15, 16])

second_trial = cyclist_trial[1]
second_trial
##OUTPUT --> array([20, 25, 30, 45])

third_trial = cyclist_trial[1][0] #secondrow,first column
third_trial
##OUTPUT --> 20

tst = cyclist_trial[1,1] # Second-row Second column
tst
```

```
##OUTPUT --> 25

forth_trial = cyclist_trial[:,2]
forth_trial
##OUTPUT --> array([15, 30])

cyclist_trial.shape
##OUTPUT --> (2, 4) - TWO ROWS AND 4 COLUMNS


fifth_trial = cyclist_trial[:,1:3]
fifth_trial
##OUTPUT --> array([[12, 15],
##OUTPUT -->         [25, 30]])
```

2.5.3.7   Accessing Array Elements: Indexing

The user can access an entire row of an array by referencing its axis index. In addition, the indices of the elements in an array can be referred to access them. A particular index of more than one axis can also be selected.

```
import numpy  as np
a = np.arange(10,21,3)
print(a)
##OUTPUT --> [10 13 16 19] - Array sttarting from 10 and ends in 21 with the
increments in value of 3
s = slice(2,7)
s
print(a[s])
print(s)
##OUTPUT --> slice(2, 7, None)
a[2] = 3
print(a)
##OUTPUT -->[10 13  3 19] - Changed the thrid value (index value 2 from 16 to
3)

s = slice(1)
print(a[s])
##OUTPUT --> [10]

a = ("a","b","c","d","e","f","g","h")
x = slice(4,6)
print(a[x])
##OUTPUT --> ('e', 'f')

b = np.arange(2.5,6.5)
b
##OUTPUT --> array([2.5, 3.5, 4.5, 5.5])

# slice single item
a = np.arange(10)
b = a[5]
print (b)
##OUTPUT --> 5

x = np.arange(10,21)
print(x)
##OUTPUT --> [10 11 12 13 14 15 16 17 18 19 20]
```

```
a = np.arange(10)**2 # Square of number from zero to Nine
a
##OUTPUT --> array([ 0,  1,  4,  9, 16, 25, 36, 49, 64, 81], dtype=int32)

a[0:6:2] = -1000  ## Please note the elements starting from index 0 and
till index 5 in the increments of 2 will be changed to -1000
a
##OUTPUT --> array([-1000,    1, -1000,    9, -1000,   25,   36,   49,
64, 81], dtype=int32)

# slice items starting from index
a = np.arange(10)
print(a)
##OUTPUT -->[0 1 2 3 4 5 6 7 8 9]
print (a[2:])
##OUTPUT -->[2 3 4 5 6 7 8 9]

a = np.array([[1,2,3],[3,4,5],[4,5,6]])
print(a)
##OUTPUT -->[[1 2 3]
##OUTPUT --> [3 4 5]
##OUTPUT --> [4 5 6]]
a.ndim
##OUTPUT -->2
## slice items starting from index
#print ('Now we will slice the array from the index a[1:]')
print (a[1:])
##OUTPUT -->[[3 4 5]
##OUTPUT --> [4 5 6]]

print (a[1][1])
##OUTPUT --> 4
print (a[1][1:])
##OUTPUT --> [4 5]

a=np.array([[1,2,3,4,5],[1,2,4,78,8,],[3,6,8,4,3],([1,2,4],[2,3,4,4])])
print(a[2:])
##OUTPUT --> [list([3, 6, 8, 4, 3]) ([1, 2, 4], [2, 3, 4, 4])]
print(a[:1])
##OUTPUT --> [list([1, 2, 3, 4, 5])]
print(a[0:])
##OUTPUT --> [list([1, 2, 3, 4, 5]) list([1, 2, 4, 78, 8]) list([3, 6, 8, 4,
3]) ([1, 2, 4], [2, 3, 4, 4])]
a.ndim
##OUTPUT -->1

import numpy  as np
np.random.random_sample((5,)) ## return random floats in half open
interval[0.0,1.0)
##OUTPUT --> array([0.93582707, 0.45519645, 0.63904608, 0.72751779,
0.03412199])

NOTE: The random numbers will be generated when run again, and the output
will be different.

type(np.random.random_sample())
##OUTPUT --> float
```

```
a = np.random.random([2,3]) #indices(no.ofrows,no.columns)
a
##OUTPUT -->array([[0.44139017, 0.50624907, 0.68734659],
##OUTPUT -->        [0.52525588, 0.03275437, 0.52491101]])

c = a.sum()
c
##OUTPUT --> 2.7179070918025525

x = np.arange(20).reshape(5, 4)
#row, col = np.indices((2, 3))
#x[row, col]
x
##OUTPUT -->array([[ 0,  1,  2,  3],
##OUTPUT -->        [ 4,  5,  6,  7],
##OUTPUT -->        [ 8,  9, 10, 11],
##OUTPUT -->        [12, 13, 14, 15],
##OUTPUT -->        [16, 17, 18, 19]])

row, col = np.indices((3, 2))
x[row, col]

##OUTPUT -->array([[0, 1],
##OUTPUT -->        [4, 5],
##OUTPUT -->        [8, 9]])

a.min()
##OUTPUT -->   0.032754372323505976

b = np.arange(12).reshape(3,4) # New shape to an array without changing its
data.
b
##OUTPUT --> array([[ 0,  1,  2,  3],
##OUTPUT -->        [ 4,  5,  6,  7],
##OUTPUT -->        [ 8,  9, 10, 11]])

b[2][1] # 2nd-Row 1st-column
##OUTPUT --> 9

b.sum() # Sum of numbers in array b
##OUTPUT --> 66

b.sum(axis=0) #sum across column
##OUTPUT --> array([ 6, 22, 38])

A = np.array([[1,1],
              [0,1]])
B = np.array([[2,0],
              [3,4]])

type(A)
##OUTPUT --> numpy.ndarray

A*B    #Elementwise product
##OUTPUT --> array([[2, 0],
##OUTPUT -->        [0, 4]])
```

```
A@B   #MatrixMultipication
##OUTPUT --> array([[5, 4],
##OUTPUT -->        [3, 4]])

A.dot(B)   #Another matrix multipication
##OUTPUT --> array([[5, 4],
##OUTPUT -->        [3, 4]])
```

Multidimensional arrays can have one index per axis. These indices are given in a tuple separated by commas:

```
a = np.fromfunction(lambda i, j: i == j, (3, 3), dtype=int)
a
##OUTPUT --> array([[ True, False, False],
##OUTPUT -->        [False,  True, False],
##OUTPUT -->        [False, False,  True]])

x = np.fromfunction(lambda i, j: i + j, (3, 3), dtype=int)
x
##OUTPUT -->array([[0, 1, 2],
##OUTPUT -->       [1, 2, 3],
##OUTPUT -->       [2, 3, 4]])

import numpy  as np
def f(x,y):
return 10*x+y
b = np.fromfunction(f,(5,5),dtype=int)#(X,Y) are coordinates
b
##OUTPUT -->array([[ 0,  1,  2,  3,  4],
##OUTPUT -->       [10, 11, 12, 13, 14],
##OUTPUT -->       [20, 21, 22, 23, 24],
##OUTPUT -->       [30, 31, 32, 33, 34],
##OUTPUT -->       [40, 41, 42, 43, 44]])

b[2,3] # 3rd row 4th Element (Please note the index starts at 0)
##OUTPUT --> 23

b[0:5, 1] # each row in the second column of b
##OUTPUT --> array([ 1, 11, 21, 31, 41])

b[-1]   # the last row. Equivalent to b[-1,:]
##OUTPUT --> array([40, 41, 42, 43, 44])
```

2.5.3.8 Shape Manipulation

The shape of the array can be manipulated and modified. This gives the orientation of the array.

```
#Shape Manipulation
#Changing the shape of an array

#An array has a shape given by the number of elements along each axis:
import numpy  as np
a = np.floor(10*np.random.random((3,4)))
##  Return the closest integer value which is less than or equal to the
specified expression
a
##OUTPUT --> array([[4., 8., 4., 3.],
```

```
##OUTPUT -->          [2., 7., 2., 8.],
##OUTPUT -->          [1., 8., 5., 2.]])

a.shape
##OUTPUT --> (3,4)

#The shape of an array can be changed with various commands.
#Note that the following three commands all return a modified array but do
not change the original array:

a.ravel() #flatened array
##OUTPUT --> array([4., 8., 4., 3., 2., 7., 2., 8., 1., 8., 5., 2.])

# ravel() function is used to create a contiguous flattened array.
# Purpose of ravel() Function
# Return only reference/view of the original array
# If you modify the array, you will notice that the value of the original
array also changes.
# Ravel is faster than flatten() as it does not occupy any memory.
# Ravel is a library-level function.

a.shape
##OUTPUT --> (3,4)

a = a.reshape(6,2)
a

##OUTPUT --> array([[4., 8.],
##OUTPUT -->         [4., 3.],
##OUTPUT -->         [2., 7.],
##OUTPUT -->         [2., 8.],
##OUTPUT -->         [1., 8.],
##OUTPUT -->         [5., 2.]])

a.T #Transpose:value of row changes to column
##OUTPUT -->   array([[4., 4., 2., 2., 1., 5.],
##OUTPUT -->          [8., 3., 7., 8., 8., 2.]])

a
##OUTPUT -->   array([[4., 8.],
##OUTPUT -->          [4., 3.],
##OUTPUT -->          [2., 7.],
##OUTPUT -->          [2., 8.],
##OUTPUT -->          [1., 8.],
##OUTPUT -->          [5., 2.]])

a.shape #After Reshape
##OUTPUT --> (6,2)

a.resize((2,6))
a
##OUTPUT -->array([[4., 8., 4., 3., 2., 7.],
##OUTPUT -->        [2., 8., 1., 8., 5., 2.]])

a.shape
##OUTPUT --> (2,6)
```

2.5.3.9   Universal Functions (ufunc) in Numpy

Numpy provides useful mathematical functions called Universal Functions. These functions operate element-wise on an array, producing another array as output.

```
np_sqrt =np.sqrt([2,4,9,16]) # Takes Square-root of each value
np_sqrt
#OUTPUT --> array([1.41421356, 2.        , 3.        , 4.        ])

from numpy  import pi
np.cos(0) #Returns the cosine of value passed as argument. The value passed
in this function should be in radians
##OUTPUT --> 1.0

np.sin(pi/2) # sine value of X
##OUTPUT --> 1.0

np.sin(90)
##OUTPUT --> 0.8939966636005579

np.cos(pi)
##OUTPUT --> -1.0

pi # Returns value of PI
##OUTPUT --> 3.141592653589793

np.floor([1.2,1.6,2.7,3.3,-0.3,-1.4])
##OUTPUT --> array([ 1.,   1.,   2.,   3., -1., -2.])

np.sin(90 * np.pi / 180)
```

2.5.3.10   Broadcasting

Numpy uses broadcasting to carry out arithmetic operations between arrays of different shapes. In this method, Numpy automatically broadcasts the smaller array over the larger array. Though broadcasting can help carry out mathematical operations between different-shaped arrays, they are subject to certain constraints as listed below.

When Numpy operates on two arrays, it compares their shapes element-wise. It finds these shapes compatible only if:

- Their dimensions are the same or
- One of them has a dimension of size 1.
- If these conditions are not met, a "ValueError" is thrown, indicating that the arrays have incompatible shapes.

```
import numpy  as np
a = np.array([1,2,3,4])
b = np.array([10,20,30,40])
c = a * b
c
##OUTPUT -->array([ 10,  40,  90, 160])

a = np.array([5])
a
##OUTPUT -->array([5])
```

```
d = a * b
print (d)
##OUTPUT -->[ 50 100 150 200]
type(d)
##OUTPUT -->numpy.ndarray

e = np.array([4,5,6,7])
print(e)
##OUTPUT -->[4 5 6 7]
f = d*e
f
##OUTPUT -->array([ 200,   500,   900, 1400])

f = e*7
print(f)
##OUTPUT -->[28 35 42 49]

#Args and kwargs
def sum(*args):
    s = 0
    for i in args:
        s += i
    print("sum is", s)

sum(1,2,3)
##OUTPUT --> sum is 6

sum(1,2,3,4,5,6)
##OUTPUT --> sum is 21
```

2.5.3.11 Args and Kwargs

*Args are the signature of Numpy arguments, which means that other positional arguments could be passed. The special syntax **kwargs in function definitions in Python is used to pass a keyworded, \nvariable-length argument list. We use the name kwargs with the double star.\n; the reason is that the double star allows us to pass through keyword arguments (and any number of them).

```
def sum(*args):
    s = 0
    for i in args:
        s += i
    print("sum is", s)

sum(1,2,3)
##OUTPUT --> sum is 6

sum(1,2,3,4,5,6)
##OUTPUT --> sum is 21

#kwargs allows us to pass a variable number of keyword argument like this

def my_func(**kwargs):
    for i,j in kwargs.items():
        print(i,j)
my_func(name='Suresh',sport='Cricket',Score=120)
##OUTPUT --> name Suresh
##OUTPUT --> sport Cricket
##OUTPUT --> Score 120
```

2.6 MATPLOTLIB BASICS

Creating the statistical view of the data is the most demanding; Python provides a library called "Matplotlib." It is very powerful and easily understandable for programmers who are already working with Python and Numpy. It is used with Numpy to provide a 2D graphical view.

The matplotlib is useful for data scientists who want to visualize their data to provide the best outcome. Matplotlib is the most popular module of Python of data visualization.

To use matplotlib, the user should first download its package according to the Python installed. The library which is used to draw 2D data is called **pyplot().** Matplotlib can be initialized as follows:

```
import matplotlib
import pyplot as plot
```

```
Let's take the example of a survey on food items purchased by students from
the canteen. Show the graphical representation of the most and least eaten
items by students.
```

```
import numpy  as ns
import matplotlib
import pyplot as plot
fooditems = ns. array ["Chips", "Burgers", "Sandwich", "Roll", "Patties",
"Pizza"]
students = ns.array [0, 1, 2, 3, 4,5,6]
plot.title ("Survey on food items")
plot.xlabel ("x-axis represents the food item sold in the canteen")
plot.ylabel ("y-axis represents the number of students purchase items")
plot.plot(fooditems,students)
plot.show()
```

```
Output : The output of the above code is shown in Figure 2.23.
```

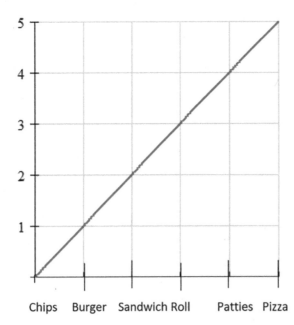

X axis : No. of Food Items

FIGURE 2.23   Output for illustration on matplotlib.

2.6.1 CREATING GRAPHS WITH MATPLOTLIB

1. **Bar graph:** It is the most commonly used graph to show the data representations. Matplotlib provides a built-in function *bar()*to create bar graphs. It takes three input variables: fields, value, and color. Let's consider the same example of a survey on students eating the same food items.

```
import numpy  as ns
Impot matplotlib
import pyplot as plot
fooditems = ns.array ["Chips", "Burgers", "Sandwich", "Roll", "Patties",
"Pizza"]
students = ns.array [ 10, 20, 30, 40,50,60]
plot.title ("Survey on food items")
plot.xlabel ("x axis represents the food item sold in canteen")
plot.ylabel ("y axis represents the number of students purchase
items")
plot.bar (fooditems,students, color = 'green')
plot.show()

Output: The output of the above code is shown in Figure 2.24.
```

2. **Pie chart:** Another type of graph is a pie chart created using a built-in function called pie(). Explode defines the fraction of the radius with which to offset each wedge. Labels define the chunks in which the chart will be distributed; shadow adds additional effects in the pie chart.

```
import numpy  as ns
Impot matplotlib
import pyplot as plot
```

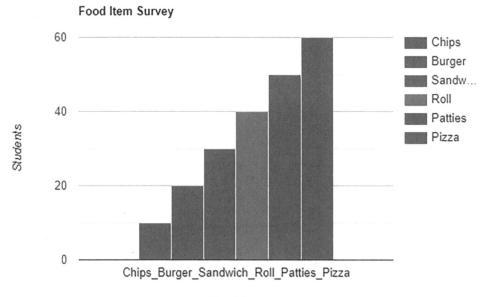

FIGURE 2.24 Output for illustration on graphs with matplotlib.

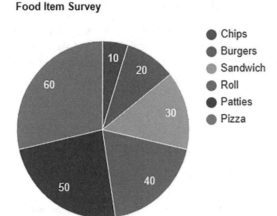

FIGURE 2.25   Output for illustration on pie chart.

```
fooditems = ns.array ["Chips", "Burgers", "Sandwich", "Roll", "Patties",
"Pizza"]
students = ns.array [ 10, 20, 30, 40,50,60]
Explode = [0,0,0,0,0,0]
plot.title ("Survey on food items")
plot.pie (students, explode = Explode,label = fooditems, shadow=
false,startangle = 45)
plot.legend(title =" Food items in canteen")
plot.show()

Output : The output of the above code is shown in Figure 2.25.
```

2.7 PANDAS BASICS

Pandas are the most well-liked Python library for data science. It helps to handle two-dimensional data tables in Python. It provides flexibility and ease of use. Pandas are used in various fields like finance, commercial, economics, and analytical.

2.7.1 GETTING STARTED WITH PANDAS

The major drawback of Python was it has very few features for data preparations and manipulation. Then, Pandas solve the problem; now, it allows preparing, manipulating, analyzing, and modeling the data.

Let's take the example of data present in the computer in a (Comma Separated Value) CSV file, and the user wants to analyze the data to conclude the results. Pandas will help the user in this by importing the data and converting the data into a meaningful manner by analyzing and cleaning the data if any missing fields are found to filter the data in rows and columns accordingly.

Pandas are easy to install. For example, the following command is written in the command line install Pandas package:

```
Conda install pandas
```

To import Pandas in the source code, use the following code:

```
import pandas as pa
```

2.7.2 DATA FRAMES

Pandas mostly deal with three data structures:

- Series
- Data Frames
- Panels

Series: It is a one-dimensional array that holds any data. It is just a column of an Excel sheet. To create a series from the array, import the numpy () function.

```
import pandas as pd
importnumpy  as ns
a = ns.array (["apple", "banana", "orange", "peach"])
series = pd.series(a)
Print series
Retrieve data from series :
Print a[0]
```

Output :

Apple
orange
banana

Data frames: It is a two-dimensional array. It is like a table with rows and columns of different data types. Let's take the example of storing student information as shown below.

Name	Age	Class	Average Marks Scored
Alice	10	6	50
Mack	5	2	20
Jason	4	1	40
Adam	9	3	50

Row

Column

The syntax used to initialize the data frame:

Pandas.DataFrame (data, index, column, data type, copy)

Let's explain each in detail:

- **Data:** The input data in the form of an array, list, set, or any other data structure.
- **Index:** Represents the row that is accessed.
- **Column:** Represents the column in the data.
- **Data type:** Data type, that is, int, string, float, etc.
- **Copy:** Used for copying the data.

Creating a Data Frame:

```
import pandas as pd
importnumpy  as ns
a = ns.array (["apple", "banana", "orange", "peach"])
dataframe= pd.DataFrame(a)
Print dataframe
```

Output :

0 Apple
1 orange
2 banana

3 peach

2.7.3 KEY OPERATIONS ON DATA FRAMES

2.7.3.1 Data Frame from List

Data frames can be created using the list. Let's take the example of displaying marks scored by students in English subject.

```
import pandas as pd
list = [['Anna', 20], ['Jhon', 30], ['Adam', 55], ['Jason', 60]]
dataframe= pd.DataFrame(list, column = ['Student Name', 'Marks Scored'],
dtype = int)
Print dataframe
```

Output:

	Student Name	Marks Scored
0	Anna	20
1	Jhon	30
2	Adam	55
3	Jason	60

2.7.3.2 Rows and Columns in Data Frame

Data are saved in the form of a table that contains rows and columns. Thus, we can perform multiple operations, for example adding, selecting, deleting, etc.

2.7.3.2.1 Selecting the Column in Data Frames

```
import pandas as ps
data = {'name' : ['Anna', 'Jhon', 'Adma', 'Jason'], 'Marks' : [20, 30, 55, 60]}
dataframe = ps.DataFrame(data, index = [0,1,2,3])
first = dataframe('name')
print (first)
```

2.7.3.2.2 Adding a Column to an Existing Data Frame

```
import pandas as ps
data = {'Name' : ['Anna', 'Jhon', 'Adam', 'Jason'], 'Marks' : [20, 30, 55, 60]}
dataframe = ps.DataFrame(data, index = [0,1,2,3])
print (dataframe)
class = [1, 2, 3, 4]
dataframe['Class'] = class# add new column
print ("after adding new column")
print (dataframe)
```

Output:

	Name	Marks
0	Anna	20
1	Jhon	30
2	Adam	55
3	Jason	60

After adding a new column

	Name	Marks	Class
0	Anna	20	1
1	Jhon	30	2
2	Adam	55	3
3	Jason	60	4

2.7.3.2.3 Deleting a Column from a Data Frame

```
import pandas as ps
data = {'Name' : ['Anna', 'Jhon', 'Adam', 'Jason'], 'Marks' : [20, 30, 55,
60], 'class' : [1,2,3,4]}
dataframe = ps.DataFrame(data, index = [0,1,2,3])
print (dataframe)
print ("delete the column class")
dataframe.pop('class')
print(dataframe)              #deletes the column
```

2.8 COMPUTATIONAL COMPLEXITY

Computational complexity refers to the number of resources required to complete a task. Computational complexity helps the programmers identify the level of complexity the program will face to overcome it.

The complexity of a program or algorithm varies concerning the input data; it is generally expressed in the form of "$f(n)$" where n indicates the size of the input.

Computational complexity in terms of an algorithm is how long an algorithm will take to solve the problem in the worst case. Algorithms can be analyzed as follows:

- **Asymptotic analysis:** When creating an application, various things need to be focused on. Such application should be user-friendly, fast, easily configurable, and the performance is the key to an application. No one likes to run an application that is slow in operations and works badly in a large amount of data. How can we identify the speed of an algorithm and tell whether the algorithm will work best in large input? The answer to all the above questions is asymptotic analysis.

It evaluates the algorithm's performance with large input data; it calculates how the time increases as the data input increases. When we have two algorithms for the same problem, asymptotic will help calculate and choose the best suitable algorithm.

The algorithm can be analyzed based on the following cases:

Worst-case complexity: Maximum number of steps algorithm will perform. Identify the UB on the run time of the algorithm. The case that causes a maximum number of operations. For example, searching an element in the data that is not present in it, as the loop will iterate till the end to search the element, which is why it is the worst case.

Average-case complexity: Find all the possible inputs, calculate the time consumed, add all the calculated values, and divide it with several inputs. It is not easy to do and has rarely been used.

Best-case complexity: It generates the LB of the algorithm. Calculate the case that causes the minimum number of operations to be executed.

Space complexity: Space complexity is the required memory to solve a problem. Suppose the problem requires large memory. As a result, the program will become more complex.

Time complexity: How much time the algorithm takes to solve a problem. Time includes the execution time of the program.

2.9 REAL-WORLD EXAMPLES

Based on the topics explained in this chapter, the authors have provided real-world examples to understand the concepts better.

2.9.1   IMPLEMENTATION USING PANDAS

Pandas help the data science field by boosting up the application flow. It helps to visualize the data in tabular form. Let's take the example of analyzing the data newly of milk products of different brands.

The information will contain different attributes of milk products namely pH, multi-vitamins, density and a quality score between 0 and 5. The quality score is the average of three tests by a human. First, let's explain how to save the data using Numpy.

Brand	pH	Energy	Fat	Quality Score	Carbohydrate	Protein	Sodium
Open Process Interface (OPI)	3.51	30	66	2	23	40	12
Milky	3.20	60	11	3	70	50	13

From the above table, there are three rows. The first row is the header column. Each row after the header represents a different product and its quality. For example, the first row defines the brand name, then is the pH, energy, fat, and so on.

Let's input the data using Matplotlib:

```
import pandas as ps
data = {'Brand: ['OPI, 'Milky'], 'PH': [3.51, 3.20], 'Energy' : [30,60],
'Fat' : [66, 11], 'Quality Score' : [2, 3], 'Carbohydrate' : [23, 70],
'Protein' : [40,50], 'Sodium' : 12, 13}
dataframe = ps.DataFrame(data, index = [0,1])
print (dataframe)
```

1. Find the count of several rows and columns in the data frame.
   `dataframe. Shape`
2. How to access the last-row value?
   `dataframe.tail(1)`
3. How can we access the first-row value?
   `dataframe.head(1)`

2.9.2   IMPLEMENTATION USING NUMPY

Let's solve the problem of finding the area and perimeter of five rectangles. To find the area and perimeter, we will need the length and width of the rectangle.

```
import numpy  as ns
length= ns.array ([5,10,15,20,25])
width = ns.array ([20, 22, 24, 25, 26])
area =  multiply(length, width)
perimeter1 = add(length, width)
perimeter = perimeter * 2
Print(perimeter)
print(area)
```

2.9.3   IMPLEMENTATION USING MATPLOTLIB

Matplotlib provides the graphical representation of data to visualize it. With the help of matplotlib, the user can extract the required information and plot it on the graph as per the requirement. Let's take the example of drawing a histogram with matplotlib.

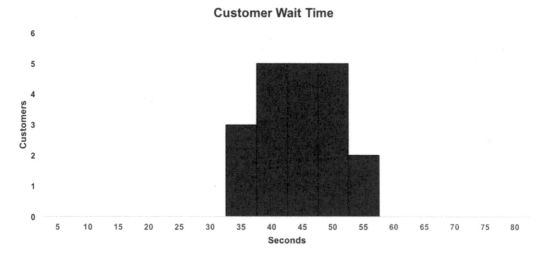

FIGURE 2.26   Histogram output.

The histogram is a common type of plot when the user is looking for the data like height, weight, and customer waiting time. Histogram data are plotted within the range against its frequency.

Adam is working in a bank; nowadays, he is receiving many complaints from clients about the wait time to register complaints to complain officers. Adam decided to observe the waiting time for each customer. Data are given below:

Customer	Time in Seconds
Customer 1	43
Customer 2	35
Customer 3	36.5
Customer 4	50.2
Customer 5	50.2

```
import numpy  as ns
import matplotlib
importpyplot as plot
time= ns.array [43, 35, 36.5, 50.2, 50.2]
customer= ns.array [ "Customer 1", "Customer 2", "Customer 3", "Customer 4",
"Customer 5"]
plot.title ("Customer Wait Ttime Observation")
plot.xlabel ("x axis represents the time in seonds")
plot.ylabel ("y axis represents the customers")
plot.hist (time,customer)
plot.show()
```

Output - The output of the above code is shown in Figure 2.26.

SUMMARY

- **Python:** It is a high-level, interactive, and object-oriented language. Python is easy to understand. Most of the ML and artificial intelligence algorithms are written in Python.

- **Major uses of Python:** It is used as Object Oriented Programming (OOP)-oriented language and scripting language, and it is easily integrated with other languages like C, C++, and JAVA. It is used heavily in data science, ML, and deep learning.
- **Control flow statement:** Control flow describes the order of the program in which the code will be executed. The control statements are handled with the help of conditional statements like a loop and function calls.
- **List:** List is the data structure that is changeable and ordered list. Each element of the list is called an item. The list is initiated using brackets.
- **Tuple:** A tuple is a sequence of absolute objects separated by a comma. Tuples are accessed with their index.
- **Dictionary:** It is the data structure used to map and store data with a key that acts as an index. Key will be a single element, whereas value can be array or list.
- **Set:** It is the same as sets in mathematics; it may consist of various elements, and the order of the elements is not defined.
- **Exceptional handling:** Errors are of different types that need to be handled to create a smooth application. Exceptional handling is the process of overcoming the unexpected error that occurs during the execution of the program. Whenever an error occurs within a method, it creates an object and hands off it to an exception handler block.
- **Debugging:** The process of identifying and removing the errors from the code is called debugging. It allows identifying the exact line and function due to which error occurred.
- **Numpy:** It is the library that supports an N-dimensional array and has sophisticated functions. It has the capability of performing functions like mathematics, statistics operations.
- **Matplotlib:** It is an another library of Python that supports the graphical representation of data in 2D and 3D charts like a pie chart, a bar graph, and a histogram. Matplotlib plays a very important role in today's business as programmers use this library to show the business status graphically.
- **Pandas:** The library of Python that provides the data in tabular form and performs arithmetic functions like add, subtracts, and reciprocal.

REVIEW QUESTIONS

1. What are the in-built data types used in Python?
2. How to initialize a list?
3. Difference between list and tuple?
4. How can we initiate a dictionary?
5. What is the main purpose of the break statement?
6. What is the use of a continue statement?
7. What is the use of the pass statement?
8. Is Numpy better than a list?
9. When is the else part of the try block in exception handling executed?
10. How can we create a Boolean array using Numpy?
11. What kind of graphs can be created using matplotlib?
12. How can we drop the missing value using Pandas and Numpy?
13. How can Pandas allow to read a CSV file?
14. Read and print the first ten columns of the data.
15. What is the computational complexity?
16. What are the parameters of plot() function?
17. What does the line imply – import matplotlib.pyplot as plt?
18. Describe the importance of heatmap in matplotlib?

19. What are the plots available in matplotlib?
20. Write a code to customize the color and adding legends to the plot?
21. Write a code for scatterplot with color attribute.
22. How to add labels to graph plots?
23. Explain about bins in histogram function?
24. What is rcdefaults()?
25. Difference between bar plot, pie plot, and scatter plot?
26. What is the importance of plotting?
27. Mention the different types of data structures in Pandas?
28. Explain the series in Pandas. How to create a copy of the series in Pandas?
29. What is a Pandas data frame? How will you create an empty data frame in Pandas?
30. Explain reindexing in Pandas.
31. What are the key features of the Pandas' library?
32. What are Pandas used for?
33. Explain categorical data in Pandas.
34. What are the different ways a data frame can be created in Pandas?
35. What is time series in Pandas?
36. Which is the standard data missing marker used in Pandas?
37. Is it possible to plot a histogram in Pandas without calling Matplotlib? If yes, then write the code to plot the histogram?
38. What is the need to use Python Pandas?

EXERCISES FOR PRACTICE

Numpy

1. Convert the list [3.14, 14.22, 160, 36.36] into one-dimensional array.
2. Create a Numpy program to create a 3×3 matrix with values ranging from 5 to 14.
3. Given the array, write a program to reverse the array in Numpy
   [1,3,6,9,12,15,18,21,24,27,30]
4. Given the array, change the data type of the array to float using Numpy
   [1,3,6,9,12,15,18,21,24,27,30]
5. Given an array, write a Numpy program to create a 2d array with 0 on the border and one inside.
   Original array:
   [[1. 1. 1. 1. 1.]
   [1. 1. 1. 1. 1.]
   [1. 1. 1. 1. 1.]
   [1. 1. 1. 1. 1.]
   [1. 1. 1. 1. 1.]]

   Expected output:
   0 on the border and one inside in the array
   [[0. 0. 0. 0. 0.]
   [0. 1. 1. 1. 0.]
   [0. 1. 1. 1. 0.]
   [0. 1. 1. 1. 0.]
   [0. 0. 0. 0. 0.]]

6. Given tuple, convert that into an array using Numpy
   ([1, 3, 5], [2, 4, 6])

7. Given the array values in Fahrenheit, convert them into centigrade using the formula: C= (F-32)*5/9 (Note: F is the array of the values)

    F=[60,70,80,90,100,110]

8. Given the array, find the length of the array, element size in bytes, and total bytes of the array (Note: use size, itemsize, and nbytes keywords)

    [1,2,3,4,5,6,7,8,9,0]

9. Given the array, sort the array in ascending and descending orders using Numpy

    [13,24,54,23,4,5,6,7,1,9]

Pandas

Given an INFO.CSV file:

Voltage (mV)	Time (s)
10	2
20	3.5
33	3.8
23	2.1
55	5.8
44	4.9
200	33.5
500	89.2

1. Write a Pandas code to read the INFO.CSV file.
2. How do you get the basic statistics of the file INFO.CSV?
3. What does the following code do? –
   print(tabulate(print_table, headers=headers))
4. Write a Pandas code for dropping the missing data.
5. Write a Pandas code for replacing with value "test" the missing data in the INFO.CSV.
6. Write a Pandas code to convert float to integer and vice versa.
7. How do you convert Pandas data frame to Numpy array?
8. Write a Pandas code to get a feature (dimension) name.
9. Write a function that will multiply all values in the "height" column of the data frame by 2.5.

MatplotLib

1. Write a matplotlib code for 3D plotting.
2. Plot a sin wave graph using the "sin" function
   a. Voltage(mV) in Y-Axis
   b. Time(s) in X-Axis
3. How do you save a matplotlib graph into a file?
4. Given the INFO.CSV file (with two columns Voltage and Time), draw a line graph to plot the values.
5. What is the purpose of scaling before plotting the graphs?

3 Data Analytics Life Cycle for Machine Learning

LEARNING OBJECTIVES

At the end of this chapter, the reader will be able to:

- Comprehend the phases involved in the Data Analytics Life Cycle for machine learning (ML).
- Appreciate the aspects involved in data discovery, data preparation, and exploratory data analysis.
- Understand the requirements for model planning and model building.
- Have a deep acquaintance on communicating results, optimize and operationalize the models.
- Gain knowledge on the roles and responsibilities of the members involved throughout the phases of the Data Analytics Life Cycle.

3.1 INTRODUCTION

The data generated in the last two years are much larger than the last 50 years combined. As the data grow exponentially, it brings a huge issue. We have to manage it properly so that the data can be used for business benefits. Adopting and successfully implementing a framework will help the user to avoid data-related pitfalls. The framework also helps the user to focus their time on data analysis (inference from data) than data preparation, ensure the rigor and completeness of the data, enable the better transition to members of the cross-functional analytic teams with repeatable scale to additional analytics, and to support the validity of findings.

Several real-world data problems look complex and chaotic, but with a well-framed approach, the complex problem can be broken down into simpler modules, which can be easily addressed. Sometimes, applying a tested procedure for analyzing the data is challenging. Hence, it is required to establish a comprehensive method for performing the analysis. Once data are collected in several instants, the user starts analyzing the data, then later plans and identifies the scope and the amount of work involved. During the process, the people involved try to explore a different objective or address a different issue that differs from the objectives communicated. The documentation process helps demonstrate rigor in the exploration and provides additional credibility to the project when shared among the team. This helps the team in knowledge sharing and to adopt the methods and analysis so it can be repeated and modified slightly over the successive years.

A well-defined process exists for developing a data science project. However, it is always recommended to have a Data Analytic Life Cycle framework, which is of primary focus in this chapter. Many of the proposed framework phases will be similar. For example, the data discovery and data preparation phases will be common, with subtle differences. However, some phases would not be needed at all. For example, the model training phase of the framework requires the user to create the training and testing datasets; the business intelligence project will not have those phases. Subsequently, data science often deals with various datasets such as big data, including semi-/unstructured data and sparse datasets. Such datasets require more attentiveness in data preparation, data stitching, and enriching than projects that only focus on business intelligence.

DOI: 10.1201/9781003258803-3

Data preparation may be the most important part of a ML project. It is the most time-consuming part, although it seems to be the least discussed topic. Data preparation is also called data pre-processing and is the act of transforming raw data into a form that is appropriate for modeling. ML algorithms require input data to be numeric values, and most algorithm development and deployments maintain this expectation. So, if the data contain data types and values that are not numbers, such as labels, you will need to change the data into numbers. Further, specific ML algorithms have expectations regarding the data types, scale, probability distribution, and relationships between input variables. You may need to change the data to meet these expectations.

The viewpoint of data preparation is to discover how to best expose the unknown underlying structure of the problem to the ML algorithms. This often requires an iterative path of experimentation through a suite of different data preparation techniques to discover what works well or best. The vast majority of the ML algorithms used on a project are years-to-decades old. The implementation and application of the algorithms are well understood. So much so that they are routine, with amazing fully featured open-source ML libraries like Scikit-learn in python. The thing that is different from project to project is the data. We may acquire a new dataset for the first time in a new application setup to use a specific data set as the basis for a predictive modeling project. As such, the preparation of the data to best present it to the problem of the learning algorithms is the primary task of any modern ML project.

The challenge of data preparation is that each dataset is unique and different. Datasets differ in the number of variables (tens, hundreds, thousands, or more), the types of the variables (numeric, nominal, ordinal, Boolean), the scale of the variables, the drift in the values over time, and more. As such, this makes discussing data preparation a challenge. Either specific case studies are used, or focus is put on the general methods used across projects. The result is that neither approach is explored.

3.2   DATA ANALYTICS LIFE CYCLE

The Data Analytics Life Cycle comprises six phases, which are iterative between the steps throughout the life cycle. The Data Analytics Life Cycle shown in Figure 3.1 portrays the best practices approach for an end-to-end data analytics process starting from data discovery to project completion and operation phase. The phases also cover the process improvement based on established methods in the domain of data analytics and decision science.

3.2.1   PHASE 1 – DATA DISCOVERY

The question to answer in the data discovery phase is "Do we have enough information?". Data discovery is the process of collecting and analyzing data from various sources to realize insight from hidden patterns and trends. It is the primary step in fully harnessing an organization's data to tell critical business decisions. Through the data discovery process, data are gathered, combined, and analyzed during a sequence of steps. The goal is to form messy and scattered data clean, understandable, and user-friendly. The primary focus of this phase is to learn the business domain, including learning from past experiences and further assessing the resources required to support the project, such as human resources, time, technology, and data. The business problem has to be framed in such a way with the focus on the analytic challenge, and this would be addressed in subsequent Data Analytic Life Cycle phases. Finally, the initial hypotheses (IHs) have to be formulated to validate and begin learning the information.

Understanding the domain in-depth for the given problem we are trying to find an answer to is critical. In a few situations, data scientists are required to possess advanced computational and quantitative knowledge such that the applications can be multi-disciplinary. These scientists are expected to possess an in-depth knowledge of the techniques, methods, and models for applying heuristics to different business and conceptual problems. Experts from domain areas with quantitative expertise

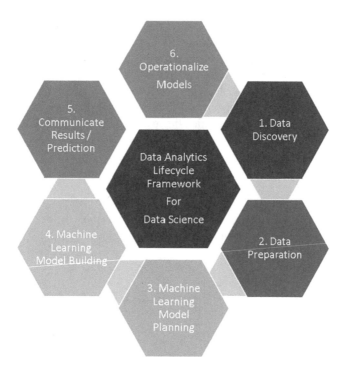

FIGURE 3.1 The Data Analytics Life Cycle.

will also partner with data scientists to address the gap between domain knowledge and analytical depth.

While assessing the resources, there should be a focus on the available tools and technology used for the process and the types of systems required for interaction with subsequent phases. It is also required to have an evaluation concerning analytical facilities available within the organization. Questions are as follows:

a. What would be the type of roles required for end-users of the model?
b. The current development model will drive success?
c. Are the roles available within the organization?

Such evaluation will help decide on the current implementation and future implementations on the type of data handling. In addition, it is necessary to validate whether the information available is sufficient to support the objectives of the current project, or whether data collection is required, whether the purchase of data from outside sources is required, or any extensions or transformations on existing data are required.

Moreover, for successful project implementation, a good project team has a proper combination of subject matter experts (SMEs), domain experts, analytic team, customers, and the project management team. Also, it is required to assess the proportion of SMEs such that there is a clear focus on the depth and breadth of skills on the working team. Once the inventory for the project is decided concerning the team, tools, data, and technology, then another set of evaluations is done to decide on the resources, else additional resources are added.

Once the interaction is complete with the stakeholder and sufficient knowledge is obtained on the domain, the business problem can be framed by considering experience. Later, the analytics problem is defined, and during this phase, the role of the stakeholders, their project requirements, their interests, and their criteria to evaluate the project. Since the analytical part of the project aims at a business perspective, it is necessary to address the weak points very clearly so that haphazard can be avoided while working on the project.

Based on the number of participants and stakeholders, we must consider using the responsible, accountable consulted, and informed (RACI) matrix. This will give a clear picture of the expectation and participation from each stakeholder, set clear expectations with the participants, and avoid delays later when we need approvals from stakeholders, rather than the supervisor of the work product. The RACI matrix is a method in which the responsibilities are documented. These responsibilities include the role of a person in the project, whether the person fits rightly in the project, etc., RACI refers to the role of people within a project:

- **Responsible:** Those individuals or groups responsible for doing the critical path activity and expected to complete the tasks actively.
- **Accountable:** Those individuals or groups who are answerable for a decision. In this case, only one accountable person/group is assigned to a given task to ensure clear ownership and accountability.
- **Consult:** Those individuals or groups who are the specific domain experts/SMEs will be in consultation throughout the project.
- **Inform:** Those individuals or groups who have to be kept informed whenever a decision or an action is taken.

A sample RACI matrix is given in Table 3.1.

Creating a framework similar to the RACI matrix will ensure that we have accountability and clear agreement on responsibilities in the project. In addition, the information to share with the right people is kept informed of progress.

Most likely, the project sponsors will start with the end goal (or the solution). The project team needs to use that as a reference and identify the problem and the desired outcomes. Thus, interviewing project sponsors (individuals like CFO, CIO, or Director) becomes a key. Here are some tips and samples for interviewing the project sponsor to frame the core business problem and project assumptions and constraints.

- What business problem are we trying to solve as part of the project?
- What industry issues (stable vs. dynamic industry, etc. – the data might be stable or changing rapidly) impact the project?
- What are the success criteria for this project (key project metrics)?
- How much historic information is needed for the analysis?
- What is in scope and out of scope for this project? (a lot of users focus on in-scope items ad ignore the out-of-scope items, and that will create a scope creep in the future)
- What are the time line and cost guidelines we should be working under (scope, time, and cost are called triple constraints. If one changes, the other two need to be evaluated and changed properly to avoid project cost overruns and delays)?

TABLE 3.1
RACI Matrix

Critical Path Activities	Stakeholder 1	Stakeholder 2	Stakeholder 3	Stakeholder 4	Stakeholder 5
Activity 1	R	R	A	C	I
Activity 2	R	C	I	A	I
Activity 3	C	R	A	C,I	I
Activity 4	R	R	A	I	I

- Where do we get the data from? (internal data sources vs. external data sources, one data source vs. many)
- Who can (internal vs. external to the organization) act as an SME to the project?
- How the scope changes will be handled (change control board, etc.)

Now, the IHs can be formed to approve or disapprove the data. It is always encouraged to develop a few IHs to test-generate additional ideas for the hypotheses. The IH formed initially serves as the basis of the tests that will be performed in later phases for analysis, and these serve as the foundation for additional learning. Hypothesis testing will be covered in greater detail in supervised and unsupervised learning chapters. Initially, the type of data required to solve a specific problem is chosen along with the data sources and their classification, such as structured, semi-structured, or unstructured data. The volume, type, and time span of the data needed to test the hypotheses must be considered. In addition to this, the data sources should be identified so that easy access is ensured. In some applications, the raw data may be required to run through the models. Hence, the possibilities to access the data have to be identified to serve as a basis for experimental analysis.

Once the hypothesis definition is complete, a thorough diagnosis of the data situation is performed. Then, the tools and techniques can be listed for the application, starting from the data preparation phase to operationalizing the model. Also, if data exploration is performed during this phase, there is clarity on the quantity of data, which helps in structuring and formatting the data. Now the scope of the information is reviewed and validated with the help of the project domain experts.

Many articles describe how to become experts in various fields, specifically the amount of practice needed to become an expert. This context is referred to as deliberate learning. To develop the required expertise, it is important to identify the possible solutions to a problem. This will lead to a set of possible solutions. If the IHs are formulated, then it is much easier to arrive at conclusions on the analytic model.

Before moving on to the next phase, the following points are to be ensured:

- Availability of sufficient information to draft the analytic plan and share for peer review.
- Whether a clear understanding of the business problem exists and whether step-by-step approach exists to address the problem.
- Sufficient SMEs are available to support in the domain area of the problem.
- Whether the success criteria for the project are detected.

With the above points, the problem definition is more clear and helps when it comes to identifying the possible choices of analytical methods used in the following phases.

3.2.2   PHASE 2 – DATA PREPARATION AND EXPLORATORY DATA ANALYSIS

The primary focus in the data discovery phase is to ensure the "availability of good quality data." In this phase, an analytic sandbox is prepared, such that it would be used for the remaining phases of the project. The extract, load, and transform (ELT) and extract, transform, and load (ETL) are performed to get the relevant data into the sandbox. Now the data get transformed so that analysis can be carried out. The basic idea is to obtain a clear understanding of the data and take the required measures to condition the data. Data analysts refer to this process as data enriching and harmonizing, and this phase is considered one of the most critical and time-consuming phases within the data life cycle.

In this phase, a space is defined to explore the data without interfering with the live production databases. In addition, all kinds of data should be collected in the sandbox since a high volume and variety of data would be required for the analytic project. Thus, huge data would include the summary, structured data, raw data feeds (e.g., sensors), and unstructured text data (log data). Hence, the sandbox is large and almost 10–50 times the size of an organization's enterprise data warehouse.

Due to the huge volume of data, a strong bandwidth with good network connections must be ensured to handle the data so that quick transformations and extractions from datasets can be done at ease. Now, the data analyst has a choice to make between ELT and ETL. In this context, ELT is preferred over ETL since this is a typical data approach problem. In the analytic sandbox approach with ELT, data are extracted, loaded, and then transformed. Here, the raw data are extracted and loaded into the analytics sandbox, and then the data transformation happens. This approach is followed to maintain and preserve the raw data as part of the other data in the sandbox before being subjected to any transformations. Some of the key differences between the ELT and ETL approaches are listed in Table 3.2. The data analyst makes a choice based on the data needs.

For example, let us consider an analysis for fraud detection on credit card usage. Frequently, the outliers in this data population can represent higher-risk transactions that may be flag fraudulent credit card activity. Using ETL, these outliers could be unintentionally filtered out or transformed and cleaned before being loaded into the database. This might cause bias in the data. Due to this, the extraction load and then transform method (ELT) is encouraged to have the data in its raw state and the ability to transform it after loading in the staging or operational data store ODS area. This approach will give us clean data to analyze that is available in the database and also, the data in its original form for finding hidden features in the data.

The Hadoop, Alpine Miner, and SAS are some of the tools we can use to inject the data into analytics sandbox. Hadoop can perform parallel ingest and custom analysis for parsing web traffic, GPS location analytics, proteomic analysis, sensor data collection, genomic analysis, and combining massive unstructured data feeds from multiple sources. Alpine Miner provides a user-friendly graphical interface for creating analytic workflows, including data manipulations and a series of analytic events such as staged data mining techniques (e.g., select top 100 customers, then run descriptive statistics and clustering) on PostgresSQL and other big data sources. We can use Python libraries to bring data from various sources. For example, using the Python Pandas library, we can ingest data from various sources.

```
#Load the libraries
import pandas as pd
```

TABLE 3.2
Comparison of ELT and ETL Approaches

Extract, Transform, and Load	Extract, Load, and Transform
Used for compute-intensive transformations and a small amount of data	Preferred and used for high amounts of data
Transformations are done at the staging/ETL server area	Transformations are performed in the target system (e.g., analytics sandbox)
No data duplication; if we need to perform another transformation, we need to load it again	Data duplication; copy of the raw data available for further transformation and use
Data are first loaded into the staging layer and later pushed into the target system. Time-intensive	Data loaded into target system directly only once. So faster
High maintenance since we need to select data to load and transform	Low maintenance as data are already available in the target system
Implementation complexity is low comparatively	ELT process requires the user to have deep knowledge of tools and expert skills
Supports only structured data; no support for data lakes	Allows use of data lakes (analytics sandbox) with unstructured data

Reading data from Flat file sources:

Read_table(filepath_or_buffer[, sep, …])	Read general delimited file into DataFrame.
read_csv(filepath_or_buffer[, sep, …])	Read a comma-separated values (csv) file into DataFrame.
read_fwf(filepath_or_buffer[, colspecs, …])	Read a table of fixed-width formatted lines into DataFrame.

For example:

```
dataset = pd.read_csv('C:/Python Files/50_Startups.csv')
```

Reading data from Clipboard:

read_clipboard([sep])	Read text from clipboard and pass to read_csv.

Reading data from Excel:

read_excel(*args, **kwargs)	Read an Excel file into a Pandas DataFrame.
ExcelFile.parse([sheet_name, header, names, …])	Parse specified sheet(s) into a DataFrame.
ExcelWriter(path[, engine])	Class for writing DataFrame objects into Excel sheets.

Reading data from JSON Files:

read_json(*args, **kwargs)	Convert a JSON string to a Pandas object.
json_normalize(data[, record_path, meta, …])	Normalize semi-structured JSON data into a flat table.
build_table_schema(data[, index, …])	Create a table schema from data.

Reading data from HTML Files:

read_html(*args, **kwargs)	Read HTML tables into a list of DataFrame objects.

Reading data from Hadoop (HDFS files)

read_hdf(path_or_buf[, key, mode, errors, …])	Read from the store, close it if we open it.
HDFStore.put(key, value[, format, index, …])	Store object in HDFStore.
HDFStore.append(key, value[, format, axes, …])	Append to table in file.
HDFStore.get(key)	Retrieve Pandas object stored in the file.
HDFStore.select(key[, where, start, stop, …])	Retrieve Pandas object stored in the file, optionally based on where criteria.
HDFStore.info()	Print detailed information on the store.
HDFStore.keys([include])	Return a list of keys corresponding to objects stored in HDFStore.
HDFStore.groups()	Return a list of all the top-level nodes.
HDFStore.walk([where])	Walk the pytables group hierarchy for Pandas objects.

Reading data from Structured Query Language (SQL) tables

read_sql_table()	Read SQL database table into a DataFrame.
read_sql_query()	Read SQL query into a DataFrame.
read_sql()	Read SQL query or database table into a DataFrame.

We can ingest data from other sources like Google BigQuery, SAS, STATA, and SPSS. The user can refer to the Pandas library help for the updated list of supported file types.

In data preparation, the people involved are as important as much as the tools employed. Proper guidance and assistance are required from IT analysts and database analysts. As illustrated earlier, this phase is critical within the analytics life cycle; if there is a lack of quality in the acquired data, it would be difficult to perform the subsequent steps in the life cycle process. In addition to data preparation, this phase also ensures that additional data aspects are considered, and common pitfalls are avoided. A few considerations in the data preparation phase are listed as follows:

- Identify the required data sources. Whether all the identified data sources are available? Proper clarity on the target fields is to be ensured.
- Whether the required data are clean?
- Whether the contents and files are consistent?

While preparing the data, there is a need to identify the amount of missing/inconsistent data that can be considered for the project, in other words, to understand the degree of allowance for blank/inconsistent data. In addition, if consistent data are available and are found deviating from normal, then the consistency of the data types has to be assessed. For example, if data are expected to be numeric, then it has to be confirmed that any special character such as an alpha numeric character can be allowed or not. A crucial and critical review has to be conducted on the data columns to ensure they make sense and are in the right form. Also, the chances of occurrence of systematic errors have to be verified. Systematic error may occur due to the sensor data or unsupervised data. This may lead to irregular data or missing data. The data have to be reviewed to gauge if the definition of the data is uniform over the repeated measurements.

3.2.2.1   Exploratory Data Analysis

Data visualization: Once we get the data from the sources to the analytics sandbox, it is important to understand the data further through the visualization techniques. Python has a lot of visualization libraries like Matplotlib (we have discussed that in Chapter 2) to Seaborn, which is based on Matplotlib and has advanced data visualization functions that help us understand the data behaviors visually. Seaborn library has multiple features, including an application programmable interface that allows comparing multiple variables, multi-plot grids to build easy visualizations, univariate (analysis with one variable), and bivariate to compare between subsets of data. These multiple color pallets allow showing various kinds of patterns. In addition, there are mandatory dependency libraries that are needed for Seaborn to work. They are Numpy, Pandas, Matplotlib, SciPy, and Statsmodels.

Like any in python, before start using the library, we need to import the Seaborn library to your model to use the functions of that library.

```
import seaborn as sns # Importing the library
```

Seaborn has in-built datasets for the user to get familiarity with the functions of liberty. To see what are the datasets are available, use the following command:

```
sns.get_dataset_names() # returns a list of all the available datasets
```

The output shows as follows:

```
Out[2]:
['anagrams',
'anscombe',
'attention',
'brain_networks',
```

```
'car_crashes',
'diamonds',
'dots',
'exercise',
'flights',
'fmri',
'gammas',
'geyser',
'iris',
'mpg',
'penguins',
'planets',
'tips',
'titanic']
```

We will be using some of the existing datasets to understand the plotting and visualizing statistical relationships, the process of understanding the relationship variables in a given dataset, and how these relationships depend on other variables. The first Seaborn function to explore is relplot(). This is a two-dimensional data visualization function. First, let us use the flights dataset that is available with the Seaborn.

```
#improting the required libraries
import numpy as np
import pandas as pd
import matplotlib.pyplot as plt
import seaborn as sns
sns.set(style="darkgrid") #style attribute is customizable and can take
any value like darkgrid, ticks, etc.

fl = sns.load_dataset("flights") #Using fl as variable to denote Flights
dataset. The user can use any var.
sns.relplot(x="passengers", y="month", data=fl);
```

Output is shown in Figure 3.2:

This is the basic plot. We can convert this plot into line, scatter, or violin plot using a parameter called "kind" in the relplot() function. This is discussed in the later part of this section. Before that, we need to explore another parameter of the replot() function. The next important semantic is hue. Using hue, we can add another dimension – year.

```
fl = sns.load_dataset("flights")
sns.relplot(x="passengers", y="month", hue="year", data=fl);
```

The output of the code snippet is shown in Figure 3.3 (the year is added to the graph).

The other parameters such as color, size, and style can be customized as shown in the below code snippet. The corresponding output is shown in Figures 3.4 and 3.5 with a slight variation in parameter "palette."

```
sns.set(style="darkgrid")
fl = sns.load_dataset("flights")
sns.relplot(x="passengers", y="month", hue="year",palette="ch:r=
-.5,l=.75", data=fl);

sns.set(style="darkgrid")
fl = sns.load_dataset("flights")
sns.relplot(x="passengers", y="month", hue="year",palette="ch:r=1,l=.9",
data=fl);
```

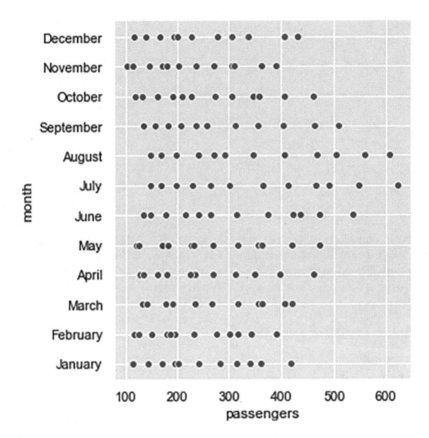

FIGURE 3.2   Basic plot using Matplotlib.

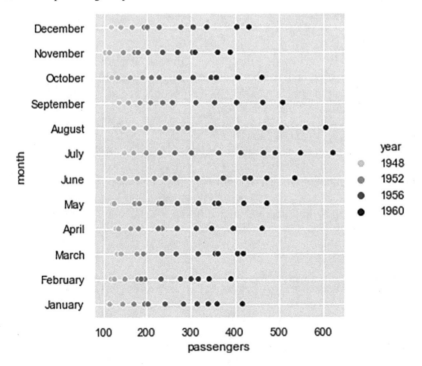

FIGURE 3.3   Illustration for function replot().

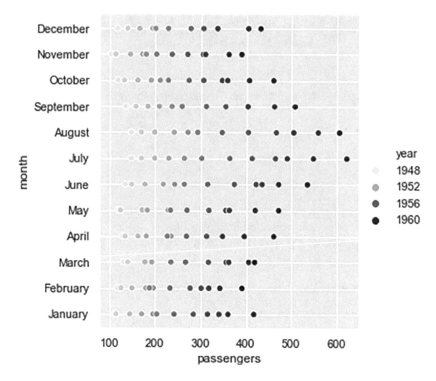

FIGURE 3.4 Illustration for function replot() with palette="ch:r=-.5,l=.75".

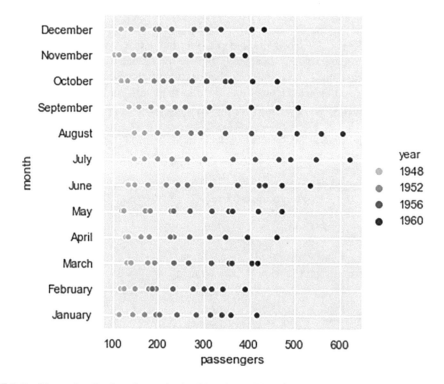

FIGURE 3.5 Illustration for function replot() with palette="ch:r=1,l=.9".

FIGURE 3.6   Output using the function palplot().

There are color palettes available in Seaborn. To understand that,

```
import numpy as np
import seaborn as sns
import matplotlib.pyplot as plt
sns.set()
presentcolors = sns.color_palette()
sns.palplot(presentcolors)
```

The output of these lines of code is presented in Figure 3.6.

To illustrate the conversion of a graph to a line graph, let us create a dataframe using Pandas as our data source.

```
gr=pd.DataFrame({'Day':[1,2,3,4,5,6,7],'Grocery':[30,80,45,50,51,90,76],
'Clothes':[13,40,34,75,54,67,98],'Utensils':[12,32,27,56,87,54,34]},
index=[1,2,3,4,5,6,7])
g = sns.relplot(x="Day", y="Clothes", kind="line", data=gr)
g.fig.autofmt_xdate()
```

```
gr=pd.DataFrame({'Day':[1,2,3,4,5,6,7],'Grocery':[30,80,45,50,51,90,76],
'Clothes':[13,40,34,75,54,67,98],'Utensils':[12,32,27,56,87,54,34]},
index=[1,2,3,4,5,6,7])
g = sns.relplot(x="Day", y="Grocery", kind="line", data=gr)
g.fig.autofmt_xdate()
```

The plot in Figures 3.7 and 3.8 shows the line graph for the data extracted from a dataframe.

Until now, we have used continuous data; let us explore the categorical data. The catplot() function is used for categorical data. This is similar to the function relplot() that is discussed earlier. This function can be categorized as scatter plots that include stripplot() and swarmplot(), distribution plots that include boxplot(), violinplot(), and boxenplot(), and estimate plots that include pointplot(), barplot(), and countplot().

We will be using a tips dataset that is also available in Seaborn.

```
import seaborn as sns
import matplotlib.pyplot as plt
sns.set(style="ticks", color_codes=True)
tp = sns.load_dataset("tips")
sns.catplot(x="day", y="total_bill", data=tp);
```

The default output is shown in Figure 3.9.

Let us convert the above graph to a violin graph by using the "kind" parameter.

```
import seaborn as sns
import matplotlib.pyplot as plt
sns.set(style="ticks", color_codes=True)
tp = sns.load_dataset("tips")
sns.catplot(x="day", y="total_bill", kind="violin", data=tp);
```

The output for the above code is shown in Figure 3.10.

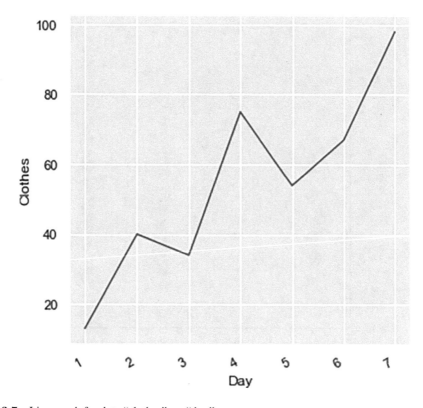

FIGURE 3.7   Line graph for data "clothes" vs. "day."

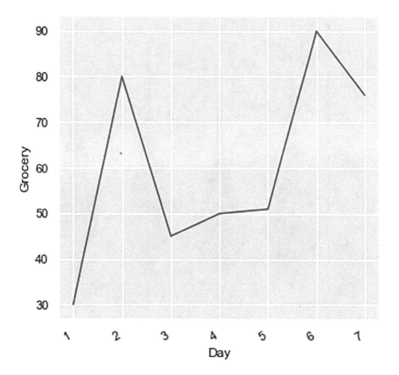

FIGURE 3.8   Line graph for data "grocery" vs. "day."

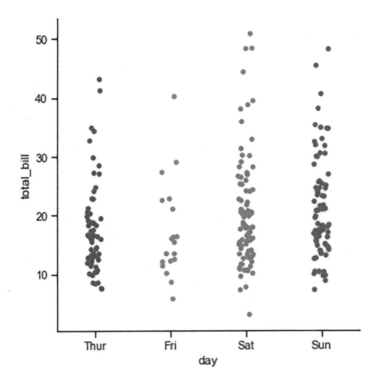

FIGURE 3.9　Line graph for data "clothes" vs. "day."

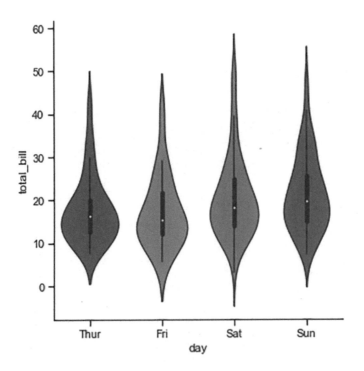

FIGURE 3.10　Illustration using the function catplot() with parameter kind = "violin."

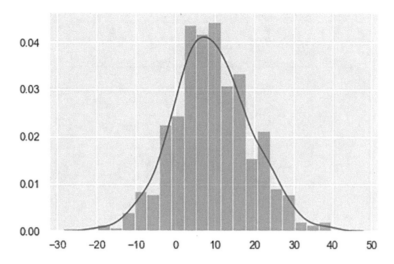

FIGURE 3.11   Illustration using the function distplot() – univariate.

Now that we have explored the basic visualizing features, let us focus on understanding the data in the context of univariate and bivariate. The distribution plot function, distplot(), is used for this purpose. Let us import all the required libraries.

```
import numpy as np
import pandas as pd
import seaborn as sns
import matplotlib.pyplot as plt
from scipy import stats
sns.set(color_codes=True)
tst = np.random.normal(loc=10,size=500,scale=10) #Univariate data
sns.distplot(tst);
```

The output is shown in Figure 3.11.
    To illustrate the bivariate, let us create two dataframes and assign them to the variables x and y.

```
x=pd.DataFrame({'Day':[1,2,3,4,5,6,7],'Accessaries':[30,80,90,23,60,46,76
],'Cloths':[13,40,60,23,54,67,98],'Shoes':[12,32,27,56,87,54,34]},
index=[1,2,3,4,5,6,7])
y=pd.DataFrame({'Day':[8,9,10,11,12,13,14],'Accessaries':[30,90,45,23,60,
46,76],'Cloths':[13,40,60,23,54,67,98],'Shoes':[12,32,27,56,87,54,34]},in
dex=[8,9,10,11,12,13,14])
mean, cov = [0, 1], [(1,.5), (.5, 1)]
data = np.random.multivariate_normal(mean, cov, 200)
with sns.axes_style("white"):
sns.jointplot(x=x, y=y, kind="kde", color="g");
```

The output is shown in Figure 3.12.
    So far, all our discussions have covered only plots with single grids. However, Seaborn allows multiple grids side by side to be plotted to visualize and infer the data better. The function, FacetGrid(), will help us to accomplish this.
    Let us use a simple dataset IRIS. The sample data are shown in Table 3.3.

```
sns.set(style="darkgrid")
ir = sns.load_dataset("iris")
```

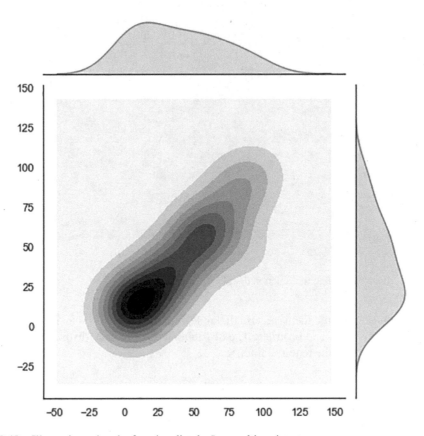

FIGURE 3.12 Illustration using the function distplot() – multi-variate.

TABLE 3.3
Sample IRIS Data

A	B	C	D	E
Sepal. Leng	Sepal. Width	Petal. Length	Petal. Width	Species
5.1	3.5	1.4	0.2	Setosa
4.9	3	1.4	0.2	Setosa
4.7	3.2	1.3	0.2	Setosa
4.6	3.1	1.5	0.2	Setosa
5	3.6	1.4	0.2	Setosa
5.4	3.9	1.7	0.4	Setosa
4.6	3.4	1.4	0.3	Setosa
5	3.4	1.5	0.2	Setosa
4.4	2.9	1.4	0.2	Setosa
4.9	3.1	1.5	0.1	Setosa
5.4	3.7	1.5	0.2	Setosa
4.8	3.4	1.6	0.2	Setosa
4.8	3	1.4	0.1	Setosa

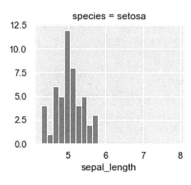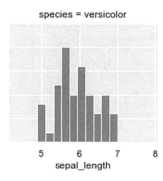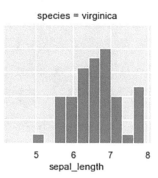

FIGURE 3.13   Correlation between the sepal length and the species.

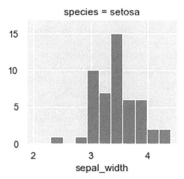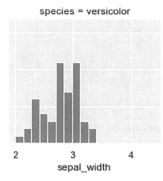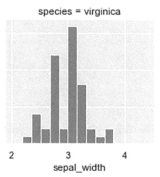

FIGURE 3.14   Correlation between the sepal width and the species.

```
mp = sns.FacetGrid(ir, col="species")
mp.map(plt.hist, "sepal_length", color="g");
```

The correlation between the sepal length and the species in the above code is shown clearly in Figure 3.13.

```
sns.set(style="darkgrid")
ir = sns.load_dataset("iris")
mp = sns.FacetGrid(ir, col="species")
mp.map(plt.hist, "sepal_width", color="g");
```

The correlation between the sepal width and the species in the above code is shown clearly in Figure 3.14.

To compare the pair of values, the PairGrid() function can be used.

```
sns.set(style="ticks")
a = sns.load_dataset("flights")
b = sns.PairGrid(a)
b.map(plt.scatter, color = "g");
```

The graph shown in Figure 3.15 compares the number of passengers and the years in different slices and dices.

We have explored the basic graphs/visualization samples in Seaborn. It is important to have a presentable graph when communicating quantitative insights. The technique is called controlling figure aesthetics.

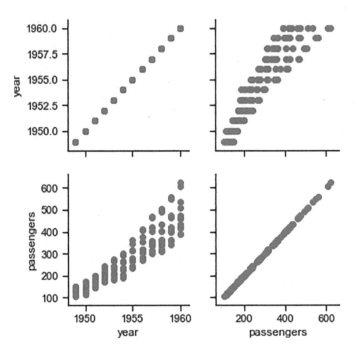

FIGURE 3.15   Comparing pair values using the function PairGrid().

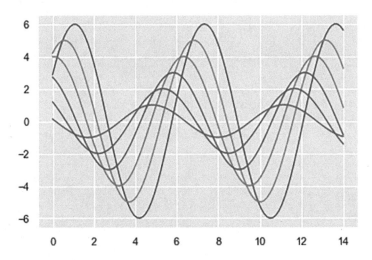

FIGURE 3.16   Illustration using the function sinplot().

```
import numpy as np
import seaborn as sns
import matplotlib.pyplot as plt

def sinplot(flip=1):
    ng = np.linspace(0, 14, 100)
    for i in range(1, 7):
        plt.plot(ng, np.sin(ng + i * .5) * (7 - i) * flip)
sinplot()
```

In Seaborn, we can use the following code to generate a sine wave, and the output is shown in Figure 3.16.

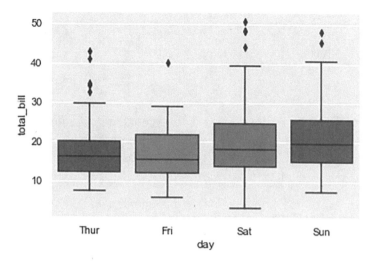

FIGURE 3.17 Illustration using the function boxplot().

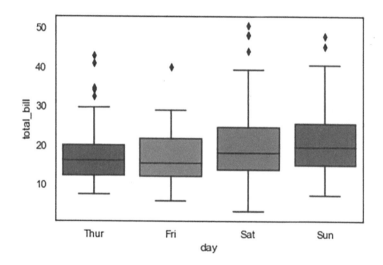

FIGURE 3.18 Illustration using the function boxplot() with white background.

```
sns.set()
sinplot()
```

Another graph available is box plot. Below is the sample code snippet, and the output is shown in Figure 3.17.

```
import seaborn as sns
import matplotlib.pyplot as plt
sns.set(color_codes=True)
a = sns.load_dataset("tips")
sns.boxplot(x="day", y="total_bill", data=a);
```

The following code illustrates the steps to remove the background and present it in white background, and the corresponding output is shown in Figure 3.18.

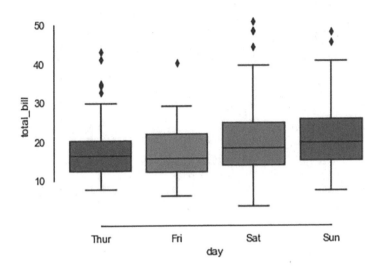

FIGURE 3.19   Illustration using the function despine().

```
import seaborn as sns
import matplotlib.pyplot as plt
sns.set(style="white",color_codes=True)
a = sns.load_dataset("tips")
sns.boxplot(x="day", y="total_bill", data=a);
```

In the above graph, we can notice the theme or the background is changed to white. We can explore further using the other themes as well (e.g., dark, darkgrid, white, and whitegrid). In the previous graph, there are axes; the rectangular line is present all around the graph. This can also be customized further using the despine() function. The code is presented below, and the corresponding output is shown in Figure 3.19.

```
import seaborn as sns
import matplotlib.pyplot as plt
sns.set(style="white",color_codes=True)
a = sns.load_dataset("tips")
sns.boxplot(x="day", y="total_bill", data=a);
sns.despine(offset=10, trim=True);
```

In multi-variate data exploration, correlation analysis is one of the primary techniques the data analysts use to understand the data. It is also known as a correlation matrix, auto-covariance matrix, variance matrix, or dispersion matrix. It is a matrix where the i-j position defines the correlation between the ith and jth parameters in the dataset.

When the data points result in a roughly straight-line trend, the variables have an approximately linear relationship. In other cases, the data points fall close to a straight line, but frequently there is quite a bit of variability of the points around the straight-line trend. A synopsis measure called the correlation describes the strength of the linear association. Correlation summarizes the strength and the linear (straight-line) association between two quantitative variables. Denoted by r, it takes values between −1 and +1. A positive r value indicates a positive association, and a negative r value indicates a negative association. The closer the r value is to 1, the closer the data points fall to a straight line. Thus, the linear association is stronger. On the other hand, the closer the r value is to 0, making the linear association weaker.

To demonstrate, let us take a House Price dataset. The sample data in the CSV file are shown in Figure 3.20.

Id	MSSubClas	MSZoning	LotFrontag	LotArea	Street	Alley	LotShape	LandContc	Utilities	LotConfig	LandSlope	Neighborh	Condition1	Condition2	BldgType	HouseStyle	OverallQu	OverallCor	YearBuilt	YearRemo	RoofStyle	RoofMatl	Exterior1st	Exterior2n	MasVnrTyp
1	60	RL	65	8450	Pave	NA	Reg	Lvl	AllPub	Inside	Gtl	CollgCr	Norm	Norm	1Fam	2Story	7	5	2003	2003	Gable	CompShg	VinylSd	VinylSd	BrkFace
2	20	RL	80	9600	Pave	NA	Reg	Lvl	AllPub	FR2	Gtl	Veenker	Feedr	Norm	1Fam	1Story	6	8	1976	1976	Gable	CompShg	MetalSd	MetalSd	None
3	60	RL	68	11250	Pave	NA	IR1	Lvl	AllPub	Inside	Gtl	CollgCr	Norm	Norm	1Fam	2Story	7	5	2001	2002	Gable	CompShg	VinylSd	VinylSd	BrkFace
4	70	RL	60	9550	Pave	NA	IR1	Lvl	AllPub	Corner	Gtl	Crawfor	Norm	Norm	1Fam	2Story	7	5	1915	1970	Gable	CompShg	Wd Sdng	Wd Shng	None
5	60	RL	84	14260	Pave	NA	IR1	Lvl	AllPub	FR2	Gtl	NoRidge	Norm	Norm	1Fam	2Story	8	5	2000	2000	Gable	CompShg	VinylSd	VinylSd	BrkFace
6	50	RL	85	14115	Pave	NA	IR1	Lvl	AllPub	Inside	Gtl	Mitchel	Norm	Norm	1Fam	1.5Fin	5	5	1993	1995	Gable	CompShg	VinylSd	VinylSd	None
7	20	RL	75	10084	Pave	NA	Reg	Lvl	AllPub	Inside	Gtl	Somerst	Norm	Norm	1Fam	1Story	8	5	2004	2005	Gable	CompShg	VinylSd	VinylSd	Stone
8	60	RL	NA	10382	Pave	NA	IR1	Lvl	AllPub	Corner	Gtl	NWAmes	PosN	Norm	1Fam	2Story	7	6	1973	1973	Gable	CompShg	HdBoard	HdBoard	Stone
9	50	RM	51	6120	Pave	NA	Reg	Lvl	AllPub	Inside	Gtl	OldTown	Artery	Artery	1Fam	1.5Fin	7	5	1931	1950	Gable	CompShg	BrkFace	Wd Shng	None
10	190	RL	50	7420	Pave	NA	Reg	Lvl	AllPub	Corner	Gtl	BrkSide	Artery	Artery	2fmCon	1.5Unf	5	6	1939	1950	Gable	CompShg	MetalSd	MetalSd	None
11	20	RL	70	11200	Pave	NA	Reg	Lvl	AllPub	Inside	Gtl	Sawyer	Norm	Norm	1Fam	1Story	5	5	1965	1965	Gable	CompShg	HdBoard	HdBoard	None
12	60	RL	85	11924	Pave	NA	IR1	Lvl	AllPub	Inside	Gtl	NridgHt	Norm	Norm	1Fam	2Story	9	5	2005	2006	Hip	CompShg	WdShing	Wd Shng	Stone
14	20	RL	NA	12968	Pave	NA	IR2	Lvl	AllPub	Inside	Gtl	Sawyer	Norm	Norm	1Fam	1Story	5	6	1962	1962	Hip	CompShg	HdBoard	Plywood	None
15	20	RL	91	10652	Pave	NA	IR1	Lvl	AllPub	Inside	Gtl	CollgCr	Norm	Norm	1Fam	1Story	7	5	2006	2007	Gable	CompShg	VinylSd	VinylSd	Stone
16	45	RM	NA	10920	Pave	NA	IR1	Lvl	AllPub	Corner	Gtl	BrkSide	Norm	Norm	1Fam	1.5Unf	6	8	1929	2001	Gable	CompShg	Wd Sdng	Wd Sdng	None
17	20	RL	NA	11241	Pave	NA	IR1	Lvl	AllPub	CulDSac	Gtl	NAmes	Norm	Norm	1Fam	1Story	6	7	1970	1970	Gable	CompShg	Wd Sdng	Wd Sdng	BrkFace
18	90	RL	72	10791	Pave	NA	Reg	Lvl	AllPub	Inside	Gtl	Sawyer	Norm	Norm	Duplex	1Story	4	5	1967	1967	Gable	CompShg	MetalSd	MetalSd	None
19	20	RL	66	13695	Pave	NA	Reg	Lvl	AllPub	Inside	Gtl	SawyerW	RRAe	Norm	1Fam	1Story	5	5	2004	2004	Gable	CompShg	VinylSd	VinylSd	None
20	20	RL	70	7560	Pave	NA	Reg	Lvl	AllPub	Inside	Gtl	NAmes	Norm	Norm	1Fam	1Story	5	6	1958	1965	Hip	CompShg	BrkFace	Plywood	None
21	60	RL	101	14215	Pave	NA	IR1	Lvl	AllPub	Corner	Gtl	NridgHt	Norm	Norm	1Fam	2Story	8	5	2005	2006	Gable	CompShg	Wd Sdng	Wd Sdng	BrkFace
22	45	RM	57	7449	Pave	Grvl	Reg	Bnk	AllPub	Inside	Gtl	IDOTRR	Norm	Norm	1Fam	1.5Unf	7	7	1930	1950	Gable	CompShg	Wd Sdng	Wd Sdng	None
23	20	RL	75	9742	Pave	NA	Reg	Lvl	AllPub	Inside	Gtl	CollgCr	Norm	Norm	1Fam	1Story	8	5	2002	2002	Hip	CompShg	VinylSd	VinylSd	BrkFace
24	120	RM	44	4224	Pave	NA	Reg	Lvl	AllPub	Inside	Gtl	MeadowV	Norm	Norm	TwnhsE	1Story	5	7	1976	1976	Gable	CompShg	CemntBd	CmentBd	None
25	20	RL	NA	8246	Pave	NA	IR1	Lvl	AllPub	Inside	Gtl	Sawyer	Norm	Norm	1Fam	1Story	5	8	1968	2001	Gable	CompShg	Plywood	Plywood	None

FIGURE 3.20 Sample data in CSV file format.

Once we load the file to our model, we can explore the file in detail before all the necessary libraries need to be imported as shown below.

```
#import libraries
import numpy as np
import pandas as pd
import seaborn as sns
import matplotlib.pyplot as plt
from scipy.stats import norm

#load data file
data = pd.read_csv("House Price.csv")
data.shape
```

The output for the data.shape command is shown below.

```
(1460, 81)
```

This means the CSV file has 1460 records with 81 columns.
Let us explore the file much more closer.

```
Data.columns
```

The output is shown below, and it is showing all the columns in that file.

```
Index(['Id', 'MSSubClass', 'MSZoning', 'LotFrontage', 'LotArea', 'Street',
       'Alley', 'LotShape', 'LandContour', 'Utilities', 'LotConfig',
       'LandSlope', 'Neighborhood', 'Condition1', 'Condition2', 'BldgType',
       'HouseStyle', 'OverallQual', 'OverallCond', 'YearBuilt',
'YearRemodAdd',
       'RoofStyle', 'RoofMatl', 'Exterior1st', 'Exterior2nd', 'MasVnrType',
       'MasVnrArea', 'ExterQual', 'ExterCond', 'Foundation', 'BsmtQual',
       'BsmtCond', 'BsmtExposure', 'BsmtFinType1', 'BsmtFinSF1',
       'BsmtFinType2', 'BsmtFinSF2', 'BsmtUnfSF', 'TotalBsmtSF', 'Heating',
       'HeatingQC', 'CentralAir', 'Electrical', '1stFlrSF', '2ndFlrSF',
       'LowQualFinSF', 'GrLivArea', 'BsmtFullBath', 'BsmtHalfBath',
'FullBath',
       'HalfBath', 'BedroomAbvGr', 'KitchenAbvGr', 'KitchenQual',
       'TotRmsAbvGrd', 'Functional', 'Fireplaces', 'FireplaceQu',
'GarageType',
       'GarageYrBlt', 'GarageFinish', 'GarageCars', 'GarageArea',
'GarageQual',
       'GarageCond', 'PavedDrive', 'WoodDeckSF', 'OpenPorchSF',
       'EnclosedPorch', '3SsnPorch', 'ScreenPorch', 'PoolArea', 'PoolQC',
       'Fence', 'MiscFeature', 'MiscVal', 'MoSold', 'YrSold', 'SaleType',
       'SaleCondition', 'SalePrice'],
      dtype='object')
```

```
data.head(10)   #gives the top ten records in that file
```

Id	MSSubClass	MSZoning		...		SaleType	SaleCondition	SalePrice
0	1	60	RL	...		WD	Normal	208500
1	2	20	RL	...		WD	Normal	181500
2	3	60	RL	...		WD	Normal	223500
3	4	70	RL	...		WD	Abnorml	140000

4	5	60	RL	...	WD	Normal	250000
5	6	50	RL	...	WD	Normal	143000
6	7	20	RL	...	WD	Normal	307000
7	8	60	RL	...	WD	Normal	200000
8	9	50	RM	...	WD	Abnorml	129900
9	10	190	RL	...	WD	Normal	118000

Data.tail() # gives the bottom five records by default.

	Id	MSSubClass	MSZoning	...	SaleType	SaleCondition	SalePrice
1455	1456	60	RL	...	WD	Normal	175000
1456	1457	20	RL	...	WD	Normal	210000
1457	1458	70	RL	...	WD	Normal	266500
1458	1459	20	RL	...	WD	Normal	142125
1459	1460	20	RL	...	WD	Normal	147500

data['SalePrice'].describe() # gives the description of the SalePrice column only.

```
count       1460.000000
mean      180921.195890
std        79442.502883
min        34900.000000
25%       129975.000000
50%       163000.000000
75%       214000.000000
max       755000.000000
Name: SalePrice, dtype: float64
```

To get the description of all the columns,

```
Data.describe()
              Id    MSSubClass     ...          YrSold       SalePrice
count  1460.000000  1460.000000    ...     1460.000000     1460.000000
mean    730.500000    56.897260    ...     2007.815753   180921.195890
std     421.610009    42.300571    ...        1.328095    79442.502883
min       1.000000    20.000000    ...     2006.000000    34900.000000
25%     365.750000    20.000000    ...     2007.000000   129975.000000
50%     730.500000    50.000000    ...     2008.000000   163000.000000
75%    1095.250000    70.000000    ...     2009.000000   214000.000000
max    1460.000000   190.000000    ...     2010.000000   755000.000000
```

Now plotting the data in graphs.
   Histogram graph (Figure 3.21):

```
plt.figure(figsize = (9, 5))
data['SalePrice'].plot(kind ="hist", color= "g")
```

   Line graph (Figure 3.22):

```
plt.figure(figsize = (9, 5))
data['SalePrice'].plot(kind ="line",color= "r")
```

   Now let us get the correlation matrix, tabular data representing the 'correlations' between pairs of variables in given data.

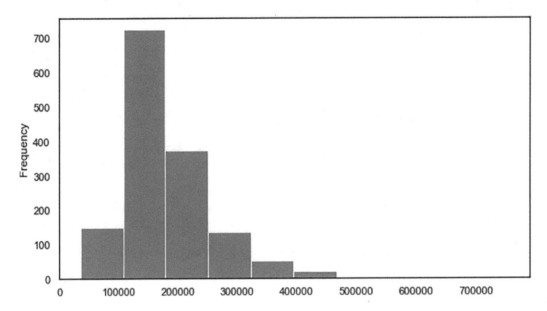

FIGURE 3.21   Illustration of data in histogram graph.

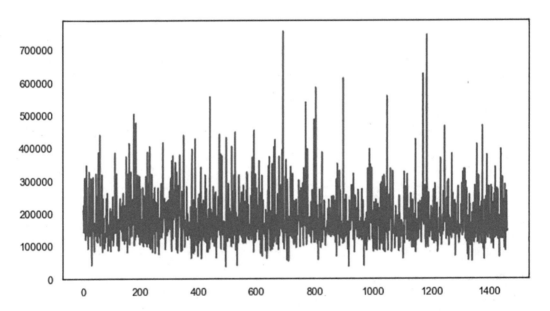

FIGURE 3.22   Illustration of data in line graph.

```
corr = data.corr()
f, ax = plt.subplots(figsize =(9, 8))
sns.heatmap(corr, ax = ax, cmap ="YlGnBu", linewidths = 0.2) #YlGnBu is
the color pellet schema
```

The output is shown in Figure 3.23.

```
<matplotlib.axes._subplots.AxesSubplot at 0x2549578ff60>
```

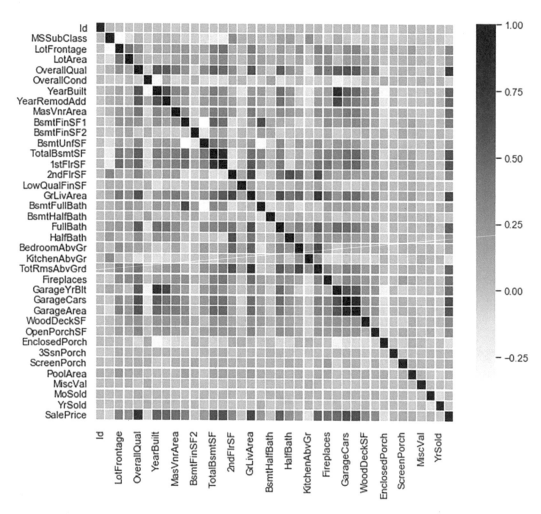

FIGURE 3.23 Correlation matrix.

Another form of visualizing the data is a grid correlation matrix.

```
corr = data.corr()
cg = sns.clustermap(corr, cmap ="YlGnBu", linewidths = 0.1);
plt.setp(cg.ax_heatmap.yaxis.get_majorticklabels(), rotation = 0)
cg
```

The output is shown in Figure 3.24.

Now that we have explored the correlation between all variables, let us focus on the SalePrice column, and on how it is correlating with other columns (Figure 3.25).

$k=20$ #k: number of variables for heatmap – the # of variables that will be compared against SalePrice.

```
cols = corr.nlargest(k, 'SalePrice')['SalePrice'].index
cm = np.corrcoef(data[cols].values.T)
f, ax = plt.subplots(figsize =(12, 10))
sns.heatmap(cm, ax = ax, cmap ="YlGnBu",
            linewidths = 0.1, yticklabels = cols.values,
                            xticklabels = cols.values)
```

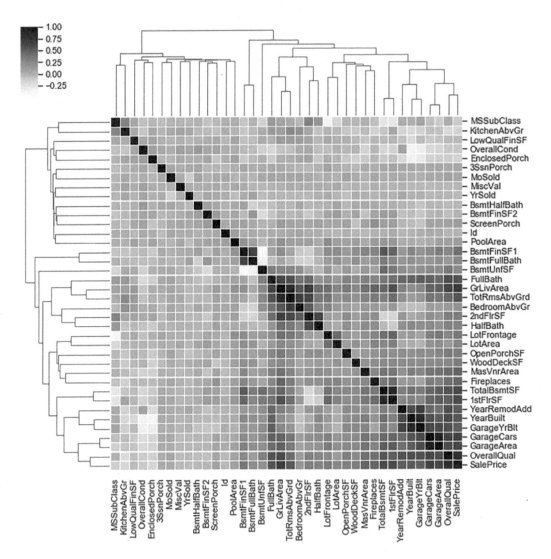

FIGURE 3.24   Grid correlation matrix.

Another technique to clean and enrich the data is typecasting. It is the technique to convert the data into a different type than the source data. For example, a variable in the source data may be coded as string/character even though the permissible values in the variable are only numeric (integers and float types). Simply put, typecasting is converting one data type to another. There are basic functions that are int(), string(), and float(), and they are used for typecasting. Int() function is used for integer literal, and float() is for decimal numbers. In python, it is very straightforward to convert from one data type to another.

```
Here is the code snippet -
x=float(2)
y=float(30.0)
z=float("20")
print(x)
print(y)
print(z)
```

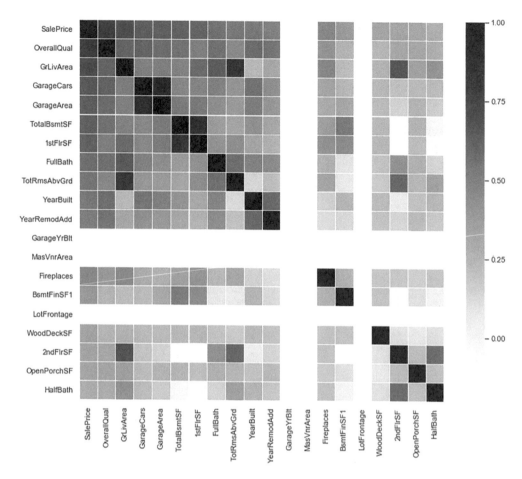

FIGURE 3.25   Correlation matrix with other columns.

The output is:

```
2.0
30.0
20.0
```

To understand the data type of the variable, use the function type().

There are two types of typecasting, that is implicit and explicit. In implicit conversion, python automatically converts one data type to another. This process doesn't need any user involvement at all. When you add one integer and another float number, the result will be automatically casted as a float without the user specifying it. For example,

```
num_int = 123
num_float = 1.23

num_new = num_int + num_float

print("datatype of num_int:",type(num_int))
print("datatype of num_flo:",type(num_float))
```

```
print("Value of num_new:",num_new)
print("datatype of num_new:",type(num_new))
```

The output is:

```
datatype of num_int: <class 'int'>
datatype of num_flo: <class 'float'>
Value of num_new: 124.23
datatype of num_new: <class 'float'>
```

In explicit conversion, the users had to explicitly convert the data type of an object to the required data type. We use the predefined functions like int(), float(), and str() to perform explicit type conversion.

```
num_int = 123
num_str = "123"

print("Data type of num_int:",type(num_int))
print("Data type of num_str before Type Casting:",type(num_str))

num_str = int(num_str) # WE ARE EXPICITELY CONVERTING THE datatype
print("Data type of num_str after Type Casting:",type(num_str))

num_sum = num_int + num_str

print("Sum of num_int and num_str:",num_sum)
print("Data type of the sum:",type(num_sum))

The output is :
Data type of num_int: <class 'int'>
Data type of num_str before Type Casting: <class 'str'>
Data type of num_str after Type Casting: <class 'int'>
Sum of num_int and num_str: 246
Data type of the sum: <class 'int'>
```

Even though typecasting is a handy tool in data pre-processing, we need to have few cautions in mind when using it. For example, when the Python interpreter does the implicit conversion, the loss of data is prevented automatically by the Python. But when there is an explicit conversion, there could be data loss depending on the data types that might impact processes requiring data accuracy.

When complaining about the multiple despaired datasets, we need to employ joins. For example, there are datasets with one master and transaction data; to combine these datasets (tables), we need to use joins. The different types of joins are illustrated in Figure 3.26. We can use the Python Pandas library to use inner joins, full joins, left joins, and right joins. Inner joins get the results set that are common in both tables. For example, you have two tables from different sources with the customer data, and the inner join will bring only the common data available in both tables. The full join or outer join returns all records when there is a match in dataset1 and dataset2. Left join returns all records from the left table (dataset1) and the matched records from the right table (dataset2).

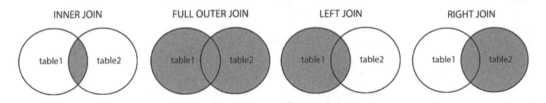

FIGURE 3.26 Types of joins.

Finally, the right join returns all records from the right table (dataset2) and the matched records from the left table (dataset1).

For example, let us create a customer DataFrame in Pandas as follows:

```
Import pandas as pd
customer=pd.DataFrame({
    'id':[1,2,3,4,5,6,7,8,9,10],

'name':['John','Joe','Cory','Steve','Richard','Tyler','Samuel','Daniel','Jeremy','Stephan'],
    'age':[20,25,15,10,40,55,35,18,23,20],
    'Product_ID':[101,0,106,0,103,104,0,0,107,105],

'Purchased_Product':['Watch','NA','Oil','NA','Shoes','Smartphone','NA','NA','Laptop','smartwatch'],

'City':['Delhi','Mumbai','Kolkatta','Chennai','Chennai','Coimbatore','Bangalore','Bangalore','Mumbai','Coimbatore']
})
Customer
```

The output is shown below.

	Id	Name	Age	Product_ID	Purchased_Product	City
0	1	John	20	101	Watch	Delhi
1	2	Joe	25	0	NA	Mumbai
2	3	Cory	15	106	Oil	Kolkata
3	4	Steve	10	0	NA	Chennai
4	5	Richard	40	103	Shoes	Chennai
5	6	Tyler	55	104	Smartphone	Coimbatore
6	7	Samuel	35	0	NA	Bangalore
7	8	Daniel	18	0	NA	Bangalore
8	9	Jeremy	23	107	Laptop	Mumbai
9	10	Stephan	20	105	Smartwatch	Coimbatore

```
Another dataframe product
product=pd.DataFrame({
    'Product_ID':[101,102,103,104,105,106,107],

'Product_name':['Watch','Bag','Shoes','Smartphone','smartwatch','Oil','Laptop'],

'Category':['Fashion','Fashion','Fashion','Electronics','Study','Grocery','Electronics'],
    'Price':[299.0,1350.50,2999.0,14999.0,145.0,110.0,79999.0],

'Seller_City':['Delhi','Mumbai','Chennai','Kolkata','Delhi','Chennai','Bengalore']
})
Product
```

The output of the product DataFrame is as follows:

	Product_ID	Product_name	Category	Price	Seller_City
0	101	Watch	Fashion	299.0	Delhi
1	102	Bag	Fashion	1350.5	Mumbai
2	103	Shoes	Fashion	2999.0	Chennai
3	104	Smartphone	Electronics	14999.0	Kolkata
4	105	Smartwatch	Study	145.0	Delhi
5	106	Oil	Grocery	110.0	Chennai
6	107	Laptop	Electronics	79999.0	Bangalore

Now let us combine the product with the customer using the merge() function in Pandas. By default, the merge function performs inner joins unless we specify different join types.

```
pd.merge(product,customer,on='Product_ID')
```

The results bring only six rows matching in both dataframes.

	Product_ID	Product_name	...	Purchased_Product	City
0	101	Watch	...	Watch	Delhi
1	102	Shoes	...	Shoes	Chennai
2	103	Smartphone	...	Smartphone	Coimbatore
3	104	Smartwatch	...	Smartwatch	Coimbatore
4	105	Oil	...	Oil	Kolkata
5	106	Laptop	...	Laptop	Mumbai

[6 rows × 10 columns]

To force the join type, we need to specify the left_on, right_on keywords.

```
pd.merge(product,customer,left_on='Product_name',right_on='Purchased_
Product')
```

	Product_ID_x	Product_name	...	Purchases_Product	City
0	101	Watch	...	Watch	Delhi
1	103	Shoes	...	Shoes	Chennai
2	104	Smartphone	...	Smartphone	Coimbatore
3	105	Smartwatch	...	Smartwatch	Coimbatore
4	106	Oil	...	Oil	Kolkata
5	107	Laptop	...	Laptop	Mumbai

One another data harmonization technique is data wrangling. When we get the data in various formats, this technique is helpful. Data wrangling allows us to merge, group, and concatenate the data for analyzing or provisioning them with another dataset. Python has built-in functions and features to apply these wrangling techniques to despaired datasets to achieve the analytical goal. We will look at few examples characterizing these methods. As we discussed, the merge() function helps do the data wrangling. Another method is called grouping. Grouping datasets is a recurring need in data analysis where we need the result in terms of various groups present in the dataset. Pandas has in-built methods/functions that can roll the data into various groups.

```
# import the pandas library
import pandas as pd
ipl_data = {'Team': ['CSK', 'RCB', 'KKR', 'KKR', 'DD',
        'DD', 'DD', 'DD', 'SRH', 'MI', 'MI', 'MI'],
        'Rank': [1, 2, 2, 3, 3,4 ,1 ,1,2 , 4,1,2],
        'Year': [2020,2015,2014,2015,2014,2020,2016,2017,2016,2014,2020,
2017],
        'Totalruns':[876,789,863,673,741,812,756,788,694,701,804,690]}
df = pd.DataFrame(ipl_data)

grouped = df.groupby('Year')
print (grouped.get_group(2014))
```

The output is shown below.

```
   Team   Rank   Year   Totalruns
2   KKR    2     2014      863
4   DD     3     2014      741
9   MI     4     2014      701
```

Another useful Pandas function for data wrangling is concatenating the data using the concat() function. Pandas provides various tools to combine Series, DataFrame, and Panel objects easily together. The example below depicts the concat function performing concatenation operations along an axis.

```
import pandas as pd
first_set = pd.DataFrame({
        'Name': ['Alex', 'Amy', 'Allen', 'Alice', 'Ayoung'],
        'subject_id':['sub1','sub2','sub4','sub6','sub5'],
        'Marks_scored':[98,90,87,69,78]},
        index=[1,2,3,4,5])
second_set = pd.DataFrame({
        'Name': ['Billy', 'Brian', 'Bran', 'Bryce', 'Betty'],
        'subject_id':['sub2','sub4','sub3','sub6','sub5'],
        'Marks_scored':[89,80,79,97,88]},
        index=[1,2,3,4,5])
print (pd.concat([first_set,second_set]))
```

The output is shown below.

```
    Name      subject_id    Marks_scored
1   Alex        sub1            98
2   Amy         sub2            90
3   Allen       sub4            87
4   Alice       sub6            69
5   Ayoung      sub5            78
1   Billy       sub2            89
2   Brian       sub4            80
3   Bran        sub3            79
4   Bryce       sub6            97
5   Betty       sub5            88
```

A review process is performed to improve the data to ensure the calculations remain consistent within columns for a given data field. Some of the considerations are as follows:

- Ensure data distribution is consistent over the entire dataset. If not, the data preparation team proposes a new plan to handle the situation.
- Assess the granularity of the data, the range of values, and the level of aggregation of the data.
- For time-related variables, are the time measurements daily, weekly, monthly? Is that good enough? Is time measured in seconds everywhere? Or is it in milliseconds in some places? This will cause the data level mismatch when we combine the data and harmonizing it. Ensure the lowest level of data is consistent across data sources.
- Are the data standardized/normalized? Are the scales consistent? If not, how normal or irregular is the data? In this case, a scaling function is applied to smoothen the data.
- If geospatial datasets are considered, are country codes, state abbreviations, and postal codes consistent across the data? Are personal names normalized? Whether English units are considered? Whether standards metric units are considered?
- How is the data deduplication handled? When combining multiple sources due to various factors such as incorrect abbreviations, using the last name instead of the full name, the same records appear as duplicate records in the target database.

Gaining more deep knowledge about the data is essential while considering time-series analysis or running ML models. If a good amount of quality data is available, the project moves to the planning phase, where the focus lies on building the model.

Using Python libraries, we can do the data processing better. Below is the code snippet for the data processing.

```
# Import pandas
import pandas as pd
import numpy as np

# Read the file into a DataFrame: df
df=pd.read_csv('C:/Users/srajappa/Desktop/MLn
using Python/dob_job_application_filings_subset.csv')

# Print the head of df
print(df.head(2))

# Print the tail of df
print(df.tail())

# Print the shape of df
print(df.shape)

# Print the columns of df
print(df.columns)

##.describe() method to calculate summary statistics of your data
print(df.describe())

df.info()
##.value_counts() method, which returns the frequency counts for each
unique value in a column!
# Print the value counts for 'Borough'
print(df['Borough'].value_counts(dropna=False))

# Print the value counts for 'State'
print(df['State'].value_counts(dropna=True))
```

```python
# Print the value counts for 'Site Fill'
print(df['Site Fill'].value_counts(dropna=True))

df.dtypes
df.get_dtype_counts()


##seperating string and numerical columns
df_string=df.select_dtypes(include=['object'])
df_numerical=df.select_dtypes(exclude=['object'])

df_string.shape
df_numerical.shape


df_string.info()
```

##ensuring all categorical variables in a DataFrame are of type category reduces memory usage.

```python
df_string['Job Type'] = df_string['Job Type'].astype('category')

##converting datatypes

tips = pd.read_csv('C:/Users/srajappa/Desktop/ML using Python/tips.csv')
print(tips.info())

# Convert the sex column to type 'category'
tips.sex = tips.sex.astype('category')

# Convert the smoker column to type 'category'
tips.smoker = tips.smoker.astype('category')

##for numeric directly
#df['column'] = df['column'].to_numeric()


# Print the info of tips
print(tips.info())
##numerica data conversion

tips.tip = tips.tip.astype('object')

#tips.tip = tips.tip.astype('float')
tips['tip'] = pd.to_numeric(tips['tip'], errors='coerce') ##incase some
char values result into nan

def recode_gender(gender):

    # Return 0 if gender is 'Female'
    if gender == 'Female':
        return 0
    # Return 1 if gender is 'Male'
    elif gender == 'Male':
        return 1
    # Return np.nan
    else:
        return np.nan
```

```
# Apply the function to the sex column
tips['recode'] = tips.sex.apply(recode_gender)

# Print the first five rows of tips
print(tips.head())


# Feature Scaling
from sklearn.preprocessing import StandardScaler
sc_X = StandardScaler()
X_train = sc_X.fit_transform(X_train)
X_test = sc_X.transform(X_test)
#sc_y = StandardScaler()
#y_train = sc_y.fit_transform(y_train)
```

3.2.3   PHASE 3 – MODEL PLANNING

The next phase, ML model planning, is to understand whether a good model is available for the data chosen for the respective project. In this phase, the methods, model, approaches, and flow expected are finalized. In addition to this, the relationship between variables in the data, primary variables, and suitable models is explored. Since this phase executes just before executing the analytical model, care should be taken in understanding the features and choosing the model. At this phase, there is a need to refer to the hypotheses developed in the first phase, from where we get to know the data and understand the business problem. The IH helps in framing the analytics to be executed in the next phase and to choose the correct methods to meet the objectives. At this stage, there are some considerations based on the data listed as follows:

- The type of data is a major factor that will prescribe and confine the tools and analytical techniques in the next phase. Different tools and approaches are applied based on the data chosen, whether it is textual data or transactional data (e.g., tumor prediction using clinical data in Hadoop – contains structured, semi-structured, and unstructured while forecasting weather is based on structured data).
- There should be an assurance whether the analytical techniques will meet the business objectives and prove/disprove the working hypotheses.
- Understand if the solution to the business problem requires a single test or a series of techniques for analytic workflow. Tools such as SAS Miner will help set up a series of steps and analyses and serve as a user-friendly interface for manipulating larger data sources.

With the type of data and resources available, the review has to be performed to check whether smaller approaches are suitable or whether new approaches are required. On several occasions, ideas arise based on analogous problems solved in industry verticals.

There are a few guidelines and recommendations on choosing ML and deep learning models based on the question we are trying to answer. The specific algorithms are explained in detail in the further chapters: supervised, unsupervised, and deep learning model chapters.

We need to understand the border classification of ML models. There are three categories as follows:

- **Supervised learning**: The answer to the question is specific, for example, what is the salary of a 5-year-experienced ML engineer? The data are labeled, and this type of model predicts the outcome/future. Direct feedback is given to the model. Ground Truth (input) and Answer Key (output) are also given to the model.
- **Unsupervised learning**: The data are cumbersome and not labeled. The intention is to find the hidden patterns in the data. No feedback is given to the model.

- **Reinforcement learning**: This type of model is based on the rewards systems. Suitable action is to maximize reward in a particular situation. These algorithms are learnt based on a series of actions.

Now that we understand the types of the algorithm, let us discuss the other factors that dictate a model type selection.

Size of training set: We all know that when the training dataset is not enough, it always results in poor estimation. An over-constrained model on the insufficient training dataset will always end in underfitting; on the other hand, an under-constrained model will probably lead to overfitting the dataset; in both the cases, the outcome will turn to be poor performance. Thus, the size of the training dataset may be a factor that plays a significant role for us when deciding the algorithm of our choice. For a little training dataset, as the low-bias/high-variance classifiers (such as k-nearest neighbors) are likely to overfit the training dataset, the high-bias/low-variance classifiers are at an advantage over this.

Training time: Time taken to coach the model varies for every algorithm. This time correlates with the size of the dataset and the accuracy we are aiming for.

The number of parameters: Parameters are one of the foremost important factors in an honest-performing model. Therefore, the components like an error tolerance level and a complete number of iterations depend on the algorithm's nature. Usually, the foremost number of trail and errors is needed to seek an honest combination within the algorithms that have an enormous number of parameters. Although having many parameters typically gives more versatility, the time taken to train the model using a particular algorithm and the same accuracy may be sensitive in obtaining just the right setup.

The number of features: Compared with the number of data points, the number of features of certain datasets may be quite large. We face the same situation when dealing with the Natural Language Processing (NLP) datasets, which are more textual datasets. Some learning algorithms can consume a longer training time when dealing with many features and make the work unrealistic. Some ML algorithms like support vector machines are especially well designed for this situation. These assumptions we make based on past experiences do not work for all situations, and we are required to have a better understanding of such algorithms to apply the best one for a specific problem.

Accuracy: The ML algorithms we use to make realistic decisions and greater accuracy on model results lead to better decisions. The expense of errors may be enormous, so we need to minimize that cost by improving the model's accuracy. The accuracy needed will be distinct, depending on the requirement. The approximation is often sufficient, which can result in a massive decrease in processing time. However, approximate techniques are likely to result in overfitting of the training dataset.

Based on the factors described above, there are heuristics on the recommended type of model based on the situation (Table 3.4).

There are many tools available, and let us discuss few popular ones.

Python is very popular nowadays and has an entire range of modeling abilities, including a satisfactory environment for building ML models with sophisticated code. In addition, Python also can work with SQL and run statistical analysis and tests on big data through open-source connectivity. Some of these abilities have made Python suitable for building models. Moreover, it contains more than 2000 packages and rapidly expanding everyday with the latest graphical features, thus making it user-friendly and more robust.

SAP HANA and Microsoft SQL Server provide SQL services such as in-database analysis of common data mining functions, basic predictive models, and involved aggregations.

TABLE 3.4

Heuristics and Their Applications

ML/Deep Learning Strategy	Description
Resampling strategy	Use this when there is an unbalanced dataset
Principal component analysis	Use this for reducing dimensionality, create new features
Autoencoding	To create new features
Regularization techniques	To prevent overfitting, outliers, and noise in linear regression and lasso regression
Random forest	Use this to overcome the outliers
Linear regression	Use this when predicting continuous variables
Logistic regression or simple vector machine	Use this when predicting a binary outcome
Random forest	Use this when predicting multi-class classification
Convolutional neural networks (CNNs)	Use this when doing image classification, object detection, and image segmentation
RNNs (typically LSTM)	Use this when doing sequence modeling such as natural language processing or text classifications

SAS provides a strong integration between SAS and databases through multiple data connectors, OBDC, JDBC, and OLE DB. Though SAS is used on file extracts, it can also be used to interface relational databases (Teradata or Oracle), data warehouse applications (snowflake), files, and also enterprise applications (SAP, JD Edwards).

The next step in the model selection process is data exploration. In this phase, it is critical to explore the data and observe the relationships among the variables in the data. The choice of variables and the methods for a corresponding problem are also challenging. Tools used for data visualization can be applied to review the data and assess the relationships between variables. Simultaneously, variable selection is also an important factor for successful model selection. In most cases, stakeholders/SMEs will have a strong knowledge of the data that has to be considered for analysis.

Initially, the inputs and the data required for the problem are taken and reviewed to check whether these inputs are related to the proposed outcomes used in prediction and analysis. Some models properly handle such tasks. However, based on the proposed solutions, a different model may also be considered after examining the inputs and transforming the inputs. This enables the selection of the best model. Generally, the model should aim to capture the best features so that the outcome is as expected. The process involves several iterations to obtain the most critical variables for the analysis chosen. Then, testing is performed on the range of possible variables and features in the data, and the most prominent features are selected.

In case regression problems are handled, candidate features have to be identified concerning the model's outcome. Here case should be taken in terms of correlation and collinearity between the data, such that they do not affect the model's outcome.

The last step in this phase is model selection. The model created in Python or any other equivalent tool should be converted to SQL so that the expected operation can be carried out in the database. Such interaction with the database and the model is required for optimal performance during runtime. In addition, during the model selection, the user has to be vigilant about the various data mining and prediction techniques, namely classification, association rules, and regression. Finally, the user needs to determine the techniques based on the data type, such as structured, unstructured, or hybrid combination.

Some of the analytical methods used across multiple market segments for churn prediction are listed in the table. Most of these methods will be covered in the remaining chapters of this book. But for the benefit of readers, we have created a table (Table 3.5) with specific industries and the analytics methods used for churn prediction.

TABLE 3.5

Analytics Techniques Used in Industry

Industry Sector	Analytics Techniques Used
Wireless telecom	Neural networks, logistic regression, and decision tree
Retail	Logistic regression, automatic relevance determination, and decision tree
Retail banking	Multiple regression
Grocery stores	Multiple linear regression and decision tree

3.2.4 Phase 4 – Model Building

The objective of this phase is to understand whether the ML model is robust enough. Here the datasets are developed and categorized as testing, training, production, and validation. In addition, there is a need to ensure a suitable environment for executing models and workflows, which includes fast hardware and parallel processing.

The model will be fitted on the training data and evaluated against the testing data during this phase. This exercise is usually done in a sandbox rather than in a live production environment. ML model planning and model building have a lot of overlap. We can iterate between the two phases for a long time before agreeing on a final ML model. Some methods necessitate using a training dataset (and, in some cases, a validation dataset), depending on the method.

Although the modeling techniques and logic necessary to develop this step can be complex, the actual duration of this phase can be very brief compared to all of the data pretreatment and approach definition work. In general, project phases 1 and 2 will require more time in the actual world to prepare and study the data and construct a presentation of the data.

As part of this phase, the following steps are conducted:

- Put the models created in Phase 3 into action.
- Wherever possible, convert the models to SQL or another appropriate database language and run them as in-database functions. This is far faster and more efficient than running them in memory. (Use SQL to run Python models on huge datasets) SAS Scoring Accelerator allows us to run SAS models in the browser if we are using SAS software.
- For testing and tiny datasets, use Python (or SAS) models on file extracts.
- Assess the model's validity and outcomes (for example, does it account for most of the data and has strong predictive power?)
- Adjust variable inputs to fine-tune the models for best results.
- Keep a record of the model's outcomes and logic.

During these iterations and refinement of the model, document the answers to the questions below to access the model efficiency:

- Does the model look plausible and accurate on the test and validation data?
- Does the model output/behavior make sense to the domain experts and SMEs? In other words, does it look like the model is providing "the right answers" or answers that make sense in the business context?
- Does the model accurate enough to meet the success criteria? (efficiency, performance, and other key performance matrix defined in phase1)
- Does the model avoid the kind of mistakes it needs to avoid? Depending on the context, false positives may be more serious or less serious than false negatives, for instance.
- Do the parameter values of the fitted model make sense in the context of the business domain?

- Do we need more data or more inputs? Do we need to transform or eliminate any of the inputs?
- Do we need a different form of the model? Then, we will need to go back to the ML model planning phase (Phase 3) and revise the modeling approach.

3.2.5   Phase 5 – Communicating Results

The question to answer in the prediction and communicating results phase is, "Is the model robust enough that predicts the results accurately (within the error value)?" First, based on the criteria we created in the data discovery phase (the key performance matrix for success criteria), we decide if the model succeeded or failed in this phase in partnership with the key stakeholders. Next, identify the most important results, quantify the business value, and write a narrative to synthesize and communicate the findings to key stakeholders.

Based on the criteria we created in the data discovery phase (the key performance matrix for success criteria), we decide if the model succeeded or failed in this phase in partnership with the key stakeholders. Identify the most important results, quantify the business value, and write a narrative to synthesize and communicate the findings to key stakeholders. Because the findings will most likely be disseminated throughout the business at multiple levels, from executive to operations, consider how to frame the findings and effectively describe the consequences.

The project team will provide recommendations for future work or improvements to existing processes as part of the project exit, taking into account what each team member and stakeholder require from you to complete their tasks and numerous new use cases for the enriched data. In addition, this is the stage where we may emphasize the project's business benefits. Finally, this stage will serve as the checkpoint for moving the models into production and operationalizing them.

As a final step in this phase, now that the model is successfully run, the following activities are conducted to document the lessons learned from the project:

- Evaluate the models' outcomes.
  - Do the findings appear to be statistically significant and consistent? If that's the case, what characteristics/attributes of the outcomes stand out? If not, what changes do we need to make to the model to refine and iterate it to make it more sustainable?
  - Which facts/details surprised you, and which were consistent with your arriving hypotheses from Phase 1? Correlating the confirmed outcomes to the ideas we formulated early on usually results in additional ideas and insights that would have been missed if we hadn't taken the effort to formulate IHs early on.
- What data have been observed as a result of the analytics?
  - What are the most important discoveries from those?
  - Do these discoveries have any commercial value or significance? We may need to spend time quantifying the business implications of the results to help prepare for the presentation, depending on what emerged as a consequence of the model.

We will document the important findings and major insights due to the analysis at the end of this phase. In addition, this phase's end product will be the most visible part of the process to outside stakeholders and sponsors, so properly articulate the findings' outcomes, methodology, and business value.

3.2.6   Phase 6 – Optimize and Operationalize the Models

The question to answer in the operationalize models' phase is, "Are technical predictions from the model are translated into the business language so that business team members can interpret the results and act on them?" The project team delivers final reports, briefings, code, and technical documents throughout this project phase. Finally, we undertake a pilot project and put the models to the test in a real-world setting. It is vital to make sure that once we've run the models and gotten the results, we frame them in a way that's appropriate for the audience who hired us and that provides demonstrable value. People will not perceive the value of a technically accurate analysis if we cannot interpret the data into a language they can understand. A lot of work will have been wasted.

In this phase, we'll evaluate the work's benefits and set up a pilot so we may launch the work in a controlled manner before expanding it to a larger enterprise or ecosystem of consumers. We scored the model in the sandbox in step 4, and most analytics approaches implementing new analytical methods or models in a production environment for the first time in Phase 6. Therefore, instead of deploying this on a large scale, we advocate starting with a small pilot rollout. This approach will allow us to limit the risk relative to full-enterprise-wide deployment, learn about the performance and related constraints on a small scale, and make fine-tune adjustments before a full deployment.

As we scope this effort, consider running the model in a production environment for a discrete set of single products or a single line of business, which will test the model in a live setting. This will allow the team to learn from the deployment and make adjustments before launching across the enterprise. Keep in mind that this phase can bring in a new set of team members, namely those responsible for the production environment, who have a new set of issues and concerns. The production support team and administrators want to ensure that the model can be incorporated into downstream processes and that it runs well in the production environment. Be on the lookout for input irregularities before feeding them to the model when running the model in the production environment. Evaluate run times and resource competition with other processes in the manufacturing environment.

Once the model is deployed, the project team conducts follow-ups to re-evaluate the model after it has been in production for a period of time. Assess whether the model is meeting goals and expectations and whether desired changes (such as an increase in revenue, reduction in churn) are occurring. If these final results are not occurring, determine if this is due to a model inaccuracy or if its predictions are not being acted on appropriately. If needed, automate the retraining/updating of the model. In any case, we will need ongoing monitoring of model accuracy, and if accuracy degrades, we will need to retrain the model. If possible, design alerts for when the model is operating "out-of-bounds." This includes situations when the inputs are far beyond the range that the model was trained on, which can cause the model's outputs to be inaccurate. If this happens regularly, retraining is called for.

Analytical projects often yield new insights about a business, a problem, or a concept that individuals may have taken at face value or thought was impossible to big into. If appropriate, hold a post-mortem with your analytic team to discuss the process or project you would change if we had to do it again.

Presenting the results to various groups is a daunting task. However, because each group will require a unique set of data, here are some general principles for preparing the analysis' findings for sharing with the major sponsors.

For a Business Audience: The more business-oriented the audience, the more succinct we must be. The majority of executive sponsors receive numerous briefings throughout the day and week. So, make sure the presentation gets to the point quickly and frames the results in terms of value to the sponsor's organization. For instance, if we are working with a bank to analyze cases of credit card fraud, highlight the frequency of fraud, the number of cases in the last month or year, and the way much cost or revenue impacts the bank (or the main focus on the reverse, how much more revenue they might gain if they address the fraud problem). This will showcase the business impact better than deep dives on the methodology. We will need to include supporting information about analytical methodology and data sources. Still, generally, we took to analyze the data only as supporting detail or to ensure the audience has confidence in the approach.

For Analysts Audience: If you're giving a presentation to other analysts, spend more time on the process and results. Coevals will be more interested in the techniques if we establish a brand-new way of processing or evaluating data that will be reused in the future or applied to comparable problems. When possible, use photos and screenshots. People tend to recall mental images to illustrate extended lists of bullets to some extent.

SUMMARY

There are many Data Analytics Life Cycle frameworks available in the market; they tend to have few variations with the same basic structure. Following the phases and the activities will alleviate the known pitfalls in implementing the ML projects. However, the users need to be mindful of the iterative nature between the phases. Without putting a solid foundation in the previous phase, the next phase's activities will be impacted. Therefore, we cannot emphasize the importance of data discovery and pre-processing data phases in the Data Analytics Life Cycle. A recent survey of data scientists from Gartner Inc. suggests that they spend over 80% of their time capturing, cleaning, and organizing data. The remaining less than 20% of their time was spent creating and optimizing the ML models. More than 75% also reported that preparing data was the least enjoyable part of their process. Table 3.6 shows the breakup of time consumed per activity in the data analytics projects.

TABLE 3.6
Time Consumption for Each Activity in a Project

Project Activity	% of Project Time Allocated
Collecting data	19%
Building training datasets	3%
Cleaning, enriching, and organizing the data	60%
Mining data for patterns	9%
Refining algorithms	5%
Other activities	4%

Table 3.7
Key Roles and Responsibilities of Team Members

Key Project Role	Description
Project sponsor	A person responsible for the project's existence, motivating, solving the core business problem, and providing funding
Business users	Members who benefit from the end result of the project/product. They can advise and be consulted on the value of the end results
SMEs/subject matter advisors (SMAs)	Members who had domain knowledge and could guide the project team in Phase 1 and Phase 2 primarily. They can be internal or external to the organization
Project manager	Key member responsible for delivering the project on time and under budget with expected quality
Business intelligence analyst	A member who has a deep understanding of the data, KPIs, and other key metrics and a clear vision of the data visualization aspects
Data engineers	Members who have deep technical skills to assist with data ingest queries and technically responsible for bringing the data into the analytics sandbox
Data scientists	Members who provide subject matter expertise in analytical techniques, applying efficient analytical techniques for the given business problem and ensuring the overall analytical goal of the project, are met
Administrators	Member of the Database Administrators Team, platform administrators, and cloud engineers who provisions and configures the environments to support the analytical team

TABLE 3.8

Analyst Wish List

Data and workspaces	Access to all the data, including raw and aggregated levels from various sources in structured, semi-structured, and unstructured data sources
	Updated data dictionary and metadata for the data elements
	Area for development, staging, testing, and production datasets
	Move data between workspace and staging/testing area
	Analytic sandbox with computer power to handle large dataset using complex ML models
Tools set	Statistical /mathematical and analytics tools with visualization capabilities such as Python, SAS, Matlab, Tableau, and Alteryx
	Collaboration tools like SharePoint
	Error logging tools like Jira

For the successful implementation of the project, there are many roles involved. Table 3.7 presents the roles and responsibilities of the team members.

Finally, the "analyst wish list" refers to suggestions for tools, data access, and working conditions that will ensure that employees are productive on the project and boost your chances of a good outcome. These requirements reflect the need for more adaptable ecosystems for storing data and performing complex, iterative analysis. In addition to the technical requirements outlined above, the project would benefit from quick access to key stakeholders and domain experts. Table 3.8 illustrates a few examples of the "analyst wish list."

REVIEW QUESTIONS

1. Explain the importance of the Data Analytics Life Cycle framework.
2. Describe the phases of the analytical life cycle and how these phases interact with other phases.
3. Describe various techniques used for data pre-processing.
4. What is the significance of correlation matrix in data preparation?
5. What is data wrangling?
6. What are data visualization techniques to understand the data better?
7. What types of files and data can be brought into the analytical sandbox?
8. What is the difference between traditional programming and ML model building?
9. How do you ensure the results of the analytics project to executives and other analysts are communicated properly?
10. What is the difference between ELT and ETL?
11. Explain few use cases where ML can be effectively implemented.
12. Explain the join types and what is the significance of those.

4 Unsupervised Learning

LEARNING OBJECTIVES

At the end of this chapter, the reader will be able to

- Understand different types of clustering algorithms, namely k-means, fuzzy k-means, hierarchical (agglomerative and divisive), and DBSCAN algorithms
- Implement the algorithms using Python
- Analyze the performance of the algorithms based on several evaluation metrics
- Appreciate the limitations of clustering algorithms and adapt suitable ones based on the working dataset

4.1 INTRODUCTION

One of the promising areas to learn systems formally is machine learning. Machine learning algorithms are used mostly in interdisciplinary areas by combining the thoughts from several fields, such as optimization theory, cognitive science, mathematics, statistics, and computer science. In this chapter, the reader would benefit from the broad underlying area of machine learning known as unsupervised learning. The present-day data scientists apply various machine learning algorithms to extract valuable information from the data provided. Most of the learning algorithms are supervised learning problems since we have a priori knowledge of the output of the type of data presented.

On the contrary, unsupervised learning is a complex and challenging approach to machine learning algorithms. Despite its complexity, the advantages of unsupervised learning algorithms are numerous. This class of algorithms has proven to be potential enough to provide solutions to previously unsolvable problems and has gained a lot of popularity in machine learning and deep learning. This chapter will explain the basics of unsupervised learning, distance measures, the concept of clustering, the most commonly used clustering algorithms, their applications to solve problems in real time, and their limitations.

4.2 UNSUPERVISED LEARNING

The class of unsupervised learning is a kind of self-organized learning that helps us identify patterns or similarities in our data related to various features. The three main categories of machine learning are supervised learning, unsupervised learning, and reinforcement learning.

Consider a machine or a system that receives a sequence of inputs $x_1, x_2, x_3,...,$ from a sensor where x_t is the sensory input at time t. This input that is received sequentially concerning time is called the data. Data can be any real-time measurement such as an image from a camera and voltage or current values from a solar panel.

In supervised learning, the system is also presented with a sequence of desired outputs $y_1, y_2,...,$ along with the received input data. The goal of the system is to learn to produce the correct output upon receiving successive inputs.

In reinforcement learning, the system interacts with its environment by producing a set of actions. These actions, in turn, impact the environment, and this change results in the system receiving a few scalar rewards or penalties corresponding to every action. Thus, the system's goal is to act in such a way as to maximize future rewards or minimize future penalties.

DOI: 10.1201/9781003258803-4

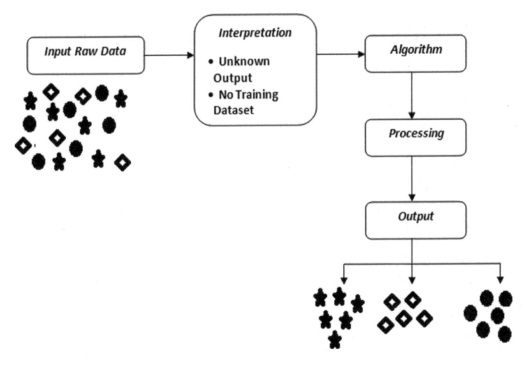

FIGURE 4.1   Block diagram of unsupervised learning.

In unsupervised learning, the system, as shown in Figure 4.1, receives the set of sensory inputs $x_1, x_2, \ldots$, but does not obtain the target outputs (like supervised learning), nor rewards or penalties from its environment (like reinforcement learning). Though it seems mysterious to imagine what the system could learn without any feedback from its environment, it is possible to develop a systematic framework for unsupervised learning. The framework's goal is to build representation models similar to the input data, which can be used for prediction, decision-making, etc.

It is important to understand the need for unsupervised learning at this point. In situations such as speech recognition, the interpretation of large datasets is very costly. Unsupervised learning has been proving to be efficient in such application areas. In data mining, there may be a situation where the user cannot predict the number of classes the data can be divided into. Unsupervised learning has been proving to be successful in such situations as well.

Unsupervised learning is classified into two categories, namely parametric unsupervised learning and non-parametric unsupervised learning.

- **Parametric unsupervised learning**

    When the given data can be represented in terms of parametric distribution, the case is referred to as *parametric unsupervised learning*. The algorithm assumes that the data is obtained from a probability distribution-based population that follows a fixed set of parameters. These fixed sets of parameters are usually mean and standard deviation. Using these parameters on normal distribution data, the probability of any future observation can be predicted easily. This learning algorithm involves structuring Gaussian mixture models with expectation-maximization (EM) algorithm to predict the class of the sample data taken for classification. This unsupervised learning approach is much more complex than any supervised learning approach, and research has not identified any standard measure of accuracy to validate the algorithm's outcome.

- **Non-parametric unsupervised learning**

  In non-parameterized unsupervised learning, the data obtained from the real world is assembled to form groups or clusters. Here, each cluster holds some information about the data present in its group. This approach is mostly used to analyze and mold data into a smaller set of samples. Here, the learning does not use any assumptions regarding the population distribution and hence is also known as a distribution-free method.

Two of the main methods used in unsupervised learning are principal component analysis and cluster analysis, but the most commonly used method is clustering.

4.2.1 CLUSTERING

One of the popular unsupervised learning problems is clustering. It evolves in determining a structure from a collection of data. The structure is comprised of a group of objects in which the members have some similar relation. Thus, a cluster can be defined as a group of objects with "similar" properties among them and "dissimilar" properties concerning the objects in other clusters.

There are several definitions for the term clustering in the literature, and some of the common ones are as follows:

- The method of identifying groups in data.
- The method of segregating the data into homogeneous groups.
- The method of segregating the data into groups, with similar points in each group -.
- The method of segregating the data into groups, where points within each group are similar while points of different groups are dissimilar.
- The method of segregating the population space into areas with a comparatively high density of points, separated by areas with a comparatively low density of points.

There is certainly a wide difference between clustering and classification. In unsupervised learning, clustering is applied on a set of unlabeled data without any knowledge about the dataset. On the contrary, in the classification approach, the grouping or class is formed on a set of unlabeled data after applying a suitable supervised learning algorithm.

Hence, a cluster is usually formed by grouping similar data points concerning a center called the centroid. Boundaries are usually not well defined for a cluster. Based on the boundaries, clusters are classified into crisp clusters and fuzzy clusters. Crisp clusters have a well-defined boundary, while fuzzy clusters do not have a well-defined boundary.

The main criteria for grouping objects into clusters are as follows:

- Each cluster should consist of objects similar to each other
- Each cluster should be unlike the other, which implies that the objects in one cluster are different from those present in other clusters.

The clustering technique provides many advantages, but the two most important benefits of clustering can be outlined as follows:

1. Identification and analysis of noisy data are comparatively easier.
2. Clustering facilitates the user to handle data with different types of variables.

4.3 EVALUATION METRICS FOR CLUSTERING

The main objective of clustering is to find an intrinsic grouping pattern among a set of unlabeled data. But how does anyone conclude that the grouping is the best? Or what constitutes a good

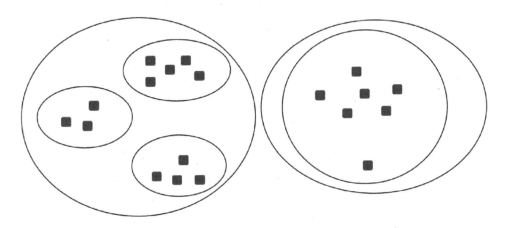

FIGURE 4.2   A sample clustering process.

clustering? As far as the literature is concerned, there has not been the best criterion evolved as a result of clustering. It has been observed that the results of clustering mainly vary from application to application and are based on the user's requirements.

In Figure 4.2, a sample clustering process is shown. How do we know what the best clustering solution is? Some of the evaluation metrics that govern the process of clustering are discussed in this section.

4.3.1 DISTANCE MEASURES

According to the clustering process, we have discussed that similar objects are grouped. The parameter that governs this similarity is the *distance measure*, which is one of the vital properties measuring the distance between two points. Thus, two or more objects are grouped into a cluster based on the closeness of objects concerning each other. This concept of grouping objects based on the geometric distance is called *distance-based clustering*.

Evaluating the distance between objects is completely dependent on the type of attributes of the data. According to Kaufman and Rousseeuw (2005), the distance function used to form clusters must satisfy the following criteria:

- The distance between any two objects should always be positive
- The distance from an object to itself is always zero
- The distance is symmetric
- The distance should always satisfy the triangle inequality. The distance from objects a to b to c should be greater than the direct distance from a to c.

Suppose the dataset consists of objects having the same physical units. In that case, the distance can be evaluated using the simple Euclidean distance metric to group the objects into different clusters. The Euclidean distance between two objects x_i and x_j in a D-dimensional space is expressed as follows:

$$d\left(x_i, x_j\right) = \sqrt{\sum_{k=1}^{D}\left(x_i^k - x_j^k\right)^2} = \left\|x_i - x_j\right\| \tag{4.1}$$

If the dataset consists of components represented in similar physical units, then the Euclidean distance metric is the best choice to group the data instances successfully. Euclidean distance is mostly used in cases where the attributes of the data vectors are color components, coordinates, or numeric types in D-dimensional Euclidean space.

4.3.1.1 Minkowski Metric

If the D-dimensional space is large, then the Minkowski metric is used to evaluate the distance. The Minkowski metric is expressed as follows:

$$d\left(x_i, x_j\right) = \left(\sum_{k=1}^{D} \left|x_i^k - x_j^k\right|^p\right)^{1/p} \tag{4.2}$$

where D is the dimensionality of the data. In *Euclidean* distance, $p = 2$, while *Manhattan* metric has $p = 1$. As reported in the literature, there are no standard theoretical guidelines for choosing a measure for any given application. Researchers have formulated an appropriate measure using domain knowledge.

4.3.2 SIMILARITY MEASURES

There are a set of similarity measures (proximity measures) to obtain a specific clustering solution to a given set of data:

Proximity Measures

A proximity measure can be defined between two data points in clustering. The term proximity refers to the similarity or dissimilarity of the samples concerning each other. Assume x_i and x_j are the two data points in a set of D-dimensional data as shown in Figure 4.3:
- Similarity measure $S\left(x_i, x_j\right)$ is large if x_i and x_j are similar
- Dissimilarity(or distance) measure $D\left(x_i, x_j\right)$ is small if x_i and x_j are dissimilar

Several similarity measures exist in the literature that can be used to evaluate the similarity or dissimilarity.

- **Vectors: cosine distance**
    If the data is represented in the form of vectors, then the similarity measure is evaluated using the cosine distance according to the equation

$$S\left(x_i, x_j\right) = \frac{x_i x_j}{\|x_i\|\|x_j\|} \tag{4.3}$$

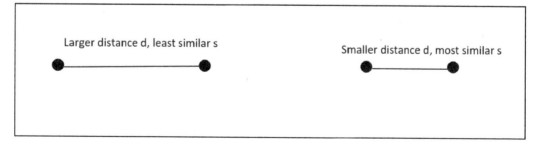

FIGURE 4.3   Similarity metrics based on distance.

- **Sets: Jaccard distance**

  If the data is represented in the form of sets, then the similarity measure is evaluated using the Jaccard distance given by the equation

  $$J(A,B) = \frac{A \cap B}{A \cup B} = \frac{A \cap B}{|A| + |B| - |A \cap B|}, \text{ where } 0 \leq J(A,B) \leq 1 \qquad (4.4)$$

  If sets A and B are empty, then $J(A,B) = 1$.

- **Points: Euclidean distance**

  If the data is represented in the form of points, then the similarity measure is evaluated using the Euclidean distance given by the equation

  $$d(x_i, x_j) = \left(\sum_{k=1}^{D} \left| x_i^k - x_j^k \right|^p \right)^{1/p} \qquad (4.5)$$

  where $p = 2$.

Generally, good proximity measures are also application-dependent. For example, for good proximity measures, the clustering user should not normalize the data drawn from multiple distributions.

4.4 CLUSTERING ALGORITHMS

In this section, a broad classification of the clustering algorithms is presented. The classification is performed based on the orthogonal characteristics of the data available for clustering.

4.4.1 HIERARCHICAL AND PARTITIONAL CLUSTERING APPROACHES

In hierarchical clustering, similar objects in a dataset are grouped into clusters and can be represented as *trees* of clusters. Here, any two clusters are displaced, or one cluster includes the other like branches of a tree, hence the term hierarchical.

In partitional clustering, multiple groups or partitions are formed from the given dataset. Here, the user has to specify the number of partitions or clusters as required for the application.

4.4.2 AGGLOMERATIVE AND DIVISIVE CLUSTERING APPROACHES

The agglomerative and divisive **clustering methods belong to the hierarchical clustering family** work in a reverse fashion concerning each other. In the agglomerative approach, each object in the dataset is assigned to its cluster based on the pairwise distance, and then, the clusters are merged. On the contrary, in the divisive approach, all the objects in the dataset are assigned to a unique cluster, and then, the clusters are split further from the unique cluster.

4.4.3 HARD AND FUZZY CLUSTERING APPROACHES

Each data object must belong to a single cluster while determining a clustering output for a given set of data. This approach is called hard clustering. But in a real-time scenario, the data can belong to more than one cluster since there may be many similarity relations between the data among clusters. To address this issue, fuzzy clustering algorithms are used with the concepts of fuzzy set theory. The algorithm allows objects to belong to different clusters based on certain degrees of membership. This approach is referred to as the fuzzy clustering approach.

All the algorithms discussed so far will find a clustering result, such that each data object must belong to a single cluster (called hard clustering). However, in real-time scientific and industrial applications, a data object may belong to one or more clusters. The existing clustering methods have been extended with the concepts of fuzzy set theory to address such issues. Fuzzy clustering algorithms allow objects to belong to several clusters simultaneously with different degrees of membership Kutner et al. (2005).

4.4.4   MONOTHETIC AND POLYTHETIC CLUSTERING APPROACHES

Monothetic and polythetic *clustering* are mostly suitable for obtaining solutions to problems in taxonomy. The monothetic clustering algorithm uses the features or objects of the dataset one by one for clustering. In contrast, the polythetic clustering algorithm uses all the dataset features at one for clustering.

4.4.5   DETERMINISTIC AND PROBABILISTIC CLUSTERING APPROACHES

In the deterministic clustering approach, the data objects are grouped into clusters in a deterministic manner, while in the probabilistic approach, an object is assigned to a certain cluster based on probability.

Though there are different approaches used for clustering, as discussed in the previous section, only a few successful and popular algorithms are derived from these approaches. Therefore, the following sections will deal with the most common clustering algorithms such as k-means clustering, fuzzy k-means clustering, mixture of Gaussians, and density-based clustering, used for real-time applications.

4.5   k-MEANS CLUSTERING

One of the simplest and most commonly used unsupervised learning algorithms is the k-means clustering algorithm proposed by MacQueen in 1967. The algorithm classifies the given set of unlabeled data into a pre-defined number of k clusters.

4.5.1   GEOMETRIC INTUITION, CENTROIDS

The basic aim of the k-means clustering algorithm is to define k centroids, each cluster with one centroid, respectively. These pre-defined centroids should be placed cleverly since the different locations of centroids give different outputs. The better approach is to maintain the centroids as far away from each other. Once the centroids' location is identified, the points in the dataset have to be associated with the nearest centroid. The process is repeated until no points are left free without association. This is specified as the first stage of grouping or clustering. Once the first stage is done, then a new set of k new centroids are computed. Once again, clustering is done according to the new k centroids. The iterative process is repeated until no change is observed between the k new centroids in the current iteration and the k centroids evaluated in the previous iteration. Once the final clusters are formed, then the objective function is evaluated; in this case, the objective function is to minimize the squared error function given by the equation

$$J = \sum_{j=1}^{k} \sum_{i=1}^{n} \left\| x_i^j - c_j^2 \right\| \tag{4.6}$$

where $\left\| x_i^j - c_j \right\|^2$ is the distance evaluated between the data point x_i^j and the cluster center c_j. The above equation gives us the information of the n data points from their respective k cluster centers.

To minimize the objective function, the k-means clustering algorithm should satisfy the following criterion:

Criterion 1: If a cluster sample c is considered among the set of clusters in the set, then the sample should be the point that minimizes.

$$\sum_{j=1}^{k}\sum_{i=1}^{n}\left\|x_i^j - c_j\right\|^2 \tag{4.7}$$

In simple words, the objective function should be minimized over the samples of the cluster.

Criterion 2: A point x_i^j must be assigned to the cluster whose centroid $c*(x)$ is the closest to $c*(x) = \arg\min_{k}\left\|x_i^j - c_j\right\|^2$. In simple words, the objective function should be minimized over the samples of x.

4.5.2   THE ALGORITHM

The steps of the k-means clustering algorithm are explained as follows:

Step 1: Determine the value of k and place the k centroids in the data space consisting of the dataset to be clustering. These k points represent the initial group of centroids.

Step 2: Once the centroids are fixed, assign each object in the dataset to the cluster with the closest centroid.

Step 3: Verify if all objects of the dataset have been assigned. Then, recompute the positions of the k centroids.

Step 4: Repeat steps 2 and 3 until there is no change in the new centroids and the previous centroids. Now we get a set of clusters with objects grouped. Next, evaluate the objective function based on the equation.

4.5.3   CHOOSING k

While finding the solution to a given dataset using the k-means algorithm, there always raises how to fix the value of initial k centroids. Based on research experiments on various datasets, there are several approaches to find the optimal value of k. The optimal value of k is required for proper convergence of the algorithm. The following are the various approaches to choose the value of k:

Elbow method

The elbow method is one of the common and popular approaches used in the k-means clustering algorithm to find the optimal value of k. First, for each k value, we will initialize k-means and identify the sum of squared distances of samples to the nearest cluster center. Then, a graph is plotted between various values of k and the sum of squared distances. Finally, a point on the graph corresponding to k is identified, beyond which the sum of squared distances starts declining. This point is known as the elbow point, and the k value is chosen as the optimal value of k.

Silhouette method

The silhouette method is a better approach to determine the number of clusters to be formulated from the dataset. We assume that the data has already been clustered into k clusters by k-means clustering. With the available information on the clusters, the silhouette coefficient $s(i)$ is given according to Equation 4.8:

$$s(i)\frac{x(i) - y(i)}{\max\left(x(i), y(i)\right)} \tag{4.8}$$

where $x(i)\dfrac{1}{c(i)-1}$. Then for each data point, we define the following:

- $C(i)$ represents the cluster allocated to the ith data object
- $|C(i)|$ is the number of data objects in the cluster allotted to the ith data point
- $a(i)$ is a measure of how good the ith data object is grouped to its cluster

$$a(i) = \frac{1}{|C(i)|-1} \sum_{C(i), i \neq j} d(i, j) \tag{4.9}$$

- $b(i)$ is the average dissimilarity to the nearest cluster, which is not its cluster

$$b(i) = \min_{i \neq j} \left(\frac{1}{|C(j)|} \sum_{j \in C(j)} d(i, j) \right) \tag{4.10}$$

The silhouette coefficient $s(i)$ is given as follows:

$$s(i) = \frac{b(i) - a(i)}{\max(a(i), b(i))} \tag{4.11}$$

In unsupervised learning, the optimal number of clusters is determined by the value of k, which has a maximum value of $s(i)$.

4.5.4 Space and Time Complexity

In terms of space, the k-means algorithm requires only storage of data points and centroids. Therefore, the space requirement is defined as $O((m+k)n)$, where k is the number of clusters, m is the number of data points, and n is the number of attributes.

In terms of time, k-means is a linear algorithm concerning the number of data points. Therefore, the time required for the k-means algorithm is $O(i*k*m*n)$, where i is the number of iterations required for the algorithm to converge, k is the number of clusters, m is the number of data points, and n is the number of attributes.

4.5.5 Advantages and Disadvantages of k-Means Clustering

4.5.5.1 Advantages

1. Highly **scalable** when the volume of data is large.
2. **Simpler** to implement.
3. Suitable for many new real-world examples
4. **Faster convergence** by minimizing optimization function that is given in terms of sum of squared error(SSE)
5. Faster and more effective based on the computational cost

4.5.5.2 Disadvantages

1. **Choice of k:** One major factor that plays a very important role in the algorithm's convergence is the optimal choice of k, which is tricky for different kinds of problems.
2. **Size and density of data:** The algorithm cannot perform well with clusters of varying sizes, shapes, and densities. The algorithm has to be generalized in such cases.

3. **Points not belonging to a cluster:** The points that are not part of any cluster have to be removed. Otherwise, upon iterations, these points tend to form another centroid due to a new cluster. This affects the performance of the algorithm.
4. **Dependence on initial values:** The value of k is limited in the case of the k-means algorithm. The performance of the algorithm decreases for higher values of k.
5. **Overlapping between clusters:** Since the k-means clustering algorithm does not have a clear measure for uncertainty, it is difficult to identify the points in the overlapping region and becomes a complex task to assign them to a cluster.

4.5.6   k-MEANS CLUSTERING IN PRACTICE USING PYTHON

Before starting the clustering process, the data points from the raw unlabeled data have to be well separated from each other. The raw data has to be scaled or standardized before applying the k-means algorithm. The user should ensure that the data points are most similar to their centroid and dissimilar to the other centroids. Over several clustering iterations, one centroid can be chosen randomly, and the next centroid can be placed as far as possible from the chosen centroid. This helps to attain the objective function.

k-Means is a simpler and more efficient, unsupervised technique suitable for various real domains such as natural language processing, computer vision, and medical analysis. Let us start with a simple example for the fuzzy k-means algorithm.

4.5.6.1   Illustration of the k-Means Algorithm Using Python

Let us consider the following dataset consisting of two variables along with their scores on ten individuals:

The Python code for initializing the dataset is given below:

Subject	I	II
1	1.5	1.0
2	1.5	2.0
3	2.5	2.0
4	2.5	5.0
5	3.0	4.0
6	6.0	7.0
7	3.5	5.0
8	1.0	1.0
9	3.5	4.5
10	4.5	5.0

```
import random
import math

noOfClusters = 2
noOfDataSet = 10
low_range_sample = 7 #element 0 of DATA_SET.
high_range_sample = 5 #element 3 of DATA_SET.
high_number = math.pow(10, 10)

DATA_SET = [[1.5, 1.0], [1.5, 2.0], [2.5, 2.0], [2.5, 5.0], [3.0, 4.0],
[6.0, 7.0], [3.5, 5.0], [1.0, 1.0], [3.5, 4.5], [4.5, 5.0]]

data = []
centroids = []
```

The objective of this example is to group the given data into two clusters. The initial partition is chosen such that data I and II of the two individuals are far apart based on the Euclidean distance. The centroid coordinates for this example are set to (1.5, 1.0) and (6.0, 7.0). The Python code segment relevant to this step is given below:

	Individual	Mean Vector (Centroid)
Group 1	8	(1.0, 1.0)
Group 2	6	(6.0, 7.0)

```
def init_centroids():
    centroids.append(Centroid(DATA_SET[low_range_sample][0], DATA_
SET[low_range_sample][1]))
    centroids.append(Centroid(DATA_SET[high_range_sample][0], DATA_
SET[high_range_sample][1]))

    print("Initial Centroids are at:")
    print("(", centroids[0].get_x(), ", ", centroids[0].get_y(), ")")
    print("(", centroids[1].get_x(), ", ", centroids[1].get_y(), ")")
    return
```

The remaining coordinates are taken in sequence, and the Euclidean distance is evaluated with respect to the initial centroid chosen. The illustration is shown below:

```
def initialize_datapoints():
    for i in range(noOfDataSet):
        newPoint = DataPoint(DATA_SET[i][0], DATA_SET[i][1])

        if(i == low_range_sample):
            newPoint.set_cluster(0)
        elif(i == high_range_sample):
            newPoint.set_cluster(1)
        else:
            newPoint.set_cluster(None)

        data.append(newPoint)
    return
```

Calculation of Euclidean distance

```
def get_distance(dataPointX, dataPointY, centroidX, centroidY):
    # Calculate Euclidean distance.
    return math.sqrt(math.pow((centroidY - dataPointY), 2) + math.
pow((centroidX - dataPointX), 2))
```

The centroids chosen initially are recomputed, and we find that the initial partition is modified. Even at this stage, to ensure correct assignment to each cluster, the distance of each individual is computed to its cluster and that of the opposite cluster. The centroids are recomputed as illustrated in the code snippet.

```
def recompute_centroids():
    xSum = 0
    ySum = 0
    sumInCluster = 0
```

```
        for j in range(noOfClusters):
            for k in range(len(data)):
                if(data[k].get_cluster() == j):
                    xSum += data[k].get_x()
                    ySum += data[k].get_y()
                    sumInCluster += 1

            if(sumInCluster > 0):
                centroids[j].set_x(xSum / sumInCluster)
                centroids[j].set_y(ySum / sumInCluster)


    return


def cluster_updation():
    isStillMoving = 0

    for i in range(noOfDataSet):
        bestMinimum = high_number
        currentCluster = 0

        for j in range(noOfClusters):
            distance = get_distance(data[i].get_x(), data[i].
get_y(), centroids[j].get_x(), centroids[j].get_y())
            if(distance < bestMinimum):
                bestMinimum = distance
                currentCluster = j

        data[i].set_cluster(currentCluster)

        if(data[i].get_cluster() is None or data[i].
get_cluster() != currentCluster):
            data[i].set_cluster(currentCluster)
            isStillMoving = 1


    return isStillMoving
def kmeans():
    isStillMoving = 1

    init_centroids()

    initialize_datapoints()

    while(isStillMoving):
        recompute_centroids()
        isStillMoving = cluster_updation()

    return

def print_output():
    for i in range(noOfClusters):
        print("Data grouped under cluster", i, "are:")
        for j in range(noOfDataSet):
            if(data[j].get_cluster() == i):
                print("(", data[j].get_x(), ", ", data[j].get_y(), ")")
        print()
```

```
    return

kmeans()
print_output()
```

The iterative process continues until a suitable number of iterations have been reached, and the following were the observations obtained:

The output of the code:

```
Initial Centroids are at:
( 1.0 ,   1.0 )
( 6.0 ,   7.0 )

Data grouped under cluster 0 are:
( 1.5 ,   1.0 )
( 1.5 ,   2.0 )
( 2.5 ,   2.0 )
( 1.0 ,   1.0 )

Data grouped under cluster 1 are:
( 2.5 ,   5.0 )
( 3.0 ,   4.0 )
( 6.0 ,   7.0 )
( 3.5 ,   5.0 )
( 3.5 ,   4.5 )
( 4.5 ,   5.0 )
```

4.5.7 Fuzzy k-Means Clustering Algorithm

In fuzzy k-means clustering, the points or objects in the data to be clustered have a probability that defines its association with each cluster. This is contradictory to the conventional k-means algorithm where data points belong to a cluster. Fuzzy k-means particularly deals with the degree of belonging. The degree of belonging is defined in terms of probability. This is achieved by replacing distance with probability, which can be a function of distance, such as having probability relative to the inverse of the distance. The fuzzy k-means clustering algorithm uses a weighted centroid based on the defined probabilities.

The algorithm of fuzzy k-means is similar to the conventional k-means algorithm in terms of initialization, iteration, and convergence. The clusters obtained at each stage are evolved based on the probabilistic distributions. The probability function in fuzzy k-means is defined within a range of [0,1], where "0" indicates that the data point is far away from the centroid while "1" indicates that the data point is closest to the centroid.

The fuzzy k-means algorithm was developed by Dunn in 1973 [27] and later improvised by Peizhuang in 1981 [28]. The clustering is performed by exploring a set of fuzzy groups, W, and the associated cluster centers, C, that define the structure of the data point as best as possible iteratively. The partition matrix obtained after clustering would be expressed as W with size $k \times m$, where k denotes the cluster number and m defines the number of data points in each cluster. W can also be expressed as $W = [w_{ab}]$, where w_{ab} is the membership defined concerning the probability of a data point u_b from a cluster center c_a, where a denotes the cluster number varying from 1 to k, and b denotes the number of data points in each cluster varying from 1 to m. In the case of crisp partitioning, $W = [w_{ab}] = 0$. The final objective of the fuzzy k-means clustering algorithm is to minimize the sum of the squared error function $E_s(C,W)$ according to Equation 4.12:

$$Es(C,W) = \sum_{b=1}^{m} \sum_{a=1}^{k} (w_{ab})^s \|u_b - c_a\|^2, s \in [1, \infty] \qquad (4.12)$$

where s is a real number and is the fuzziness coefficient. It is a very important factor that influences the membership grades, thus aiding the algorithm's performance. As the value of s increases, the algorithm becomes fuzzier, and researchers have proved that the fuzzy k-means algorithm converges for s value in the range $[1, \infty]$. Here, w_{ab} is the membership degree of u_b in cluster a, c_a is the cluster center, and the $\|\cdot\|$ operator indicates the inner product showing the similarity between the data points and the cluster. The error function is mainly dependent on W and C, subject to two main constraints as follows:

$$\sum_{a=1}^{k} w_{ab} = 1, \text{ for } b = 1, 2, \ldots m \tag{4.13}$$

and

$$0 < \sum_{b=1}^{m} w_{ab} < k, \text{ for } a = 1, 2, \ldots k$$

The algorithm is iterated to minimize the error function defined above.

4.5.7.1   The Algorithm

The steps of the fuzzy k-means clustering algorithm are explained as follows:

- **Step 1:** Choose an optimal value of k, which indicates the number of clusters.
- **Step 2:** Initialize the k-means membership μ_k associated with the clusters and evaluate the probability such that each data point x_i is assigned to a cluster k, $P(\mu_k \mid x_i, k)$.
- **Step 3:** Recompute the centroid of the cluster according to the equation.
- **Step 4:** Repeat steps 2 and 3 until convergence or until a specified number of iterations have been reached, and the error function is minimized.

4.5.8   ADVANTAGES AND DISADVANTAGES OF FUZZY K-MEANS CLUSTERING

Since the fuzzy k-means clustering algorithm works similarly to the k-means clustering, most of the advantages and limitations of the fuzzy k-means clustering algorithm are common. Still, we differentiate the two clustering algorithms as follows:

Advantages:
- For classification problems pertinent to hard classes, the k-means algorithm performs better than fuzzy k-means, despite an exploratory data analysis.
- The underlying benefit of the fuzzy k-means clustering algorithm becomes evident based on the membership values of the fuzzy clustering. The membership values show a powerful skewed bimodal distribution for classification problems. This is a major benefit for having proper clustering between classes in a clustering algorithm.
- For huge datasets, the fuzzy k-means clustering algorithm is recommended for analyzing the substructure of the data, for existing known patterns, and unexplored data in the available dataset.

Disadvantages:
- The fuzzy k-means clustering algorithm requires more computation time (slower than k-means clustering). When compared to k-means clustering, it is observed in various studies that the computation time increases more rapidly for the fuzzy k-means clustering algorithm as the number of clusters increases.

4.6 HIERARCHICAL CLUSTERING

Hierarchical clustering algorithm, otherwise called hierarchical cluster analysis, is a method used to create a tree of clusters by grouping homogeneous data points. The endpoint is a set of cluster in which each cluster is unique from every other.

For the given input of six raw data points {A,B,C,D,E,F}, hierarchical cluster analysis computes the distance matrix.

Let's see how hierarchical clustering works with an example. Initially, each observation is considered as a group or cluster. Execute the following two steps repetitively until all the clusters are merged:

B	16				
C	47	37			
D	72	57	40		
E	77	65	30	31	
F	79	66	35	23	10
	A	B	C	D	E

- Identify the two closer clusters
- Merge the identified two clusters

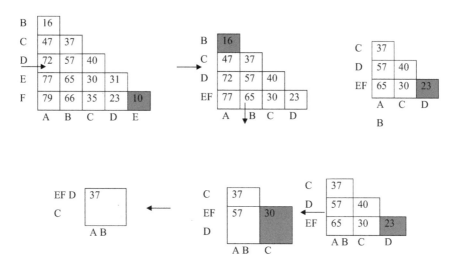

Treelike dendrograms represent the cluster relationship. The dendograms for the example considered is shown in Figure 4.4.

Types of Hierarchical Clustering

Hierarchical clustering is classified (Figure 4.5) as agglomerative or divisive based on how hierarchical decomposition is performed.

4.6.1 AGGLOMERATIVE HIERARCHICAL CLUSTERING

In agglomerative hierarchical clustering, dendrograms are built from the bottom level. Then, the two most similar or nearest clusters from the bottom are merged. The algorithm stops the merging process when all the data points are merged into a single cluster. The following steps (Figure 4.6) describe how to build a dendrogram based on agglomerative hierarchical clustering:

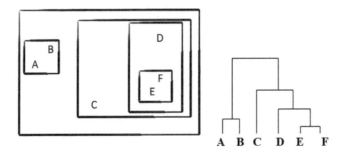

FIGURE 4.4　Dendrogram representation.

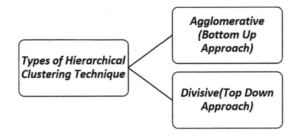

FIGURE 4.5　Classification of hierarchical clustering.

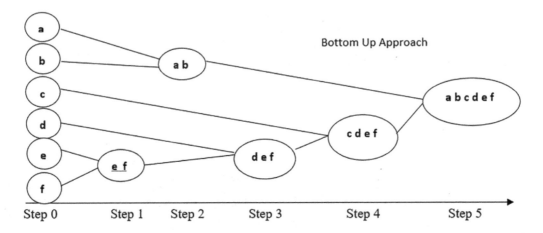

FIGURE 4.6　Step-by-step procedure in agglomerative hierarchical clustering.

- **Step 1:** Initialization – initially, each data point forms a separate cluster
- **Step 2:** Compute distance/proximity matrix of the cluster
- **Step 3:** Repeat
  - **Step 3.1:** Merge the two most similar or nearest clusters from the bottom
  - **Step 3.2:** Update the distance matrix
- **Step 4:** Repeat step 3 until a single cluster remains

Distance or proximity matrix can be constructed in different ways, as shown below:

- **Single linkage:** Similarity of the most similar data points
- **Complete linkage:** Similarity of the least similar data points
- **Average linkage:** Average cosine between pair of elements.

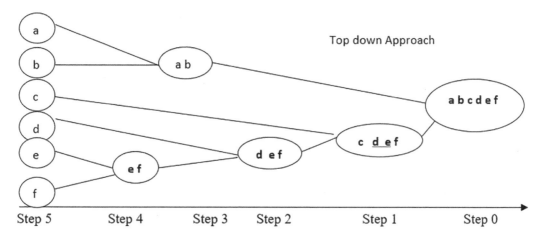

FIGURE 4.7   Step-by-step procedure in divisive hierarchical clustering.

4.6.2 DIVISIVE HIERARCHICAL CLUSTERING

In divisive hierarchical clustering, the clustering process starts from the top or root of the dendrogram where all data points are in one single cluster. Then, it starts to split the root into a set of child clusters. The process of splitting is continuously performed for each child cluster. The process of splitting stops only when a singleton cluster of one data point is present. Moreover, top-down divisive hierarchical clustering is more complex than the bottom-up approach because it uses a flat clustering algorithm. The most extensively used flat clustering algorithm is k-means clustering.

The top-down approach as shown in Figure 4.7 is more accurate as it gives a complete idea from global distribution, whereas the bottom-up approach decides from the local distributions. The following are the steps to perform divisive clustering:

Initialization: Initially start from the top or root of the dendrogram, which contains one single cluster with all data points.
Repeat
   • Choose which cluster to split
   • Determine how to split: Split that cluster by the flat clustering algorithm such as k-means clustering, and
Until termination condition: Each data is in its singleton cluster.

4.6.3 TECHNIQUES TO MERGE CLUSTER

To define inter-cluster distance for merging two clusters, the following approaches are used widely:

   • Min or single link
   • Max or complete link
   • Group average or average link
   • Centroid distance
   • Ward's method

Single linkage: The distance between two clusters C1 and C2 is represented by the distance of the closest pair of data objects belonging to different clusters, as shown in Figure 4.8. The single-link method is sensitive to outliers because they lie far away from the rest of the data points.

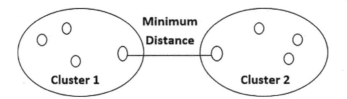

FIGURE 4.8 Minimum distance between two data objects in two different clusters.

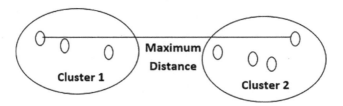

FIGURE 4.9 Maximum distance between two data objects in two different clusters.

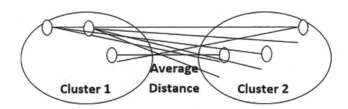

FIGURE 4.10 Average distance between two data objects in two different clusters.

$$d_{\min}(C_1,C_2) = \min_{x \in C_1,\, y \in C_2} d(x,y) \tag{4.14}$$

Complete linkage: The distance between two clusters C1 and C2 is represented by the distance of the farthest pair of data objects belonging to different clusters, i.e., the maximum distance between two data objects (Figure 4.9).

$$d_{\min}(C_1,C_2) = \max_{x \in C_1,\, y \in C_2} d(x,y) \tag{4.15}$$

The complete link method is less sensitive to outliers because they lie far away from the rest of the data points.

Average linkage: The similarity of two clusters is determined by the average similarity (Figure 4.10) between all pairs of data objects belonging to different clusters.

$$d_{\min}(C_1,C_2) = \operatorname*{avg}_{x \in C_1,\, y \in C_2} d(x,y) \tag{4.16}$$

The average link method is robust to noise and outlier. However, the limitation of average linkage is biased toward global clusters.

Centroid distance: The distance between two clusters is represented by the distance between the means (Figure 4.11) of the clusters.

$$d_{\mathrm{mean}}(C_1,C_2) = d(m_1,m_2) \tag{4.17}$$

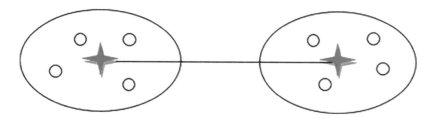

FIGURE 4.11   Mean distance between two different clusters.

Ward's method: The sum of squares of the distance of P_i and P_j is calculated in Ward's method based on the relation

$$\text{sim}(C_1, C_2) = \sum \left(\text{dist}(P_i, P_j)^2 \right) \Big/ |C_1| * |C_2| \qquad (4.18)$$

It performs well with noisy data, and the problem of Ward's method is biased toward global clusters.

4.6.4   SPACE AND TIME COMPLEXITY

Space complexity: The space complexity remains high when the number of data points is more because more space is required to store the proximity matrix.
Space complexity $S = O(n^2)$, where n is the total count of input data objects.
Time complexity: The time complexity is also high as we need to update the similarity matrix in every iteration.
Time complexity $= O(n^3)$, where n is the total count of input data objects.

4.6.5   LIMITATIONS OF HIERARCHICAL CLUSTERING

- Highly sensitive to scaling
- Difficulty in handling noise data and not efficient with outliers
- High space and time complexity

4.6.6   HIERARCHICAL CLUSTERING IN PRACTICE USING PYTHON

An example is presented in this section to cluster a random dataset of data points (Figure 4.12) using the agglomerative hierarchical clustering. Initially, all the libraries required are imported.

```
import random
import math
import matplotlib.pyplot as plt
import numpy as np
from numpy import random
```

The next step is to obtain the data. Here, a random data ranging from 0 to 100 with 30 rows and two columns is generated. The dataset is also plotted for more clarity of the data points.

```
DATA_SET=random.randint(100, size=(30, 2))
print(DATA_SET)

labels = range(1, 100)
plt.figure(figsize=(10, 7))
```

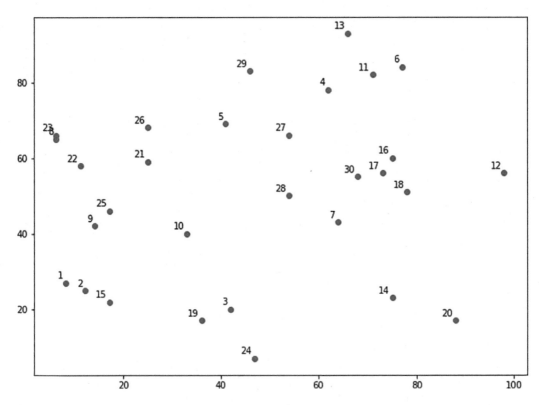

FIGURE 4.12   Distribution of the random dataset generated.

```
plt.subplots_adjust(bottom=0.1)
plt.scatter(DATA_SET[:,0],DATA_SET[:,1], label='True Position')

for label, x, y in zip(labels, DATA_SET[:, 0], DATA_SET[:, 1]):
    plt.annotate(
        label,
        xy=(x, y), xytext=(-3, 3),
        textcoords='offset pixels', ha='right', va='bottom')
plt.show()
```

Now the class for Clustering AgglomerativeClustering is imported from the sklearn cluster library. Here, the cluster number is set to three, with affinity set to Euclidean and linkage set to "ward."

```
from sklearn.cluster import AgglomerativeClustering
cluster = AgglomerativeClustering(n_
clusters=3, affinity='euclidean', linkage='average')
cluster.fit_predict(DATA_SET)
print(cluster.labels_)
plt.scatter(DATA_SET[:,0],DATA_SET[:,1], c=cluster.
labels_, cmap='rainbow')
```

4.6.6.1   DATA_SET

[[8 27] [12 25] [42 20] [62 78] [41 69] [77 84] [64 43] [6 65] [14 42] [33 40] [71 82] [98 56] [66 93] [75 23] [17 22] [75 60] [73 56] [78 51] [36 17] [88 17] [25 59] [11 58] [6 66] [47 7] [17 46] [25 68] [54 66] [54 50] [46 83] [68 55]]

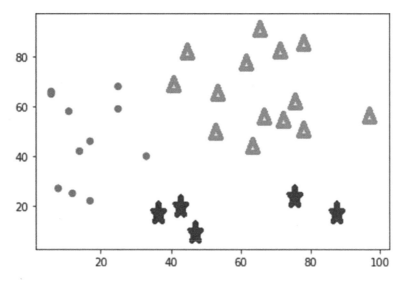

FIGURE 4.13 Clustered output based on agglomerative hierarchical clustering.

The following array shows the pattern in which the data points are clustered:
[2 2 0 1 1 1 1 2 2 2 1 1 1 0 2 1 1 1 0 0 2 2 2 0 2 2 1 1 1 1]
It is a one-dimensional array with 30 elements corresponding to the cluster assigned to 30 data points. The clustered output is shown in Figure 4.13.

4.7 MIXTURE OF GAUSSIAN CLUSTERING

The Gaussian clustering algorithm is probability-based which is highly suitable for unlabeled or unsupervised data. The Gaussian clustering algorithm performs similar to k-means clustering. However, the k-means clustering algorithm doesn't take care of the distribution of data or variance. Moreover, the k-means algorithm only works well when the data is circular and unsuitable for oblong data distribution. But the Gaussian method can handle more elongated clusters.

Let's understand with a simple example of classifying images based on their RGB intensity. In Figure 4.14, images of the sea (dark-shaded circles), forest (dark gray-shaded circles), and desert (light gray circles) without any labels are considered.

Select a data point x_i that is circled in Figure 4.14, and associate probability π_k with each Gaussian component. In this case, the π is represented as

$$\pi = \left[\pi_1 = 0.8, \pi_2 = 0.2, \pi_3 = 0 \right]$$

The prior probability of the data point x_i to be associated with the kth cluster is given as

$$p(z_i = k) = \pi_k \tag{4.19}$$

The likelihood of seeing the data point x_i in cluster sea is given as

$$p\left(x_i | z_i = k, \mu_k \sigma_k^2\right) \tag{4.20}$$

To maximize the likelihood, we can use the EM algorithm.

The main advantages of model-based clustering are as follows:

- Less sensitive to scalability
- Highly flexible for any data distribution

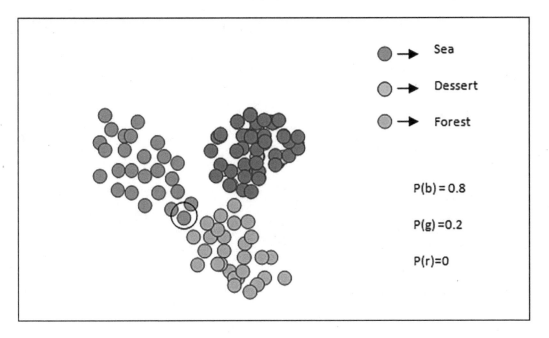

FIGURE 4.14   Example to understand the mixture of Gaussian clustering.

- Efficient in handling outliers
- Faster convergence
- A more effective method for noisy real-world data.

4.7.1   EXPECTATION MAXIMIZATION

To maximize the likelihood of Gaussian clustering, EM algorithm comes into the picture. Let us understand this with a simple example. EM proceeds iteratively with two steps. The expectation treats the Gaussian parameters, Mean μ, and covariance $\sum_c$, while π for the cluster is fixed.

Expectation step (E step):

For each data point x_i and cluster c, compute relative probability r_{ic} of data point x_i such that it belongs to cluster c, using the equation below.

$$r_{ic} = \frac{\pi N\left(x_i; \mu_c, \sum_c\right)}{\sum_{c'} \pi N\left(x_i; \mu_{c'}, \sum_{c'}\right)} \tag{4.21}$$

If x_i is very likely to be the cth cluster, then it will get high values. So the denominator is just to normalize, i.e., to make the sum to one.

Maximization step (M step):

Start with the relative probability r_{ic} and update the parameter of the clusters mean μ, covariance $\sum_c$, and π.

For each cluster, $z = c$. Update the parameters using the weighted data points.

$$m_c = \sum_i r_{ic} \left(\text{Total responsibility allocated to cluster} c\right)$$

$$\pi_c = \frac{m_c}{m}\left(\text{Fraction of total assigned to cluster } c\right)$$

$$\mu_c = \frac{1}{m_c}\sum_i r_{ic}x^{(i)} \quad \left(\text{Weighted mean of assigned data}\right)$$

$$\Sigma_c = \frac{1}{m_c}\sum_i r_{ic}\left(x^{(i)} - \mu_c\right)^T\left(x^{(i)} - \mu_c\right)\left(\text{Weighted covariance of assigned data}\right)$$

Example: Suppose x_k are the student marks and $p(x_k)$ are their probability.

$$x_1 = 30 \quad P(x_1) = \frac{1}{2}$$

$$x_2 = 18 \quad P(x_2) = \mu$$

$$x_3 = 0 \quad P(x_3) = 2\mu$$

$$x_4 = 23 \quad P(x_4) = \frac{1}{2} - 3\mu$$

First case: We observe that the marks are so distributed among students:
x_1: a students
x_2: b students
x_3: c students
x_4: d students

$$P(a,b,c,d|\mu) \propto \left(\frac{1}{2}\right)^a * (\mu)^b * (2\mu)^c * \left(\frac{1}{2} - 3\mu\right)^d \tag{4.22}$$

Maximize by deriving $\frac{\partial P}{\partial \mu} = 0$. Derive the logarithm of the function and maximize it:

$$P_L = \log\left(\frac{1}{2}\right)^a + \log(\mu)^b + \log(2\mu)^c + \log\left(\frac{1}{2} - 3\mu\right)^d$$

$$\frac{\partial P_L}{\partial \mu} = \frac{b}{\mu} + \frac{2c}{2\mu} - \frac{3d}{\frac{1}{2} - 3\mu} = 0 \tag{4.23}$$

$$\Rightarrow \mu = \frac{b+c}{6(b+c+d)}$$

Suppose $a = 14$, $b = 6$, $c = 9$, and $d = 10$, and we can calculate $\mu = \frac{1}{10}$.

Second case: We observe that marks are so distributed among students:
$x_1 + x_2$: h students
x_3: c students
x_4: d students

$$\text{expectation:} \mu \rightarrow a = \frac{\frac{1}{2}}{\frac{1}{2} + \mu}h, b = \frac{\mu}{\frac{1}{2} + \mu}h \tag{4.24}$$

$$\text{maximization: } a,b \rightarrow \mu = \frac{b+c}{6(b+c+d)} \qquad (4.25)$$

This circularity can be solved iteratively.

The time complexity of the EM algorithm is $O(NKD^3)$, where N is the number of data objects, K is the number of Gaussian components, and D is number of dimensions.

Advantages of EM

- Convergence is guaranteed
- Likelihood increases in every iteration

Disadvantages of EM

- It is highly complex when the number of dimensions increases and thus of limited use.

4.7.2 MIXTURE OF GAUSSIAN CLUSTERING IN PRACTICE USING PYTHON

This example applies GMM to a random dataset using the GaussianMixture from the sklearn library. All the necessary libraries are imported accordingly. A random dataset of size 100 is generated using the random function from the numpy library with 100 rows and two columns.

```
import numpy as np
import matplotlib.pyplot as plt
from sklearn.mixture import GaussianMixture
from numpy import random

DATA_SET=random.randint(100, size=(100, 2))
print(DATA_SET)
plt.plot(DATA_SET[:,0], DATA_SET[:,1], 'gx')
plt.axis('equal')
plt.show()

gmm = GaussianMixture(n_components=2)
gmm.fit(DATA_SET)
print(gmm.means_)
print('\n')
print(gmm.covariances_)

X, Y = np.meshgrid(np.linspace(-200, 400), np.linspace(-200,400))
XX = np.array([X.ravel(), Y.ravel()]).T
Z = gmm.score_samples(XX)
Z = Z.reshape((50,50))

plt.contour(X, Y, Z)
plt.scatter(DATA_SET[:, 0], DATA_SET[:, 1])

plt.show()
```

The output of the above code is presented below:

The random data generated in the range between 0 and 100 are listed. The plot of the data is shown in Figure 4.15.

```
[[ 1 59] [32 88] [11 56] [79 47] [27 45] [87 71] [30 77] [93 31] [58 55]
[31 97] [36 77] [10 11] [93 33] [32 50] [88 82] [12 78] [26  4] [70 10] [66
```

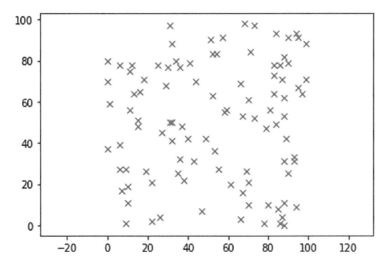

FIGURE 4.15   Distribution of the random data generated for a mixture of Gaussians.

3] [83 78] [52 63] [15 51] [22 2] [67 16] [38 22] [9 27] [83 64] [13 64]
[86 1] [84 49] [69 26] [40 42] [68 98] [52 83] [6 39] [88 11] [70 61] [55
27] [7 17] [73 52] [44 70] [88 31] [0 37] [32 41] [10 19] [31 50] [22
21] [36 32] [66 69] [51 90] [94 93] [49 42] [25 78] [84 93] [87 4] [70 21]
[95 91] [90 25] [6 27] [61 20] [54 83] [90 79] [41 79] [29 68] [47 7] [43
31] [89 42] [88 62] [19 26] [83 73] [99 71] [88 53] [90 91] [0 70] [9 1]
[85 8] [78 1] [95 67] [67 53] [37 48] [35 25] [18 71] [73 97] [57 91]
[0 80] [71 84] [15 48] [16 65] [53 36] [80 10] [94 9] [97 64] [11 75] [86
78] [34 80] [6 78] [81 56] [99 88] [88 0] [59 56]]

In this case, the input is a set of 2D data points. Hence, the Gaussians will be the same plot of the two Gaussians overlapping. Once the model has converged, the means and the covariances are determined and given as follows:

μ1 = [[43.89912658 36.92423653] [71.38718383 76.86583559]]

Σ1 = [[[931.53709452 -284.48772158]   [-284.48772158 602.82022267]]

μ2 = [[513.42101497 -31.36462194]   [-31.36462194 188.92292275]]]

This example creates a grid with X- and Y-coordinates ranging from −200 to 400 to compute the GMM using the EM algorithm. GMM is then plotted as contours over the original data, as represented in Figure 4.16. It can be observed that with normal distribution, most of the data points are found around the mean and less as we move away.

4.8   DENSITY-BASED CLUSTERING ALGORITHM

A density-based clustering algorithm is a non-parametric approach of unsupervised learning used to cluster unlabeled data. Various density-based clustering algorithms are DBSCAN, OPTICS, DENCLUE, and CLIQUE. In this section, the DBSCAN algorithm is discussed in detail with relevant Python implementation.

4.8.1   DBSCAN (DENSITY-BASED SPATIAL CLUSTERING OF APPLICATIONS WITH NOISE)

The widely used density-based technique is DBSCAN, which was introduced by Ester et al. (1996). The main objective of DBSCAN is to identify the dense region. The main high-level idea of DBSCAN is as follows:

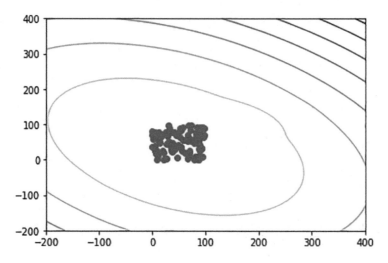

FIGURE 4.16   Clustering using the GMM algorithm.

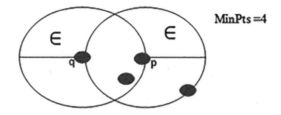

FIGURE 4.17   Illustration for density with MinPts=4.

- Partition the data into three types of points (core, boundary, and noise). The core points are the high-density points at the center with lots of neighbors around them.
- Connect the core points to create clusters
- Assign boundary points to each cluster

Two parameters involved are eps and MinPts. $\in$ Neighborhood refers to the objects within the radius $\in$. The $\in$ Neighborhood is defined as follows:

$$\in \text{Neighborhood}(x) = \{y \in D : d(x,y) \leq \in\}$$

where D is the dataset and d is the distance between data objects.

The higher density of objects should hold at least MinPts of objects. For example, as shown in Figure 4.17, let us consider MinPts=4. It is inferred from the figure that the density of p is higher than the density of q.

For Figure 4.18, the assigned parameters are eps=1 unit and MinPts=5. Based on the given parameters, the data points are classified into three points: core, border, and outlier points, as shown in Figure 4.18.

The core point is the data point if it has more objects than MinPts within the radius $\in$. Border point has fewer objects than MinPts within the radius $\in$, but it lies nearer to the core point. Outliers are the ones that are extreme data objects. The two approaches in DBSCAN are as follows:

- Density reachable
- Density-connected

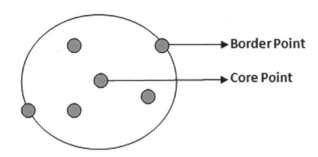

FIGURE 4.18   Illustration for density with MinPts = 5.

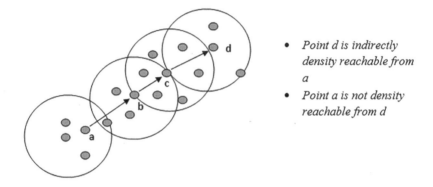

- *Point d is indirectly density reachable from a*
- *Point a is not density reachable from d*

FIGURE 4.19   Illustration for density-reachable.

> ***Density reachable:*** The two variants of density-reachable are directly and indirectly density-reachable. As shown in Figure 4.19, data point d is directly density-reachable from data point c. Point c is directly density-reachable from b. Similarly, point b is directly density-reachable from a. Chain of objects from data point d to data point a is directly density-reachable.
>
> ***Density-connected:*** Data point a is density-connected to the point c if there is an intermediate data object b from which both a and b are density-reachable.

4.8.2   Space and Time Complexity

Time complexity is $O(n^2)$ for each data point; it has to be determined whether it is a core point or not. Therefore, space complexity is $O(n)$.

4.8.3   Advantages and Disadvantages of DBSCAN

4.8.3.1   Advantages

It can handle outliers and noise.
    It works well for any shape and size.

4.8.3.2   Disadvantages

It cannot handle varying densities and is sensitive to parameters.
    Identifying the correct value for the parameter is not easy.

4.8.4   DBSCAN in Practice Using Python

The application of DBSCAN using Python is illustrated in this section. Here, a random cluster data is generated using the make_blobs function from the sklearn library. The data is transformed in this case. Compared to the k-means algorithm, it has been observed that in k-means, data clusters only around the nearest cluster center, whereas in DBSCAN, the entire plane of the data can be clustered. To illustrate this feature, the random data generated is transformed.

The total number of samples generated was 500, with four centers, center_box parameter set in the range [−20, 20]. The required functions are imported from the respective libraries. While using the DBSCAN function, the parameter "eps" plays a significant role in clustering. All the data points resulted in a single cluster when "eps" was set to a large value. At the same time, setting "eps" to small values resulted in data labeled as noise. Several experiments were conducted to have a trade-off, and in this example, "eps" is set to 0.2. Thus, the readers can explore different values of "eps" and observe the data clustering.

```python
import numpy as np
import matplotlib.pyplot as plt
from sklearn.datasets import make_blobs
from sklearn.cluster import DBSCAN
from sklearn.preprocessing import StandardScaler
from sklearn import metrics

# generate some random cluster data
X, labels_true = make_blobs(n_samples=500, n_
features=2,  centers=4, cluster_std=1.0, center_box=(-
20.0, 20.0), shuffle=True, random_state=100)
rng = np.random.RandomState(74)

# transform the data to be stretched
transformation = rng.normal(size=(2, 2))
X = np.dot(X, transformation)

scaler = StandardScaler()
X_scaled = scaler.fit_transform(X)
# cluster the data into five clusters
dbscan = DBSCAN(eps=0.123, min_samples = 2)
clusters = dbscan.fit_predict(X_scaled)
# plot the cluster assignments
plt.scatter(X[:, 0], X[:, 1], c=clusters, cmap="plasma")
plt.xlabel("Feature 0")
plt.ylabel("Feature 1")

core_samples_mask = np.zeros_like(dbscan.labels_, dtype=bool)
core_samples_mask[dbscan.core_sample_indices_] = True
labels=dbscan.labels_
n_clusters_ = len(set(labels)) - (1 if -1 in labels else 0)
n_noise_ = list(labels).count(-1)

print('Estimated number of clusters: %d' % n_clusters_)
print('Estimated number of noise points: %d' % n_noise_)
print("Adjusted Mutual Information: %0.3f"
      % metrics.adjusted_mutual_info_score(labels_true, labels))
print("Adjusted Rand Index: %0.3f"
      % metrics.adjusted_rand_score(labels_true, labels))
```

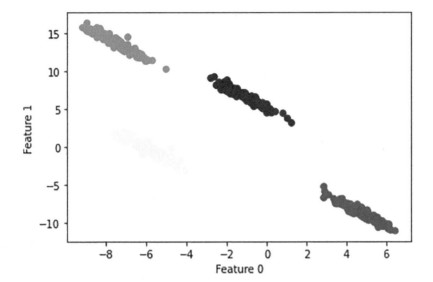

FIGURE 4.20 DBSCAN clustering for "eps"=0.2.

```
print("Completeness: %0.3f" % metrics.
completeness_score(labels_true, labels))
print("Homogeneity: %0.3f" % metrics.
homogeneity_score(labels_true, labels))
print("V-measure: %0.3f" % metrics.v_measure_score(labels_true, labels))
```

When it comes to analysis, it is important to understand the metrics involved in a code. In the example considered for implementing DBSCAN, the metrics function from the sklearn library is used to evaluate all the metrics corresponding to clustering. The output of the above code is presented below with all the metrics shown for "eps"=0.2. Figure 4.20 shows the clustering for the random data chosen for clustering.

 Estimated number of clusters: 4
 Estimated number of noise points: 0
 Adjusted Mutual Information: 1.000
 Adjusted Rand Index: 1.000
 Completeness: 1.000
 Homogeneity: 1.000
 V-measure: 1.000

The value of "eps" was then changed to 0.05, and the results are presented below with clustering shown in Figure 4.21. It is observed that though the number of clusters required was 4, the algorithm has estimated the number of clusters as 9. The number of noise points estimated has also increased considerably to 19. There is a variation concerning all the other evaluation metrics.

 Estimated number of clusters: 9
 Estimated number of noise points: 19
 Adjusted Mutual Information: 0.858
 Adjusted Rand Index: 0.866
 Completeness: 0.777
 Homogeneity: 0.964
 V-measure: 0.860

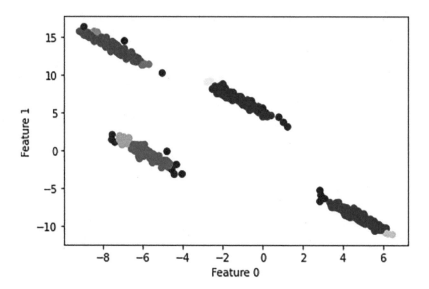

FIGURE 4.21   DBSCAN clustering for "eps" = 0.05.

SUMMARY

Unsupervised learning is a machine learning technique where the model does not require supervision. The unknown patterns of data can be explored based on the concept of clustering and association. This chapter has discussed several clustering algorithms, namely the k-means clustering, fuzzy k-means clustering, hierarchical (agglomerative and divisive) clustering, and DBSCAN clustering. These algorithms were discussed in detail with the implementation of examples using Python. Unsupervised machine learning helps you to find all kinds of unknown patterns in data. The major limitation of unsupervised learning is the lack of precise information from the clustering process. This can be overcome by exploring and conducting several additional experiments by varying the model parameters.

REVIEW QUESTIONS

1. Suppose we want to build a neural network that classifies two-dimensional data (i.e., $X = [x_1, x_2]$) into two classes: diamonds and crosses. The dataset has 1000 samples, including diamonds and crosses. Use k-means clustering and DBSCAN clustering algorithms to cluster the data and evaluate the clustering metrics. Compare the performance of the algorithms. List your observations by varying the model parameters.
2. What is the role of principal component analysis in unsupervised learning? Explain in detail.
3. List out all the unsupervised clustering algorithms and identify the model parameters relevant to each algorithm. Then, generate a random dataset, and explain the observations for each algorithm to vary the model parameter for at least five settings covering the minimum and maximum range.
4. What are the limitations of the fuzzy k-means algorithm?
5. Discuss the differences between agglomerative hierarchical and divisive hierarchical clustering algorithms. Then, implement these algorithms on a random dataset and observe the output.
6. Does clustering using unsupervised learning algorithms require data cleaning? If so, what would be the suitable approach for data cleaning? Discuss.

7. For performing a clustering analysis, what is the minimum number of features required?

8. Suppose the k-means algorithm is run twice on the same dataset. Do you observe the same results? Justify your answer.

9. What are dendrograms? Generate a dendrogram for random data. Is it possible to have two different dendrograms using agglomerative clustering for the same dataset? Discuss in detail.

10. Is it possible to obtain dendrograms using k-means clustering algorithms? Discuss.

11. What are all the evaluation metrics used to evaluate a clustering algorithm? List them and explain with relevant equations.

5 Supervised Learning
Regression

LEARNING OBJECTIVES

At the end of this chapter, the reader will be able to

- Know the basic paradigms and their underlying mathematical concept of supervised learning technique
- Understand the concepts of supervised learning for classification and regression problems
- Identify the appropriate supervised learning approaches for regression – linear regression
- Understand and implement linear regression using Python for practical problems

5.1 INTRODUCTION

Supervised learning is a variant of a machine learning algorithm to learn about the input–output paired samples. Medical image analysis, predictive analysis, and computer vision applications utilize these supervised algorithms for classifying data. To get useful insights and discover the patterns, data scientists utilize various types of machine learning algorithms. In general, these algorithms are categorized into two types depending on the method of learning about data to predict the future: supervised and unsupervised learning. A user teaches the supervised learning algorithm to learn about big data in the desired fashion. Supervised learning is a widely used machine learning algorithm that is used to learn the relationship between the independent input variable (X) and dependent output variable (Y) by determining the approximate mapping function $Y=f(X)$. This is shown in Figure 5.1. The objective is to learn an optimal mapping function to know how well it works to extrapolate for the new unknown input data (X).

Supervised learning techniques are support vector machines (SVMs), linear regression, logistic regression, multi-class classification, and decision trees. Training a supervised learning algorithm for each input requires a correct output label. For example, a classification algorithm needs to classify images of digits from 1 to 10 after being trained on a dataset of digit images that are properly labeled with the corresponding digits (1–10). Regression and classification are the two groups of the problem that can be efficiently learned using a supervised algorithm. The difference between the regression and classification problem is that the output variable is continuous or numerical for regression, whereas it is discrete or categorical for classification. This chapter introduces essential ideas behind all supervised algorithms in machine learning. The mathematical concept behind supervised algorithms with worked examples and implementation using Python is given in detail. Supervised algorithm for regression problem is well explained in this chapter with Python implementation. Linear regression is the fundamental regression algorithm to predict the output y-coordinate from the input x. Multiple linear regressions such as simple and multiple regression are discussed in this chapter.

5.2 SUPERVISED LEARNING – REAL-LIFE SCENARIO

Supervised learning is the task of uncovering hidden patterns and structures from labeled data. Successful supervised learning requires technical expertise to label data. In real-life applications, supervised learning is used widely, such as object detection, language processing, spoken word recognition, anomaly detection, product recommendation, credit risk analysis, optical character recognition, medical diagnosis, protein structure prediction, and biometrics.

DOI: 10.1201/9781003258803-5

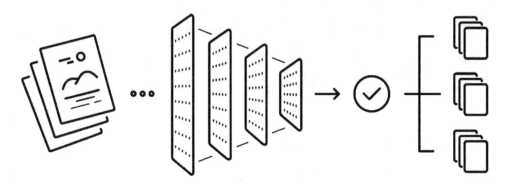

FIGURE 5.1 Mapping between input and output.

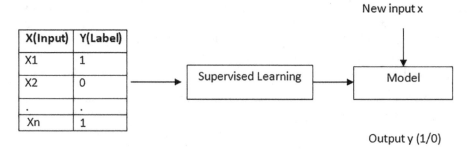

FIGURE 5.2 Prediction using supervised learning.

5.3 TYPES OF SUPERVISED LEARNING

Supervised techniques train the model using labeled data. The training process should continue until the level of performance is high enough. After training, the system should predict new unseen data correctly, as shown in Figure 5.2.

There are two types of supervised learning techniques: regression and classification. Classification separates the data, whereas regression fits the data.

5.3.1 SUPERVISED LEARNING – CLASSIFICATION

Classification is the process of categorizing the given input data into different classes. The output of the classification problem is a discrete or categorical value such as positive or negative, spam or not spam. Classifying the tumor as malignant or benign and classifying whether the account of a person is hacked or not are few examples of classification problems. Classification can be either binary or multi-class classification. Logistic regression is the best example for binary classification. Multi-class classification is a problem with more than two output classes; for example, alphabet character recognition is a multi-class classification problem. The various classification techniques are decision tree, logistic regression, random forest, gradient boosted tree, SVM, and naïve Bayes algorithm.

Which of the following is/are classification problem(s)?

- Predicting the sales of a newly introduced SUV over the next 6 months.
- Predicting whether a customer account is hacked or not.

Solution: Predicting the sale of car output is a continuous value and therefore it is not a classification problem. Predicting whether an account is hacked or not is a classification problem where the output value is categorical.

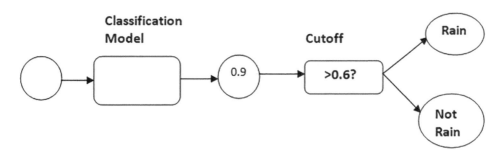

FIGURE 5.3   A simple classification example.

5.3.1.1   Classification – Predictive Modeling

Classification predictive modeling is the process of approximating a mapping function (*f*) from input variables (*X*) to discrete output variables (*y*). The mapping function f predicts the class or category for a given observation.

A classification problem needs that input data to be categorized into one of two or more classes. The input data can be either discrete or continuous values. A problem with two distinct classes is called a two-class or binary classification problem, such as true or false. A problem with more than two classes is often called a multi-class classification problem, such as sentiment analysis with angry, sad, and happy labels.

In general, the classification models predict a continuous probability value for the given input corresponding to each output class. The probabilities can be interpreted as the likelihood or confidence of a given input belonging to each output class. A predicted probability can be converted into a class value by selecting the class label with the highest probability. For example, for specific input data to predict whether it will rain tomorrow or not, assign the probability for the input data and select the label whose probability is greater than the cutoff value as it has the highest likelihood, as shown in Figure 5.3. There are many ways to measure the performance of a predictive classification model, but perhaps the most common is to calculate the classification accuracy. The classification accuracy is the percentage of correctly classified examples out of all predictions made.

For example, if a classification predictive model made ten predictions and seven of them were correct and three of them were incorrect, then the classification accuracy of the model based on just these predictions would be as follows:

accuracy = correct predictions / total predictions * 100
accuracy = 7 / 10 * 100 = 70%

5.3.2   Supervised Learning – Regression

Regression is the process of identifying a model or function for fitting the data into continuous real values instead of using classes or discrete values. For example, a regression problem is quantity based where the output variable is a real or continuous value, such as salary, age, sales rate, speed, and weight. The simplest form is the linear regression that tries to fit data (Figure 5.4) with the optimal hyperplane or line that goes through the points.

Which of the following is the regression task?

* Predicting credit risk analysis
* Predicting nationality of a person
* Predicting tomorrow's wind speed in a specific site
* Predicting the sentiment of a product review

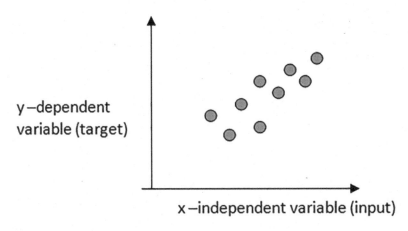

FIGURE 5.4   Data fitting.

Solution: Predicting tomorrow's wind speed in a specific site (because it is a real value, predicting nationality and credit risk(low or high risk) is categorical, and predicting the sentiment is again discrete a good/bad answer).

5.3.2.1   Regression Predictive Modeling

Regression predictive modeling is the process of approximating a mapping function (f) from input variables (X) to a continuous output variable (Y). A continuous output variable is a real value, such as an integer or floating-point value. These are often quantities, such as amounts and sizes.

A regression problem requires the prediction of a continuous value, such as predicting the amount of rainfall. Real values or discrete input variables can be used for regression analysis. A problem with a single input variable is simple regression, and a problem with multiple input variables is called a multivariate regression problem. Time series forecasting problem is a type of regression problem with an input ordered time value.

Because a predictive regression model predicts a quantity, the model's performance must be calculated using error in predictions. There are many ways to estimate the performance of the predictive regression model. The most widely used is to calculate the root mean squared error (RMSE).

Sample RMSE calculation for regression predictive model which made two predictions, one of 1.5 where the expected value is 1.0 and another of 3.3 and the expected value is 3.0, then the RMSE would be:

$$RMSE = sqrt\left(average\left(error^2 \right) \right) \tag{5.1}$$

$$RMSE = sqrt\left(\left((1.0 - 1.5)^2 + (3.0 - 3.3)^2 \right) / 2 \right) = 0.412$$

5.3.3   Classification vs. Regression

Based on the target value, classification problems can be differentiated from regression, as shown in Figure 5.5. Both classification and regression problems can be learned using some algorithms with slight changes, such as decision trees and artificial neural networks. Linear regression is a regression predictive modeling algorithm, whereas logistic regression is a binary classification algorithm. Classification algorithm can be evaluated using accuracy, whereas regression algorithm can be estimated using RMSE.

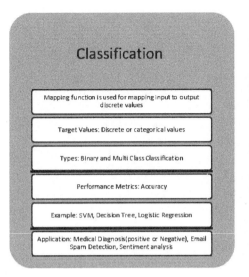 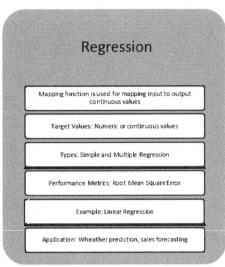

FIGURE 5.5 Differences between classification and regression.

5.3.4 Conversion between Classification and Regression Problems

In certain cases, a regression problem can be used to predict discrete values. This can be achieved using the discretization technique that converts continuous values between $0 and $1000 into two discrete class labels: class 1 (range from $0 to $499) and class 2 (range from $500 to $1000).

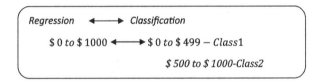

Similarly, a classification problem can be used to predict a numerical value. For example, the target output label can be converted into a continuous numerical range.

If there is a natural ordinal relationship, then the conversion from classification problem to regression learns well, or it may result in poor performance.

5.4 LINEAR REGRESSION

Regression analysis is an extensively used forecasting technique of supervised learning algorithms. Linear regression is the simplest form of regression analysis to analyze the trend behind the input data points. In this section, the working of regression and its types with real-time examples are explained.

Linear regression is a supervised learning technique in which we have a collection of training samples with a labeled output. It is a simple statistical technique and an interpretable method and is very widely used in prediction analysis. The main advantage of linear regression is to forecast the trend more feasibly. Linear regression can be used to predict the continuous target variable given the value of input variables. Regression analysis is used for analyzing the relationship among data to predict the continuous output variable. In other words, linear regression identifies the relationship between dependent and independent variables via a sloped straight line. The sloped straight line is known as the regression line or best-fit line. The representation of the regression model is given in Figure 5.6.

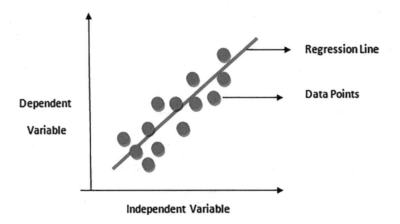

FIGURE 5.6   Representation of regression.

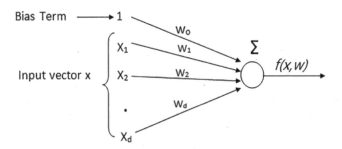

FIGURE 5.7   Linear regression visualization.

To understand the math behind linear regression, let's see a simple example. Given a set of n data, samples can be represented as $D = \{D_1, D_2, \ldots, D_n\}$ as shown in Figure 5.7. The single data point is represented as $D_i = \langle x_i, y_i \rangle$, where $x_i = (x_{i,1}, x_{i,2}, \ldots, x_{i,d})$ is an input vector of size d and y_i is the desired output. And the idea is to find the best linear relationship function $x_i \sim f(x_i)$ such that $y_i \sim f(x_i)$ for all $i = 1, 2, \ldots, n$.

The regression problem is defined as given a sample instance x and y we have to learn a function such that

$$fn : x \rightarrow y$$

$$f(x) = w_0 + w_1 x_1 + w_2 x_2 + \cdots + w_d x_d = w_0 + \sum_{i=1}^{d} w_i x_i \tag{5.2}$$

where $w_0, w_1, \ldots, w_d$ are the weight parameters.

Definition of linear regression: Given a training dataset comprising N observations $\{x_n\}$ where $n = 1, 2, \ldots, N$ and their corresponding target values are $\{t_n\}$. The goal is to predict the value of t for a new value of x.

5.4.1 Types of Linear Regression

The variants of linear regression are simple and multiple linear regressions further classified as linear and non-linear, as shown in Figure 5.8. For simple regression, the input or independent variable is one, whereas for multiple regression, it is two or more.

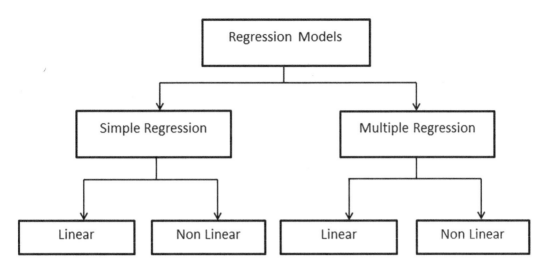

FIGURE 5.8   Regression types.

5.4.1.1   Simple Linear Regression

The simple linear regression consists of only one input or independent variable. The form of the simple linear regression model is given in Equation 5.3:

$$y = \beta_0 + \beta_1 \cdot x \tag{5.3}$$

where y is the independent output variable, x is the dependent input variable, β_0 is bias, and β_1 is the slope of the regression line.

There are three possible cases.

Case 1: $\beta_1 < 0$, which indicates the variable x has a negative impact on y. In this case, if x increases, y decreases, and vice versa.

Case 2: $\beta_1 = 0$, which implies the variable x has no impact on y.

Case 3: $\beta_1 > 0$, which indicates the variable x has a positive impact on y. In this case, if x increases, y increases, and vice versa.

To understand the linear regression model, let us see a simple linear model. For instance, if we want to predict the peak electricity demand of a city based on the high temperature recorded, a simple linear model can be constructed for predicting peak demand for tomorrow.

$$y_i = \theta_1 \cdot x_i + \theta_2 \tag{5.4}$$

i.e., Predicted Peak Demand$=\theta_1$. high temperature$+\theta_2$

where

y_i is the output or independent variable,

x_i is the input or dependent variable,

$\theta_1 = 0.046$ and $\theta_2 = -1.46$ are model parameters.

For instance, if the high temperature recorded is 80°F, then the predicted output is

$$y_i = \theta_1 . x_i + \theta_2$$

$$y_i = 0.046 * 80 - 1.46$$

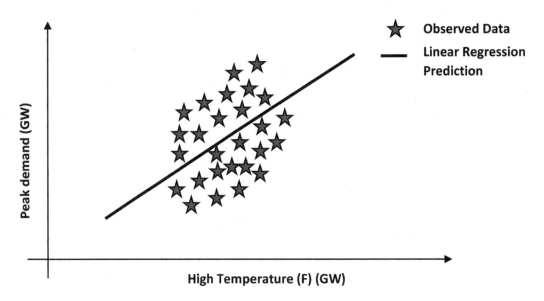

FIGURE 5.9   High temperature vs. peak demand.

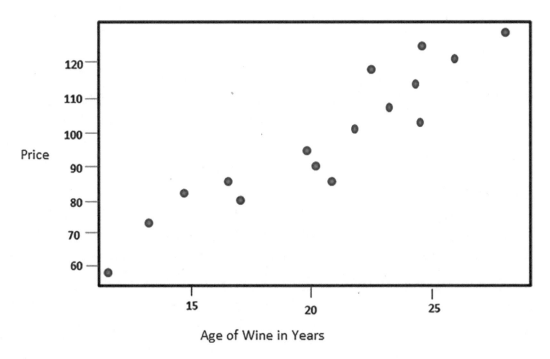

FIGURE 5.10   Age of wine vs. price.

Then, the predicted output of peak demand is 2.19 GW. There is a positive correlation between temperature and peak demand (Figure 5.9).

5.4.1.2   Multiple Linear Regression

The multiple linear regression consists of multiple input or independent variables. For example, let's create a model for predicting the price of wine based on the age of the wine. Here, the dependent variable is the age of the wine, and the independent variable is the price of wine (Figure 5.10).

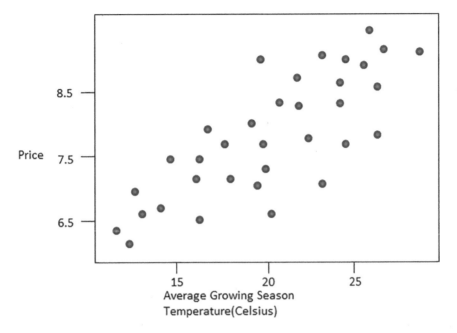

FIGURE 5.11   Average growing-season temperature (Celsius) vs. price.

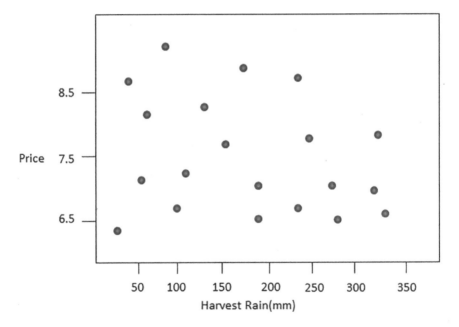

FIGURE 5.12   Harvest rain (mm) vs. price.

$$\text{Wine Price} = \beta_0 + \beta_1 \cdot \text{Age of Wine}$$

Similarly, we can predict the price of wine based on multiple independent variables such as average growing-season temperature (Figure 5.11), harvest rain (Figure 5.12), and winter rain (Figure 5.13).

$$\text{Wine Price} = \beta_0 + \beta_1 \cdot \text{Average Growing-Season Temperature}$$

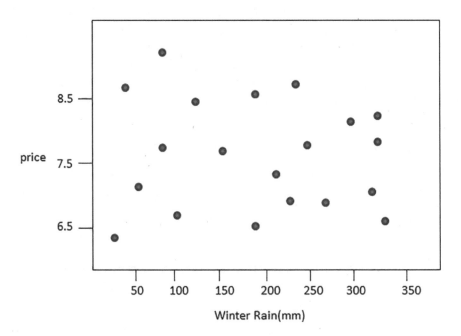

FIGURE 5.13 Winter rain (mm) vs. price.

$$\text{Wine Price} = \beta_0 + \beta_1 \cdot \text{Harvest Rain}$$

$$\text{Wine Price} = \beta_0 + \beta_1 \cdot \text{Winter Rain}$$

The multiple linear regression is

$$\text{Wine Price} = \beta_0 + \beta_1 \cdot \text{Age of Wine} + \beta_2 \cdot \text{Average Growing-Season Temperature}$$

$$+ \beta_3 \cdot \text{Harvest Rain} + \beta_4 \cdot \text{Winter Rain} > + \varepsilon$$

5.4.2 GEOMETRIC INTUITION

Given an input x, the goal is to compute an output y. The linear function can be the optimal line function where the line can be characterized by a slope and intercept with x- or y-axis, as represented in Figure 5.14.

Let us consider these blue points as input data points, and we want to fit a linear function. For example, predict height y from given age x. Similarly, predict the house price value from the given house area.

Figure 5.15 shows the parameters, and the population line is the actual line, and it is given as Equation 5.5:

$$y = \beta_0 + \beta_1 x + \in \tag{5.5}$$

where y is the linear dependent function, β_0 is the population y-intercept, β_1 is the population slope, and $\in$ is the random error. The mean and the variance of the distribution are as follows:

$$E(y \mid x) = \beta_0 + \beta_1 x \tag{5.6}$$

$$\text{var}(y \mid x) = \text{var}(\beta_0 + \beta_1 x + \in) = \sigma^2 \tag{5.7}$$

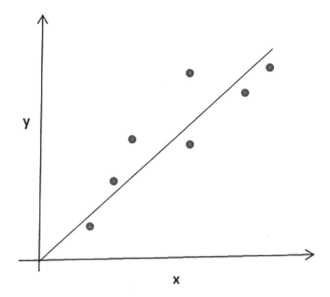

FIGURE 5.14   Linear regression scatter plot.

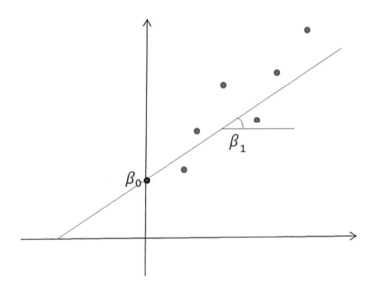

FIGURE 5.15   Parameters of linear regression.

5.4.3   MATHEMATICAL FORMULATION

The equation of the line mathematically drives the statistical theory of linear regression technique is given as in equation 5.8:

$$y_i = \beta_0 + \beta_1 x_i + \epsilon_i \text{ for } i = 1,2,\ldots n \tag{5.8}$$

To estimate the two unknown parameters β_0 and β_1, the least-squares criteria are

$$S(\beta_0,\beta_1) = \sum_{i=1}^{n} (y_i - \beta_0 - \beta_1 x_i)^2 \tag{5.9}$$

The least-squares estimators of β_0 and β_1, say $\hat{\beta}_0$ and $\hat{\beta}_1$, must satisfy

$$\frac{\partial S}{\partial \beta_0}\Big|_{\hat{\beta}_0,\hat{\beta}_1} = -2\sum_{i=1}^{n}\left(y_i - \hat{\beta}_0 - \hat{\beta}_1 x_i\right) = 0 \tag{5.10}$$

And

$$\frac{\partial S}{\partial \beta_1}\Big|_{\hat{\beta}_0,\hat{\beta}_1} = -2\sum_{i=1}^{n}\left(y_i - \hat{\beta}_0 - \hat{\beta}_1 x_i\right)x_i = 0 \tag{5.11}$$

Simplifying these two equation yields

$$n\,\hat{\beta}_0 + \hat{\beta}_1\sum_{i=1}^{n} x_i = \sum_{i=1}^{n} y_i \tag{5.12}$$

$$\hat{\beta}_0\sum_{i=1}^{n} x_i + \hat{\beta}_1\sum_{i=1}^{n} x_i^2 = \sum_{i=1}^{n} y_i x_i \tag{5.13}$$

The above equation is the least-squares normal equation; the solution to the normal equation is

$$\hat{y} = \hat{\beta}_0 + \hat{\beta}_1\bar{x} \tag{5.14}$$

where

$$\bar{y} = \frac{1}{n}\sum_{i=1}^{n} y_i \tag{5.15}$$

$$\bar{x} = \frac{1}{n}\sum_{i=1}^{n} x_i \tag{5.16}$$

$$\hat{\beta}_1 = \frac{S_{xx}}{S_{xy}} \tag{5.17}$$

where

$$S_{xx} = \sum_{i=1}^{n} x_i^2 - \frac{\left(\sum_{i=1}^{n} x_i\right)^2}{n} = \sum_{i=1}^{n} y_i(x_i - \bar{x})^2$$

$$S_{xy} = \sum_{i=1}^{n} x_i y_i - \frac{\left(\sum_{i=1}^{n} y_i\right)\left(\sum_{i=1}^{n} x_i\right)}{n} = \sum_{i=1}^{n} y_i(x_i - \bar{x}) \tag{5.18}$$

The residual e is the difference between the observed value y_i and their fitted value $\hat{y}_i$

$$e = y_i - \hat{y}_i \quad \text{for } i = 1, 2\ldots,n \tag{5.19}$$

Example 5.1

The rocket propellant data is given in Table 5.1, and the corresponding scatter diagram is shown in Figure 5.16. There exists a relationship between shear strength and the age of the propellant. First, find the residual and equation of a line.

$$S_{xx} = \sum_{i=1}^{n} x_i^2 - \frac{\left(\sum_{i=1}^{n} x_i\right)^2}{n} = 4677.69 - \frac{71,422.56}{20} = 1106.56$$

$$S_{xy} = \sum_{i=1}^{n} x_i y_i - \frac{\left(\sum_{i=1}^{n} y_i\right)\left(\sum_{i=1}^{n} x_i\right)}{n} = 528,492.64 - \frac{(267.25)(42,627.15)}{20} = -41,112.65$$

$$\hat{\beta}_1 = \frac{S_{xy}}{S_{xx}} = \frac{-41,112.65}{1106.56} = -37.15$$

$$\hat{\beta}_0 = \bar{y} - \hat{\beta}_1 \bar{x} = 2131.3575 - (37.15)13.3625 = 2627.82$$

The results computed for the rocket propulsion data in terms of observed value, fitted value, and residual are presented in Table 5.2.

TABLE 5.1
Rocket Propellant Data

Observation, i	Shear Strength, y_i (psi)	Age of Propellant, x_i (weeks)
1	2158.70	15.50
2	1678.15	23.75
3	2316.00	8.00
4	2061.30	17.00
5	2207.50	5.50
6	1708.30	19.00
7	1784.70	24.00
8	2575.00	2.50
9	2357.90	7.50
10	2256.70	11.00
11	2165.20	13.00
12	2399.55	3.75
13	1779.80	25.00
14	2336.75	9.75
15	1765.30	22.00
16	2053.50	18.00
17	2414.40	6.00
18	2200.50	12.50
19	2654.20	2.00
20	1753.70	21.50

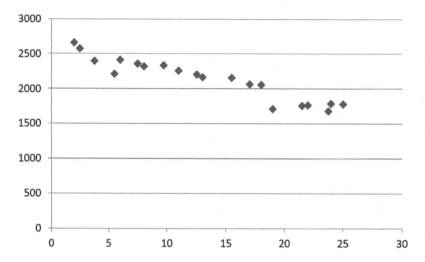

FIGURE 5.16   Scatter plot of rocket propellant data.

TABLE 5.2
Results for Rocket Propellant Data

Age of Propellant, x_i (weeks)	Observed Value, y_i	Fitted Value, $\widehat{y}_i$	Residual, e_i
15.50	2158.70	2051.94	106.76
23.75	1678.15	1745.42	−67.27
8.00	2316.00	2330.59	−14.59
17.00	2061.30	1996.21	65.09
5.50	2207.50	2423.48	−215.98
19.00	1708.30	1921.90	−213.60
24.00	1784.70	1736.14	48.56
2.50	2575.00	2534.94	40.06
7.50	2357.90	2349.17	8.73
11.00	2256.70	2219.13	37.57
13.00	2165.20	2144.83	20.37
3.75	2399.55	2488.50	−88.95
25.00	1779.80	1698.98	80.82
9.75	2336.75	2265.58	71.17
22.00	1765.30	1810.44	−45.14
18.00	2053.50	1959.06	94.44
6.00	2414.40	2404.90	9.50
12.50	2200.50	2163.40	37.10
2.00	2654.20	2553.52	100.68
21.50	1753.70	1829.02	−75.32
	$\sum y_i = 42{,}627.15$	$\sum \widehat{y}_i = 42{,}627.15$	$\sum e_i = 0.00$

Example 5.2

Predict the linear regression model based on the data given below in Table 5.3, and Figure 5.17 is the corresponding scatter plot.

TABLE 5.3
Hydrocarbon Level versus Oxygen Purity Data

S. No.	Hydrocarbon Level, x (%)	Oxygen Purity, y (%)
1	0.99	90.01
2	1.02	89.05
3	1.15	91.43
4	1.29	93.74
5	1.46	96.73
6	1.36	94.45
7	0.87	87.59
8	1.23	91.77
9	1.55	99.42
10	1.40	93.65
11	1.19	93.54
12	1.15	92.52
13	0.98	90.56
14	1.01	89.54
15	1.11	89.85
16	1.20	90.39
17	1.26	93.25
18	1.32	93.41
19	1.43	94.98
20	0.95	87.33

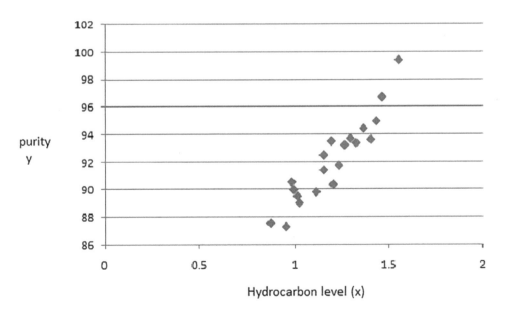

FIGURE 5.17   Scatter plot of hydrocarbon level vs. oxygen purity.

Solution:

$n=20$

$$\sum_{i=1}^{20} x_i = 23.92 \sum_{i=1}^{20} y_i = 1843.21$$

$$\bar{x} = 1.1960 \; \bar{y} = 92.1605$$

$$\sum_{i=1}^{20} x_i^2 = 29.2892$$

$$\sum_{i=1}^{20} y_i^2 = 170,044.5321$$

$$\sum_{i=1}^{20} x_i y_i = 2214.6566$$

$$S_{xx} = \sum_{i=1}^{20} x_i^2 - \frac{\left(\sum_{i=1}^{20} x_i\right)^2}{20} = 29.2892 - \frac{(23.92)^2}{20} = 0.68088$$

and

$$S_{xy} = \sum_{i=1}^{20} x_i y_i - \frac{\left(\sum_{i=1}^{20} x_i\right)\left(\sum_{i=1}^{20} y_i\right)}{20}$$

$$= 2214.6566 - \frac{(23.92)(1843.21)}{20} = 10.17744$$

Therefore, the least-squares estimates of the slope and intercept are

$$\beta_1 = \frac{S_{xy}}{S_{xx}} = \frac{10.17744}{0.68088} = 14.94748$$

and

$$\beta_0 = \bar{y} - \beta_1\bar{x} = 92.1605 - (14.94748)1.196 = 74.28331$$

The linear regression model is

$$y = 74.28331 + 14.94748x$$

Example 5.3

To understand mathematically behind regression, let's see an example where 15 samples of houses of a region are given in Table 5.4. The idea is to predict the price y given area of the house x.

   The 15 data points are plotted in a graph (Figure 5.18) where the x-axis is the house size in terms of 100 square feet and the y-axis is the prize. So given these 15 points, we have to find the equation of the line. This is a linear regression problem that consists of 15 independent variables.

$$\text{Prize} = \beta_0 + \beta_1 * \text{House Size}$$

TABLE 5.4
Actual Housing Prize versus House Size Data

House Number	Actual Housing Price (Y)	House Size (X)
1	89.5	20.0
2	79.9	14.8
3	83.1	20.5
4	56.9	12.5
5	66.6	18.0
6	82.5	14.3
7	126.3	27.5
8	79.3	16.5
9	119.9	24.3
10	87.6	20.2
11	112.6	22.0
12	120.8	.019
13	78.5	12.3
14	74.3	14.0
15	74.8	16.7
Average	88.84	18.17

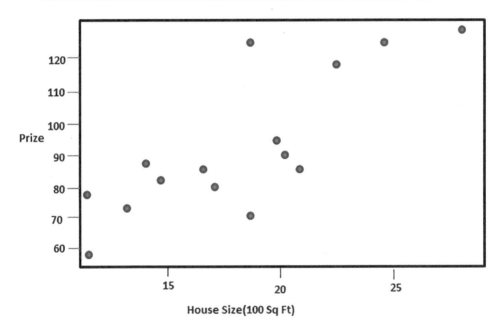

FIGURE 5.18   Scatter plot of house size vs. prize.

The equation of the above regression problems is given below:

$$y = \beta_0 + \beta_1 x_1 + \beta_2 x_2 + \beta_3 x_3 + \beta_4 x_4 + \beta_4 x_5 + \cdots + \beta_p x_p + \in$$

where p is the predictor or independent variable. Let us assume that the expected value of y given x is given by the population line.

$$E(Y|X) = \beta_0 + \beta_1 x_1 + \beta_2 x_2 + \beta_3 x_3 + \beta_4 x_4 + \beta_4 x_5 + \cdots + \beta_p x_p$$

To minimize the sum of squared errors based on the training points, the least-squares line equation is as follows:

$$\text{Least-Square Line} = \widehat{\beta}_0 + \widehat{\beta}_1 x_1 + \widehat{\beta}_2 x_2 + \widehat{\beta}_3 x_3 + \cdots + \widehat{\beta}_p x_p$$

Now the data we may have may not form a perfect line. The error function is used to determine the deviation between actual and predicted. So, the assumptions about the errors are given as follows:

- $E(\varepsilon_i) = 0$ for $i = 0,1,2,\ldots n$

- $\sigma(\varepsilon_i) = \sigma_\varepsilon$, where σ_ε is unknown

- The errors ε_i are independent to each other
- The errors ε_i are normally distributed (with mean 0 and standard deviation σ_ε)

So, this kind of noise is called Gaussian noise or white noise.

The least-squares regression line is the unique line such that the sum of squared vertical (y) distances between the data points (dark colored circles) and the line is the smallest possible. The gray vertical lines are errors, as given in Figure 5.19.

Let us consider for a training point $d_i = (x_i, y_i)$ where y_i is the actual value. The idea is to minimize these errors. There are different methods to identify the error of the model. The mean absolute error is the simple one that calculates the average of the absolute value of errors and is given as

$$\text{MAE} = \frac{1}{n} \sum_{i=1}^{n} |y_i - \hat{y}_i| \tag{5.20}$$

where y_i is the actual value and $\hat{y}_i$ is the predicted value.

The mean squared error is given as MSE:

$$\text{MSE} = \frac{1}{n} \sum_{i=1}^{n} (y_i - \hat{y}_i)^2 \tag{5.21}$$

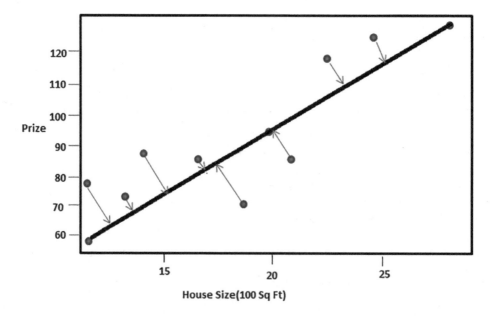

FIGURE 5.19 Measuring the distance between hyperplane and data points.

where y_i is the actual value and $\hat{y}_i$ is the predicted value.

The root mean squared error is given as RMSE:

$$\text{RMSE} = \sqrt{\frac{1}{n} \sum_{i=1}^{n} \left(y_i - \hat{y}_i\right)^2} \tag{5.22}$$

The rooted absolute error, also known as the residual sum of squares, is given as RAE:

$$\text{RAE} = \frac{\sum_{i=1}^{n} \left|y_i - \hat{y}_i\right|}{\sum_{i=1}^{n} y_i - \bar{y}} \tag{5.23}$$

where y_i is the actual value, $\hat{y}_i$ is the predicted value, and $\bar{y}$ is average value of y.

The rooted square error is RSE, which is similar to RAE:

$$\text{RSE} = \frac{\sum_{i=1}^{n} \left(y_i - \hat{y}_i\right)^2}{\sum_{i=1}^{n} \left(y_i - \bar{y}\right)^2} \tag{5.24}$$

The least-squares regression line equation for n data points is given as

$$y = ax + b \tag{5.25}$$

where a and b are

$$a = \frac{n \sum_{i=1}^{n} x_i y_i - \sum_{i=1}^{n} x_i \sum_{i=1}^{n} y_i}{n \sum_{i=1}^{n} x_i^2 - \left(\sum_{i=1}^{n} x_i\right)^2} \tag{5.26}$$

$$b = \frac{1}{n}\left(\sum_{i=1}^{n} y_i - a \sum_{i=1}^{n} x_i\right) \tag{5.27}$$

Example 5.4

Find the least-squares regression line for the following set of data points {(−1, 0), (0, 2), (1, 4), (2, 5)} given in Table 5.5. Plot the given points and identify the regression line.

TABLE 5.5
Sample Data Points

x	y	Xy	x^2
−1	0	0	1
0	2	0	0
1	4	4	1
2	5	10	4
$\sum x = 2$	$\sum y = 11$	$\sum xy = 14$	$\sum x^2 = 6$

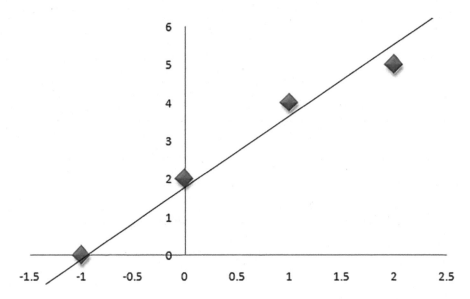

FIGURE 5.20   Least-squares regression line.

The least-squares regression line equation for n data points is given as

$$y = ax + b$$

where a and b are

$$a = \frac{n\sum_{i=1}^{n} x_i y_i - \sum_{i=1}^{n} x_i \sum_{i=1}^{n} y_i}{n\sum_{i=1}^{n} x_i^2 - \left(\sum_{i=1}^{n} x_i\right)^2}$$

$$b = \frac{1}{n}\left(\sum_{i=1}^{n} y_i - a\sum_{i=1}^{n} x_i\right)$$

$$a = \frac{4*14 - 2*11}{4*6 - 2^2}$$

$$a = 17/10 = 1.7$$

$$b = \frac{1}{4}(11 - 1.7*2)$$

$$b = 1.9$$

The least-squares regression line for the given problem is shown in Figure 5.20.

$$y = 1.7x + 1.9$$

Example 5.5

The values of x and their corresponding values of y are shown in Table 5.6.

     i. Find the least-squares regression line $y = ax + b$
     ii. Estimate the value of y when $x = 10$.

TABLE 5.6
Data for Example 5.5

x	0	1	2	3	4
y	2	3	5	4	6

Solution:

The least-squares regression line equation for n data points is given as

$$y = ax + b$$

where a and b are

$$a = \frac{n \sum_{i=1}^{n} x_i y_i - \sum_{i=1}^{n} x_i \sum_{i=1}^{n} y_i}{n \sum_{i=1}^{n} x_i^2 - \left(\sum_{i=1}^{n} x_i \right)^2}$$

$$b = \frac{1}{n} \left(\sum_{i=1}^{n} y_i - a \sum_{i=1}^{n} x_i \right)$$

---

x	y	xy	x^2
0	2	0	0
1	3	3	1
2	5	10	4
3	4	12	9
4	6	24	16
$\sum x = 10$	$\sum y = 20$	$\sum xy = 49$	$\sum x^2 = 30$

$$a = \frac{5 * 49 - 10 * 20}{5 * 30 - 10^2}$$

$$a = 0.9$$

$$b = \frac{1}{5}(20 - 0.9 * 10)$$

$$b = 2.2$$

Thus, the least-squares regression equation is

$$y = 0.9x + 2.2$$

Substitute the value of $x = 10$; then

$$y = 0.9 * 10 + 2.2$$

$$y = 11.2$$

The output for the example is presented in Figure 5.21.

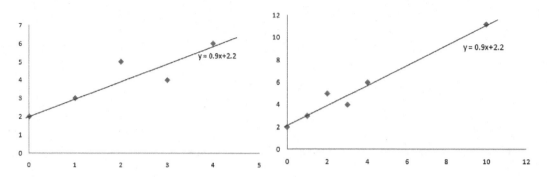

FIGURE 5.21   (a) Least-squares regression line and (b) predicting the new data point for Example 5.5.

TABLE 5.7

Year vs. Sales Data

x(year)	2005	2006	2007	2008	2009
y(sales)	12	19	29	37	45

Example 5.6

The sales of a company (in million dollars) for each year are shown in Table 5.7.

    i. Find the least-squares regression line $y = ax + b$
    ii. Use the least-squares regression line as a model to estimate the sales of the company in 2012.

Solution:

First, we can normalize the data for easy computation. Subtract 2005 from x values.

x(year)	0	1	2	3	4
y(sales)	12	19	29	37	45

x	y	xy	x^2
0	12	0	0
1	19	19	1
2	29	58	4
3	37	111	9
4	45	180	16
$\sum x = 10$	$\sum y = 142$	$\sum xy = 368$	$\sum x^2 = 30$

The least-squares regression line equation for n data points is given as

$$y = ax + b$$

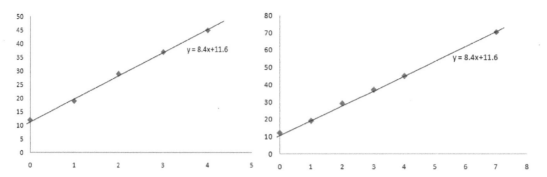

FIGURE 5.22   (a) Least-squares regression line and (b) predicting the new data point for Example 5.6.

where a and b are

$$a = \frac{n \sum_{i=1}^{n} x_i y_i - \sum_{i=1}^{n} x \sum_{i=1}^{n} y_i}{n \sum_{i=1}^{n} x_i^2 - \left(\sum_{i=1}^{n} x_i \right)^2}$$

$$b = \frac{1}{n} \left(\sum_{i=1}^{n} y_i - a \sum_{i=1}^{n} x_i \right)$$

$$a = \frac{5 * 368 - 10 * 142}{5 * 30 - 10^2}$$

$$a = 8.4$$

$$b = \frac{1}{5}(142 - 8.4 * 10)$$

$$b = 11.6$$

The least-squares regression equation is

$$y = 8.4x + 11.6$$

To estimate the sales of the company in 2012, substitute $x = 2012 - 2005 = 7$ in the least-squares regression equation:

$$y = 8.4 * 7 + 11.6$$

$$y = 70.4 \text{ million dollars}$$

The output for the given example is shown in Figure 5.22.

Example 5.7

Predict CO_2 emission vs. engine size and cylinders of cars for the data shown in Table 5.8. Find the mean absolute error.

   Independent variables (x): engine size, cylinders, and fuel consumption
   Dependent variables (y): CO_2 emission

TABLE 5.8

CO_2 Emission Data

S. No.	Enginesize	Cylinders	Fuelconsumption_Comb	CO_2 Emissions
0	2.0	4	8.5	196
1	2.4	4	9.6	221
2	1.5	4	5.9	136
3	3.5	6	11.1	255
4	3.5	6	10.6	244
5	3.5	6	10.0	230
6	3.5	6	10.1	232
7	3.7	6	11.1	255
8	3.7	6	11.6	267
9	2.4	4	9.2	?

$$CO_2 \text{ emission} = \beta_0 + \beta_1 \text{ Engine size} + \beta_2 \text{ Cylinders} + \beta_3 \text{ Fuel consumption \_Comb}$$

$$\hat{y} = \beta_0 + \beta_1 x_1 + \beta_2 \beta_2 + \beta_3 \beta_3$$

$$\hat{y} = \beta^T X$$

$$\beta^T = [\beta_0, \beta_1, \beta_2, \beta_3] X = \begin{bmatrix} 1 \\ x_1 \\ x_2 \\ x_3 \end{bmatrix}$$

$$\beta^T = [125, 6.2, 14, 1.98]$$

For the ninth instance, the CO_2 emissions are

$$CO_2 \text{ emission} = 125 + 6.2 * 2.4 + 14 * 4 + 1.98 * 9.2$$

$$CO_2 \text{ emission for ninth instance} = 214.1$$

S. No.	x_1	x_2	x_3	y_i	RMSE = sqrt$\left(\text{average}\left(\text{error}^2\right)\right)$
0	2	4	8.5	196	210.23
1	2.4	4	9.6	221	214.888
2	1.5	4	5.9	136	201.982
3	3.5	6	11.1	255	252.678
4	3.5	6	10.6	244	251.688
5	3.5	6	10	230	250.5
6	3.5	6	10.1	232	250.698
7	3.7	6	11.1	255	253.918
8	3.7	6	11.6	267	254.908
9	2.4	4	9.2	214	214.096

5.4.4 SOLVING OPTIMIZATION PROBLEM

The optimization problem can be solved using two different strategies

- Deriving a closed-form solution, and
- Gradient descent

To understand the method of deriving a closed-form solution, let's take a partial derivative of the mean squared error J_n. For the optimal set of parameters, derivatives of the error concerning each parameter must be 0.

$$\frac{\partial}{\partial w_j} J_n(w) = -\frac{2}{n} \sum_{i=1}^{n} \left(y_i - w_0 x_{i,0} - w_1 x_{i,1} - \cdots - w_d x_{i,d}\right) x_{i,j} = 0 \qquad (5.28)$$

The vector of derivatives

$$\text{grad}_w J_n(w) = \nabla_w \left(J_n(w)\right) = -\frac{2}{n} \sum_{i=1}^{n} \left(y_i - w^T x_i\right) x_i = 0 \qquad (5.29)$$

5.4.4.1 Maxima and Minima

In Figure 5.23, the peaks in the data are called maxima. The global maxima are the highest peak in the entire data. The global minima are the lowest trough in the entire data.

For finding minima, let us see an example and set $f'(z) = 0$ and solve z:

$$f(\mathbf{z}) = \mathbf{z}^2 \qquad (5.30)$$

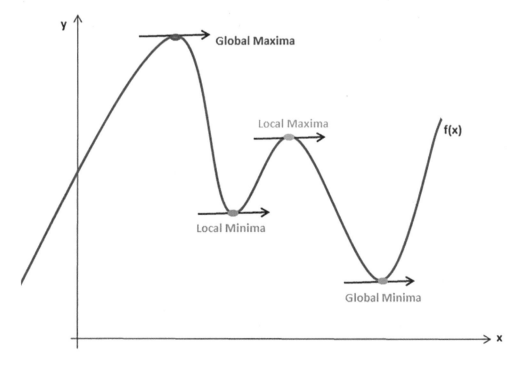

FIGURE 5.23 Representation of maxima and minima.

The derivative of $f(z) = z^2$ is $f'(z)$, and it can be written as

$$f'(z) = 2z \qquad (5.31)$$

If $z = 0$, then the derivative function becomes zero, and this point is known as local maxima or local minima:

$$f'(z) = 0 \qquad (5.32)$$

If the derivative is greater than zero or positive, the function increases, which implies that it is moving away from the trough. Else if the derivative is lesser than zero or negative, the function decreases, which means the function moves toward the trough.

Finding minima by assuming $z = -1$, then the function $f'(z) = 2z$ becomes $f'(-1) = 2 * -1 = -2$, which is decreasing and moving toward the trough (Figure 5.24). Then, increase z by the size of the gradient. If the size of the gradient is 2, then z becomes 1.

$$z = -1 + 2 = 1$$

For the second iteration, by assuming $z = 1$, then the function $f'(z) = 2z$ becomes $f'(1) = 2 * 1 = 2$, which is increasing and moving away from the trough. Then, increase z by the size of the gradient. If the size of the gradient is 2, then z becomes 1.

$$z = 1 - 2 = -1$$

Thus, it is kept jumping between the same two points, which can be overcome by using the appropriate learning rate or step size.

5.4.4.2 Gradient Descent

Gradient descent is an optimization algorithm used to minimize the error function in machine learning. Gradient descent is used to solve linear regression problems iteratively, as shown in Figure 5.25.

The objective of gradient descent is to minimize the error function. The simple example of the parabola for minimizing the error using gradient descent is explained below in Figure 5.26. If we

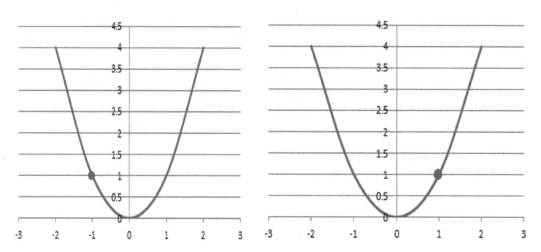

FIGURE 5.24   Finding minima.

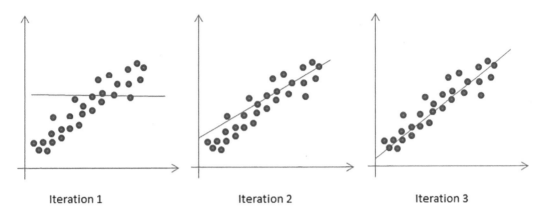

FIGURE 5.25   Geometric intuition of gradient descent.

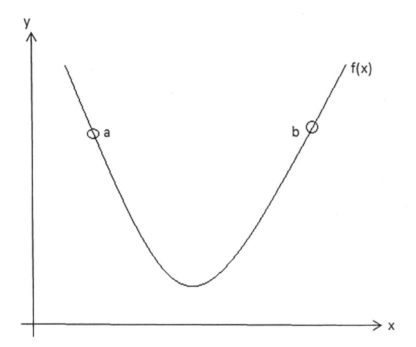

FIGURE 5.26   Minimizing error in a parabola using gradient descent.

start at point a and move left, the function f is increasing, and if we move right, it is decreasing. Therefore, choose the direction where it is decreasing.

But not all the functions are like a parabola. The other example is shown in Figure 5.27, where the local minima and global minima are depicted clearly. In this graph, if b moves right, it will reach local minima.

Define a cost function $J(\theta)$:

$$J(\theta) = \frac{1}{2}\left(\sum_{i=1}^{m} h(x)^{(i)} - y^{(i)}\right)^2 \tag{5.33}$$

$$h(x) = \sum_{i=0}^{n} \beta_i x_i \tag{5.34}$$

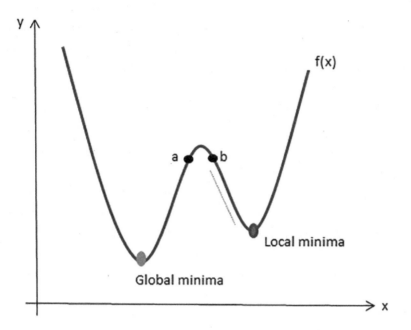

FIGURE 5.27   Minimizing error using an irregular function other than the parabola.

where $h(x)^{(i)}$ is the predicted value and $y^{(i)}$ is the actual value. The main objective is to learn θ, which minimizes cost function $J(\theta)$.

Algorithm for Gradient Descent
Begin

Step 1: Initialize θ Randomly
Step 2: Do
{
Step 3: $\theta = \theta - \alpha \nabla_\theta J(\theta)$
}
Step 4: while$\left(\alpha \|\nabla J\| > \varepsilon\right)$

The algorithm for gradient descent is as follows. First, initialize θ randomly or often set to zero and then iterate. The learning rate is denoted as α. The stopping condition is that either J is not changing quickly or the gradient is sufficiently small. Then, the process is repeated until it reaches minimal error or no further improvement is possible.

In gradient descent, the learning rate α is used to ensure whether gradient descent is working correctly or not. The smaller the learning rates α, the slower the convergence. Choose α as 0.001, 0.01, 0.1, and 1.

$$\theta_j = \theta_j - \alpha \frac{\partial}{\partial \theta_j} J(\theta) \tag{5.35}$$

Let the x-axis denote the number of iterations in gradient descent. $J(\theta)$ should decrease at every iteration, as observed in Figure 5.28.

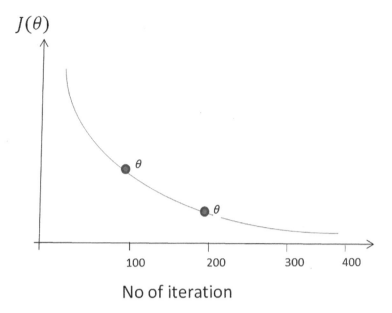

FIGURE 5.28   Learning rate.

5.4.4.3   LMS (Least Mean Square) Update Rule

Apply derivative to the cost function $J(\theta)$:

$$\frac{\partial}{\partial\theta}J(\theta) = \frac{\partial}{\partial\theta_j}\frac{1}{2}(h(x)-y)^2$$

$$= 2.\frac{1}{2}(h(x)-y)\frac{\partial}{\partial\theta_j}(h(x)-y)$$

$$= (h(x)-y).\frac{\partial}{\partial\theta_j}\left(\sum_{i=0}^{n}\theta_i x_i - y\right)$$

$$= (h(x)-y)x_j \tag{5.36}$$

5.4.4.4   SGD Algorithm

Stochastic gradient descent (SGD) is a widely used variant of gradient descent.
    Algorithm for Stochastic Gradient Descent
    Begin

    Step 1: Repeat{
    Step 2: For $I=1$ to m do
    Step 3: $\theta_j = \theta_j + \alpha\left(y^i - h(x^i)\right)x_j^{(i)}$(for every j)
    Step 4: End for
    }
    Step 5: until convergence

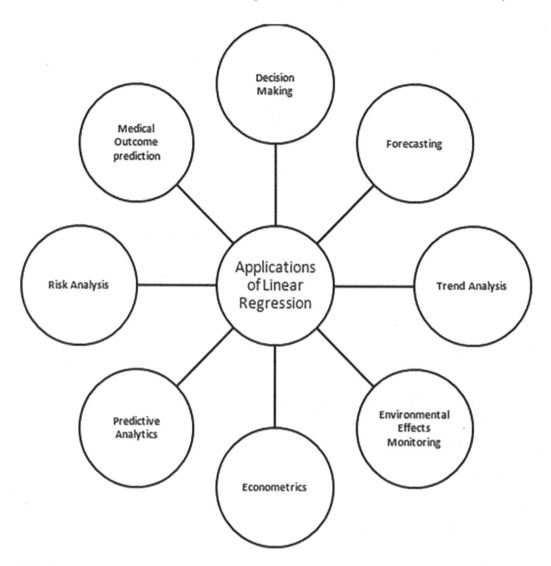

FIGURE 5.29   Applications of linear regression.

5.4.5   REAL-WORLD APPLICATIONS

Many real-world applications make use of linear regression techniques, as shown in Figure 5.29. To analyze the trend overtime -plays an important role in business sectors. The analyses of GDP, oil price, and stock prices are well-known examples of trend analysis. With the help of statistical analysis, the business can gather new insights and achieve operational efficiency.

5.4.5.1   Predictive Analysis

It can be used to generate insights on customer behavior, understanding business, and factors influencing profitability. Linear regressions can be used in business to evaluate trends and make estimates or forecasts. Linear regression can also analyze the marketing effectiveness, pricing, and promotions on sales of a product. Linear regression can also be used to assess risk in the financial services or insurance domain. The risk can be assessed based on the attributes of the car, driver information, or demographics. The results of such an analysis might guide important business decisions.

TABLE 5.9
E-Commerce Data

Online Store	Monthly E-Commerce Sales (in 1000 s)	Online Advertising Dollars (1000 s)
1	368	1.7
2	340	1.5
3	665	2.8
4	954	5
5	331	1.3
6	556	2.2
7	376	1.3

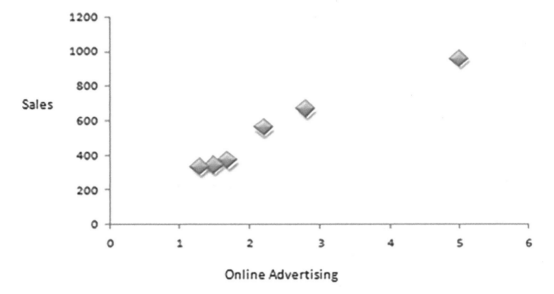

FIGURE 5.30   Online advertising versus sales.

In the credit card industry, a financial company may be interested in minimizing the risk portfolio and understanding the top five factors that cause a customer to default. Then, based on the results, the company could implement specific EMI options to minimize default among risky customers.

To study the relationship between monthly e-commerce sales and online advertising costs, the survey results for seven online stores for the last year are given in Table 5.9. Identify the impact of online advertising in e-commerce sales.

Solution:

The scatter plot in Figure 5.30 clearly shows a positive relationship between the independent variable online advertising and the dependent variable e-commerce sales.

$$\text{Monthly Sales} = \beta_0 + \beta_1 \cdot \text{Online Advertising}$$

The regression line is given as

$$\text{Monthly Sales} = 125.8 + 171.5 * \text{Online Advertising}$$

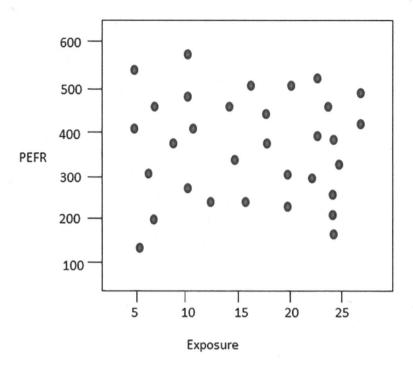

FIGURE 5.31   Exposure vs. PEFR.

5.4.5.2   Medical Outcome Prediction

Linear regression plays an important role in medical analysis. For instance, smoking reduces the life span, and linear regression analyzes the relationship between these two variables. In this scenario, the relationship can be defined using the simple linear regression such as the following:

$$\text{Life Span} = \beta_0 + \beta_1 \text{Smoking}$$

where life span is the dependent variable and smoking is the independent variable. Similarly, it can also be represented using multiple linear regression form by adding another independent variable socioeconomic status:

$$\text{Life Span} = \beta_0 + \beta_1 \text{Smoking} + \beta_1 \text{Socioeconomic status}$$

For another instance, to measure the lung capacity based on the exposure of dust, consider the scatter plot in Figure 5.31, where the x-axis is the exposure to dust, and the y-axis is the measure of lung capacity (PEFR or PEAK expiratory flow rate).

$$\text{PEFR} = \beta_0 + \beta_1 \cdot \text{Exposure}$$

The regression line for this model is shown in Figure 5.32.

5.4.5.3   Wind Speed Prediction

Wind energy is one of the key renewable energies which is clean and exhaustive. Wind speed prediction plays a key role in wind farms, disaster management, and aviation. Therefore, it is an important technology in the wind power field. Due to their chaotic and fluctuating nature, predicting wind

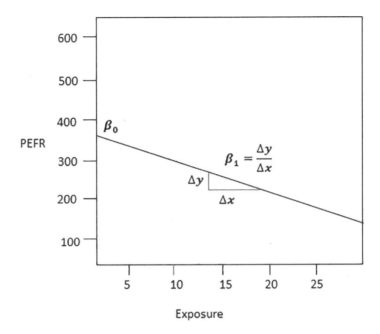

FIGURE 5.32   Regression line.

speeds accurately is difficult. The wind speed depends on various aspects. Therefore, multiple linear regression models can be utilized to design the model. Typically, there are two general methods for wind prediction: Short-term prediction involves timescales of minutes and hours, while long-term involves a timescale of months or years.

5.4.5.4   Environmental Effects Monitoring

Time series regression is widely used in environmental epidemiology. Exposure to air pollution may lead to acute respiratory infections in humans. The regression analysis can be carried out to know the impact of exposure to air pollution on respiratory infection in humans. This is represented as

$$\text{Exposure to air pollution} = \beta_0 + \beta_1 \text{ Respiratory Infection}$$

In Canada, the Environmental Effects Monitoring program uses statistical linear regression techniques to measure the effects of pulp mill or metal mine effluent on the aquatic ecosystem.

5.4.6   LINEAR REGRESSION IN PRACTICE USING PYTHON

5.4.6.1   Simple Linear Regression Using Python

Before implementing regression, let us understand the data file. The sample data file we have used is shown below. It has two columns – years of experience and salary. Our goal is to predict the salary based on the number of years of experience.

Salary_Data.csv

A sample screenshot of the file is shown below:

A	B
Years of Experience	**Salary**
1.1	39,343
1.3	46,205
1.5	37,731
2	43,525
2.2	39,891
2.9	56,642
3	60,150
3.2	54,445
3.2	64,445
3.7	57,189
3.9	63,218
4	55,794
4	56,957
4.1	57,081
4.5	61,111
4.9	67,938
5.1	66,029
5.3	83,088
5.9	81,363
6	93,940

```
# Coding →
# Importing the libraries
import numpy as np
import matplotlib.pyplot as plt
import pandas as pd

#For this example, we have created a sample file, Salary_Data.CSV file. I
have placed it in my C:/Python #Files/ directory

# Importing the dataset
dataset = pd.read_csv('C:/Python Files/Salary_Data.csv')
X = dataset.iloc[:, :-1].values
y = dataset.iloc[:, 1].values

# Splitting the dataset into the Training set and Test set
from sklearn.cross_validation import train_test_split
X_train, X_test, y_train, y_test = train_test_split(X, y, test_size =
1/3, random_state = 0)

# Feature Scaling - It means changing the range of values without
changing the shape of the distribution. The range is often set to 0 to 1

from sklearn.preprocessing import StandardScaler
sc_X = StandardScaler()
X_train = sc_X.fit_transform(X_train)
X_test = sc_X.transform(X_test)
```

```
#sc_y = StandardScaler()
#y_train = sc_y.fit_transform(y_train)

# Fitting Simple Linear Regression to the Training set
from sklearn.linear_model import LinearRegression
regressor = LinearRegression()
regressor.fit(X_train, y_train)

# regression coefficients
print('Coefficients: \n', regressor.coef_)

# OUTPUT →
Coefficients:
[23651.14412001]

print(regressor.intercept_)

# OUTPUT →
71022.5

# Predicting the Test set results
y_pred = regressor.predict(X_test)

# Visualizing the Training set results
plt.scatter(X_train, y_train, color = 'red')
plt.plot(X_train, regressor.predict(X_train), color = 'blue')
plt.title('Salary vs Experience (Training set)')
plt.xlabel('Years of Experience')
plt.ylabel('Salary')
plt.show() #Figure 5.33

# Visualizing the Test set results
plt.scatter(X_test, y_test, color = 'red')
plt.plot(X_train, regressor.predict(X_train), color = 'blue')
```

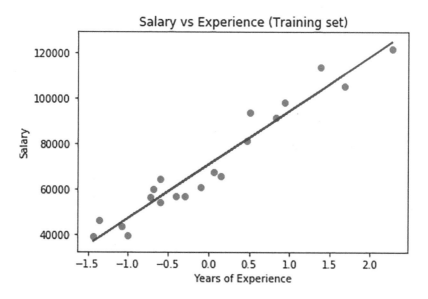

FIGURE 5.33 Training set results.

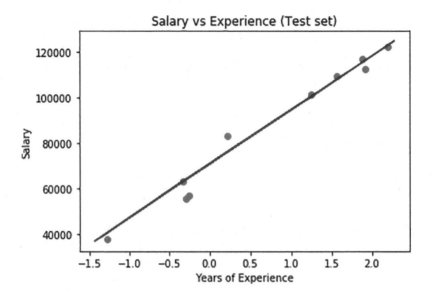

FIGURE 5.34   Test set results.

```
plt.title('Salary vs Experience (Test set)')
plt.xlabel('Years of Experience')
plt.ylabel('Salary')
plt.show() ###Figure 5.34

from sklearn.metrics import mean_squared_error
mean_squared_error(y_test,y_pred)#mse
print(np.sqrt(mean_squared_error(y_test, y_pred))) #rmse

#OUTPUT →
4585.4157204675885

# print the R-squared value for the model
regressor.score(X_test, y_test)#rsquare

#OUTPUT →
0.9749154407708353
```

5.4.6.2   Multiple Linear Regression Using Python

Let us understand the data file for multiple linear regression. The sample data file we have used is shown below. It has five columns, as shown below. Our goal is to predict the profit based on multiple variables – spending on R&D, administrative spending, marketing spending, and the state in which the start-up is located.

The sample screenshot of the file is given in Figure 5.35.

50_Startups.csv

R&D Spend	Administration	Marketing Spend	State	Profit
165349.2	136897.8	471784.1	New York	192261.8
162597.7	151377.59	443898.53	California	191792.1
153441.51	101145.55	407934.54	Florida	191050.4
144372.41	118671.85	383199.62	New York	182902
142107.34	91391.77	366168.42	Florida	166187.9
131876.9	99814.71	362861.36	New York	156991.1
134615.46	147198.87	127716.82	California	156122.5
130298.13	145530.06	323876.68	Florida	155752.6
120542.52	148718.95	311613.29	New York	152211.8
123334.88	108679.17	304981.62	California	149760
101913.08	110594.11	229160.95	Florida	146122
100671.96	91790.61	249744.55	California	144259.4
93863.75	127320.38	249839.44	Florida	141585.5
91992.39	135495.07	252664.93	California	134307.4
119943.24	156547.42	256512.92	Florida	132602.7
114523.61	122616.84	261776.23	New York	129917
78013.11	121597.55	264346.06	California	126992.9
94657.16	145077.58	282574.31	New York	125370.4
91749.16	114175.79	294919.57	Florida	124266.9
86419.7	153514.11	0	New York	122776.9
76253.86	113867.3	298664.47	California	118474
78389.47	153773.43	299737.29	New York	111313
73994.56	122782.75	303319.26	Florida	110352.3

FIGURE 5.35 Screenshot of sample dataset.

```
# Multiple Linear Regression

# Importing the libraries
import numpy as np
import matplotlib.pyplot as plt
import pandas as pd

# Importing the dataset
dataset = pd.read_csv('C:/Users/mpandey1/Desktop/ML using Python
Training/day4/Section 5 - Multiple Linear Regression/50_Startups.csv')
X = dataset.iloc[:, :-1].values
y = dataset.iloc[:, 4].values

# Encoding categorical data - since we cannot use the text values as it
is.
from sklearn.preprocessing import LabelEncoder, OneHotEncoder
labelencoder = LabelEncoder()
X[:, 3] = labelencoder.fit_transform(X[:, 3])
onehotencoder = OneHotEncoder(categorical_features = [3])
X = onehotencoder.fit_transform(X).toarray()

# Avoiding the Dummy Variable Trap
X = X[:, 1:]

# Splitting the dataset into the Training set and Test set
from sklearn.cross_validation import train_test_split
```

```
X_train, X_test, y_train, y_test = train_test_split(X, y, test_size =
0.2, random_state = 0)

# Feature Scaling
from sklearn.preprocessing import StandardScaler
sc_X = StandardScaler()
X_train = sc_X.fit_transform(X_train)
X_test = sc_X.transform(X_test)
sc_y = StandardScaler()
y_train = sc_y.fit_transform(y_train)

# Fitting Multiple Linear Regression to the Training set
from sklearn.linear_model import LinearRegression
regressor = LinearRegression()
regressor.fit(X_train, y_train)

# Predicting the Test set results
y_pred = regressor.predict(X_test)

# regression coefficients
print('Coefficients: \n', regressor.coef_)

#OUTPUT →
#Coefficients:
# [ -415.38222603 333.57777773 35726.28774249 851.30163448
# 4519.88277698]

print(regressor.intercept_)

#OUTPUT →
109446.44724999998

from sklearn.metrics import mean_squared_error
mean_squared_error(y_test,y_pred)#mse

print(np.sqrt(mean_squared_error(y_test, y_pred))) #rmse

#OUTPUT →
9137.99015279494

# print the R-squared value for the model
regressor.score(X_test, y_test)#rsquare

#OUTPUT →
0.9347068473282425

from sklearn.linear_model import Ridge
ridgeReg = Ridge(alpha=0.05, normalize=True)
ridgeReg.fit(X_train,y_train)
pred = ridgeReg.predict(X_test)
mean_squared_error(y_test,pred)#mse
ridgeReg.score(X_test, y_test)

#OUTPUT →
0.9091504993722859
```

```
from sklearn.linear_model import Lasso
lassoReg = Lasso(alpha=0.8, normalize=True)
lassoReg.fit(X_train,y_train)
pred1 = lassoReg.predict(X_test)
mean_squared_error(y_test,pred1)#mse
lassoReg.score(X_test, y_test)

#OUTPUT →
0.934827712684663
```

SUMMARY

This chapter introduced the concepts of supervised learning and the types of supervised learning. A detailed analysis of supervised learning for regression is covered in this chapter. The simple and multiple linear regression methods with solved examples are illustrated to depict the procedure to find the optimal regression line clearly. In addition, the various error functions to converge the error between actual and predicted values are also shown clearly. Various real-world applications such as sales forecasting, medical prediction, and wind speed prediction are exemplified. Finally, simple and multiple linear regression implementation using Python is comprehensively demonstrated, starting from handling data to feature scaling, thus determining the output.

REVIEW QUESTIONS

1. Estimate the cost of oil well drilling based on the depth. The data is collected from Philippines offshore oil wells and given in Table 5.10. Draw the scatter plot. Based on a scatter plot, predict a linear regression model.
2. Calculate the residual for the above problem.
3. Find the difference between simple linear regression and multiple linear regression with appropriate example.

TABLE 5.10
Oil Well Drilling Data

Depth	Cost
5000	2596.8
5200	3328.0
6000	3181.1
6538	3198.4
7109	4779.9
7556	5905.6
8005	5769.2
8207	8089.5
8210	4813.1
8600	5618.7
9026	7736.0
9197	6788.3
9926	7840.8
10,813	8882.5
13,800	10,489.5
14,311	12,506.6

TABLE 5.11
Advertisement Data

TV	Radio	Newspaper	Sales
230.1	37.8	69.2	22.1
44.5	39.3	45.1	10.4
17.2	45.9	69.3	9.3
151.5	41.3	58.5	18.5
180.8	10.8	58.4	12.9

TABLE 5.12
Water Pollution Variables

Variable	Description
Y	Mean nitrogen concentration (mg/liter)
x_1	Percentage of agriculture land
x_2	Percentage of forest land
x_3	Percentage of residential land
x_4	Percentage of industrial land

TABLE 5.13
Water Pollution Data in New York Rivers

S. No.	River	Y	x_1	x_2	x_3	x_4
1	Olean	1.10	26	63	1.2	0.29
2	Cassadaga	1.01	29	57	0.7	0.09
3	Oatka	1.90	54	26	1.8	0.58
4	Neversink	1.00	2	84	1.9	1.98
5	Hackensack	1.99	3	27	29.4	3.11
6	Wappinger	1.42	19	61	3.4	0.56
7	Fishkill	2.04	16	60	5.6	1.11
8	Honeoye	1.65	40	43	1.3	0.24
9	Susquehanna	1.01	28	62	1.1	0.15
10	Chenango	1.21	26	60	0.9	0.23
11	Tioughnioga	1.33	26	53	0.9	0.18
12	West Canada	0.75	15	75	0.7	0.16
13	East Canada	0.73	6	84	0.5	0.12
14	Saranac	0.80	3	81	0.8	0.35
15	Ausable	0.76	2	89	0.7	0.35
16	Black	0.87	6	82	0.5	0.15
17	Schoharie	0.80	22	70	0.9	0.22
18	Raquette	0.87	4	75	0.4	0.18
19	Oswegatchie	0.66	21	56	0.5	0.13
20	Cohocton	1.25	40	49	1.1	0.13

TABLE 5.14
Quiz Mark Data

Student	x_i	y_i
1	95	85
2	85	95
3	80	70
4	70	65
5	60	70

4. Find the impact of advertising in TV, radio, and newspaper on sales as shown in Table 5.11. Identify the regression line.
5. Find the multiple regression model for the given data in Table 5.13. Variables in the study of water pollution in New York rivers are given in Table 5.12.
6. Find the least-squares regression line using data points {(−2, −1), (1, 1), (3, 2)}. Plot the given data points and the regression line in the graph.
7. Students attended an entrance quiz for a machine learning course. Quiz marks and the ML grades are given in Table 5.14.

   Perform least-squares regression and plot it in a graph.

6 Supervised Learning
Classification

LEARNING OBJECTIVES

At the end of this chapter, the reader will be able to

- Understand the difference between supervised learning algorithms used for regression and classification
- Comprehend the various supervised learning algorithms related to classification problems
- Know the basic mathematical concepts involved in logistic regression, decision trees, random forests, and support vector machines
- Solve examples based on the algorithms covered in this chapter
- Implement the supervised learning algorithms using Python for practical problems

6.1 INTRODUCTION

The idea of the classification problem is to classify the outcome variable into one or more categories. Then, the supervised learning method learns from the labeled data. Logistic regression, decision tree, and support vector machine (SVM) are the various supervised learning classification algorithms widely used. In this chapter, a detailed description of these algorithms, their mathematical modeling, merits and demerits, solved examples, and real-world applications are provided with step-by-step implementation in Python.

6.2 USE CASES OF CLASSIFICATION

Classification techniques are used for predictive analysis, image classification, and text analysis. In addition, many real-world applications such as handwritten character recognition, self-driving cars, remote sensing, marketing, and biomedical analysis utilize classification algorithm. As we walk through this chapter, several real-world examples are illustrated in the context of the classification algorithm.

6.3 LOGISTIC REGRESSION

Logistic regression is a supervised classification technique widely used to solve many real-world problems by data scientists. For example, various useful insights about big data can be obtained using logistic regression. Logistic regression is a simpler and powerful algorithm for both binary classification and multiclass classification problems. Some examples of binary classification problems are detecting spam email or not, whether an online transaction is fraudulent or not, and whether the examined tumor is malignant. In all of these above classification problems, we are trying to predict the output label y is either 0 (negative class) or 1 (positive class).

$$y \in \{0,1\} \begin{cases} 0 & \text{Negative class}\left(\text{e.g., not a fraudulent transaction}\right) \\ 1 & \text{Positive class}\left(\text{e.g., fraudulent transaction}\right) \end{cases}$$

Logistic regression is not a regression problem, as the name implies. It is different from linear regression, as given in Table 6.1.

DOI: 10.1201/9781003258803-6

TABLE 6.1
Linear Regression Versus Logistic Regression

Linear Regression	Logistic Regression
• Predicts continuous output value • The aim is to identify the best fit line	• Predicts categorical output value • The aim is to identify an S-shaped curve
$Y = \beta_0 + \beta_1 x_1$	$\ln\left(\dfrac{p}{1-p}\right) = \beta_0 + \beta_1 x_1$
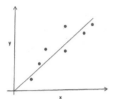	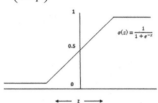
• Used to solve regression analysis • Uses least squares regression for estimating parameters • Applications: stock value prediction, wind speed prediction	• Used to solve the classification problem • Uses MLE to estimate parameters • Applications: spam email classification, customer churn prediction

6.3.1 GEOMETRIC INTUITION

Logistic regression makes use of the sigmoid function for separating two classes, as given in Equation 6.1. The logistic sigmoid function is otherwise called logit.

$$\sigma(z) = \frac{1}{1 + e^{-z}} \tag{6.1}$$

The value of sigmoid function $\sigma(z)$ is bounded between 0 and 1, which looks like S as in Figure 6.1. The hypothesis function or the threshold $h_\theta(x)$ is at 0.5.

$$0 \le h_\theta(x) \le 1$$

$$h_\theta(x) = \sigma(\theta^T x) = \frac{1}{1 + e^{-(\theta^T x)}} \tag{6.2}$$

If $h_\theta(x) \ge 0.5$, then predict output label y as 1. Else if $h_\theta(x) < 0.5$, then predict output label y as 0.

Let us consider weight vector as β_i, observations say x_i and bias β_0 as intercept in linear regression. Assume for a binary classification problem, one class is 0, and another class is one, and the formula for predicting probabilities is given below.

$$P(Y = 0 \mid X) = \frac{1}{1 + \exp\left[\beta_0 + \sum \beta_i x_i\right]} \tag{6.3}$$

$$P(Y = 1 \mid X) = \frac{\exp\left[\beta_0 + \sum \beta_i x_i\right]}{1 + \exp\left[\beta_0 + \sum \beta_i x_i\right]} \tag{6.4}$$

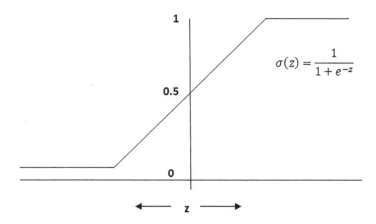

$$\sigma(z) = \frac{1}{1 + e^{-z}}$$

FIGURE 6.1 Sigmoid curve.

where exp[x] is similar to e^x. More simply, it can be rewritten as

$$P(Y = 0 \mid X) = \sigma\left(-\beta_0 + \sum \beta_i x_i\right) \tag{6.5}$$

$$P(Y = 1 \mid X) = 1 - \left[\sigma\left(-\beta_0 + \sum \beta_i x_i\right)\right] \tag{6.6}$$

where

$$\sigma(z) = \frac{1}{1 + e^{-z}}$$

With a simple example, let us understand whether a person has a lung disease based on age and smoking habit.

$$P\left(D = 1 \middle| \text{age, smoking habit}\right) = \frac{1}{1 + e^{-(\beta_0 + \beta_1 \text{age} + \beta_2 \text{smoking habit})}}$$

$$P\left(D = 1 \middle| x_1, x_2\right) = \frac{1}{1 + e^{-(\beta_0 + \beta_1 x_1 + \beta_2 x_2)}}$$

$$P\left(D = 0 \middle| \text{age, smoking habit}\right) = \frac{e^{-(\beta_0 + \beta_1 \text{age} + \beta_2 \text{smoking habit})}}{1 + e^{-(\beta_0 + \beta_1 \text{age} + \beta_2 \text{smoking habit})}}$$

$$P\left(D = 0 \middle| x_1, x_2\right) = \frac{e^{-(\beta_0 + \beta_1 x_1 + \beta_2 x_2)}}{1 + e^{-(\beta_0 + \beta_1 x_1 + \beta_2 x_2)}}$$

where
  D = presence of lung disease, discrete value {1 – Yes and 0 – No}
  x_1 = age, continuous value
  x_2 = smoking habit, discrete value {1 – Yes and 0 – No}
  To estimate the parameters β_0, β_1, and β_2, maximum likelihood estimation (MLE) is used

$$\ln\left(\frac{p}{1-p}\right) = \beta_0 + \beta_1 x_1 \tag{6.7}$$

TABLE 6.2

Example Illustration

Heart Attack	Anger Treatment		Total
	Yes (1)	No (0)	
Yes(1)	$3(R_{11})$	$7(R_{12})$	10
No(0)	$6(R_{21})$	$4(R_{22})$	10
	9	11	20

where $p/1-p$ is the odds ratio and $\ln(p/1-p)$ is the logit odds ratio.

$$\text{Odds} = \frac{p(\text{event})}{1- p(\text{event})} \tag{6.8}$$

The odds ratio is the ratio between the probability of success and the probability of failure. Let us understand how to calculate the odds ratio with a simple illustration using Table 6.2.

Odds that a person who had anger treatment got a heart attack $= R_{11}/R_{21} = 3/6 = 0.5$

Odds that a person who had not undergone anger treatment got a heart attack $= R_{12}/R_{22} = 7/4 = 1.75$

Relative odds/odds ratio $= (R_{12}/R_{22})/(R_{11}/R_{21}) = 1.75/0.5 = 0.285$

To estimate the probability of heart attack with respect to anger treatment, logistic function is used

$$\ln\left(\frac{p}{1-p}\right) = \beta_0 + \beta_1 x_1$$

where β_0 and β_1 are regression coefficients and p is the probability of a person who has suffered a heart attack.

6.3.2 Variants of Logistic Regression

The major types of logistic regression (Figure 6.2) are

- Simple logistic regression
- Multiple logistic regression
- Binary logistic regression

6.3.2.1 Simple Logistic Regression

It is a simpler form with only one independent variable. The general form of simple logistic regression is $\ln\left(\frac{p}{1-p}\right) = \beta_0 + \beta_1$. To predict the presence of heart disease (Yes/No) based on only one variable, say a smoking habit is a simple logistic regression type. The variable description for heart disease y and smoking habit x_1 is

$$\text{Presence of heart disease } y = \begin{cases} 1 & \text{Yes} \\ 0 & \text{No} \end{cases}$$

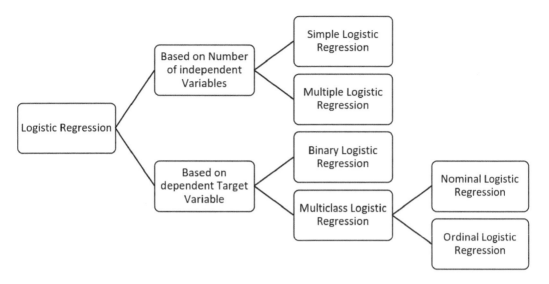

FIGURE 6.2   Variants of logistic regression.

$$\text{Smoking habit } x_1 = \begin{cases} 1 & \text{Smoker} \\ 0 & \text{Non smoker} \end{cases}$$

The simple logistic function for predicting heart disease y based on smoking habit x_1 is given as

$$\ln\left(\frac{p(y=1|x_1)}{1-p(y=1|x_1)}\right) = \beta_0 + \beta_1 x_1$$

6.3.2.2   Multiple Logistic Regression

If we have more than one independent variable, say $\{x_1, x_2, \ldots, x_n\}$, then, it is called multiple logistic regression. The general form of multiple logistic regression is in Equation 6.3

$$\ln\left(\frac{p}{1-p}\right) = \beta_0 + \beta_1 x_1 + \cdots + \beta_n x_n \tag{6.9}$$

To predict the presence of heart disease y (Yes/No) based on more than one variable, say smoking habit x_1 and age-group x_2 are examples of multiple logistic regression.

$$\ln\left(\frac{p(y=1|x_1, x_2)}{1-p(y=1|x_1, x_2)}\right) = \beta_0 + \beta_1 x_1 + \beta_2 x_2 \tag{6.10}$$

6.3.2.3   Binary Logistic Regression

It tries to predict the probability of binary target (0, 1). Binary logistic regression is a simpler method that makes use of the sigmoid function. For instance, as shown in Figure 6.3, to predict whether it will rain tomorrow or not based on humidity, the target-dependent variable "Will it Rain" contains exactly two classes, say rain (1) and no rain (0).

$$P(\text{rain} = 1 \,|\, \text{humidity}) = \frac{1}{1 + e^{-(\beta_0 + \beta_1 \text{humidity})}}$$

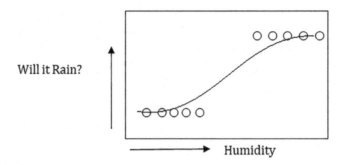

FIGURE 6.3 Binary logistic regression.

$$P\left(\text{rain} = 0 \mid \text{humidity}\right) = \frac{e^{-(\beta_0 + \beta_1 \text{humidity})}}{1 + e^{-(\beta_0 + \beta_1 \text{humidity})}}$$

Few other examples of binary logistic regression classification:

- What factors influence a person's decision to travel for leisure?
  $Y = 1$ if visit for leisure, 0 if not
- What factors determine baby birth weight?
  $Y = 1$ if baby birth weight is low, 0 if not
- Which demography is more likely to vote in favor of new legislation?
  $Y = 1$ if a person voted Yes, 0 if not
- Which customers are more likely to buy a new car?
  $Y = 1$ if a new car is bought, 0 if not

6.3.2.4 Multiclass Logistic Regression

Multiclass logistic regression tries to predict the probability of more than two target classes. Instead of using the sigmoid function, the softmax function is used for multiclass classification problems. Examples of multiclass logistic regression classification are given below.

Which party is a person going to vote for?

$$\left\{ \begin{array}{l} \text{Republican} - 1 \\ \text{Democratic} - 2 \\ \text{Independent} - 3 \end{array} \right.$$

What kind of symptoms does a person have?

$$\text{Symptoms} \left\{ \begin{array}{l} \text{None} - 0 \\ \text{Mild} - 1 \\ \text{Moderate} - 2 \\ \text{Severe} - 3 \end{array} \right.$$

The two types of multiclass logistic regression are ordinal and nominal logistic regressions.

6.3.2.5 Nominal Logistic Regression

It is a type of multiclass logistic regression, where the target-dependent variable consists of more than two class labels. There is no inherent or natural ordering present in nominal class variables.

Examples of the nominal variable are

$$
\text{Occupational status}
\begin{cases}
\text{Self employed} - 0 \\
\text{Government employee} - 2 \\
\text{Private employee} - 3 \\
\text{Unemployed} - 1
\end{cases}
$$

For instance, let us consider a nominal variable called the type of a target variable. We aim to classify the target variable based on the input variables age-group and smoking.

$$
\text{Target dependent variable } Y = \text{Cancer type}
\begin{cases}
\text{Lung cancer} - 0, \\
\text{Mouth cancer} - 1 \\
\text{other} - 2
\end{cases}
$$

$$
\text{Independent variable } x_1 = \text{Age group}
\begin{cases}
0 & \text{if} \leq 50 \\
1 & \text{if} > 50
\end{cases}
$$

$$
\text{Independent variable } x_2 = \text{Smoking}
\begin{cases}
0 - \text{Non smoker} \\
1 - \text{Smoker}
\end{cases}
$$

To perform multiclass logistic regression, let us assume any category as a reference and then separately compare with the other two categories. For example, let us consider lung cancer {0} as a reference category and first compare mouth cancer {1} versus lung cancer {0} and later other {2} versus lung cancer {0}. Then, the odds ratio (OR) needs to be calculated for each separate comparison.

$$
\text{OR}_{1vs0} = \frac{P(Y=1)}{P(Y=0)}
$$

$$
\text{OR}_{2vs0} = \frac{P(Y=2)}{P(Y=0)}
$$

The logit expression for two comparisons is given as

$$
\ln\left(\frac{P(Y=1)}{P(Y=0)}\right) \text{ and } \ln\left(\frac{P(Y=2)}{P(Y=0)}\right)
$$

The logistic function for category mouth cancer {1} versus lung cancer {0} is

$$
\ln\left(\frac{P(Y=1|x_1,x_2)}{P(Y=0\pi|x_1,x_2)}\right) = \frac{1}{1+e^{-(\beta_0+\beta_1 \text{ age group}+\beta_2 \text{ smoking})}}
$$

The logistic function for category other {2} versus carcinoma {0} is

$$
\ln\left(\frac{P(Y=2|x_1,x_2)}{P(Y=0|x_1,x_2)}\right) = \frac{1}{1+e^{-(\beta_o+\beta_1 \text{ age group}+\beta_2 \text{ smoking})}}
$$

6.3.2.6 Ordinal Logistic Regression

It is a type of multiclass logistic regression, where the target variable consists of more than two class labels. The natural order is present in the ordinal class variable. Examples of the ordinal variable are the performance of students and tumor grade.

$$\text{Tumor grade} \begin{cases} \text{Well differentiated} \\ \text{Modrately differentiated} \\ \text{Poorly differentiated} \end{cases}$$

$$\text{Performance of student} \begin{cases} \text{Good} \\ \text{Average} \\ \text{Poor} \end{cases}$$

6.3.3 Optimization Problem

Optimization is a minimization or maximization problem. Let the actual output be y and the predicted output be $\hat{y}$, and the objective is to minimize the difference between the predicted output and actual output as given in Equation 6.4.

$$\text{Objective is to} \min(\hat{y} - y) \tag{6.11}$$

Cross-entropy loss function L_{CE} is the function used in logistic models

$$L_{CE} = -\log p(y|x) \tag{6.12}$$

$$\log p(y \mid x) = y \log \hat{y} + (1 - y) \log(1 - \hat{y}) \tag{6.13}$$

$$L_{CE} = -\left[y \log \hat{y} + (1 - y) \log(1 - \hat{y}) \right] \tag{6.14}$$

6.3.4 Regularization

The model performs well for training data and does not classify new unseen data, which is known as the overfitting problem. Overfitting occurs when our model fits with too much data. This can be resolved by using regularization term to generalize the logistic regression model. Regularization can be done by adding a penalty to the weight parameters. L_1 and L_2 regularizations are the two forms of regularizations. L_2 regularization is a widely used one, and the general form is in Equation 6.15.

$$\frac{\lambda}{2} ||w||^2 = \frac{\lambda}{2} \sum_{j=1}^{m} w_j^2 \tag{6.15}$$

where λ is the regularization parameter.

6.3.5 REAL-WORLD APPLICATIONS

6.3.5.1 Medical Diagnosis

Several studies utilized logistic regression for disease diagnosis. Evans County dataset collected by cohort study predicts the presence of heart disease using the logistic regression model. Some of the variables of the Evans County dataset are given in Table 6.3.

The multiple logistic regression form to predict coronary heart disease is given in Figure 6.4.

$$\ln\left(\frac{P(\text{CHD}=1\mid\text{CAT},\text{CHL},\text{SMK},\text{ECG})}{1-P(\text{CHD}=1\mid\text{CAT},\text{CHL},\text{SMK},\text{ECG})}\right) = \frac{1}{1+e^{-(\beta_0+\beta_1\text{CAT}+\beta_2\text{CHL}+\beta_3\text{SMK}+\beta_4\text{ECG})}}$$

Several studies on cancer survival utilized the cancer dataset and performed multiclass ordinal logistic regression, as shown in Figure 6.5. Some of the variables of the cancer dataset are given in Table 6.4.

6.3.5.2 Text Classification

Data scientist widely uses logistic regression for text analysis and classification. Several applications such as sentiment analysis, Twitter data classification, spam email identification, and recommendation system utilize logistic regression. For example, you have a movie review, says "Very Boring," and the aim is to predict whether this review has a positive or negative review, as given in Figure 6.6.

6.3.5.3 Marketing

The logistic regression technique is widely used to analyze customer behavior, retain the customer, and check a customer's creditworthiness. Customer churn prediction application uses logistic

TABLE 6.3
Evans County Dataset Variables Description

Variable	Value	Type
CHD (coronary heart disease)	1 – present 0 – absent	Discrete, binary value
CAT (catecholamine level)	1 – high 0 – normal	Discrete, binary value
CHL (cholesterol)	-	Continuous
SMK (smoking)	1 – ever smoked 0 – never smoked	Discrete, binary value
ECG (ECG abnormality)	1 – presence 0 – absence	Discrete, binary value

FIGURE 6.4 Binary multiple logistic regression.

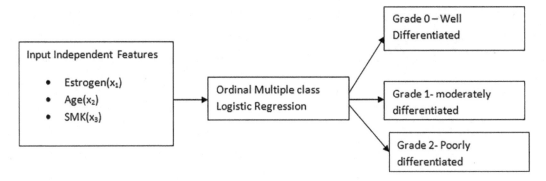

FIGURE 6.5   Ordinal multi-class logistic regression.

TABLE 6.4

Endometrial Cancer Dataset

Variable	Value	Type
Grade	0 – well-differentiated 1 – moderately differentiated 2 – poorly differentiated	Discrete, multiclass ordinal
Estrogen	1 – ever used 0 – never used	Discrete, binary value
Age	-	Continuous
SMK(smoking)	1 – current smoker 0 – not a current smoker	Discrete, binary value

---

FIGURE 6.6   Logistic regression in text classification.

regression technique more efficiently. In churn prediction, the logistic regression model classifies customers into three types, namely newly acquired customer, existing customer, and churn customer (who decided to end their relation). The customer can end their relationship based on various factors such as customer service. The variable description of churn prediction is given in Table 6.5.

6.3.6   Logistic Regression in Practice using Python

Logistic regression is named for the function used at the core of the tactic, the logistic function. The logistic function, also called the sigmoid function, is developed by statisticians to elucidate properties of an increase in population, rising quickly and maxing out at the environment's carrying capacity. It's an S-shaped curve that assumes any real-valued number and maps it into a worth between 0 and 1 but never exactly at those limits.

$$1/\left(1 + e^{\hat{}} - \text{value}\right)$$

TABLE 6.5
Churn Prediction

Variable	Value	Type
Customer (y)	0 – new customers	Discrete, multiclass
	1 – existing customer	
	2 – churn customer	
Customer service (x_1)	1 – satisfied	Discrete, binary value
	0 – not satisfied	

where e is that the base of the natural logarithms (Euler's number or the EXP() function in your spreadsheet) and value is that the particular numerical value that you just simply want to remodel. Below might be a plot of the numbers between −5 and 5 transformed between the range 0 and 1 using the logistic function.

Logistic regression could also be a linear method, but the predictions are transformed using the logistic function. The impact of this is often that we will not understand the predictions as a linear combination of the inputs as we will with linear regression; for instance, continuing from the above, the model is often stated as

$$p(X) = e^{\wedge(b_0+b_1X)}\big/\left(1 + e^{\wedge(b_0+b_1X)}\right)$$

We don't want to dive into the math an excessive amount, but we will rotate the above equation as follows (remove the exponent term by adding a logarithm (ln) to the other):

$$\ln\big(p(X)/1 - p(X)\big) = b_0 + b_1 * X$$

This is beneficial since we'll notice that the output on the right is calculated linearly again (just like linear regression), and the input on the left might be a log of the default class's probability. This ratio on the left is known as the default class's chances (we've always used odds instead of probabilities; for example, odds are used in horse racing instead of probabilities). Odds are calculated as a ratio of the probability of an event divided by the probability of not occurring; for example, 0.8/(1−0.8) has a probability of 4. So instead, we could write:

$$\ln(\text{odds}) = b_0 + b_1 * X$$

We call this left side the log-odds or the probit since the chances are log-converted. Of course, other types of functions can be used for the transform (which is beyond the scope of this article). Still, it's customary to ask for the transformation that relates the linear regression equation to the probabilities due to the link function, such as the probit link function. Then, we can return the exponent to its appropriate place and express it as

$$\text{odds} = e^{\wedge}\left(b_0 + b_1 * X\right)$$

All of this lets us see that the model is still a linear combination of inputs but that this linear combination is related to the default class's log-odds. For explaining the logistic regression, we will be using a sample dataset called the Titanic dataset. Our goal is to predict, -the values for the variables (Pclass – Passenger class of travel, Name of the passenger, gender of the passenger, Age of the passenger, If they are related to any of other passengers – (like a spouse, sibling, or parent/child of another passenger and the fare paid) – if the person could have survived in the titanic mishap.

titanic.csv

Survived	Pclass	Name	Sex	Age	Siblings/Spouses Aboard	Parents/Children Aboard	Fare
0	3	Mr. Owen Harris Braund	Male	22	1	0	7.25
1	1	Mrs. John Bradley (Florence Briggs Thayer) Cumings	Female	38	1	0	71.2833
1	3	Miss. Laina Heikkinen	Female	26	0	0	7.925
1	1	Mrs. Jacques Heath (Lily May Peel) Futrelle	Female	35	1	0	53.1
0	3	Mr. William Henry Allen	Male	35	0	0	8.05
0	3	Mr. James Moran	Male	27	0	0	8.4583
0	1	Mr. Timothy J McCarthy	Male	54	0	0	51.8625
0	3	Master. Gosta Leonard Palsson	Male	2	3	1	21.075
1	3	Mrs. Oscar W (Elisabeth Vilhelmina Berg) Johnson	Female	27	0	2	11.1333
1	2	Mrs. Nicholas (Adele Achem) Nasser	Female	14	1	0	30.0708
1	3	Miss. Marguerite Rut Sandstrom	Female	4	1	1	16.7
1	1	Miss. Elizabeth Bonnell	Female	58	0	0	26.55
0	3	Mr. William Henry Saundercock	Male	20	0	0	8.05
0	3	Mr. Anders Johan Andersson	Male	39	1	5	31.275
0	3	Miss. Hulda Amanda Adolfina Vestrom	Female	14	0	0	7.8542
1	2	Mrs. (Mary D Kingcome) Hewlett	Female	55	0	0	16
0	3	Master. Eugene Rice	Male	2	4	1	29.125
1	2	Mr. Charles Eugene Williams	Male	23	0	0	13
0	3	Mrs. Julius (Emelia Maria Vandemoortele) Vander Planke	Female	31	1	0	18
1	3	Mrs. Fatima Masselmani	Female	22	0	0	7.225
0	2	Mr. Joseph J Fynney	Male	35	0	0	26
1	2	Mr. Lawrence Beesley	Male	34	0	0	13

```
import numpy as np
import pandas as pd
import seaborn as sb
import matplotlib.pyplot as plt
import sklearn

from pandas import Series, DataFrame
from pylab import rcParams
from sklearn import preprocessing
from sklearn.linear_model import LogisticRegression
from sklearn.cross_validation import train_test_split
from sklearn import metrics
from sklearn.metrics import classification_report
```

The first thing we are going to do is to read in the dataset using the Pandas' read_csv() function. Then, we will put this data into a Pandas DataFrame, called "titanic," and name each of the columns.

```
data = pd.read_csv("titanic.csv")
data.columns = ['Survived','Pclass','Name','Sex','Age','Siblings/Spouses
Aboard','Number of Parents/Children Aboard','Fare']
data.head()
```

The OUTPUT is shown below – top 5 values

	Survived	Pclass	Name	Sex	Age	Siblings/Spouses Aboard	Number of Parents/Children Aboard	Fare
0	0	3	Mr. Owen Harris Braund	Male	22.0	1	0	7.2500
1	1	1	Mrs. John Bradley (Florence Briggs Thayer) Cum...	Female	38.0	1	0	71.2833
2	1	3	Miss. Laina Heikkinen	Female	26.0	0	0	7.9250
3	1	1	Mrs. Jacques Heath (Lily May Peel) Futrelle	Female	35.0	1	0	53.1000
4	0	3	Mr. William Henry Allen	Male	35.0	0	0	8.0500

6.3.6.1 Variable Descriptions
Survived – Survival (0=No; 1=Yes); Pclass – Passenger Class (1=1st; 2=2nd; 3=3rd); Name – Name; Sex – Sex; Age – Age; SibSp – Number of Siblings/Spouses Aboard; Parch – Number of Parents/Children Aboard; Fare – Passenger Fare (British pound)

6.3.6.2 Checking for Missing Values
It's easy to check for missing values by calling the isnull() method, and the sum() method off of that, to return a tally of all the true values that are returned by the isnull() method.

data.isnull()

#The OUTPUT is shown below.

	Survived	Pclass	Name	Sex	Age	Siblings/Spouses Aboard	Number of Parents/Children Aboard	Fare
0	False	False	False	False	False	False	False	False
1	False	False	False	False	False	False	False	False
2	False	False	False	False	False	False	False	False
3	False	False	False	False	False	False	False	False
4	False	False	False	False	False	False	False	False
5	False	False	False	False	False	False	False	False
6	False	False	False	False	False	False	False	False
7	False	False	False	False	False	False	False	False
8	False	False	False	False	False	False	False	False
9	False	False	False	False	False	False	False	False
10	False	False	False	False	False	False	False	False
11	False	False	False	False	False	False	False	False
12	False	False	False	False	False	False	False	False
13	False	False	False	False	False	False	False	False
14	False	False	False	False	False	False	False	False
15	False	False	False	False	False	False	False	False

(Continued)

	Survived	Pclass	Name	Sex	Age	Siblings/Spouses Aboard	Number of Parents/Children Aboard	Fare
16	False	False	False	False	False	False	False	False
17	False	False	False	False	False	False	False	False
18	False	False	False	False	False	False	False	False
19	False	False	False	False	False	False	False	False
20	False	False	False	False	False	False	False	False
21	False	False	False	False	False	False	False	False
22	False	False	False	False	False	False	False	False
23	False	False	False	False	False	False	False	False
24	False	False	False	False	False	False	False	False
25	False	False	False	False	False	False	False	False
26	False	False	False	False	False	False	False	False
27	False	False	False	False	False	False	False	False
28	False	False	False	False	False	False	False	False
29	False	False	False	False	False	False	False	False
...	...	...	...	...	...	...	...	...
857	False	False	False	False	False	False	False	False
858	False	False	False	False	False	False	False	False
859	False	False	False	False	False	False	False	False
860	False	False	False	False	False	False	False	False
861	False	False	False	False	False	False	False	False
862	False	False	False	False	False	False	False	False
863	False	False	False	False	False	False	False	False
864	False	False	False	False	False	False	False	False
865	False	False	False	False	False	False	False	False
866	False	False	False	False	False	False	False	False
867	False	False	False	False	False	False	False	False
868	False	False	False	False	False	False	False	False
869	False	False	False	False	False	False	False	False
870	False	False	False	False	False	False	False	False
871	False	False	False	False	False	False	False	False
872	False	False	False	False	False	False	False	False
873	False	False	False	False	False	False	False	False
874	False	False	False	False	False	False	False	False
875	False	False	False	False	False	False	False	False
876	False	False	False	False	False	False	False	False
877	False	False	False	False	False	False	False	False
878	False	Pclass	Name	False	Age	False	False	False
879	False	False	False	False	False	False	False	False
880	False	False	False	False	False	False	False	False
881	False	False	False	False	False	False	False	False
882	False	False	False	False	False	False	False	False
883	False	False	False	False	False	False	False	False
884	False	False	False	False	False	False	False	False
885	False	False	False	False	False	False	False	False
886	False	False	False	False	False	False	False	False

887 rows×8 columns

```
data.isnull().sum()
```

#The output is shown below.

```
Survived                         0
Pclass                           0
Name                             0
Sex                              0
Age                              0
Siblings/Spouses Aboard      0
Number of Parents/Children Aboard      0
Fare                             0
dtype: int64
data.info()
```

```
<class 'pandas.core.frame.DataFrame'>
RangeIndex: 887 entries, 0 to 886
Data columns (total 8 columns):
Survived                     887 non-null int64
Pclass                       887 non-null int64
Name                         887 non-null object
Sex                          887 non-null object
Age                          887 non-null float64
Siblings/Spouses Aboard      887 non-null int64
Number of Parents/Children Aboard      887 non-null int64
Fare                         887 non-null float64
dtypes: float64(2), int64(4), object(2)
memory usage: 55.5+ KB
```

So let's just go ahead and drop all the variables that aren't relevant for predicting survival. We should at least keep the following:

Survived: This variable is relevant.
Pclass: Does a passenger's class on the boat affect their survivability?
Sex: Could a passenger's gender impact their survival rate?
Age: Does a person's age impact their survival rate?
SibSp: Does the number of relatives on the boat (siblings or a spouse) affect a person's survivability? Probability
Parch: Does the number of relatives on the boat (children or parents) affect a person's survivability? Probability
Fare: Does the fare a person paid affect his survivability?
Maybe: let's keep it.

```
titanic_data = data.drop(['Pclass','Name'], 1)
titanic_data.head()
```

#The output is shown below – top 5 rows

	Survived	Sex	Age	Siblings/Spouses Abroad	Number of Parents/Children Aboard	Fare
0	0	Male	22.0	1	0	7.2500
1	1	Female	38.0	1	0	71.2833
2	1	Female	26.0	0	0	7.9250
3	1	Female	35.0	1	0	53.1000
4	0	Male	35.0	0	0	8.0500

6.3.6.3 Converting Categorical Variables to a Dummy Indicator

The next thing we need to do is reformat our variables so that they work with the model. Specifically, we need to reformat the Sex and Embarked variables into numeric variables.

```
gender = pd.get_dummies(titanic_data['Sex'],drop_first=True)
gender.head()
```

	Male
0	1
1	0
2	0
3	0
4	1

```
itanic_dmy = pd.concat([titanic_data,gender],axis=1)
titanic_dmy.head()
```

	Survived	Age	Siblings/Spouses Aboard	Number of Parents/Children Aboard	Fare	Male
0	0	22.0	1	0	7.2500	1
1	1	38.0	1	0	71.2833	0
2	1	26.0	0	0	7.9250	0
3	1	35.0	1	0	53.1000	0
4	0	35.0	0	0	8.0500	1

```
titanic_dmy.drop(['Fare'],axis=1,inplace=True)
titanic_dmy.head()
```

	Survived	Age	Siblings/Spouses Aboard	Number of Parents/Children Aboard	Male
0	0	22.0	1	0	1
1	1	38.0	1	0	0
2	1	26.0	0	0	0
3	1	35.0	1	0	0
4	0	35.0	0	0	1

```
X = titanic_dmy.ix[:,(1,2,3,4)].values
y = titanic_dmy.ix[:,0].values
X_train, X_test, y_train, y_test = train_test_split(X, y, test_size =.3,
random_state=25)
```

Deploying and evaluating the model:

```
LogReg = LogisticRegression()
LogReg.fit(X_train, y_train)
```

#The OUTPUT is shown below.

```
LogisticRegression(C=1.0, class_weight=None, dual=False,
fit_intercept=True,
intercept_scaling=1, max_iter=100, multi_class='ovr', n_jobs=1,
        penalty='l2', random_state=None, solver='liblinear', tol=0.0001,
        verbose=0, warm_start=False)
```

```
y_pred = LogReg.predict(X_test)
y_pred
```

#The OUTPUT is shown below.

```
array([0, 1, 1, 0, 0, 0, 1, 0, 0, 1, 0, 0, 1, 0, 0, 0, 1, 1, 0, 0, 1, 0,
       0, 0, 1, 0, 0, 0, 0, 0, 0, 0, 1, 0, 1, 0, 0, 0, 0, 0, 0, 0, 0, 0,
       0, 0, 1, 0, 1, 0, 1, 0, 1, 0, 1, 1, 0, 0, 1, 0, 1, 0, 0, 0, 0, 0,
       0, 1, 0, 0, 1, 1, 0, 1, 1, 0, 1, 0, 0, 0, 0, 0, 0, 0, 0, 1, 0, 0,
       1, 0, 0, 0, 0, 1, 0, 0, 1, 0, 0, 1, 1, 1, 1, 1, 0, 0, 1, 1, 0, 0,
       1, 0, 1, 1, 1, 0, 1, 0, 0, 1, 0, 1, 0, 0, 0, 1, 0, 1, 1, 1, 1, 0,
       1, 1, 0, 0, 0, 1, 1, 1, 0, 0, 0, 0, 1, 0, 1, 1, 0, 1, 0, 1, 0, 0,
       0, 0, 0, 0, 1, 1, 1, 0, 0, 0, 1, 0, 0, 0, 1, 0, 1, 0, 1, 0, 0, 1,
       1, 0, 0, 1, 1, 0, 0, 0, 1, 1, 1, 0, 0, 0, 0, 1, 1, 0, 0, 1, 1, 0,
       0, 0, 0, 1, 0, 0, 1, 1, 0, 1, 0, 0, 1, 0, 0, 0, 0, 0, 0, 1, 0, 1,
       1, 0, 0, 0, 0, 0, 0, 0, 0, 0, 0, 1, 0, 0, 0, 0, 0, 1, 0, 0, 0, 1,
       0, 1, 1, 0, 0, 1, 0, 1, 0, 0, 1, 0, 0, 1, 0, 0, 0, 1, 0, 1, 1, 0,
       0, 0, 0], dtype=int64)
```

```
from sklearn.metrics import confusion_matrix
confusion_matrix = confusion_matrix(y_test, y_pred)
confusion_matrix
```

#The OUTPUT is shown below.

```
array([[140, 23],
       [ 31, 73]], dtype=int64)
```

The confusion matrix results tell us that 137 and 69 are the numbers of correct predictions. Conversely, 34 and 27 are the numbers of incorrect predictions.

```
print(classification_report(y_test, y_pred))
```

#The OUTPUT is shown below.

	Precision	Recall	F1-score	Support
0	0.82	0.86	0.84	163
1	0.76	0.70	0.73	104
Avg/total	0.80	0.80	0.80	267

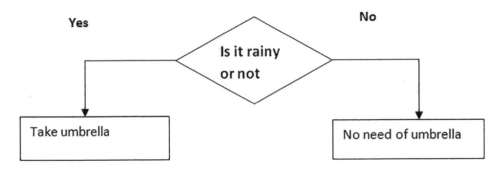

FIGURE 6.7   Sample decision tree.

6.4   DECISION TREE CLASSIFIER

The decision tree belongs to the nonparametric supervised learning. A decision tree is one of the most popular classification and prediction algorithms. It is used in data mining, operation research, and machine learning (ML). A decision tree is a tree-structured classifier. The decision node and leaf node are the two nodes in the decision tree. A test is done on the decision node. A leaf node represents the class label. The path from the root to the leaf represents the classification rule. A decision tree is a flowchart-like structure. The test is conducted on each node of the decision tree, and the branch represents the outcome of the test. The last node or leaf node represents the class label. The path from the root node to the leaf node represents the classification rule. The goal of the decision tree is to create a decision model from the dataset that predicts the value of a target variable by using a simple decision rule. A decision tree is a visual representation of the decision. The real data have many features (i.e., in iris flower, the features are petal width and length). These features are represented clearly in the decision tree. The relationship between the features can be easily identified by using the decision tree. A decision tree can be built efficiently by using the decision tree algorithm.

The decision tree problem can be solved from the starting node (i.e., root node) to the end node. Figure 6.7 shows the sample decision tree. The decision tree can be used for classification or regression. A decision tree is very easy to understand because it has a graphical representation.

The decision trees are constructed based on the attributes. The attribute for Figure 6.7 is whether the climate is rainy or not. Based on the attribute, the decision trees are constructed. This section explains in detail about the selection of attributes for using a decision tree algorithm. The performance of decision trees is affected by the overfitting and underfitting problem. The detailed procedure for solving these problems is also discussed in this section. Nowadays, the decision trees play a vital role in medical, library management, healthcare management, business management, banking sector, etc.; these applications are discussed in detail.

6.4.1   IMPORTANT TERMINOLOGY IN THE DECISION TREE

Figure 6.8 represents a simple decision tree. The various terminologies used in the decision tree are as follows:

Root node: The entire population of the tree is represented by the root node. The root node is divided into two or more nodes.
Decision node: The subnode dividing into a further subnode is called a decision node.
Splitting: The process of splitting a node into two or more nodes.
Leaf/terminal node: This node is also called a terminal node. A node that does not split further is called a terminal node.
Pruning: The removal of a subnode in a decision tree is called pruning.

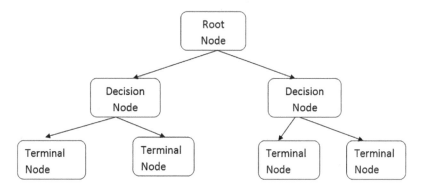

FIGURE 6.8   Decision tree with terminology.

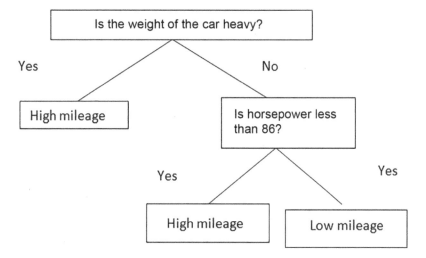

FIGURE 6.9   Decision tree for buying a car.

Branch/subtree: A subsection of the entire tree is called a branch or subtree.

Parent node/child node: A node dividing into subnodes is called a parent node. A subnode is called a child node.

Information gain: The amount of energy that cannot be used to do work or a measure of disorder in the system.

$$E(s) = \sum_{i=1}^{c} P \log P \qquad (6.16)$$

where

   s is the training dataset

   c is the number of the target class

   P is the proportion of training data belonging to the target class

6.4.2   EXAMPLE FOR DECISION TREE

The decision tree in Figure 6.9 represents the sample decision tree for the selection of cars. From the decision tree, we can easily identify the car having high mileage (i.e., heavy weighted car and less weighted car with horse power >86) selected for buying a car.

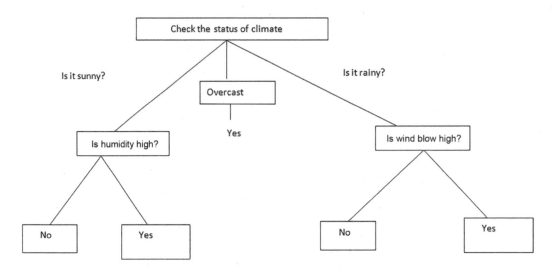

FIGURE 6.10   Decision tree for weather forecast.

TABLE 6.6
Weather Forecast Data

Attribute	Condition
Yes	Overcast
	Sunny and high humidity
	Rainy and high wind blow
No	Sunny and less humidity
	Rainy and low wind blow

The decision tree in Figure 6.10 represents the decision for playing tennis. The status of climate is checked at the root node. The climate may be sunny, rainy, and overcast. The tennis player can select the leaf node having Yes for playing tennis. Table 6.6 represents the condition for playing tennis.

6.4.3   Sample Decision Tree

Let us consider a simple example of creating a decision tree for crediting a loan, as shown in Figure 6.11. First, the data are spitted into two parts based on the employment status at the root node (i.e., employed or not employed).

Decision tree classification for unemployed: The decision tree goes to node A if the applicant is not employed. Again, the data are divided based on the credit score (i.e., high or low). The loans are approved for the applicant having a high credit score.

Decision tree classification for unemployed: The decision tree goes to node B if the applicant is employed. Again, the data are divided based on the income (i.e., high or low). The loans are approved for the applicant having a high income.

6.4.4   Decision Tree Formation

Let us consider a dataset having four attributes, namely A1, A2, A3, and A4. Let us assume that the decision tree is started with attribute A1 (i.e., root node). The data are divided into two parts at the root node based on attribute A1. Data d1 represent the data satisfying the attribute A1. Data d2 represent the data that are not satisfying attribute A1, as shown in Figure 6.12.

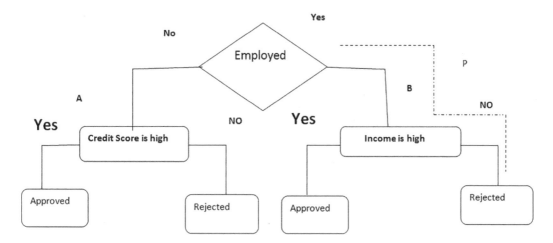

FIGURE 6.11   Decision tree for crediting loan.

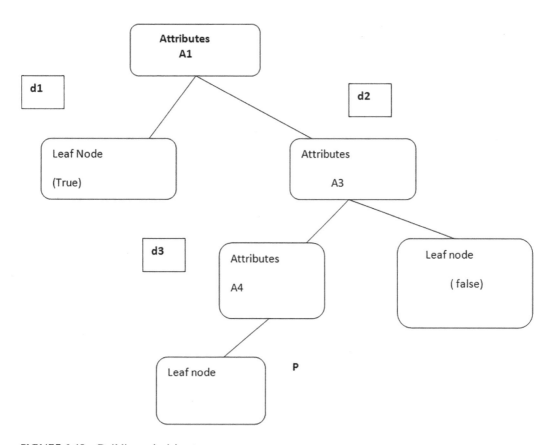

FIGURE 6.12   Building a decision tree.

Data d1: All the data in d1 belong to the same class. So it becomes a leaf node.

Data d2: The data d2 belong to a different class. So the data are divided further based on the attribute A3. d3 represent the data satisfying the condition A3. d4 represent the data that are not satisfying condition A3.

Data d3: The data d3 belong to a different class. So the data are divided further based on the attribute A4. d5 represent the data satisfying attribute A4, and d6 represent the data that are not satisfying the condition A4.

Data d5, d6, and d3: The data in d5, d6, and d3 belong to the same class. So these data belong to a leaf node.

6.4.5 ALGORITHMS USED FOR DECISION TREES

The dataset having many attributes (i.e., bank loans are given based on the attributes like employment status and salary) for root nodes are calculated from the following algorithm:

1. CART 4.5
2. ID3
3. C 4.5

In the ID3 algorithm, the information gain is used for the selection of root attributes. The information gain is calculated for each attribute, and the attributes having high information gain are selected as the root node. In C 4.5 algorithm, the gain information is used for the calculation of root attributes. The attributes having maximum gain ratio are selected as the root node. The CART 4.5 algorithm uses the Gini index to identify the attributes for the root node. The attribute having a low Gini index is selected as the root node.

S.No.	Algorithm	Parameter	Maximum/Minimum
1	ID3 algorithm	Information gain	Maximum
2	C 4.5	Gain index	Maximum
3	CART	Gini index	Minimum

6.4.5.1 ID3 Algorithm

If the decision tree has multiple attributes, then root node attributes can be selected using entropy and information gain.

Entropy: Entropy is a measure of disorder. Entropy is small for the sample with only positive or negative values. It is high for the half-positive or half-negative value of the sample. Entropy is defined as the average optimal number of bits to encode information about certainty and uncertainty about Sample S.

Information gain: Gain is a measure of uncertainty reduction. The sample having different classes has less information gain. Information gain is expressed in entropy.

Let S be the sample of training examples, $p+$ be the number of positive samples, and $p-$ be the number of negative samples. Then, sample entropy is shown in Figure 6.13.

$$\text{Entropy(S)} = p_+\left(-\log_2 p_+\right) + p_-\left(-\log_2 p_-\right)$$
$$= -p_+\left(\log_2 p_+\right) - p_-$$

(6.17)

Information gain of samples concerning attribute a is given as

$$\text{Gain(S, A)} = \text{Entropy(s)} - \sum \frac{Sv}{S}\text{entropy}\left(s_v\right)$$

(6.18)

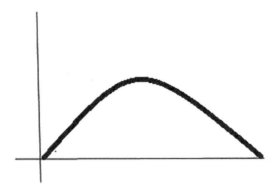

FIGURE 6.13   Entropy curve.

6.4.5.2   C 4.5 Algorithm

C 4.5 algorithm is used to generate decision tree, and it's developed by Ross Quinlan. It is an extension of the ID3 algorithm. The decision tree developed by using C 4.5 is used for classifications; it is called a statistical classifier. The data are split by using the gain ratio. The attributes having the highest gain ratio are used as root nodes. The C 4.5 is similar to the ID3 algorithm, but additionally, normalization is applied in this algorithm.

$$\text{Gain ratio} = \text{Gain of the attribute/Splitinfo}(A).$$

$$\text{Split info(A)} = \sum \frac{D_j}{D} \log_2 \left(\frac{D_j}{D} \right) \tag{6.19}$$

6.4.5.3   CART Algorithm

CART represents the classification and regression tree algorithm. Breiman discovered this algorithm in 1984. It's a simple binary tree where a tree has one root node and two child nodes. This algorithm can be used in classification and regression problems. The classification is done by using the Gini index. The Gini index represents the squared probability of each class.

$$\text{Gini index} = 1 - \sum_{k=0}^{n} p^2 \tag{6.20}$$

where n represents the number of probabilities.

6.4.6   Overfitting and Underfitting

Overfitting is the phenomenon in which the learning process matches exactly with all the training data. As a result, the model's accuracy is high for trained data and low for untrained data. Overfitting (Figure 6.14) occurs in decision trees when the tree is designed to fit all samples in the training dataset perfectly. Underfitting occurs when the training model does not capture the underlying pattern. Underfitting (Figure 6.14) is destroying the accuracy of our model of ML.

6.4.6.1   Overfitting

- Overfitting is a scenario in which the system is learned with the entire training data.
- It results in an inaccurate prediction of the data.
- Overfitting can be solved by using pruning (i.e., remove the decision node from the leaf node without reducing the accuracy).

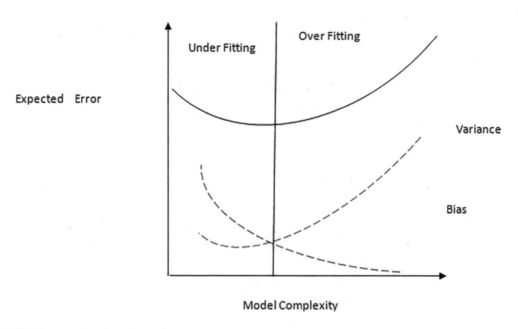

FIGURE 6.14   Overfit and underfit curve.

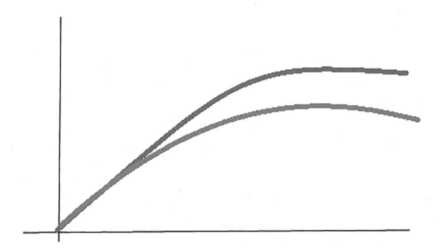

FIGURE 6.15   Accuracy of decision tree.

6.4.6.2   Underfitting

- Underfitting model is not a suitable model, and it will result in poor performance on training data.

A more splitting of data will result in a larger decision tree. The larger decision tree has less error rate. The overfitting results in a higher error on training data and a low error on test data. The accuracy is high on the training data but less on test data, as shown in Figure 6.15.

The overfitting occurs due to the following condition:

- Due to noise in the data
- Not enough data

Due to noise

In Figure 6.16, the noise point occurs in the training data. The system is trained with noise points on overfitting. This will produce an error in the test data "Not enough data."

The above training sample has two classes (one represents a circle and another represents a star). The number of data belonging to star classification is less at the bottom, as shown in Figure 6.17. This leads to misclassification.

6.4.6.3 Pruning to Avoid Overfitting

Overfitting can be eliminated by the following method:

- Prepruning
- Postpruning

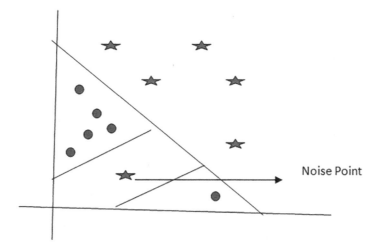

FIGURE 6.16   Decision tree with noise point.

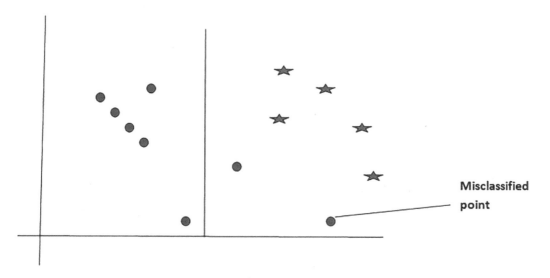

FIGURE 6.17   Decision tree with less data.

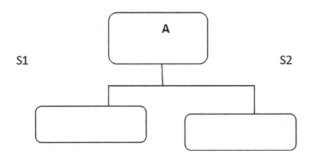

FIGURE 6.18   Prepruning at stage S1.

6.4.6.3.1   *Prepruning*

It is the process of pruning the decision tree on growing. Tree growth is stopped for negative gain or low positive benefit value. It is used to stop overfitting at an earlier stage.

Considering Figure 6.18, the root node is divided based on an attribute A. Calculate the gain of the decision tree at S1 and S2. The decision tree will be stopped at S1 and S2 for the low or negative value of gain, as shown in Figure 6.18.

6.4.6.3.2   *Postpruning*

Postpruning is also called backward pruning (Figure 6.19). First, a complete decision tree is constructed fully. Then, the accuracy of the tree is improved by removing the least significant branches. In postpruning, a decision tree is grown fully first. Several heuristics are used to delete subnodes. The error is measured on the whole tree (i.e., error (T)) and at point ST1 (i.e., error (st1)). If the error at ST1 is small than error T, then we can remove the subtree. The pruning can be done by using reduced error pruning, minimum error pruning, and cost-based pruning. The reduced error pruning is the simplest pruning algorithm.

In this method, the error is measured on the whole tree (i.e., error (T)) and at point ST1 (i.e., error (st1)). If the error at ST1 is small than error T, then we can remove the subtree. In the minimum error pruning, the error rate is calculated at each non-leaf node by pruning subtree and without pruning subtree. If the error rate of the subtree with pruning is high, then keep that subnode. In cost-based pruning, the error and cost are also considered for pruning the data.

6.4.7   ADVANTAGES AND DISADVANTAGES

6.4.7.1   Advantages

- **Interpretability**: Easy to understand. It can handle both categorical and numerical data
- Useful in data exploration and deal with missing data points
- Nonparametric method
- Capture nonlinear relationship
- Simple rule-based approach
- Feature scaling is not explicitly required for the algorithm work
- Quite useful for exploring a large dataset to pick out useful variables.
- Little effort is required for data preparation.

6.4.7.2   Disadvantages

- A highly complicated decision tree has a low bias.
- Overfitting is the major problem of decision tree
- It does not apply to the continuous variable
- Cost is high

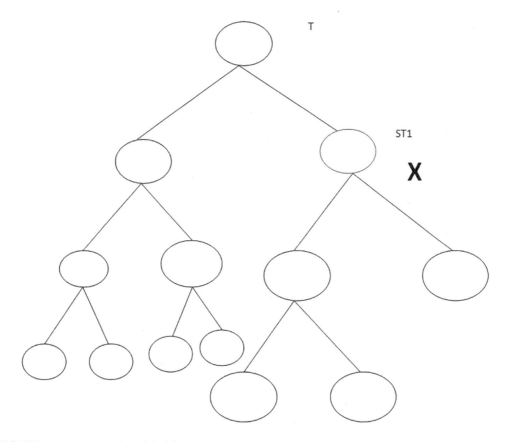

FIGURE 6.19   Postpruning of decision tree.

6.4.8   DECISION TREE EXAMPLES

Example 6.1: A Simple Decision Tree for Classification of Iris Flower

The problem describes the creation of a very simple decision tree using iris flower. The iris flower is classified based on the petal length. The iris flower with a petal length >2.45 belongs to versi-Setsoa and <1.75 belongs to Versicolor. The iris flower having petal length between 2.45 and 1.75 belongs to Verginica.

Draw a decision tree based on the data in Table 6.7 for the iris flower. The petal length of the iris flower differs for each flower. Take the petal length as an attribute for creating a decision tree.

Consider the decision tree shown in Figure 6.20 for the classification of the iris flower. The three types of iris flower are iris Versisetosa, Versicolor, and Virginica. The data are divided into two parts at the root node based on the petal width (i.e., petal width having a length >2.45 cm). A petal width >2.45 cm belongs to Versisetosa. Again at point B, the data are divided further based on the petal width. Petal widths >1.75 are classified as Versicolor, and petal widths <1.75 are classified as Virginica.

TABLE 6.7
Iris Flower Data

Flower	Petal Length
Versisetosa	>2.45 cm
Versicolor	<1.75 cm
Verginica	Between 2.45 and 1.75

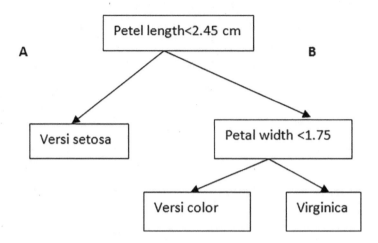

FIGURE 6.20   A decision tree for classification of iris flower.

Example 6.2: Oil Drill Using Decision Tree

Assume that you have land that you believe may have oil underground. There is only a 15% chance of having oil if you drill, but the payoff is $50,000. Therefore, it costs $15,000 to drill. Develop a decision tree for the above problem.

   Root node: In the above problem, the root node decides whether the land has oil or not. The root node has two probabilities. The land may or may not have fuel. This is referred to as a split point. The given data are divided into two parts at a split point. The land has oil, and the land does not have oil, as shown in Figure 6.21. Table 6.8 represents the profit for drilling the land having oil.

$$\text{The profit obtained for drilling the land} = 50,000 - 15,000 = 35,000$$

$$\text{The profit obtained for not drilling the land} = 0$$

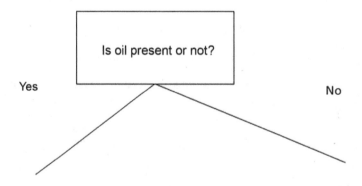

FIGURE 6.21   Decision tree for oil from the root node.

TABLE 6.8
Drilling the Land Having Oil

Status	Cost
The land is drilled	Cost=$15,000
The land is not drilled	Cost=0

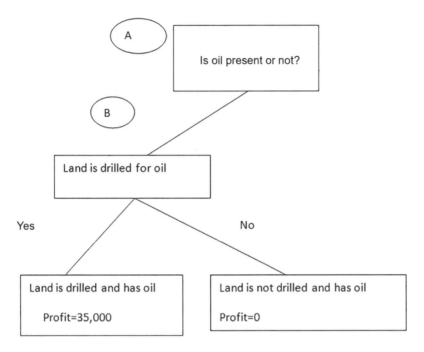

FIGURE 6.22   Decision tree for oil from the root node to leaf node.

TABLE 6.9
Drilling Land Having no Oil

Status	Cost
The land is drilled	$15,000
The land is not drilled	$0

Figure 6.22 represents the decision tree for drilling the land having oil.
   Table 6.9 represents the cost of drilling the land having no oil.

$$\text{Loss for drilling the land} = -15,000$$

$$\text{Loss for not drilling the land} = 0$$

Figure 6.23 represents the simple decision tree for drilling land. By using the decision tree, we can infer the profit and loss for drilling land for oil.

Example 6.3: Decision Tree for Purchasing Laptop

Create a decision tree for the following problem. Table 6.10 gives the details of purchasing a laptop.

CALCULATION OF MUTUAL INFORMATION

Mutual information between two random variables X and Y is given as

$$I(X;Y) = H(X) - H(X|Y)$$

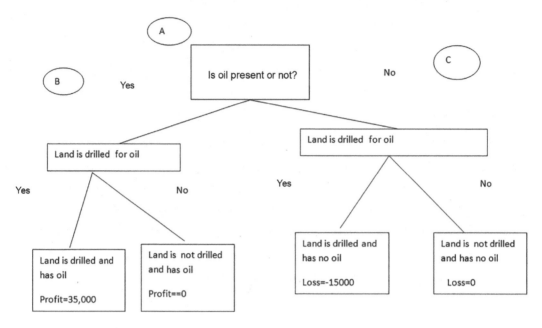

FIGURE 6.23   Decision tree for oil drill.

TABLE 6.10
Data for Purchasing Laptop

RID	Age	Earning	Class
1	≤30	High	No
2	≤30	High	No
3	31 ... 40	High	Yes
4	>40	Medium	Yes
5	>40	Low	Yes
6	>40	Low	No
7	31 ... 40	Low	Yes

where
     $I(X; Y)$ is mutual information for X and Y
     $H(X)$ is entropy of X
     $H(X|Y)$ is the conditional entropy for X given Y.

$$\text{The mutual information of two classes} = -4/7\ \log_2(4/7) - 3/7\ \log_2(3/7)$$

$$= 4/7\log_2(0.571) - 3/7\log_2(0.48)$$

$$= 4/7(0.808)\ + 3/7(1.05)$$

$$= 0.461 + 0.45$$

$$= 0.911$$

CALCULATION OF GAIN BASED ON AGE

RID	Age	Class
1	≤30	No
2	≤30	Yes
3	31 ... 40	Yes
4	>40	Yes
5	>40	Yes
6	>40	No
7	31 ... 40	Yes

For age, we have two values for ≤ 30(1 – No, 1 – Yes), 2 values for 31 ... 40 (2 – Yes, 0 – No), and 3 values for > 40(2 – Yes, 1 – No).

$$\text{Entropy} = 2/7(0) + 2/7(0) + 3/7\left(-2/7 \ \log_2(2/7) - 1/7 \ \log_2(1/7)\right)$$

$$= 3/7\left(2/7(-1.83) + 1/7(-2.81)\right)$$

$$= 3/7(0.5228 + 0.4014)$$

$$= 0.3961$$

$$\text{Gain} = 0.911 - 0.391$$

$$= 0.52$$

CALCULATION BASED ON EARNING

RID	Earning	Class
1	High	No
2	High	No
3	High	Yes
4	Medium	Yes
5	Low	Yes
6	Low	No
7	Low	Yes

For earning, we have three values for high (2 – No, 1 – Yes), one value for medium (1 – Yes, 0 – No), and three values for low (2 – Yes, 1 – No).

$$\text{Entropy} = 3/7\left(-1/7\log_2(1/7) - (2/7) \ \log_2(2/7)\right)$$

$$+ 0 + 3/7\left(-2/7 \ \log_2(-2/7) - 1/7 \ \log_2(-1/7)\right)$$

$$= 0.7922$$

$$\text{Gain} = 0.911 - 0.7922$$

$$= 0.1188$$

Since age has the highest again, the data are divided based on the age factor, as shown in Figure 6.24.

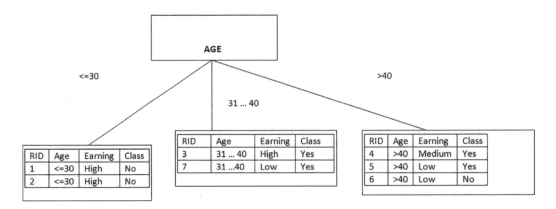

FIGURE 6.24   Decision tree for laptop purchase from the root node.

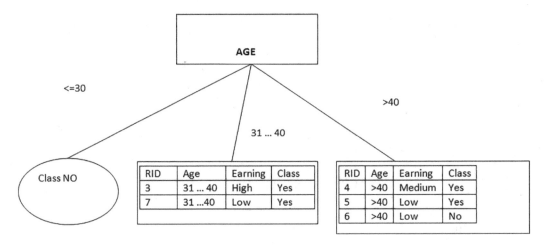

FIGURE 6.25   Decision tree for laptop purchase from the root node to leaf node.

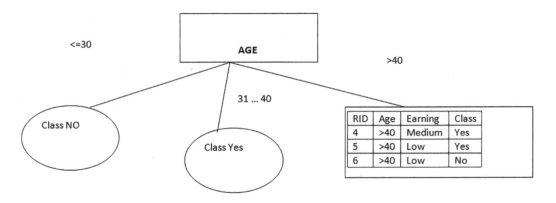

FIGURE 6.26   Decision tree for laptop purchase from the root node to leaf node.

In the above decision diagram, the age≤30 falls under No class, as shown in Figure 6.25. Similarly, the age 31–40 belongs to the Yes class, as shown in Figure 6.26.

The age >40 can be subdivided into two categories based on the earning. Using the above decision tree, we can infer the probability of purchasing a laptop, as shown in Figure 6.27.

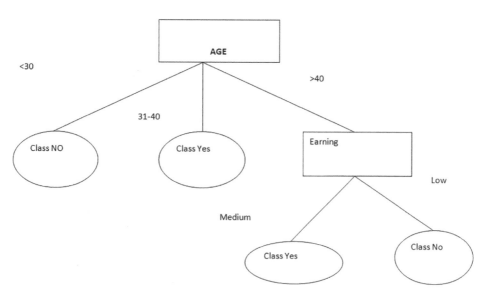

FIGURE 6.27 Decision tree for laptop purchase from the root node to leaf node.

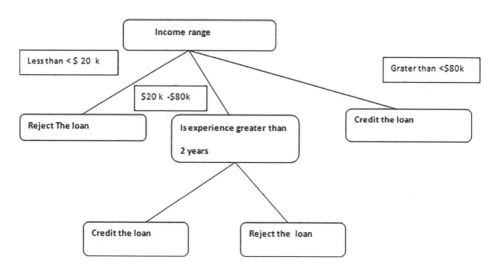

FIGURE 6.28 Decision tree for crediting the loan.

Example 6.4: A Simple Decision Tree for Crediting Loan

Create a decision tree for crediting the loan.

1. If the income is <$20k, then no need to credit the loan.
2. If income is between $20k and 80k, credit the loan if the experience is >2 years.
3. If income is >$80k, credit the loan.

A decision tree is constructed based on the income range. The application having income <$ 20k is rejected and income >$80k is credited with a loan. An applicant with a salary between $20k and $80k is divided further based on the experience details. From the decision tree shown in Figure 6.28, the loans are credited for a person having experience >2 years and having a salary >$20k to $80k and also for the person having a salary >$80.

Example 6.5: Calculate the Entropy for the Given Sample

Climate	Temperature	Humidity	Play
Sunny	Hot	High	No
Rainy	Mild	Normal	Yes
Sunny	Mild	Normal	Yes
Rainy	Mild	High	No
Sunny	Hot	Normal	Yes
Rainy	Cool	Normal	No

The entropy of the dataset is the sum of entropy for Yes and the sum of entropy for No.
There are four Yes and two No on the weather data.
The **entropy of the weather dataset**:

$$H(s) = \sum -p(c)\log_2 p(c)$$

$$= 0.3933 + 0.523$$

$$= 0.9163$$

$$P\,\text{yes} = (-4/6)\log_2(4/6) = -(0.66)(-0.599) = 0.3933$$

$$P\,\text{no} = (-2/6)\log_2(2/6) = 0.333 X 1.584 = 0.523$$

Example 6.6: Construct a Decision Tree for the Data Given in Table 6.11

There are five positive and five negative data

$$\text{Entropy} = (-5/10)\log 2(5/10) + (-5/10)\log 2(5/10) = 1$$

The results of gain based on age are presented in Table 6.12.

TABLE 6.11
Positive and Negative Data

Age	Competition	Type	Profit
Old	Yes	Software	Down
Old	No	Software	Down
Old	No	Hardware	Down
Mid	Yes	Software	Down
Mid	Yes	Hardware	Down
Mid	No	Hardware	Up
Mid	No	Software	Up
New	Yes	Software	UP
New	No	Hardware	Up
New	No	Software	Up

$$\text{Entropy}(\text{old}) = 3/3\log_2(3/3) = 0$$

$$\text{Entropy}(\text{mid}) = 2/4\log_2(2/4) + (2/4)\log 2(2/4) = 1$$

$$\text{Entropy}(\text{new}) = 3/3\log(3/3) = 0$$

$$\text{Entropy}(\text{age}) = 3/10*0 + 4/10*1 + 3/10*0 = 0.4$$

$$\text{Gain} = \text{Class entropy} - \text{Entropy}(\text{age}) = 1 - 0.4 = 0.6$$

The results based on competition are presented in Table 6.13.

$$\text{Entropy}(\text{yes}) = 1/4\log_2(1/4) + 3/4\log_2(3/4) = 0.81127$$

$$\text{Entropy}(\text{no}) = 4/6\ \log_2(4/6) + 2/6\ \log_2(2/6) = 0.918295$$

$$\text{Entropy}(\text{competition}) = 4/10*0.81127 + 6/10(0.9182) = 0.8745$$

$$\text{Gain} = \text{Class entropy} - \text{Entropy}(\text{competition}) = 1 - 0.8745 = 0.1245$$

The results based on profit are presented in Table 6.14.

$$\text{Entropy}(\text{software}) = 1/2\log_2(1/2) + 1/2\log_2(1/2) = 1$$

$$\text{Entropy}(\text{hardware}) = 1/2\log_2(1/2) + 1/2\log_2(1/2) = 1$$

$$\text{Entropy}(\text{type}) = 2/4(1) + 2/4(1) = 4/4 = 1$$

$$\text{Gain} = \text{Class entropy} - \text{Entropy}(\text{type}) = 1 - 1 = 0$$

TABLE 6.12

Calculation of Gain Based on Age

Age	Positive	Negative	$I(P_i, N_i)$
Old	0	3	0
Mid	2	2	1
New	3	0	0

TABLE 6.13

Calculation Based on Competition

Competition	Positive	Negative	$I(P_i, N_i)$
Yes	1	3	0.81127
No	4	2	0.918295

TABLE 6.14

Calculation Based on Profit

Type	Positive	Negative	$I(P_i, N_i)$
Software	1	1	1
Hardware	1	1	1

TABLE 6.15

Age and Profit

Age	Profit
Old	Down
Old	Down
Old	Down
Mid	Down
Mid	Down
Mid	Up
Mid	Up
New	UP
New	Up
New	Up

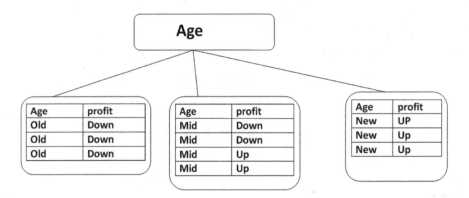

FIGURE 6.29   Decision tree for attribute age.

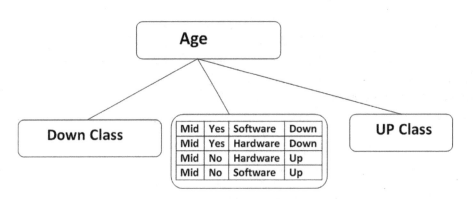

FIGURE 6.30   Decision tree with a leaf node.

Table 6.15 shows that age has high information gain. This is because the decision tree starts from the age attribute, as shown in Figure 6.29.

In the above tree, the old and new parameters have a negative sample. So it represents the leaf node as shown in Figure 6.30.

Again, the data are divided based on the competition, as shown in Figure 6.31.

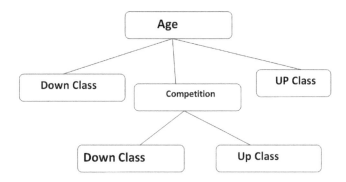

FIGURE 6.31 Decision tree for purchasing.

Example 6.7: The Toy Industry

ABC toys Pvt. Ltd is considering the addition of a new toy to its existing product line. Three alternative courses of action are available.

a. Work overtime to meet the demand for the new toy. Overtime expenses are estimated at Rs. 20,000 per month.
b. Install new equipment for which fixed expenses per month are expected at Rs.80,000.
c. Lease (rent) a machine at the rate of Rs. 35,000 per month.

Variable costs associated with the above three alternatives are Rs. 9, Rs. 7, and Rs. 8 per toy. The price per unit of the toy, which is independent of the manufacturing alternative, is fixed at Rs. 15. The expected demand for the toys is given below.

10,000 pieces with a probability of 0.5
20,000 pieces with a probability of 0.3
50,000 pieces with a probability of 0.2

Which alternatives should the company adapt to manufacture the toy?

GIVEN DATA

ABC toys had decided to add a new product. They have three alternate courses.

1. If workers work overtime, they are paid Rs. 20,000 per month with a variable cost of Rs. 9 per toy
2. If new equipment is installed, they have to pay 80,000 per month Rs. 7 per toy
3. Lease the machine at the rate of 35,000 per month Rs. 8 per toy

The sales price of toys=Rs. 15

EXPECTED DEMAND

10,000 pieces with a probability of 0.5
   20,000 pieces with a probability of 0.3
   50,000 pieces with a probability of 0.2
   There are three alternatives from a decision node as represented in Figure 6.32.
   Each alternative node has three demands, as shown in Table 6.16.

$$\text{Profit} = 10,000 \times 15 - 10,000 \times 9 - 20,000 = 15,0000 - 90,000 - 20,000$$

$$= 60,000 - 20,000 = 40,000$$

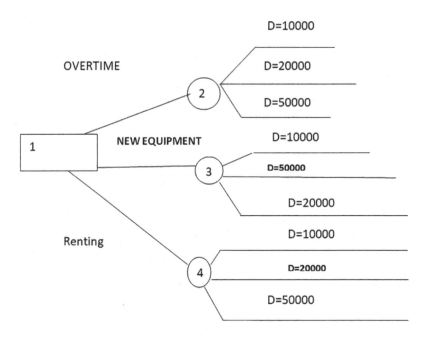

FIGURE 6.32 Decision tree for purchasing new equipment.

TABLE 6.16
Alternatives and Their Demands

Alternatives	Price per Unit	V.C/Unit	Monthly Profit		
			10,000	20,000	50,000
Overtime	15	9	40,000	100,000	280,000
New equipment	15	7	0	80,000	320,000
Leasing	15	8	35,000	105,000	315,000

The decision tree for purchasing new equipment with profit value is shown in Figure 6.33.

$$At\,point\,2 = 0.5 \times 40,000 + 0.3 \times 100,000 + 0.2 \times 280,000 = 106,000$$

$$At\,the\,point\,3 = 0.5 \times 0 + 0.3 \times 80,000 + 0.2 \times 320,000 = 88,000$$

$$At\,point\,4 = 0.5 \times 35,000 + 0.3 \times 105,000 + 0.2 \times 315,000 = 112,000$$

The decision tree for final equipment purchase is shown in Figure 6.34.

Example 6.8: Construct a Decision Tree for the Data in Table 6.17

The different nodes in the decision tree are illustrated in Figure 6.35.
First, we have to draw a decision node, as shown in Figure 6.36.
The outcome of stocks, MF, and bonds is growing and declining. Let us consider the stocks, growing at 0.4 and declining at 0.6. The payoff is 70 and −13. The decision tree is shown in Figure 6.37.
Similarly, we have to construct for other MF and bonds. The decision tree for stocks and MF is shown in Figure 6.38 and for stocks and bonds in Figure 6.39.

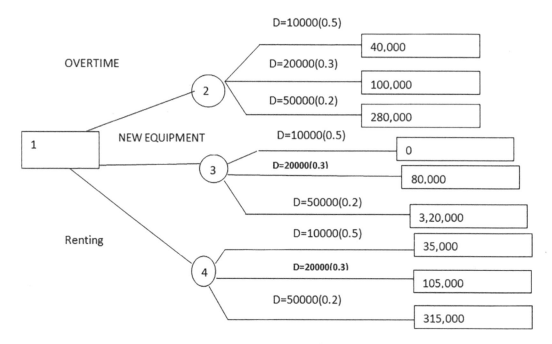

FIGURE 6.33 Decision tree for purchasing new equipment with profit value.

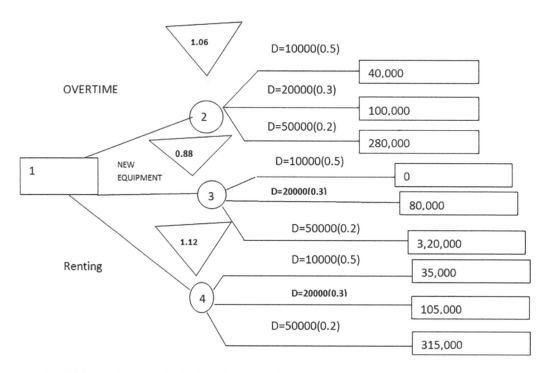

FIGURE 6.34 Decision tree for final purchasing equipment.

TABLE 6.17
Growing Declining Data

	Growing	Declining
Stock	70	−13
Mutual funds	53	−5
Bonds	20	20
Probability	0.4	0.6

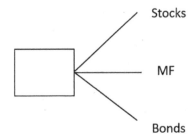

FIGURE 6.35   Symbol for decision tree.

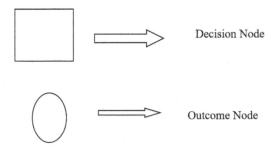

FIGURE 6.36   Root node for decision tree.

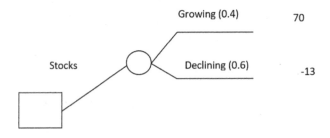

FIGURE 6.37   Decision tree for stocks.

The expected value of the tree for sticks = $0.4 \times 70 + 0.6 \times (-13) = 20.2$

The expected value of the decision tree for MF = $53 \times 0.4 + 0.6 \times (-5) = 18.2$

Since bonds have 20, no calculation is required. The expected values are given in Table 6.18. Among these values, the stocks have a high value. So the decision should be done on the stocks.

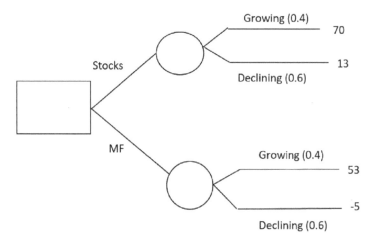

FIGURE 6.38   Decision tree for stocks and MF.

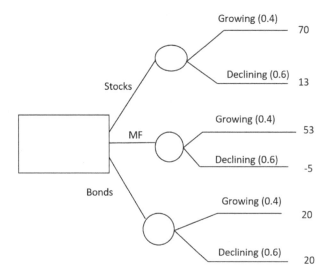

FIGURE 6.39   Decision tree for stocks, MF, and bonds.

TABLE 6.18
Expected Results for Growing Declining Data

S.No.	Company	Expected Value
1	Stocks	20.2
2.	MF	18.2
3	Bonds	20

Example 6.9: Construct a Decision Tree for the Data Given in Table 6.19

The probability for mobile production is 0.60 for profit and 0.40 for loss.
    There are two technologies, A and B (Figure 6.40). So there are two possibilities (technology A and technology B) (Figure 6.41).
$400,000 is credited for the technology A (profit)
    $200,000 is credited for the technology A (loss)

TABLE 6.19
Mobile Production Data

	Mobile Phase Production	
	Profit	Loss
Technology A	$400,000	$200,000
Technology B	$300,000	$150,000

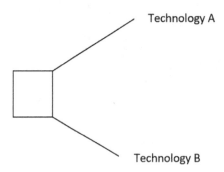

FIGURE 6.40   Classifying based on technology A and technology B.

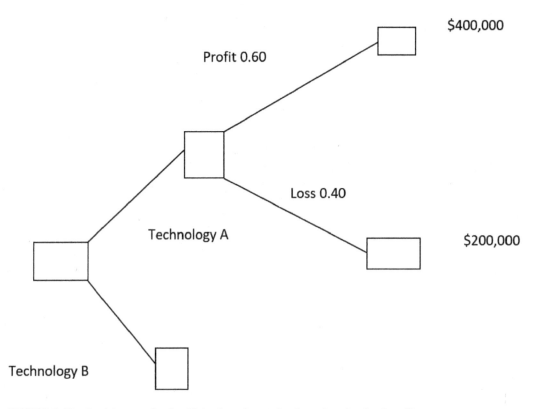

FIGURE 6.41   Decision tree for classifying based on technology A and technology B..

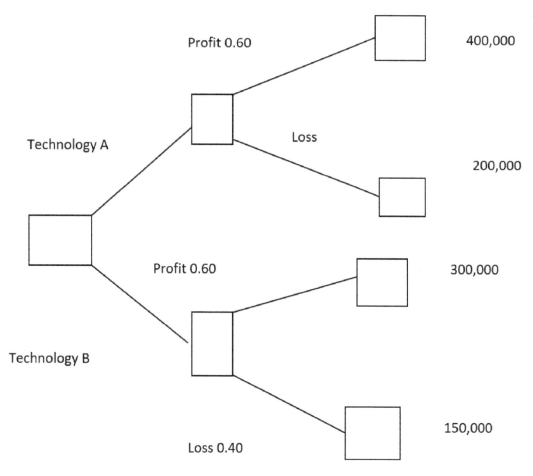

Profit 0.60   400,000

Technology A

Loss

200,000

Profit 0.60   300,000

Technology B

150,000

Loss 0.40

FIGURE 6.42 Decision tree for profit and loss.

TECHNOLOGY A

Profit		Loss	
Amount	Percentage	Amount	Percentage
$400,000	0.60	$200,000	0.40

The decision tree for profit and loss is shown in Figure 6.42
$300,000 is credited for the technology B (profit)
$150,000 is credited for the technology B (loss)

TECHNOLOGY B

Profit		Loss	
Amount	Percentage	Amount	Percentage
$300,000	0.60	$150,000	0.40

$$\text{Expected value for technology A} = 400,000 \times 0.60 + 200,000 \times 0.40$$

$$= 2,40,000 + 80,000$$

$$= 3,20,000$$

$$\text{Expected value for technology B} = 300,000 \times 0.60 + 150,000 \times 0.40$$

$$= 1,80,000 + 60,000$$

$$= 2,40,000$$

Hence, we conclude that among the groups, technology A has the highest value.

Example 6.10: Decision to Buy a New Product

A company wants to decide on a new product. They can buy a new product, or they can make new products. There may be strong demand for the product or less demand for the product. The strong demand for making the product is $25 million, and the weak demand for making the product is $20 million loss. The strong demand for making the product is $5 million and weak demand is $5 million loss. Draw the decision tree for the above problem.

The root node has two probabilities: They can either buy or make the new product. The corresponding decision tree is shown in Figure 6.43.

The decision tree is divided further for strong demand and weak demand, as presented in Figure 6.44. The cost of strong demand is $25 million, and the cost of weak demand is –$20 million.

The cost of strong demand for buying is $5 million, and the cost of weak demand is –$5 million, as shown in Figure 6.45.

$$\text{The expected value for making the product} = (25 \times 0.75) - 20(0.20)$$

$$= 18.75 - 4$$

$$= 14.75$$

$$\text{The expected value for buying the product} = (0.75 \times 5) - (5 \times 0.20)$$

$$= 3.75 - 1$$

$$= 2.75$$

6.4.9 REGRESSION USING DECISION TREE

Decision tree regression extracts the features of the object and trains the model to predict the data. The topmost node represents the root node, and the final node represents the leaf node. A decision

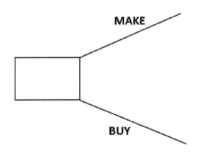

FIGURE 6.43   Root node for decision tree.

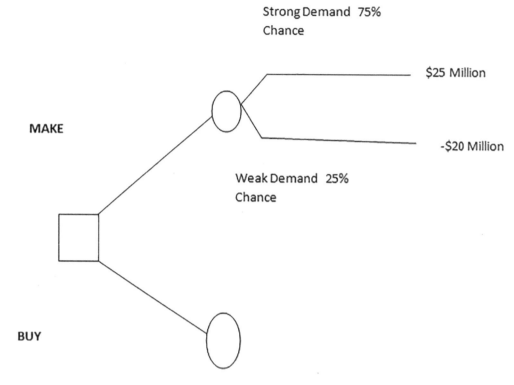

FIGURE 6.44 Decision tree for profit and loss (make).

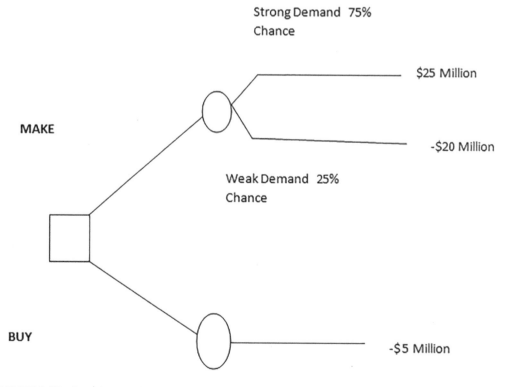

FIGURE 6.45 Decision tree for profit and loss (buy).

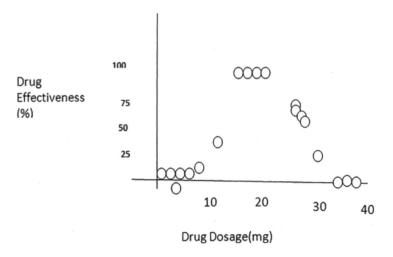

FIGURE 6.46   Medical data for nonlinear regression.

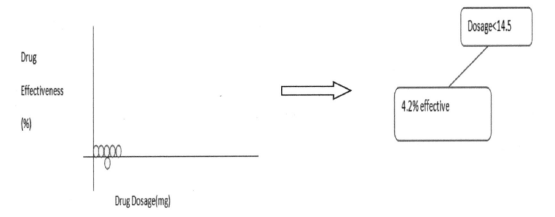

FIGURE 6.47   Dosage <14.5.

node has two or more sub-branches that represent the value to be tested. The regression tree will predict the value.

Consider the following example for the regression tree. A medical company produces a drug for the cold, and they have to determine a dosage of medicine. The medicine is given for different dosages, and effectiveness is predicted by using a regression tree.

It's difficult to solve the data in Figure 6.46 using linear regression. So it can be solved by using a non-regression tree. A regression tree classification is done using numeric values, while in a classification tree, the data are classified using true or false conditions. The above decision tree has low effectiveness for low dosage and high dosage. Introduce good results for medium dosage. The regression tree starts if the dosage is <14.5 mL. The six samples belong to the dosage <14.5 mL, and they have 4.2% of dosage effectiveness (Figure 6.47).

A dosage value >29 mL has 2.5% dosage effectiveness. The medium dosage has 52.8% effectiveness. A dosage value >23.5mL has 100% dosage effectiveness. The corresponding decision tree is shown in Figure 6.48.

A regression tree is used for the prediction. In Figure 6.49, a regression decision tree is constructed for the iris flower. Data are divided into the root node based on the condition $x1 \geq 0.1973$. Again, the data are divided further until it reaches the leaf node. Suppose if you want to predict the value 0.71, it traverses along the path and it reaches the value 0.1106.

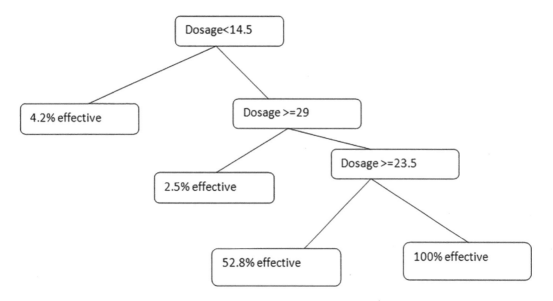

FIGURE 6.48   Decision tree for medical data.

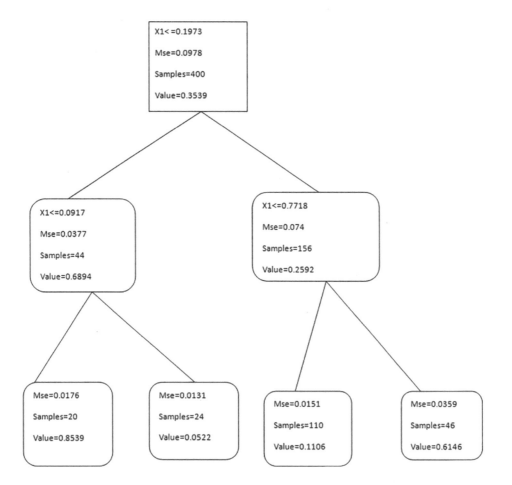

FIGURE 6.49   Regression decision tree.

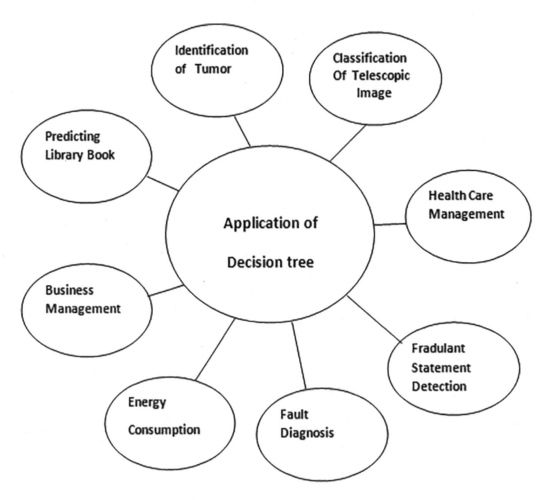

FIGURE 6.50   Application of decision tree.

6.4.10   REAL-WORLD EXAMPLES

A decision tree can be used in real-world problems. Some of the applications of the decision tree (Figure 6.50) covered in this section are as follows:

1. Predicting library book usage
2. Identification of tumor
3. Classification of telescope image
4. Healthcare management
5. Fault diagnosis
6. Energy consumption
7. Fraudulent statement detection

6.4.10.1   Predicting Library Book

A decision tree is used to predict the future use of the library book. Harvard College Library uses this decision tree algorithm to move the book to off-site storage. The library has short storage space and stores the low-demand book into remote storage. The wider library in Harvard College has a lack of space problem. So they have to remove the old book and less useful modern book to remote storage. The books having lower expected future usage have to be moved to the remote storage.

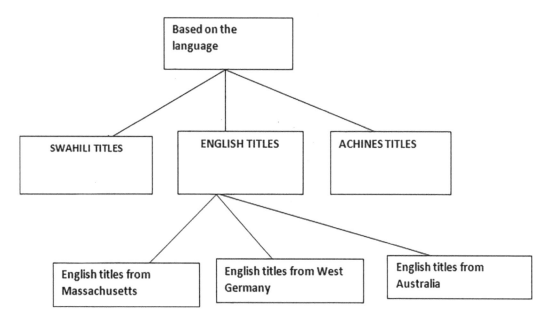

FIGURE 6.51 A simple decision tree for predicting books in the library.

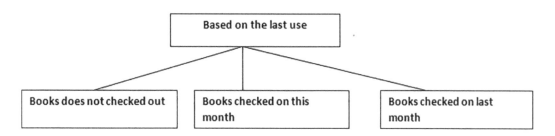

FIGURE 6.52 A decision tree based on the single criteria.

Comprehensive statistics have to be automated to select the book. The six attributes, such as check-out details (number of past and last use), publication date, last use, language, country, and alphabetic prefix, are taken. Based on the EAR value, the book is moved to the off-site storage.

Figure 6.51 represents the simple decision tree. First, the tree is classified based on the language and then classified based on the publication country. The trees are also constructed based on the single criteria (i.e., last use) as shown in Figure 6.52.

Figure 6.53 represents the decision tree classification based on Fussler and Simon's choice policy. First, a decision tree is constructed based on the root nodes divided between the language attribute and children of the root node divided based on the publication date.

The ID3 algorithm is used for designing a decision tree. First, the information gain is calculated for the different attributes, and the tree with the greatest gain is selected to divide the data. Then, the nodes are created based on the checkout. Finally, the smoothed tree is evaluated by using pruning.

6.4.10.2 Identification of Tumor

The decision tree plays a major role in medical decision-making. The single decision tree boosted the decision tree, and the decision tree forest is used in the decision tree. Decision tree classification provides an effective method of categorizing datasets. Decision-making can be done at the training and testing stages. For example, breast cancer is the most commonly diagnosed cancer among

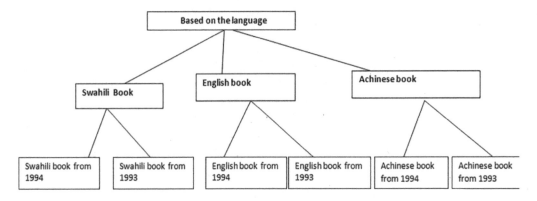

FIGURE 6.53 Fussler and Simon's choice policy-based decision tree.

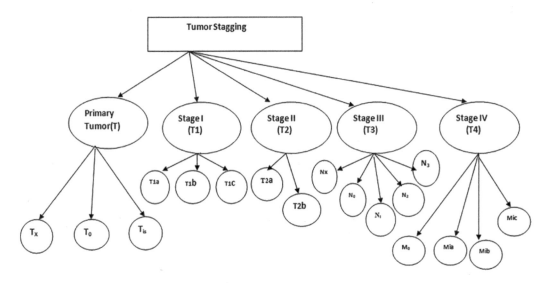

FIGURE 6.54 Decision tree for tumor identification.

women, and early breast cancer diagnosis plays a major role in reducing mortality. On the other hand, mammograms have a high percentage of missed cancer cases. These can be identified properly by using the decision support system.

The brain tumor is a cluster of brain-growing abnormal cells. It can happen at almost any age in any person. It may even vary from one therapy session to the next, but it may not have the same effects for each patient. MRI images are preprocessed for feature extraction. First, the noise is introduced by applying median filtering techniques. Next, power law transformation is used to enhance the image. Finally, the preprocessed image is given to the decision tree for further classification. Tumors can be identified by the following features such as tumor differentiation, cellularity, mitotic count, age, location, and cell type. The decision tree approach produces higher accuracy compared to the other classifications.

Figure 6.54 represents the identification of tumor in lungs. If the lung tumor is <3 cm, it belongs to class primary tumor and stage I. The tumor measuring 3–5 cm belongs to the stage II tumor. The tumor measuring 5–7 cm belongs to the stage III tumor. The tumor measuring >7 cm belongs to the stage IV tumor. The tumors are further classified based on the length, as shown in Table 6.20.

TABLE 6.20
Tumor Type and Length

S. No.	Tumor Type	Description
1	T1a	<1 cm
2	T1b	1–2 cm
3	T1C	2–3 cm
4	T2a	3–4 cm
5	T2b	4–5 cm

6.4.10.3 Classification of Telescope Image

The telescopic images are stars, galaxies, cosmic rays, plate defects, and other types of objects in the sky. A decision tree classifier is used to identify cosmic rays hit in telescope images. The decision tree is used to classify the stars and cosmic rays from a telescopic image. The features are extracted from the telescopic images and are classified further by using a decision tree. The correct attributes are selected by using the CART algorithm. Figure 6.55 represents the decision tree for the classification of telescope image.

The x_{20} and x_{16} are attributes for the decision tree. This method produces 95% of accuracy.

6.4.10.4 Business Management

In recent years, most of the companies have their database. We can extract the data from the database using a decision tree because data can be extracted based on the domain. It can also be used in fraud detection or customer relationship management. Customer relationship management is used to investigate the frequency of accessing online services. The usage of data collects the information, and corresponding information is used for user recommendation. The online shopping users are divided into two equal parts: the user using online shopping frequently and rarely. The time needed by the customer for the transaction, degree of human resources, price of the product, and how urgent the product is needed are also considered in this model. Decision trees produce a successful result in online shopping.

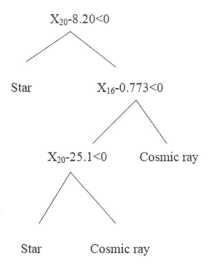

FIGURE 6.55 Decision tree for classification of telescope image.

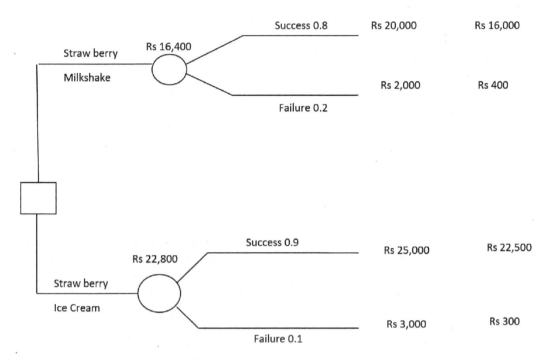

FIGURE 6.56 Decision tree for business management.

TABLE 6.21

Success Rate and Cost

S.No.	Description	Rate	Cost
1	Strawberry milkshake – success	0.8	20,000
2	Strawberry milkshake – failure	0.2	2,000
3	Strawberry ice cream – success	0.9	25,000
4	Strawberry ice cream – failure	0.1	3,000

The decision tree in Figure 6.56 is used for selecting the strawberry milkshake or strawberry ice cream business. Among the two businesses, the success and failure rate and cost are given in Table 6.21.

$$\text{Total estimated cost for strawberry milkshake} = 0.8 \times 20,000 + 0.2 \times 2,000$$

$$= 16,000 + 400$$

$$= 16,400$$

$$\text{Total estimated cost for strawberry ice cream} = 0.9 \times 25,00 + 0.1 \times 3,000$$

$$= 22,500 + 300$$

$$= 22,800$$

Among these two estimations, it's proved that the production of strawberry ice cream has more profit than the production of strawberry milkshake.

6.4.10.5 Fault Diagnosis

Faults should be detected, identified, and removed as quickly as possible on transmission lines. In power transmission line safety, error detection and defective phase identification (fault classification) are important. The measured voltage and current data at the relay point are used to identify and diagnose the fault with or without fault resistance in the line. A three-phase fault current is given as input to the decision tree for fault detection. In the case of fault classification, the three-phase currents and the zero-sequence current samples for half cycle are used as inputs to the decision tree to categorize all ten types of faults. The decision tree (Figure 6.57) has provided accurate results to identify and classify defects in the power system. DT also provides higher classification accuracy compared to SVM. The DT-based approach is validated for wide variations in the power system network operating conditions and can thus be applied to online fault detection for large power system networks.

6.4.10.6 Healthcare Management

A decision tree may be used in the management of health care. Data mining is used to collect and view useful information in easy-to-interpret visualizations from large datasets. The medical use of decision trees includes the diagnosis of a symptom-specific medical disorder. The categories identified by the decision tree could be either separate clinical subtypes or a disease. With the advent of electronic data processing, the number of regularly tracked variables in clinical settings has increased dramatically. Many of these variables are of limited significance and should therefore likely not be included in experiments on data mining. However, many important input variables are to be used in decision-making tree models. Figure 6.58 represents the decision tree for fault identification.

6.4.10.7 Decision Tree in Data Mining

Data mining can be done on the decision tree on segmented images. Image segment is a process of extracting useful information from the image. The pixel with gray value ranges from 180 to 240, and its local variation >80 and its slope variation >0.5 are selected for segmentation. For example, the image in Figure 6.59a is segmented into Figure 6.59b using the decision tree.

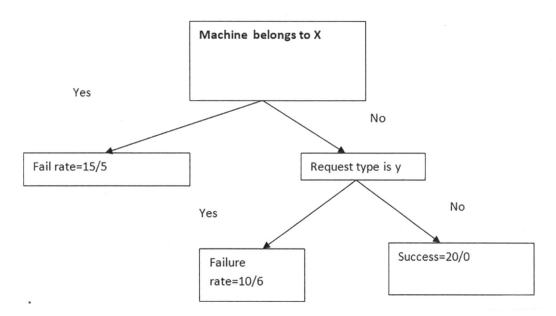

FIGURE 6.57 Fault detection using decision tree.

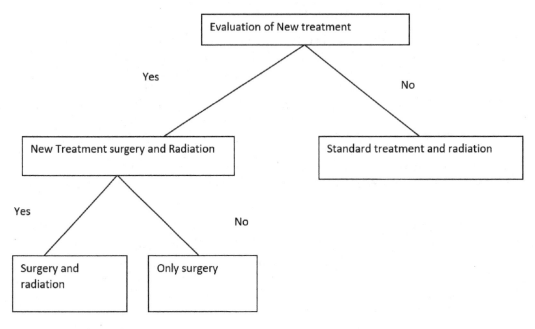

FIGURE 6.58   Healthcare management in decision tree.

FIGURE 6.59   Segmenting data noise.

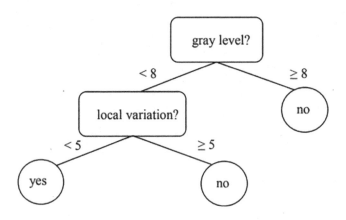

FIGURE 6.60   Segmenting data noise decision tree.

The outside contour is identified by checking the gray level, as shown in Figure 6.60. If the gray level is greater than eight and local variation is greater than five then the output of the decision tree is "no".

6.4.11 DECISION TREES IN PRACTICE USING PYTHON

Decision trees are widely used supervised models for classification and regression tasks. These classifiers build a sequence of straightforward if/else rules on the training data through which they predict the target value. Decision trees are simple to interpret thanks to their structure and, therefore, visualize the modeled tree.

By using the sklearn export_graphviz function, we can display the tree within a Jupyter Notebook. For this demonstration, we'll use the sklearn wine dataset.

```python
# Import packages for Decision Tree& GRAPHVIZ
from sklearn.tree importDecisionTreeClassifier, export_graphviz
from sklearn import tree
from sklearn.datasets import load_wine
from IPython.display import SVG  #Scalable Vector Graphics
from graphviz import Source
from IPython.display import display


# load Dataset
Data = load_wine() ## Since the data set is part of the package; we can
directly load it
```

The OUTPUT is shown below. Previewing gives all kinds of information about the dataset. #(Please note: the result contains actual data sample, Array information, Data set #Characteristics, Summary Statistics, Attributes Values to name a few. This will help the user to #understand the dataset.)

```
{'data': array([[1.423e+01, 1.710e+00, 2.430e+00, ..., 1.040e+00,
3.920e+00,1.065e+03],
    [1.320e+01, 1.780e+00, 2.140e+00, ..., 1.050e+00, 3.400e+00,1.050e+03],
    [1.316e+01, 2.360e+00, 2.670e+00, ..., 1.030e+00, 3.170e+00, 1.185e+03],
    ...,
    [1.327e+01, 4.280e+00, 2.260e+00, ..., 5.900e-01, 1.560e+00,8.350e+02],
    [1.317e+01, 2.590e+00, 2.370e+00, ..., 6.000e-01, 1.620e+00,8.400e+02],
    [1.413e+01, 4.100e+00, 2.740e+00, ..., 6.100e-01, 1.600e+00,5.600e+02]]),
 'target': array([0, 0, 0, 0, 0, 0, 0, 0, 0, 0, 0, 0, 0, 0, 0, 0, 0, 0,
0, 0, 0, 0,
        0, 0, 0, 0, 0, 0, 0, 0, 0, 0, 0, 0, 0, 0, 0, 0, 0, 0, 0, 0, 0, 0,
        0, 0, 0, 0, 0, 0, 0, 0, 0, 0, 0, 0, 0, 0, 0, 1, 1, 1, 1, 1, 1, 1,
        1, 1, 1, 1, 1, 1, 1, 1, 1, 1, 1, 1, 1, 1, 1, 1, 1, 1, 1, 1, 1, 1,
        1, 1, 1, 1, 1, 1, 1, 1, 1, 1, 1, 1, 1, 1, 1, 1, 1, 1, 1, 1, 1, 1,
        1, 1, 1, 1, 1, 1, 1, 1, 1, 1, 1, 1, 1, 1, 1, 1, 1, 1, 1, 1, 2, 2,
        2, 2, 2, 2, 2, 2, 2, 2, 2, 2, 2, 2, 2, 2, 2, 2, 2, 2, 2, 2, 2, 2,
        2, 2, 2, 2, 2, 2, 2, 2, 2, 2, 2, 2, 2, 2, 2, 2, 2, 2, 2, 2, 2, 2,
        2, 2]),
'target_names': array(['class_0', 'class_1', 'class_2'], dtype='<U7'),
 'DESCR': '.. _wine_dataset:\n\nWine recognition dataset\n--------------
----------\n\n**Data Set Characteristics:**\n\n    :Number of Instances:
178 (50 in each of three classes)\n    :Number of Attributes: 13 numeric,
predictive attributes and the class\n    :Attribute Information:\n \t\t-
Alcohol\n \t\t- Malic acid\n \t\t- Ash\n\t\t- Alcalinity of ash  \n
\t\t- Magnesium\n\t\t- Total phenols\n \t\t- Flavanoids\n \t\t-
Nonflavanoid phenols\n \t\t- Proanthocyanins\n\t\t- Color intensity\n
\t\t- Hue\n \t\t- OD280/OD315 of diluted wines\n \t\t- Proline\n\n    -
class:\n          - class_0\n          - class_1\n              -
class_2\n\t\t\n    :Summary Statistics:\n      \n===========================
```

```
==== ===== ======= =====\n                                        Min   Max
Mean      SD\n      ============================ ==== ===== ======= =====\n
Alcohol:                          11.0  14.8   13.0   0.8\n    Malic Acid:
0.74  5.80   2.34  1.12\n   Ash:                                1.36  3.23
2.36  0.27\n      Alcalinity of Ash:           10.6  30.0   19.5   3.3\n
Magnesium:                        70.0 162.0   99.7  14.3\n    Total
Phenols:                    0.98  3.88   2.29  0.63\n    Flavanoids:
0.34  5.08   2.03  1.00\n   Nonflavanoid Phenols:               0.13  0.66
0.36  0.12\n      Proanthocyanins:             0.41  3.58   1.59  0.57\n
Colour Intensity:                 1.3  13.0    5.1   2.3\n    Hue:
0.48  1.71   0.96  0.23\n   OD280/OD315 of diluted wines: 1.27  4.00
2.61  0.71\n      Proline:                     278  1680    746   315\n
============================ ==== ===== ======= =====\n\n    :Missing
Attribute Values: None\n    :Class Distribution: class_0 (59), class_1
(71), class_2 (48)\n    :Creator: R.A. Fisher\n    :Donor: Michael
Marshall (MARSHALL%PLU@io.arc.nasa.gov)\n    :Date: July, 1988\n\nThis is
a copy of UCI ML Wine recognition datasets.\nhttps://archive.ics.uci.edu/
ml/machine-learning-databases/wine/wine.data\n\nThe data is the results
of a chemical analysis of wines grown in the same\nregion in Italy by
three different cultivators. There are thirteen different\nmeasurements
taken for different constituents found in the three types of\nwine.\n\
nOriginal Owners: \n\nForina, M. et al, PARVUS - \nAn Extendible Package
for Data Exploration, Classification and Correlation. \nInstitute of
Pharmaceutical and Food Analysis and Technologies,\nViaBrigata Salerno,
16147 Genoa, Italy.\nCitation:\n\nLichman, M. (2013). UCI Machine
Learning Repository\n[http://archive.ics.uci.edu/ml]. Irvine, CA:
University of California,\nSchool of Information and Computer Science.
\n\n..topic:: References\n\n  (1) S. Aeberhard, D. Coomans and O. de Vel,
\n  Comparison of Classifiers in High Dimensional Settings, \n  Tech.
Rep. no. 92-02, (1992), Dept. of Computer Science and Dept. of  \n
Mathematics and Statistics, James Cook University of North Queensland. \n
(Also submitted to Technometrics). \n\n  The data was used with many
others for comparing various \n  classifiers. The classes are separable,
though only RDA \n  has achieved 100% correct classification. \n  (RDA :
100%, QDA 99.4%, LDA 98.9%, 1NN 96.1% (z-transformed data)) \n  (All
results using the leave-one-out technique) \n\n  (2) S. Aeberhard, D.
Coomans and O. de Vel, \n  "THE CLASSIFICATION PERFORMANCE OF RDA" \n
Tech. Rep. no. 92-01, (1992), Dept. of Computer Science and Dept. of \n
Mathematics and Statistics, James Cook University of North Queensland. \n
(Also submitted to Journal of Chemometrics).\n',
 'feature_names': ['alcohol',
  'malic_acid',
  'ash',
  'alcalinity_of_ash',
  'magnesium',
  'total_phenols',
  'flavanoids',
  'nonflavanoid_phenols',
  'proanthocyanins',
  'color_intensity',
  'hue',
  'od280/od315_of_diluted_wines',
  'proline']}
# Understand the Data Better - feature matrix
X=data.data
```

```
# target vector
y=data.target

# class labels
labels=data.feature_names

# print dataset description
print(data.DESCR)

estimator=DecisionTreeClassifier()
estimator.fit(X,y)

graph=Source(tree.export_graphviz(estimator,out_file=None,feature_names=labels,
class_names=['0','1','2'],filled=True))

display(SVG(graph.pipe(format='svg')))
# The OUTPUT is shown below.


.. _wine_dataset:
Wine recognition dataset
------------------------


**Data Set Characteristics:**

:Number of Instances: 178 (50 in each of three classes)
:Number of Attributes: 13 numeric, predictive attributes and the class
:Attribute Information:
            - Alcohol
            - Malic acid
            - Ash
            - Alcalinity of ash
            - Magnesium
            - Total phenols
            - Flavanoids
            - Nonflavanoid phenols
            - Proanthocyanins
            - Color intensity
            - Hue
            - OD280/OD315 of diluted wines
            - Proline


    - class:
            - class_0
            - class_1
            - class_2

: Summary Statistics:
```

	Min	Max	Mean	SD
Alcohol:	11.0	14.8	13.0	0.8
Malic Acid:	0.74	5.80	2.34	1.12
Ash:	1.36	3.23	2.36	0.27
Alcalinity of Ash:	10.6	30.0	19.5	3.3
Magnesium:	70.0	162.0	99.7	14.3

Total Phenols:	0.98	3.88	2.29	0.63
Flavanoids:	0.34	5.08	2.03	1.00
Nonflavanoid Phenols:	0.13	0.66	0.36	0.12
Proanthocyanins:	0.41	3.58	1.59	0.57
Colour Intensity:	1.3	13.0	5.1	2.3
Hue:	0.48	1.71	0.96	0.23
OD280/OD315 of diluted wines:	1.27	4.00	2.61	0.71
Proline:	278	1680	746	315

```
:Missing Attribute Values: None
:Class Distribution: class_0 (59), class_1 (71), class_2 (48)
:Creator: R.A. Fisher
:Donor: Michael Marshall (MARSHALL%PLU@io.arc.nasa.gov)
:Date: July, 1988
```

This is a copy of UCI ML Wine recognition datasets.
https://archive.ics.uci.edu/ml/machine-learning-databases/wine/wine.data

The data results from a chemical analysis of wines grown in the same
region in Italy by three different cultivators. There are thirteen
different
measurements taken for different constituents found in the three types of
wine.

Original Owners:

Forina, M. et al, PARVUS -
An Extendible Package for Data Exploration, Classification, and
Correlation.
Institute of Pharmaceutical and Food Analysis and Technologies,
Via Brigata Salerno, 16147 Genoa, Italy.

Citation:

Lichman, M. (2013). UCI Machine Learning Repository
[http://archive.ics.uci.edu/ml]. Irvine, CA: University of California,
School of Information and Computer Science.

.. topic:: References

   (1) S. Aeberhard, D. Coomans and O. de Vel,
   Comparison of Classifiers in High Dimensional Settings,
   Tech. Rep. no. 92-02, (1992), Dept. of Computer Science and Dept. of
   Mathematics and Statistics, James Cook University of North Queensland.
   (Also submitted to Technometrics).

   The data was used with many others for comparing various
   classifiers. The classes are separable, though only RDA
   has achieved 100% correct classification.
   (RDA : 100%, QDA 99.4%, LDA 98.9%, 1NN 96.1% (z-transformed data))
   (All results using the leave-one-out technique)

   (2) S. Aeberhard, D. Coomans and O. de Vel,
   "THE CLASSIFICATION PERFORMANCE OF RDA"
   Tech. Rep. no. 92-01, (1992), Dept. of Computer Science and Dept. of
   Mathematics and Statistics, James Cook University of North Queensland.
   (Also submitted to Journal of Chemometrics).

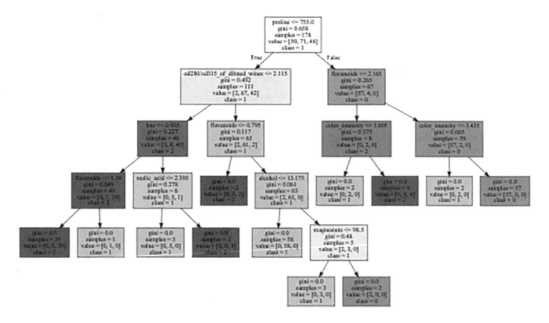

FIGURE 6.61 Tree plot for wine data.

In the tree plot shown in Figure 6.61, each node contains the condition (if/else rule) that splits the information alongside a series of other metrics of the node. For example, the Gini function refers to the Gini impurity, a measure of the impurity of the node, i.e., how homogeneous are the samples within the node. The user can say that a node is pure when all its samples belong to an equivalent class. In this case, there's no need for further split, and this node is named a leaf. Samples are the number of instances within the node, while the value array shows the distribution of those instances per class. At the very bottom, we see the majority class of the node. When the filled option of export_graphviz is set to true, each node gets colored in line with the bulk class.

Decision trees tend to overfit the info (the data) by constructing complex models. Overfitted models will presumably not generalize well in "unseen" data. Two main approaches to avoid overfitting are pre- and postpruning. Prepruning means restricting the depth of a tree before creation, while postpruning is removing non-informative nodes after the tree has been built.

Let us do the iris dataset example.

```
from sklearn.datasets import load_iris
from sklearn import tree
iris = load_iris()
clf = tree.DecisionTreeClassifier()
clf = clf.fit(iris.data, iris.target)

import os
os.environ["PATH"] += os.pathsep +
'C:\\Users\\<<USERNAME>>\\Downloads\\graphviz-2.38.zip\\release\\bin'
# Note: The user has to download and install the Graphviz add-on package.
import graphviz
from sklearn import tree

import graphviz
dot_data = tree.export_graphviz(clf, out_file=None)
graph = graphviz.Source(dot_data)
graph.render("iris")
```

```
# The output shows
'iris.pdf.'

# Plotting the tree using Graphviz
dot_data = tree.export_graphviz(clf, out_file=None,
feature_names=iris.feature_names,
class_names=iris.target_names,
                filled=True, rounded=True,
special_characters=True)
graph = graphviz.Source(dot_data)
graph


clf.predict(iris.data[:1,:])
```

#The output is shown in Figure 6.62.

```
array([0])
```

```
clf.predict_proba(iris.data[:1,:])
```
#The output is shown below.

```
array([[1., 0., 0.]])
```

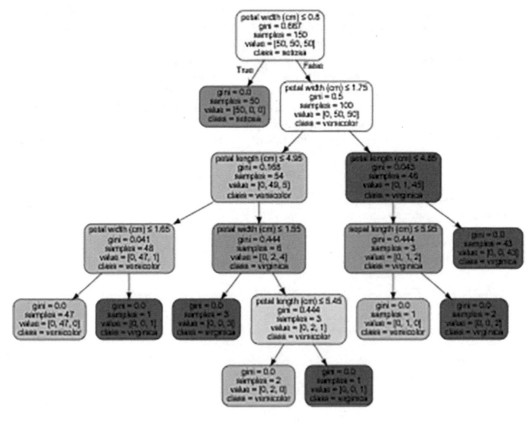

FIGURE 6.62   Tree plot using Graphviz.

sklearn decision tree classifier implements only prepruning. Prepruning is often controlled through several parameters like the utmost depth of the tree, the minimum number of samples required for a node to keep splitting, and therefore the minimum number of instances required for a leaf is selected by setting max_depth as the depth of tree the user requires.

Note to download graphviz for Windows:

https://graphviz.gitlab.io/_pages/Download/Download_windows.html

6.5 RANDOM FOREST CLASSIFIER

ML algorithms are classified into supervised learning, unsupervised learning, and reinforced learning. Supervised learning is divided into classification and regression problems. The decision tree belongs to supervised learning. The decision tree is a popular ML algorithm. It's a tree-like structure used for classification and regression problems. The decision tree is a tree-shaped diagram used to determine a course of action. Each branch of the tree represents the possible action. Entropy (i.e., the measure of randomness or unpredictability in the dataset) and information gain (i.e., a measure of the decrease in entropy after the dataset is split) are used to construct the decision tree. The testing is done on the decision node, and it has two or more branches, and the leaf node carries classification or decision. It's used in the classification and regression problem. The trees are constructed only with the relevant features. So to improve the accuracy, the tree has to construct in deep to learn a highly irregular pattern. So it leads to an overfitting problem (i.e., low bias and high variance). This overfitting problem can be solved by using random forest (RF).

The RF is a classification algorithm that consists of many decision trees. Each tree in the RF will predict the class. The class having majority voting is selected as the predicted class of the RF model. RF is an ensemble classifier first proposed by Tin Kam Ho of Bell Labs in 1995. It belongs to the classifier of the ensemble because it uses several ML algorithms for classification. If the number of trees is more, then the accuracy of the RF model is high.

RF is a method that operates by constructing multiple decision trees during the training phase. The main advantage of the RF tree is that it has less training due to multiple trees. Since we are training a large data, the system's accuracy is very high in RF. The RF chooses the decision of the majority tree, which is the final decision. RF is based on the bagging concept.

The difference between RF and decision tree is the process of finding the root node and splitting features nodes that are done randomly in RF. The rules are formed by using information gain and the Gini index.

The sample RF with a decision tree is shown in Figure 6.63. The two decision trees classify the input parameter as α, and one classifies the input parameter as β. Since α has majority voting, the input parameters are classified into class α. RF is used in ETM devices, object detection, and game because it has high accuracy and less training time.

The RF works on the concept of **bagging**. In bagging, the given training data are split into small training datasets by using the sampling method. For example, in Figure 6.64, the training data are

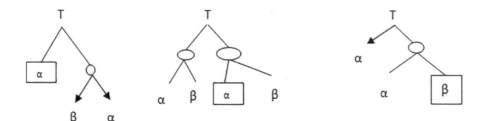

FIGURE 6.63 Voting mechanism in RF.

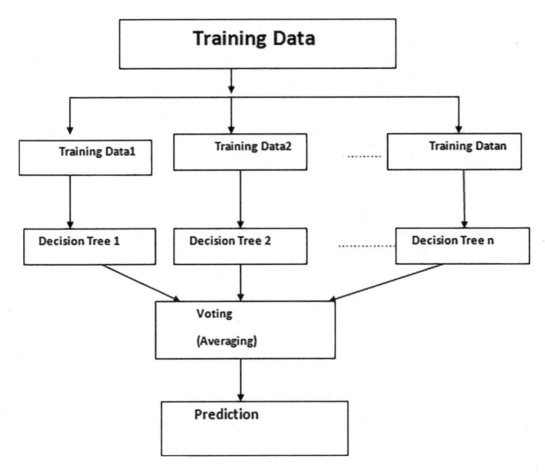

FIGURE 6.64   Representation of RF.

divided into training data 1, training data 2 up to training data each decision tree model recon-structed from the training data. Then, the n models are constructed, and prediction is done by using majority voting methods. Finally, the class having majority voting is selected as the predicted result of the model.

Important terminology used in random forest

Entropy: It is a randomness or unpredictability measure in the dataset.
Bagging: It is parallel training of a bunch of individual models. A random subset of the data is conditioned for each model.
Boosting: It is training sequentially a bunch of individual models. Each node learns from the previous model's mistake.
Gini index: Gini index measures the degree or probability of error in classifying a particular variable when selected randomly.

6.5.1   RANDOM FOREST AND THEIR CONSTRUCTION

Bagging is also called bootstrap aggregating, which is used in the creation of RFs. It is used to avoid overfitting. RF is better than bagging trees because the prediction of all subtrees is considered dur-ing classification.

$$SM = \begin{bmatrix} fa_3 & fb_3 & c_3 \\ . & . & . \\ f_{12} & f_{12} & c_{12} \end{bmatrix} \qquad (6.21)$$

Feature a is the first sample having n data, and feature b has the second sample having n data. c_1, c_2, c_3, ..., c_n represent the training class.

We can create a random subset, as shown below. For example, let S_1, S_2, S_3, ... and S_m be a random subset.

$$\text{Subset 1} \quad S_1 = \begin{bmatrix} fa_1 & fb_1 & c_1 \\ . & . & . \\ f_{35n} & f_{35n} & c_{35} \end{bmatrix}$$

$$\text{Subset 2} \quad S_2 = \begin{bmatrix} fa_2 & fb_{12}. & c_2 \\ . & . & . \\ f_{20} & f_{20} & c_{20} \end{bmatrix}$$

$$\text{Subset } M \quad SM = \begin{bmatrix} fa_3 & fb_3 & c_3 \\ . & . & . \\ f_{12} & f_{12} & c_{12} \end{bmatrix}$$

Decision trees are constructed from subset 1, subset 2, and subset M as represented in Figure 6.65. The prediction is done on this decision tree (i.e., decision tree 1, decision tree 2, and decision tree M). The given data are predicted by using the majority voting concept. The class with the highest voting is selected as the predicted class of the RF model, as shown in Figure 6.66.

Let X_1, X_2, X_3, ..., X_n be the parameter available in the dataset. Assume that the forest has 2 decision trees, as shown in Figure 6.67. X_1, X_3, X_4,..., X_n will be used to build decision tree1 and X_3, X_4, X_5, and X_n to create decision tree 2. Since we are using only partial data, the model is very efficient compared to another method. Correlation represents the relationship between two random trees (i.e., some of the variables are used in both trees). The forest error rate is high for the tree with the highest correlation. A strong classifier has a low forest error rate.

Figure 6.68 represents the sample RF. The input variable x is given to the RF. These variables are divided into the separate training set and are given to the decision tree. The decision tree output is combined, and the class with higher voting is selected for classification.

6.5.2 Sampling of the Dataset in Random Forest

Consider a dataset (Table 6.22) containing 9000 records, 8 features, and 2 classes. Each row of a table represents a record. The columns F-1, F-2, F-3, ..., F-8 represent the features. The class represents the class type. A total of k trees are constructed from the given dataset. The given dataset is

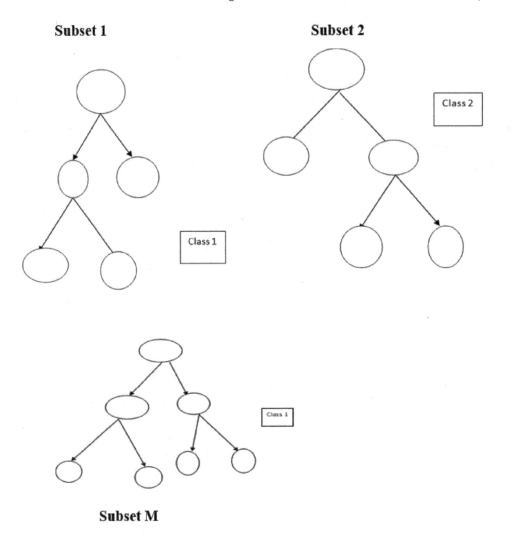

FIGURE 6.65   Decision tree constructed from subset 1, subset 2, and subset M.

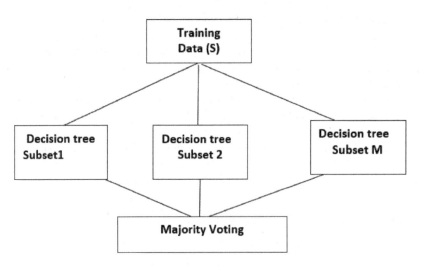

FIGURE 6.66   Creation of RF using bagging.

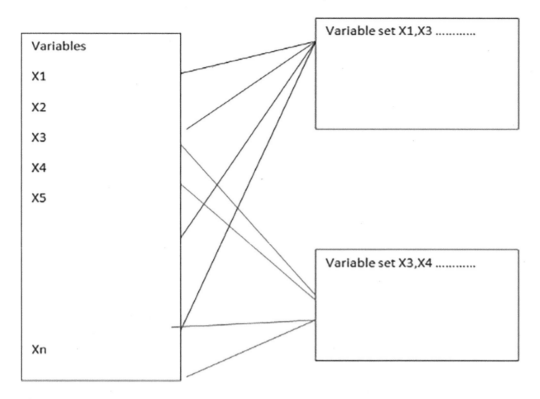

FIGURE 6.67 Dividing of data using bagging.

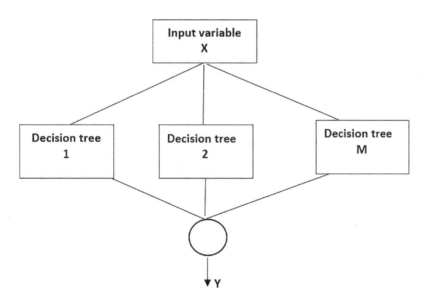

FIGURE 6.68 Diagrammatic representation of RF.

split into K sampling by using bagging or bootstrap aggregating. A standard training set D of size n bagging generates in new training set D_i each of size n' by sampling from D uniformly and with replacement. By sampling with replacement, some observations may be repeated in each D_i. In the above example, we have 9000 samples.

TABLE 6.22
Total Number of Samples

F-1	F-2	F-3	F-4	F-5	F-6	F-7	F-8	Class
Fa1	Fb1	Fc1	Fd1	Fe1	Ff1	Fg1	Fh1	Class A
Fa2	Fb2	Fc2	Fd2	Fe2	Ff2	Fg2	Fh2	Class B
Fa3	Fb3	Fc3	Fd3	Fe3	Ff3	Fg3	Fh3	Class A
Fa4	Fb4	Fc4	Fd4	Fe4	Ff4	Fg4	Fh4	Class B
Fa5	Fb5	Fc5	Fd5	Fe5	Ff5	Fg5	Fh5	Class A
Fa6	Fb6	Fc6	Fd6	Fe6	Ff6	Fg6	Fh6	Class B
Fa7	Fb7	Fc7	Fd7	Fe7	Ff7	Fg7	Fh7	Class A
Fa8	Fb8	Fc8	Fd8	Fe8	Ff8	Fg8	Fh8	Class B
Fa9	Fb9	Fc9	Fd9	Fe9	Ff9	Fg9	Fh9	Class A
-	-	-	-	-	-	-	-	-
-	-	-	-	-	-	-	-	-
-	-	-	-	-	-	-	-	-
Fai	Fbi	Fci	Fdi	Fei	Ffi	Fgi	Fhi	Class B
-	-	-	-	-	-	-	-	-
-	-	-	-	-	-	-	-	-
-	-	-	-	-	-	-	-	-
Fa9000	Fb9000	Fc9000	Fd9000	Fe9000	Ff9000	Fg9000	Fh9000	Class A

TABLE 6.23
The 6000 Sample Selected from Table 6.22

F-1	F-2	F-3	F-4	F-5	F-6	F-7	F-8	Class
Fa1	Fb1	Fc1	Fd1	Fe1	Ff1	Fg1	Fh1	Class A
Fa2	Fb2	Fc2	Fd2	Fe2	Ff2	Fg2	Fh2	Class B
Fa3	Fb3	Fc3	Fd3	Fe3	Ff3	Fg3	Fh3	Class A
Fa4	Fb4	Fc4	Fd4	Fe4	Ff4	Fg4	Fh4	Class B
Fa5	Fb5	Fc5	Fd5	Fe5	Ff5	Fg5	Fh5	Class A
-	-	-	-	-	-	-	-	-
-	-	-	-	-	-	-	-	-
-	-	-	-	-	-	-	-	-
Fai	Fbi	Fci	Fdi	Fei	Ffi	Fgi	Fhi	Class B
-	-	-	-	-	-	-	-	-
-	-	-	-	-	-	-	-	-
Fa6000	Fb6000	Fc6000	Fd6000	Fe6000	Ff6000	Fg6000	Fh6000	Class A

$$\text{No of selected sample} = 2/3 \left(\text{no of training set} \right)$$

$$= 2/3 * 9000$$

$$= 6000$$

Six thousand random samples are selected, and it's illustrated in Table 6.23.

Among this 6000 dataset, we apply attribute bagging (random subspace creation) and create the decision tree. If we have n features, then select square root (n) for creating a decision tree. In the

TABLE 6.24

Data for Decision Tree 1

F-1	F-5	F-7	Class
Fa1	Fe1	Fg1	Class A
Fa2	Fe2	Fg2	Class B
Fa3	Fe3	Fg3	Class A
Fa4	Fe4	Fg4	Class B
Fa5	Fe5	Fg5	Class A
-	-	-	-
-	-	-	-
-	-	-	-
Fai	Fei	Fgi	Class B
-	-	-	-
-	-	-	-
-	-	-	-
Fa6000	Fe6000	Fg6000	Class A

TABLE 6.25

Confusion Matrix for the Features

Total Result = 200	Predicted No	Predicted Yes	Row-wise Total
Actual No	TN = 30	FP = 25	55
Actual Yes	FN = 15	TP = 130	145
Col-wise Total	45	155	

below example, we have eight features, the square root of 8 gives around 3. So we select three features from the above dataset (Table 6.24); information gain, gain ratio, and Gini index are applied to create a decision tree from the sample.

Three features are selected from 6000 data, and decision tree 1 is constructed. Finally, a confusion matrix is created for the features, as shown in Table 6.25.

The misclassification rate is calculated from the confusion matrix.

M is classification rate:

$$\frac{FP + FN}{Total} = \frac{25 + 15}{200} = 0.2$$

The features having less misclassification rate are selected for the decision tree.

6.5.2.1   Creation of Subset Data

Let's consider the dataset as shown in Figure 6.69 with circle ● and star ★. First, we have to create a subset from the dataset by using the sampling method. Three subsets are created: Subset 1 has 6 circles and 3 stars, Subset 2 has 4 circles and 5 stars, and Subset 3 has 2 circles and 5 stars. Let us consider the subset as shown in Figure 6.70.

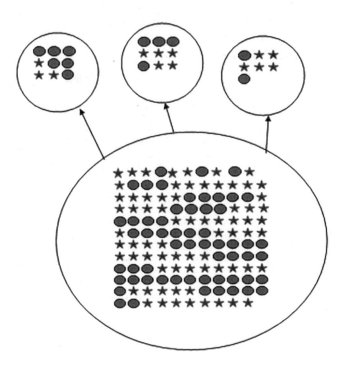

FIGURE 6.69   Creating subset from original dataset by using the sampling method.

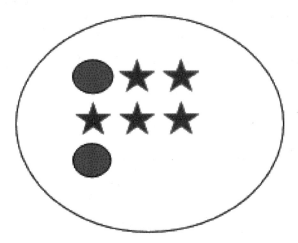

FIGURE 6.70   A sample subset.

Now, decision trees are constructed for the subsets. Next, each decision tree is obtained based on decision criteria, and finally, there are a group of decision trees. Finally, the average prediction is obtained from all the decision trees (subset), and an overall RF prediction is obtained, as illustrated in Figure 6.71.

6.5.3   PSEUDOCODE FOR RANDOM FOREST

Step 1: Randomly select K features from total M features where k is less than M
Step 2: Among K features, calculate the node "d" using the best split node
Step 3: Split the node into daughter node using the best split

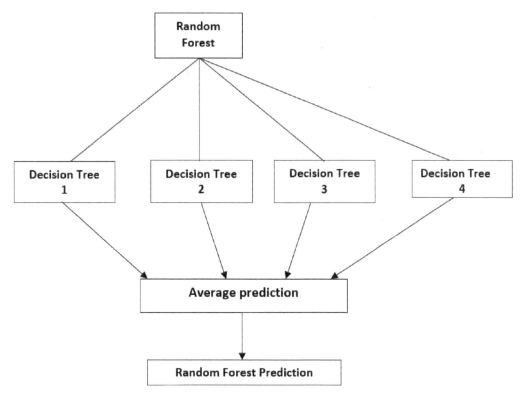

FIGURE 6.71   Creation of decision tree based on the salary.

Step 4: Repeat 1–3 steps until the "*i*" number of nodes has been reached.
Step 5: Building forest by repeating steps 1–4 for "*n*" times to create "*n*" of trees.

Let us assume a dataset that has *M* features. A *K* feature is selected from the dataset by using the sampling method. The selected *K* features should be less than *M* features in the dataset. The decision tree is constructed by using the *K* features. By using split node, first, determine the root node and daughter node. Then, the tree is constructed by using the split node concept until it reaches the leaf node. Similarly, construct another decision tree in the RF.

6.5.3.1   Pseudocode for Prediction in Random Forest

Step 1: Take the test features and use the rules of each randomly created decision tree to predict the outcome and store the predicted outcome
Step 2: Calculate the votes for each predicted target
Step 3: Consider the high voted predicted target as the final prediction from the RF algorithm.

Input is given to all the decision trees of the RF. Then, calculate the number of votes given to each class. The class having majority voting is selected as the predicted class of the model.

6.5.4   REGRESSION USING RANDOM FOREST

We can use the RF for regression also. Consider sample *X*. Sample *x* is divided into subsample 1, sample 2, sample 3, and sample. Decision tree 1, decision tree 2, decision tree 3, and decision tree *m* are constructed from the samples. Each tree can be constructed from any of the decision tree

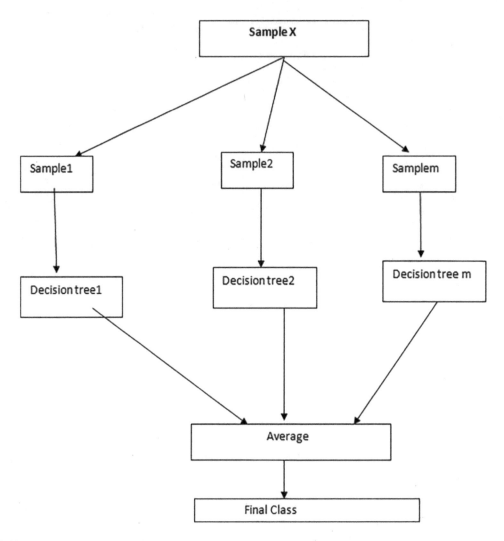

FIGURE 6.72   RF for regression.

algorithms like CART and ID3. Each decision tree will produce a value. The output of each decision tree is considered in the regression process. In the classification process, the voting mechanisms are used. The average output of each tree is taken to compute the final class, as represented in Figure 6.72.

6.5.5   Classification Using Random Forest

This section illustrates the step-by-step procedure of applying RF for a classification problem with a suitable example.

Step1: Create a bootstrap dataset

     Consider the below dataset for predicting heart disease (Table 6.26).

     The bootstrap dataset should be the same size as the original dataset and select randomly from the given dataset. The bootstrap dataset is created by randomly selecting data from the original dataset. In the above example, the data in row 2 are selected first (Table 6.27).

TABLE 6.26
Original Dataset

Chest Pain	Good Blood Circulation	Blocked Arteries	Weight	Heart Disease
No	No	No	125	No
Yes	Yes	Yes	180	Yes
Yes	Yes	No	210	No
Yes	No	Yes	167	Yes

TABLE 6.27
Random Selection of Single Data

Chest Pain	Good Blood Circulation	Blocked Arteries	Weight	Heart Disease
Yes	Yes	Yes	180	Yes

TABLE 6.28
Random Selection of Two Data

Chest Pain	Good Blood Circ.	Blocked Arteries	Weight	Heart Disease
Yes	Yes	Yes	180	Yes
No	No	No	125	No

TABLE 6.29
Random Selection of Three Data

Chest Pain	Good Blood Circulation	Blocked Arteries	Weight	Heart Disease
Yes	Yes	Yes	180	Yes
No	No	No	125	No
Yes	No	Yes	167	Yes

TABLE 6.30
Random Selection of Four Data

Chest Pain	Good Blood Circulation	Blocked Arteries	Weight	Heart Disease
Yes	Yes	Yes	180	Yes
No	No	No	125	No
Yes	No	Yes	167	Yes
Yes	No	Yes	167	Yes

Then, the data from the first row are selected (Table 6.28).
Then, the data from the last row are selected (Table 6.29).
Then again, the data from the last row are selected (Table 6.30).
So we have selected four data from the original dataset (Table 6.31).

TABLE 6.31
Bootstrap Dataset

Chest Pain	Good Blood Circulation	Blocked Arteries	Weight	Heart Disease
Yes	Yes	Yes	180	Yes
No	No	No	125	No
Yes	No	Yes	167	Yes
Yes	No	Yes	167	Yes

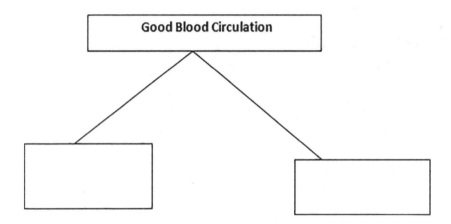

FIGURE 6.73   Selection of candidate key.

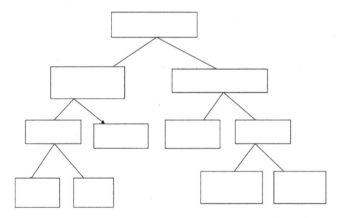

FIGURE 6.74   Decision tree from the bootstrap dataset.

Step 2: Create a decision tree using the bootstrap dataset, but only use a random variable subset at each step

In the above example, we have four variables. Instead of selecting all four variables, we will select only two variables as candidate variables (good blood circulation or blocked arteries). Even we can use the decision tree algorithm to select the candidate key. Let us take good blood circulation as a candidate key (Figure 6.73).

Then, the tree can be divided further using chest pain and weight. Figure 6.74 represents the decision tree.

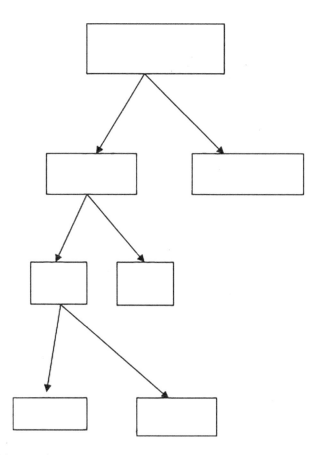

FIGURE 6.75   Decision tree 2.

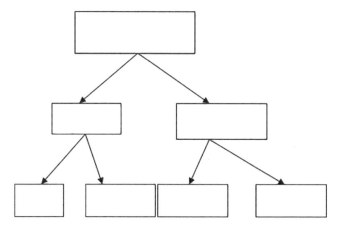

FIGURE 6.76   Decision tree 3.

Then again, we have to repeat Step 2 to create more decision trees by using different bootstrap datasets. Decision trees 2 and 3 are constructed as shown in Figures 6.75 and 6.76.

Step 3: Evaluating the random forest

After the creation of a RF, we have to evaluate the performance. Consider the sample shown in Table 6.32.

TABLE 6.32

Sample for Constructing Decision Tree 1

Chest Pain	Good Blood Circulation	Blocked Arteries	Weight	Heart Disease
Yes	No	No	168	

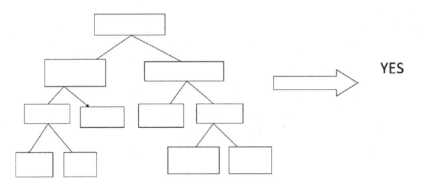

FIGURE 6.77   Classification in decision tree 1.

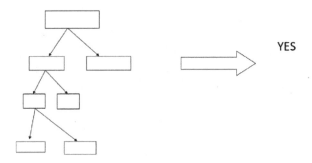

FIGURE 6.78   Classification in decision tree 2.

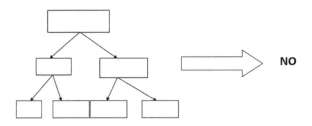

FIGURE 6.79   Classification in decision tree 3.

The above sample will be given to decision tree 1 (Figure 6.77).

From the decision trees in Figures 6.78 and 6.79, Yes is selected. Finally, the voting for the class is given in Table 6.33.

Similarly, we have to pass the variable into another decision tree also. Finally, after passing to all decision trees, the voting is represented in Table 6.34.

So the majority of voting belongs to class Yes. So the data belong to class Yes (Table 6.35).

TABLE 6.33
Voting Results

Heart Disease	
Yes	No
1	0

TABLE 6.34
Voting Results from All the Decision Trees

Heart Disease	
Yes	No
5	1

TABLE 6.35
Majority Voting Results

Chest Pain	Good Blood Circulation	Blocked Arteries	Weight	Heart Disease
Yes	No	No	168	Yes

6.5.5.1   Random Forest Problem for Classification – Examples

6.5.5.1.1   Problem 1

Construct the RF for the example in Table 6.36.

Assume that we are splitting the data based on the attribute home type. The values for home type are between 6 and 31. The possible split of the dataset is

- home type ≤ 6
- home type ≤ 10
- home type ≤ 15
- home type ≤ 30
- home type ≤ 31

TABLE 6.36
Sample Data – Home Type, Salary, and Class

Record	Attributes		Class
	Home Type	Salary	
1	31	3	1
2	30	1	0
3	6	2	0
4	15	4	1
5	10	4	0

6.5.5.1.2   Gini Index

If dataset D contains n classes, Gini index is defined as

$$\text{Gain}(D) = 1 - \sum P_i^2$$

where
P_i represents the sum of the probabilities of the positive index and negative index

Home type ≤ 6:

Record	Number of Records		
	Zero	One	$N=5$
Home type ≤ 6	1	0	$n_{1=}1$
Home type >6	2	2	$n_2=4$

Gini (home type≤ 6) $= 1-(1^2+0) = 0$
Gini (home type >6) $= 1-((2/4)^2+(2/4)^2) = 0.5$
Gini (split) $= 1/5(0)+4/5(0.5) = 0.4$

Home type ≤ 10

Record	Number of Records		
	Zero	One	$N=5$
Home type ≤ 10	2	0	$n1=2$
Home type >10	1	2	$n2=3$

Gini (home type ≤ 6) $= 1-(1^2+0) = 0$
Gini (home type >10) $= 1-((1/3)^2+(2/3)^2) = 0.4452$
Gini (split) $= 2/5(0)+3/5(0.445) = 0.2671$
Home type ≥ 10 has the lowest value.

Gini Split	Value
Home type ≤ 6	0.4000
Home type ≤ 10	0.2671
Home type ≤ 15	0.4671
Home type ≤ 30	0.3000
Home type ≤ 31	0.4800

Best Split:

$$\text{Home type} = (10+15)/2 = 12.5$$

If the home_type is <12.5, then it belongs to class 0. If home_type is >12.5, then it belongs to class 1, as shown in Figure 6.80. The next Gini index is based on salary as shown in Figure 6.81.

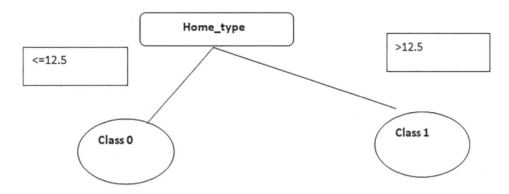

FIGURE 6.80   Creating RF based on home_type.

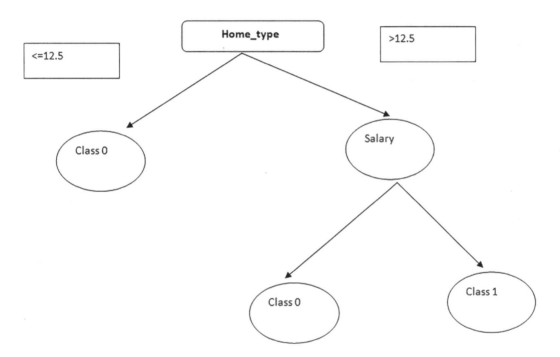

FIGURE 6.81   Creating RF based on home_type and salary.

6.5.6   FEATURES AND PROPERTIES OF RANDOM FOREST

6.5.6.1   Features

- It is the most accurate algorithm currently available, and it works quickly on huge datasets.
- It can handle tens of thousands of input variables without deleting any of them.
- It calculates the importance of several variables in the classification.
- As the forest grows, it generates an internal unbiased estimate of the generalization error.
- It offers a method for guessing missing data that works well and retains accuracy even with a considerable amount of missing data.
- It includes techniques for balancing errors in uneven datasets with a class population.
- The forests that are created can be preserved and used on other data in the future.

- Prototypes are created that reveal the relationship between the variables and the classification.
- It calculates distances between pairs of examples, which can be useful in clustering, detecting outliers, or giving fascinating views of the data (by scale).
- Unlabeled data can be used to create unsupervised clustering, data visualizations, and outlier identification using the capabilities described above.
- It provides a mechanism for finding variable interactions through experimentation.

6.5.6.2 Properties
- Each tree has maximal strength
- Each tree has a minimal correlation with the other trees.
- Ensemble of trees votes for the final result.

6.5.7 ADVANTAGES AND DISADVANTAGES OF RANDOM FOREST

6.5.7.1 Advantages
- It can be used for both classification and regression tasks.
- Handle the missing value and maintains accuracy for missing data.
- No overfitting the model.
- Handle larger datasets with higher dimensionality.

6.5.7.2 Disadvantages
- Works well for classification and does not work for regression.
- Less control on the model.

6.5.8 CALCULATION OF ERROR USING BIAS AND VARIANCE

The bias and variance represent the deviation of the result from the expected value. Let F be the true function having random noise. Then, hypothesis h is imperfect for the following reason.

6.5.8.1 Bias
H is unable to fit f perfectly because it lacks capacity or complexity.

6.5.8.2 Variance
H is fitting to the noise in the data and missing the true function f.

Let z be that arbitrary point and generated point is given as

$$¥ = f(z) + €$$ (6.22)

Expected value is given as

$$E[¥] = f(z)$$ (6.23)

Variance is given as

$$\text{var}[¥] = \text{var}[€]$$ (6.24)

Mean squared error is given as

$$R(h) = E\left[\left(h[z] - ¥\right)^2\right]$$
$$= E\left[h(z)^2\right] + E\left[¥^2\right] - 2E\left[¥h(z)\right] \tag{6.25}$$

where ¥ and (z) are independent.
Variance of ¥ and (z) is given as

$$= E\left[h(z)^2\right] + E\left[¥^2\right] - 2E\left[¥h(z)\right]$$
$$= \text{var}\left[h(z)\right] + E\left[h(Z)\right]^2 + \text{var}[¥] + E[¥]^2 - 2E[¥]E\left[h(Z)\right]$$
$$= \left(E[h(z)] - E[¥]\right)^2 + \text{var}\left[h(z)\right] + \text{var}[¥] \tag{6.26}$$
$$= \left(Eh(z) - f(Z)\right)^2 + \text{var}\left[h(z)\right] + \text{var}[€]$$

$(E[h(z)]-f(z))^2$ represents the squared bias. It represents the quantity in which the model differs from the real data distribution function.

var$[h(Z)]$ represents the variance. The variance determines the risk factors.

var$[€]$ represents the irreducible error. The error is due to the noise introduced in the input signal.

6.5.8.3 Properties of Bias and Variance
- Too much bias leads to underfitting
- Too much variance leads to overfitting.
- Training errors show bias.
- Test errors show bias and variance.
- If the n value is infinity, then the variance is zero.
- A model has sufficient modeling capacity when bias is zero when n tends to infinity
- If the number of features is increased, then there is a drop in bias.
- Noise in the test only affects var($€$). Noise in the training set affects only bias and var($€$).

6.5.9 Time Complexity

RF is a decision tree ensemble system. The time complexity for creating a complete unpruned decision tree is $O(v * n \log(n))$, where n is the record number and v is the number of variables/attributes.

Let n tree be the number of trees in the RF and m try be the number of variables at each node. Then, the time complexity of a single tree is $o(m \text{ try} * n \log(n))$.

The time complexity of n tree is $o(n \text{ tree} * m \text{ try} * n \log(n))$. Let the depth of the tree be $o(\log n)$. Let d represent the depth of the tree. Then, the time complexity is represented as $o(n \text{ tree} * m \text{ try} * d * n)$.

6.5.10 Extremely Randomized Tree

Extremely randomized trees do not use bagging to create a collection for each tree of training samples. Instead, the same set of input learning is used to train all trees. Extremely randomized trees strongly choose a split node (both a variable index and a variable split value are randomly selected). In contrast, RF considers the strongest split between random subsets of variables (optimal by variable index and variable split value). Each tree is constructed from a complete learning sample. Let k be the number of random splits at each node. K is fixed to one; the resulted tree structure is independent of the output labels of the training set. Let P be the number of features. The value of K is the square root of p for the classification problem and $k=p$ for the regression problem. The extra tree has increased bias and reduced variance; once the randomization rate is achieved, the variance will vanish, and bias will increase. If the level of randomization rises above the optimum level, the variance decreases, and the bias increases.

6.5.11 REAL-WORLD EXAMPLES

The RF is a popular ML algorithm. The accuracy of RF is high because it has multiple decision trees. So it plays a major role in classification and regression problems. A few application areas where RF is popular are as follows:

1. Machine fault diagnosis
2. Medical field
3. Banking
4. E-Commerce
5. Security

6.5.11.1 Machine Fault Diagnosis

RF algorithm is a novel assembly classifier that creates many decision trees to improve the single tree classification. While there are many current fault diagnostic techniques, such as artificial neural networks and SVMs, RF research is essential due to its fast speed, tree classifier characteristics, and high performance in computer fault diagnosis. Moreover, it is proved that by combining with other optimization methods, the RF-based diagnosis approach can produce more accurate results.

RF adopts a set of decision trees and defines by majority voting algorithm the categorical groups. To check the quality of RF, a serious consideration of overfitting is therefore required. Some of the research work is done by combining RFs with genetic algorithms. In this approach, the RF is developed by using a decision tree from the CART algorithm. The tree is built by splitting a node recursively. The tree is constructed from the sample data and the majority voting process. The class that has the highest voting is selected for classification. The RF can be strengthened by using a genetic algorithm. The rule of survival of the fittest is applied to the population of individuals. GA has a powerful search algorithm because of its simplicity and powerful features.GA is used for parameter optimization.

6.5.11.2 Medical Field

6.5.11.2.1 Diabetic Retinopathy Classification Analyses

RF methods are for evaluating the identification of data for diabetic retinopathy (DR) fundus photography. In the United States and worldwide, DR is one of the leading causes of blindness. DR is a chronic illness that may go unnoticed for effective treatment until it is too late. Early detection could therefore improve the chances of therapeutic interventions to reduce its effects. Graded fundus photography and structural data were used to estimate RF and logistic regression classifiers. The impact of sample size on classifier performance and the possibility of using conditional probabilities are generated by RF as metrics describing DR risk. Variable RF measurements are used to identify factors that affect the quality of classification. By comparing participants with or without DR, both types of data are valuable. RF-based models provided much higher classification accuracy than those based on logistical regression. Combining both data types did not increase reliability but increased statistical bias among healthy participants who subsequently had or did not have DR events over 4 years of monitoring. RF factor value parameters showed that the number of microaneurysms in both eyes seemed to play the most important role in the discrimination between the graded fundus variables and the number of medicinal products.

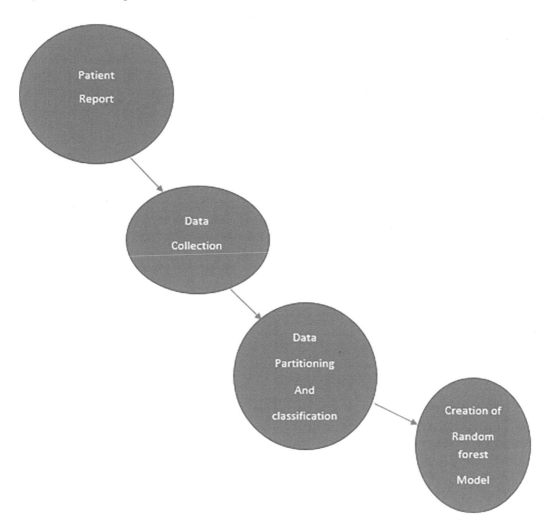

FIGURE 6.82   Disease prediction using RF.

At the initial stage, the data are collected from the patient report. There should not be any miss-ing data in the collected data. For example, among all the collected attributes, one of the attributes should represent whether the patient is suffering from liver damage or not.

Figure 6.82 represents the prediction of liver damage using RF. At the initial stage, the data are collected from the patient report. There should not be any missing data in the collected data. Among all the collected attributes, one of the attributes should represent whether the patient is suffering from liver damage or not. RF model is collected for the above model, and it produces an accuracy of 70.50%. The data are collected from the UCI ML repository. The dataset has 167 negative tests, and 416 positive test classifications are done at various decision trees. The final output is selected by using the voting mechanism. Liver damage occurs due to inhaling harmful gases, intake of con-taminated food, different kinds of drugs, and excessive alcohol consumption. Preprocessing is used for cleansing the data attributes that are selected from the data.

6.5.11.3   Banking

RF algorithms are widely used in the banking sector in two main applications. These are meant to recognize clients who are trustworthy and to find customers who are fraud. The loyal customer is not the customer who pays well, but also the customer who can take the huge amount as a loan and pay the interest on the bank loan well. As the success of the bank is purely dependent on loyal customers, bank customer data are highly evaluated to determine the pattern for the loyal customer based on customer data.

Similarly, consumers who are not important to the bank need to be identified, such as taking the loan, paying interest on the loan appropriately, and finding outgoing customers. Then, bank will have a chance not to approve this customer loan form. Also used in this case is the RF algorithm to identify customers that are not beneficial to the bank.

The RF is used to predict bank failures. The bank-level financial statement is analyzed to identify the falling of the bank. RF improves classification accuracy because classification is done at many trees rather than single tree. The RF predicts the bank failure event by analyzing bank-level financial data to distinguish active and inactive banks. The data are collected from bank scope. $8 indicators are selected from these data, and these data are classified into four groups (profitability ratio, capitalization, loan quality, and funding). This method can be applied to a commercial bank, saving bank, and cooperative bank. A threshold value or explanatory variable is used to split the active and interactive banking. First, a large number of the trees are constructed based on the given data. Then, the class is selected based on the voting mechanism. The three trees are constructed for testing: first, a single tree, second one RF with many trees, and third one with a large dataset by training multiple tree parallel. A single tree represents a decision tree, and the accuracy obtained by the single tree is less than the RF tree.

First, the RF is constructed as a single tree, RF with many trees, and RF with multiple tree parallel. Compared to single tree RF, the multiple tree RF produced higher accuracy.

The explanatory variables are

1. The average rate of interest on loans and assets
2. The average rate of a bank in deposits.

6.5.11.4   E-Commerce

For E-Commerce, the RF is used only in the small segment of the recommendation engine on various types of customers to identify the likelihood of customers who like the recommended goods. It takes high-end GPU systems to run RF algorithms on very large datasets. If GPU is not available, the ML models can also be run on the cloud hosting environment. The online cloud computing system can be used from any corner of the world to run high-end ML models.

6.5.11.5   Security

In recent times, the RF has played a major role in the intrusion detecting system. Due to advancements in the technologies like IoT, big data, and the cloud, there is increased usage of the computer system in business. A huge amount of data are transferred and processed. The IDS maintains the confidentiality and integrity of data. The IDS in the network should have a low false-positive rate. RF algorithm plays a major role in IDS because it requires less training time and fast prediction. Detection strategy type, problem domain, and software architecture are used to create a RF model. Proximity methods are used in the RF. The various data collected from the network are HOST log (i.e., operational system and system logs), application log (i.e., data generated from the application), network traffic (i.e., OSI layer 3), and wireless traffic(i.e., OSI layer 1). Data can be collected from the centralized or distributed method. In analogy-based detection, patterns different from normal patterns are identified. In signature-based detection, the misused data are identified, and in specification-based detection, the data violated from the protocol specification are identified. The detection can be done by using online, i.e., block the IP address or off-line.

6.5.12   Random Forest in Practice Using Python

Before implementing RF classifier, let us understand the data file. The sample data file we have used is shown below. It has five columns – user ID, gender, age, estimated salary, and whether they have done any purchases or not. Our goal is to classify using RF classifier.

Social_Network_Ads.
CSV

The partial data are shown below.

User ID	Gender	Age	Estimated Salary	Purchased
15624510	Male	19	19,000	0
15810944	Male	35	20,000	0
15668575	Female	26	43,000	0
15603246	Female	27	57,000	0
15804002	Male	19	76,000	0
15728773	Male	27	58,000	0
15598044	Female	27	84,000	0
15694829	Female	32	150,000	1
15600575	Male	25	33,000	0
15727311	Female	35	65,000	0
15570769	Female	26	80,000	0
15606274	Female	26	52,000	0
15746139	Male	20	86,000	0
15704987	Male	32	18,000	0
15628972	Male	18	82,000	0
15697686	Male	29	80,000	0
15733883	Male	47	25,000	1
15617482	Male	45	26,000	1
15704583	Male	46	28,000	1
15621033	Female	48	29,000	1
15649487	Male	45	22,000	1
15736760	Female	47	49,000	1
15714658	Male	48	41,000	1
15599081	Female	45	22,000	1

```
# Random Forest Classification

# Importing the libraries
import numpy as np
import matplotlib.pyplot as plt
import pandas as pd
from sklearn.metrics import confusion_matrix, classification_report,
roc_curve,auc
import statistics

# Importing the dataset
```

```python
dataset = pd.read_csv('C:/Python Files/Decision Tree/Decision Tree/Source
Files/Social_Network_Ads.csv')
X = dataset.iloc[:, [2, 3]].values
y = dataset.iloc[:, 4].values




# Splitting the dataset into the Training set and Test set
from sklearn.cross_validation import train_test_split
X_train, X_test, y_train, y_test = train_test_split(X, y, test_size =
0.25, random_state = 0)

# Feature Scaling
from sklearn.preprocessing import StandardScaler
sc = StandardScaler()
X_train = sc.fit_transform(X_train)
X_test = sc.transform(X_test)

# Fitting Random Forest Classification to the Training set
from sklearn.ensemble import RandomForestClassifier
classifier = RandomForestClassifier(n_estimators = 10, criterion =
'entropy', random_state = 0)
classifier.fit(X_train, y_train)

# Predicting the Test set results
y_pred = classifier.predict(X_test)

# Making the Confusion Matrix
from sklearn.metrics import confusion_matrix
cm = confusion_matrix(y_test, y_pred)


pd.crosstab(y_pred,y_test)

#OUTPUT ◇
#col_0 0 1
#row_0
#0 63 3
#1 5 29

total1=sum(sum(cm))

#####from confusion matrix calculate accuracy
accuracy=(cm[0,0]+cm[1,1])/total1
print ('Accuracy : ', accuracy)

#OUTPUT ◇
#Accuracy : 0.92

sensitivity = cm[0,0]/(cm[0,0]+cm[0,1])
print('Sensitivity : ', sensitivity)

#OUTPUT ◇
#Sensitivity : 0.9264705882352942
```

```
specificity = cm[1,1]/(cm[1,0]+cm[1,1])
print('Specificity : ', specificity)


#OUTPUT ◇
#Specificity : 0.90625


precision = cm[0,0]/(cm[0,0]+cm[1,0])
print('precision : ', precision)


#OUTPUT ◇
#precision : 0.9545454545454546


classifier.score(X_test, y_test)
#OUTPUT ◇
#0.92


print(classification_report(y_test, y_pred))

#OUTPUT ◇
# precision recall f1-score support
#
# 0 0.95 0.93 0.94 68
# 1 0.85 0.91 0.88 32
#
#avg /total 0.92 0.92 0.92 100


decisiontree5= classifier.estimators_[5]
from sklearn import tree
from IPython.display import Image


tree.export_graphviz(decisiontree5, out_file='C:/Python Files/Decision
Tree/Decision Tree/Source File/srandomforest_5_tree.dot')

Image(filename = 'C:/Python Files/Decision Tree/Decision Tree/Source
Files/randomforest_5_tree.png')
```

THE OUTPUT FILE IS given below and represented in Figure 6.83

randomforest_5_tree
.png

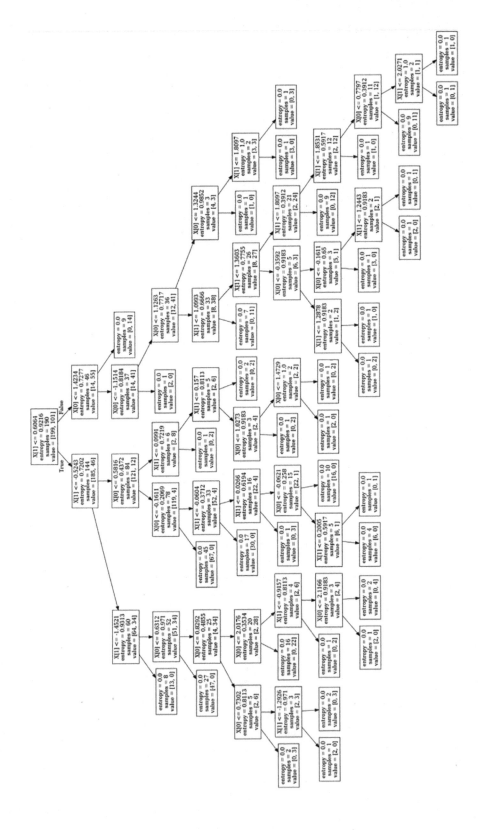

FIGURE 6.83   Decision tree for estimating the classes.

```
#################################################
##regressor

from sklearn.ensemble import RandomForestRegressor
# From the previous example in multiple regression, (50_Startups.csv) Use
a Classifier

dataset1 = pd.read_csv('C:/Python Files/50_Startups.csv')
X1 = dataset1.iloc[:, :-1].values
y1 = dataset1.iloc[:, 4].values

# Encoding categorical data
from sklearn.preprocessing import LabelEncoder, OneHotEncoder
labelencoder = LabelEncoder()
X1[:, 3] = labelencoder.fit_transform(X1[:, 3])
onehotencoder = OneHotEncoder(categorical_features = [3])
X1 = onehotencoder.fit_transform(X1).toarray()

# Avoiding the Dummy Variable Trap
X1 = X1[:, 1:]

# Splitting the dataset into the Training set and Test set
from sklearn.cross_validation import train_test_split
X_train1, X_test1, y_train1, y_test1 = train_test_split(X1, y1, test_size
= 0.2, random_state = 0)

regr = RandomForestRegressor()

regr.fit(X_train1,y_train1)

#OUTPUT ◇
# RandomForestRegressor(bootstrap=True, criterion='mse', max_depth=None,
#           max_features='auto', max_leaf_nodes=None,
#           min_impurity_decrease=0.0, min_impurity_split=None,
#          min_samples_leaf=1, min_samples_split=2,
#            min_weight_fraction_leaf=0.0, n_estimators=10, n_jobs=1,
#           oob_score=False, random_state=None, verbose=0,
warm_start=False)

# Predicting the Test set results
y_pred1 = regr.predict(X_test1)

from sklearn.metrics import mean_squared_error

mean_squared_error(y_test1,y_pred1)#mse

print(np.sqrt(mean_squared_error(y_test1, y_pred1))) #rmse

#OUTPUT ◇
8029.705866133677

# print the R-squared value for the model
regr.score(X_test1, y_test1)#rsquare

#OUTPUT ◇
0.9495843301735848
```

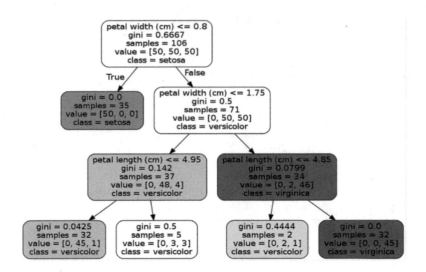

FIGURE 6.84　RF output.

```
sst=sum(np.power(y_test1-statistics.mean(y_test1),2))
sse=sum(np.power((y_test1-y_pred1),2))

rsquared=(sst-sse)/sst

adjusted_r_squared = 1 - (1-rsquared)*(len(y_test)-1)/(len(y_test)-X_
test.shape[1]-1)
dt=regr.estimators_[5]

from sklearn.tree import export_graphviz
from IPython.display import Image

export_graphviz(dt, out_file='C:/Python Files/Decision Tree/Decision
Tree/Source File/dt_regressor.dot',class_names = dataset1.Profit,
           rounded = True, filled = True)

##dot -Tpng sample_1.dot -o sample_1.png
Image(filename = 'C:/Python Files/Decision Tree/Decision Tree/Source
File/tree_limited.png')
## THE OUTPUT FILE IS ATTACHED BELOW and shown in Figure 6.84
```

tree_limited.png

6.6　SUPPORT VECTOR MACHINES

ML aims to identify the pattern behind the data and build systems that learn from the experience gained. SVM gained research interest as it utilizes optimization techniques and achieves higher performance. SVM differs from other classical ML techniques since it makes use of statistical ideas. While learning a model in ML, we generally attempt to minimize the errors in the training phase, leading to the overfitting of data. SVM has a clever way to tackle the overfitting problem with the help of maximizing margin techniques. This chapter presents the basic ideas of SVMs and kernel functions. SVM is the most effective kernel-based supervised ML classifier. This is a sophisticated classification technique that handles both linear and nonlinear data. Kernel machines have many useful properties to analyze nonlinear data. The variants of SVM are support vector regression (SVR), which can be used for solving regression analysis. SVM is a robust learning method as a piece of evidence from its usage in diverse fields of engineering. It has been applied for real-world applications, including handwritten OCR, face recognition, speaker identification, natural language processing, text mining, drug design, fault diagnosis in machines, damage assessment of bridges, and pattern recognition. The only prerequisite for understanding SVM is constrained optimization based on the Lagrangian multiplier method. In this section, working of SVM, underlying statistical concept, kernel tricks, linear and nonlinear SVM classifier, finding optimal hyperplane, maximum margin classifier, the hard and soft margin of SVM, variants of SVM, pros and cons of SVM, SVM regression analysis, and applications are discussed in detail.

6.6.1 GEOMETRIC INTUITION

SVM is a supervised learning algorithm in which the learning model is provided with the set of inputs and their associated outputs or labels. SVMs are used in classification problems. The classification problem can be viewed as the task of separating classes in feature space. To understand the mystery of SVM, a simple binary classification problem with two classes is considered as an example, as shown in Figure 6.85. It consists of a decision boundary or hyperplane that separates the two classes. The goal of SVM is to choose an optimized hyperplane for separating the classes. For example, in Figure 6.85, many possible lines separate the two classes, and the dark shaded thick line is the optimal hyperplane among all others.

The support vectors are the essential data points that are closer to the decision boundary. The *main objective of* SVM is to find an optimal hyperplane classifier for this problem. The optimal hyperplane is to identify the maximum distance between the support vectors and the hyperplane.

a. the distance to the closest negative sample d_2 is lesser than the distance to the closest positive sample d_1. In contrast to Figure 6.86,
b. the optimal hyperplane was found where the distance to the closest negative sample d_2 is equal to the distance to the closest positive sample d_1.

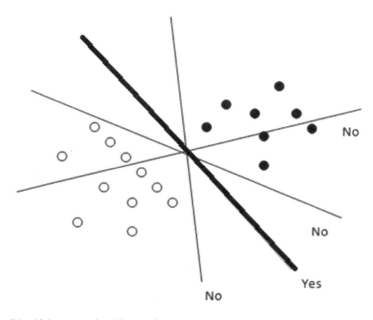

FIGURE 6.85   Identifying an optimal hyperplane.

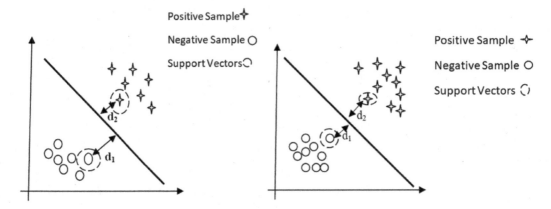

FIGURE 6.86   (a) Not an optimal hyperplane $d_1 > d_2$ and (b) optimal hyperplane $d_{1=}d_2$.

S.No	x1	x2	y
1	1	3	-1
2	2	1	-1
3	4	5	-1
4	6	9	-1
5	8	7	-1
6	5	1	1
7	7	1	1
8	9	4	1
9	12	7	1
10	13	6	1

FIGURE 6.87   Example for linearly separable.

$$\text{Optimal hyperplane : distance to the closest negative sample } d_2$$
$$= \text{Distance to the closest positive sample} \qquad (6.27)$$

Example Let us understand numerically with an example given in Figure 6.87 to find the optimal hyperplane from the given data points, which are linearly separable.

There are many possible infinite numbers of solutions available, as shown in Figure 6.88a. Therefore, the aim is to find the optimal hyperplane solution as shown in Figure 6.88b, which separates the $+$ and $-$ classes.

Figure 6.89 illustrates the concept of binary classification with another simple example. There are two features (nodes and ages) and two labels (survived and lost). The hyperplane or decision boundary will distinctly separate the two classes.

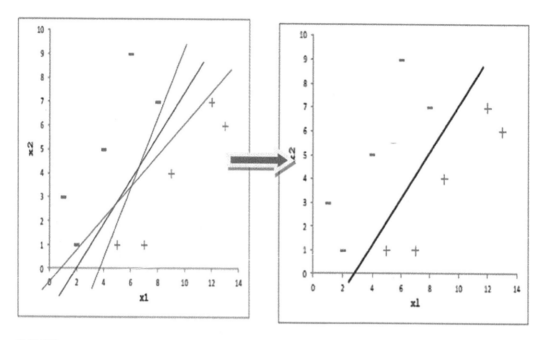

FIGURE 6.88   (a) Possible hyperplanes and (b) optimal hyperplane.

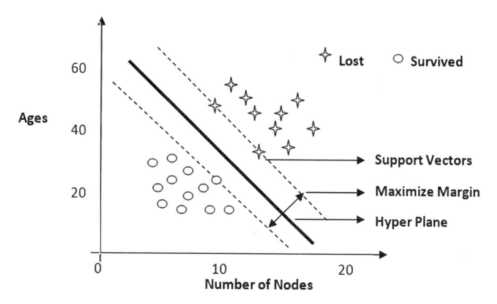

FIGURE 6.89   A simple SVM.

The distance between the closest point (support vector) and the decision boundary is defined as margin. Among all possible decision surfaces, choose the optimal decision surface for which the margin width is high. There can be a minimum of two support vectors and a maximum of any number of vectors. But typically, the number of support vectors should be extremely small. These support vectors determine the equation of a line. SVM has a clear way to prevent overfitting and works well with a relatively larger number of features without requiring too much computation.

6.6.2 MATHEMATICAL FORMULATION

Let us understand the mathematical intuition behind SVM by defining functional and geometrical margins. Functional margin is defined as the distance between the arbitrary point (x_i, y_i) and the decision boundary (w, b). Functional margin γ^i is the distance between (x_i, y_i) and the decision boundary and is derived in Equation 6.28.

$$\gamma^i = y_i\left(w^T x_i + b\right) \tag{6.28}$$

Similarly, for another point (x_j, y_j) that is farther from the decision boundary, the functional margin is as follows in Equation 6.29.

$$\gamma^j = y_j\left(w^T x_j + b\right) \tag{6.29}$$

The functional margin of point (x_i, y_i) is greater than the functional margin of point (x_j, y_j), as shown in Figure 6.90. The larger the functional margin, the higher the confidence.

And now, we can define the functional margin for a set of training points $S = \left\{(x_1, y_1), (x_2, y_2), \ldots, (x_m, y_m)\right\}$

$$\gamma = \min \gamma^i \text{ for } i = 1, 2, \ldots, m \tag{6.30}$$

If we scale w and b, the functional margin gets larger. To overcome this drawback, a geometric margin comes into the picture. Figure 6.91 shows that the **geometric margin** is invariant to the scaling of the equation. Let w be the vector normal to the decision surface.

And let $\dfrac{w}{\|w\|}$ be the unit vector normal to the decision surface. For example, let us assume $w = (2, 3)$, then $\|w\| = \sqrt{2^2 + 3^2}$

$$\frac{w}{\|w\|} = \left(\frac{2}{\sqrt{13}}, \frac{3}{\sqrt{13}}\right) \tag{6.31}$$

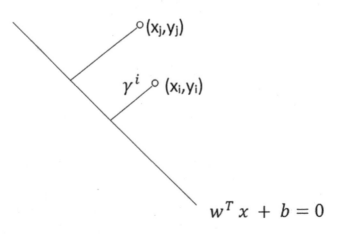

FIGURE 6.90 Functional margin.

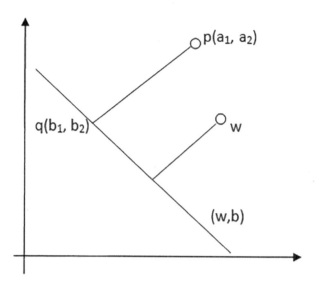

FIGURE 6.91 Geometric margin.

Now, if we want to find the distance of p from q. But the distance is in the direction of w, and we can write it as

$$p = q + \gamma \frac{w}{\|w\|} \tag{6.32}$$

The above equation 6.6 can be rewritten as

$$\left(a_1, a_2\right) = \left(b_1, b_2\right) + \gamma \frac{w}{\|w\|}$$

$$w^T \left(\left(a_1, a_2\right) - \gamma \frac{w}{\|w\|}\right) + b = 0$$

$$\gamma = y \frac{\left(w^T \left(a_1, a_2\right) + b\right)}{\|w\|} \tag{6.33}$$

Now, we can scale $\|w\| = 1$; then,

$$\gamma = y\left(w^T \left(a_1, a_2\right) + b\right) \tag{6.34}$$

After normalization, the geometric margin is

$$\frac{\gamma}{\|w\|} \tag{6.35}$$

$$w^T x_i + b \geq \gamma \quad \text{for + ve points}$$

$$w^T x_i + b < \gamma \quad \text{for - ve points}$$

and can be rewritten as

$$y_i(w^T x_i + b)1$$

$$y_i\left(w^T x_i + b\right) < 1 \text{ for } \quad i = 1, 2, \dots, m$$

$$\gamma = 1$$

$$\text{maximize} \frac{1}{\|w\|} \equiv \text{minimize} \frac{1}{2}\|w\|^2$$

Hence, the formulation for optimization problem concerning SVM subject to linear constraints is given as follows:

$$\text{minimize} \frac{1}{2}\|w\|^2 \qquad\qquad (6.36)$$

$$\text{s.t.} \quad y_i\left(w^T x_i + b\right) \geq 1$$

6.6.2.1 Maximize Margin with Noise

SVM can handle the noise in the data in a very efficient way. The optimization function is required to find the weight vector w and b such that the margin width is maximized. So the margin can be written as in Equation 6.37.

$$\max \frac{2}{\|w\|} \qquad\qquad (6.37)$$

And for each of the m training points $\left(x_i, y_i\right)$

$$\text{s.t.} \ y_i\left(w^T x_i + b\right) \geq 1$$

and can be rewritten as a minimization problem

$$\|w\|^2 = w \cdot w \ \text{is minimized}$$

And for each of the m training points $\left(x_i, y_i\right)$

$$\text{s.t.} \ y_i\left(w^T x_i + b\right) \geq 1$$

The main objective is to minimize $w \cdot w + c$ where c is the distance of error points to their correct zones.

6.6.2.2 *Slack Variable* ξ_i

In Figure 6.92, there are two wrongly classified slack variables given as ξ_1, ξ_2 and the maximum margin is given as M, which we want to maximize.

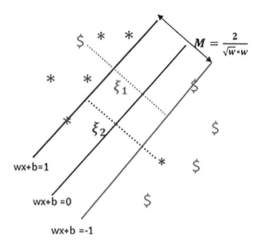

FIGURE 6.92 Maximize margin with noise.

The maximum margin with noise is defined by adding the penalty due to slack variables.

$$\text{minimize} \quad w \cdot w + c \sum_{k=1}^{n} \xi_k \qquad (6.38)$$

$$\text{s.t.} \quad y_k \left(w \cdot x_k + b \right) \geq 1 - \xi_k, \quad k = 1, \ldots, m$$

$$\xi_k \geq 0 \quad k = 1, \ldots, m$$

The Lagrangian of this quantity will be given in Equation 6.10.

$$L\left(w, b, \xi, \alpha, \beta\right) = \frac{1}{2} w \cdot w + C \sum_{i=1}^{m} \xi_i + \sum_{i=1}^{m} \alpha_i \left[y_i \left(x \cdot w + b \right) - 1 + \xi_i \right] - \sum_{i=1}^{m} \beta_i \xi_i \qquad (6.39)$$

where α_i and β_i are Lagrange multipliers ≥ 0

The soft SVM separates the positive and negative points. And the solution to the dual problem is given in Equation 6.40.

$$w = \sum_{i=1}^{m} \alpha_i y_i x_i \quad (6.40)$$

$$b = y_k \left(1 - \xi_k \right) - \sum_{i=1}^{m} \alpha_i y_i x_i x_k \qquad (6.41)$$

for any k such that $\alpha_k > 0$. And for classification, the function $f(x)$ is given as in Equation 6.42.

$$f(x) = \sum_{i=1}^{m} \alpha_i y_i x_i \cdot x + b \qquad (6.42)$$

where x is the test point and α_i is nonzero support vectors.

However, the decision surface classifier is still linear and cannot handle the nonlinear case. Overfitting is controlled by soft margin SVM. The difference between soft margin and hard margin of SVM is presented in Figure 6.93.

Let see a simple example in one-dimensional space as shown in Figure 6.94. Suppose we have three data points and one scalar feature x with two negative classes ($x=-3$ and -1) and one positive class ($x=2$). These data are easily separable with many linear classifiers ($wx+b$). So let's find the classifier with maximum margin.

$$x = -3 \quad \text{and} \quad y = -1$$

$$x = -1 \quad \text{and} \quad y = -1$$

$$x = 2 \quad \text{and} \quad y = 1$$

The margin constraints are rewritten and visualized in two-dimensional spaces as in Figure 6.95. The set of parameters that satisfy our margin constraints are shown in the green-shaded region.

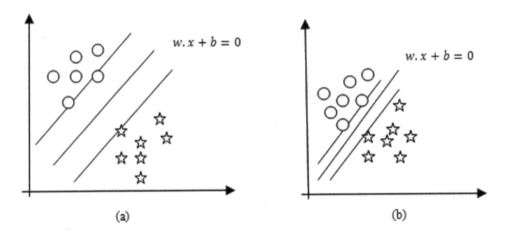

FIGURE 6.93   (a) Soft margin SVM and (b) hard margin SVM.

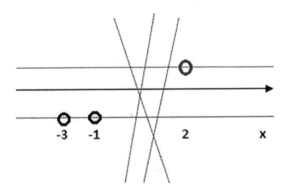

FIGURE 6.94   Points at one-dimensional space.

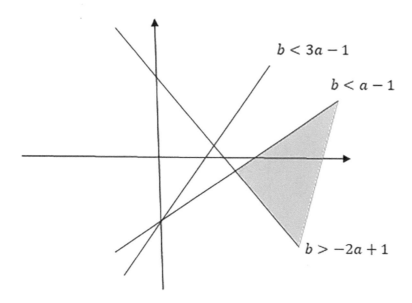

FIGURE 6.95   Visualization of margin constraints in 2D space.

$$a(-3) + b < -1 \rightarrow b < 3a - 1$$

$$a(-1) + b < -1 \rightarrow b < a - 1$$

$$a(2) + b < +1 \rightarrow b > -2a + 1$$

Finally, the objective is to minimize $\|a\|$.

6.6.3   Loss Minimization

In Figure 6.96, the data point D is misclassified, and for such instance, SVM defines slack variable ξ

$$\text{minimize} \frac{1}{2}\|w\|^2 + C\sum_i \xi$$

$$\text{s.t.} \quad y_i\left(w^T x_i + b\right)1$$

$$\text{minimize} \frac{1}{2}\|w\|^2 + C\sum_i \max\left(0, 1 - y_i\left(w^T x_i\right)\right) \qquad (6.43)$$

where C is the regularization parameter that can be set using cross-validation.

An instance may have four possible cases described in Figure 6.96 while classifying the data points.

1. The data point A is on the correct side, and far away from the margin, then the penalty is 0
2. The data point B is on the correct side, and closer tothe margin, then the penalty is 0
3. The data point C is the correct side but is in the margin lying very close to the hyperplane then the penalty is $1 - y_i\left(w^T x_i\right)$
4. The data point D is on the wrong side; then, the penalty is $1 - y_i\left(w^T x_i\right)$

And the comparison of hinge loss with 0–1 loss is shown in Figure 6.97.

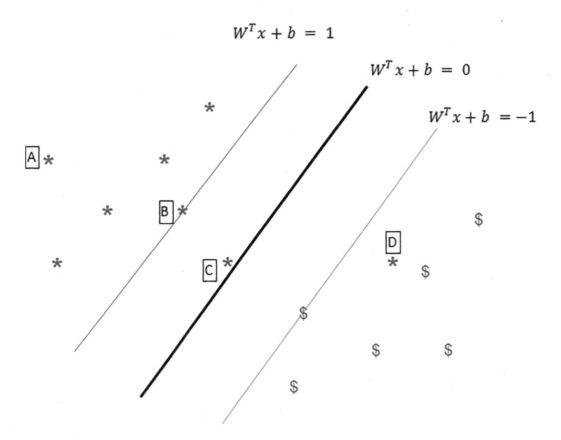

FIGURE 6.96   Four possible cases in classifying.

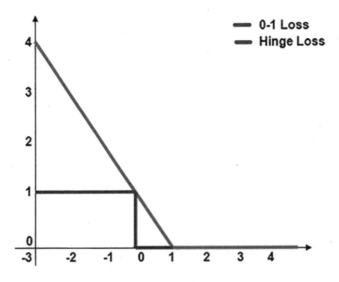

FIGURE 6.97   Comparisons of 0–1 loss and hinge loss.

6.6.4   DUAL FORMULATION

Lagrangian duality for a primal problem is to minimize $f(w)$ where w is the parameter. There are two linear constraints: inequality constraints $g(w)$ and equality constraints $h(w)$.

$$\min_w f(w) \tag{6.44}$$
$$\text{s.t. } g_i(w) \le 0, \ i = 1, 2,..,k$$
$$h(w) = 0 \ i = 1, 2,...,l$$

The generalized Lagrangian is given as $L(w,\alpha,\beta)$ where α,β are Lagrange multipliers and $\alpha \ge 0$

$$L(w,\alpha,\beta) = f(w) + \sum_{i=1}^{k} \alpha_i g_i(w) + \sum_{i=1}^{l} \beta_i h_i(w) \tag{6.45}$$

Lemma:

$$\max_{\alpha,\beta,\alpha_i \ge 0} L(w,\alpha,\beta) = \begin{cases} f(w) \ if \ w & \text{Satisfies primal constraints} \\ \infty & \text{Otherwise} \end{cases}$$

The solution to the primal problem is p^*, and the dual problem is d^*.

Theorem (Weak Duality)

$$\mathbf{p^* = \min_w \max_{\alpha,\beta,\alpha_i \ge 0} L(w, \alpha, \beta)}$$

$$\mathbf{d^* = \max_{\alpha,\beta,\alpha_i \ge 0} \min_w L(w, \alpha, \beta)}$$

$$d^* = \max_{\alpha,\beta,\alpha_i \ge 0} \min_w L(w,\alpha,\beta) \le \min_w \max_{\alpha,\beta,\alpha_i \ge 0} L(w,\alpha,\beta) = p^* \tag{6.46}$$

Theorem (Strong Duality)

If there exists a saddle point of $L(w,\alpha,\beta)$, we have $d^* = p^*$. As per the strong duality theorem, when the saddle point exists, the following Karush–Kuhn–Tucker (KKT) conditions are satisfied.

$$\frac{\partial}{\partial w_i} L(w,\alpha,\beta) = 0, \quad i = 1,...,k$$

$$\frac{\partial}{\partial b_i} L(w,\alpha,\beta) = 0, \quad i = 1,...,l$$

$$\alpha_i g_i(w) = 0, \quad i = 1,...,m$$

$$g_i(w) \le 0, \quad i = 1,...,m$$

$$\alpha_i \ge 0, \quad i = 1,...,m$$

The theorem states that if $w^*, \alpha^*,$ and β^* satisfy KKT conditions, then it is a solution to the primal and dual problems.

In SVM, as given in the above equation if α_i is nonzero, then such points are called support vectors.

$$\alpha_i g_i(w) = 0 \qquad\qquad (6.47)$$

If $\alpha_i > 0$, then $g_i(w) = 0$.

Now, let's see how to solve the optimization problem in SVM. After applying Lagrangian, the quadratic programming with linear constraints is as follows.

min w and b with fixed α.

$$minimize \; \frac{1}{2}\|w\|^2 s.t.\, y_i(w^T x_i + b) \geq 1$$

$$minimize \; L_p(w, b, \alpha_i) = \frac{1}{2}\|w\|^2 - \sum_{i=1}^{n} \alpha_i (\, y_i(w^T x_i + b) - 1)$$

$$s.t.\, \alpha_i \geq 0$$

$$\frac{\partial L_p}{\partial w} = 0 \rightarrow w = \sum_{i=1}^{n} \alpha_i y_i x_i$$

$$\frac{\partial L_p}{\partial b} = 0 \rightarrow \alpha_i y_i = 0$$

$$L_p(w, b, \alpha) = \sum_{i=1}^{m} \alpha_i - \frac{1}{2}\sum_{i,j=1}^{m} \alpha_i \alpha_j y_i y_j \left(x_i^T x_j \right) - b \sum_{i=1}^{m} \alpha_i y_i \qquad (6.48)$$

$$L_p(w, b, \alpha) = \sum_{i=1}^{m} \alpha_i - \frac{1}{2}\sum_{i,j=1}^{m} \alpha_i \alpha_j y_i y_j \left(x_i^T x_j \right)$$

Now, we have the following dual problem, and this is a quadratic programming problem where a global maxima α_i can be found at all times.

$$\max_a J(\alpha) = \sum_{i=1}^{m} \alpha_i - \frac{1}{2}\sum_{i,j=1}^{m} \alpha_i \alpha_j y_i y_j \left(x_i^T x_j \right) \qquad (6.49)$$

s.t, $\alpha_i \geq 0, \quad i = 1,\dots,k$

$$\sum_{i=1}^{m} \alpha_i y_i = 0 \qquad\qquad (6.50)$$

After getting the Lagrangian multiplier α_j, then the parameter vectors w can be reconstructed as follows:

$$w = \sum_{i=1}^{m} \alpha_i y_i x_i w = \sum_{i\in SV} \alpha_i y_i x_i \qquad\qquad (6.51)$$

TABLE 6.37
Two-Dimensional Data

x_1	x_2	y	Lagrange Multiplier α
0.3858	0.4687	1	65.5261
0.4871	0.611	−1	65.5261
0.9218	0.4103	−1	0
0.7382	0.8936	−1	0
0.1763	0.0579	1	0
0.4057	0.3529	1	0
0.9355	0.8132	-1	0
0.2146	0.0099	1	0

At last, compute with new data z

$$w^T z + b = \sum_{i \in SV} \alpha_i y_i \left(x_i^T z \right) + b \tag{6.52}$$

If the resulting sum is +ve, then classify the new data z as 1, and else, if the sum is −ve, then z is classified as 2. The discriminant function w depends on the dot product of the new data z and support vector x_i.

Example Consider the two-dimensional data as shown in Table 6.37, which contain eight instances.
Let $w = (w_1, w_2)$ and b denote the parameters of the decision boundary; using the below equation, we can solve for w_1 and w_2 in the following way:

$$w_1 = \sum_i \alpha_i y_i x_{i1} = 65.5621*1*0.3858 + 65.5621*-1*0.4871 = -6.64$$

$$w_2 = \sum_i \alpha_i y_i x_{i2} = 65.5621*1*0.4687 + 65.5621*-1*0.611 = -9.32$$

The bias term b is computed using equation

$$b^{(1)} = 1 - w \cdot x_1 = 1 - (-6.64)(0.3858) - (-9.32)(0.4687) = 7.9300$$

$$b^{(2)} = -1 - w \cdot x_2 = -1 - (-6.64)(0.4871) - (-9.32)(0.611) = 7.9289$$

$$\text{Bias } b = \frac{b^{(1)} + b^{(2)}}{2} = 7.93$$

The decision boundary corresponding to these parameters is shown in Figure 6.98.
Once the decision boundary is found, a test instance z is classified as

$$f(z) = \text{sign}(w.z + b) = \text{sign}\left(\sum_{i=1}^{N} \alpha_i y_i x_i . z + b\right)$$

If $f(z) = 1$, then the test instance is classified as a positive class; otherwise, it is classified as negative class.

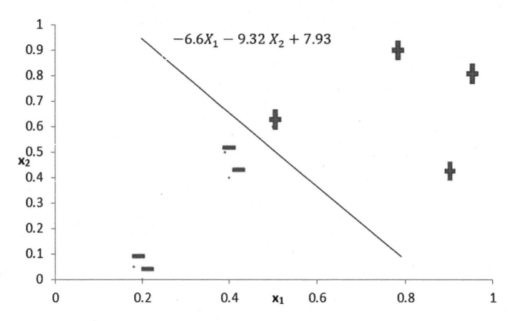

FIGURE 6.98 Decision boundary.

6.6.5 THE KERNEL TRICK

To explore the kernel trick mechanism, we must understand the math behind linearly separable and nonlinearly separable. Consider a binary classification problem with class labels 0 and 1. A linearly separable case is the one in which a single line separates the two classes, whereas nonlinearly separable case is the one in which more than one line is required to separate the two classes. Logic functions such as AND function and OR function are linearly separable, while XOR function is nonlinearly separable, as shown in Figures 6.99 and 6.100. Solved examples to understand the concept are illustrated in Section 6.6.10 of this chapter.

6.6.6 POLYNOMIAL KERNEL

The notion of the kernel function in SVM is given in Equation 6.53.

$$g(x) = w^T \varnothing(x) + b = \sum_{i \in SV} \alpha_i \varnothing(x_i)^T \varnothing(x) + b \tag{6.53}$$

A kernel function is the dot product of two feature vectors in feature space in Equation 6.54.

$$k(x_a, x_b) = \varnothing(x_a) \cdot \varnothing(x_b) \tag{6.54}$$

The idea of the kernel function is to replace the dot product with the kernel function. To prove this, we can solve an example given two-dimensional vectors $\bar{x} = [x_1, x_2]$ where x_1 and x_2 are the two attributes of the vector. Let $k(x_i, x_j) = (1 + x_i.x_j)^2$; we need to show $k(x_i, x_j) = \varnothing(x_i) \cdot \varnothing(x_j)$

$$k(x_i, x_j) = (1 + x_i \cdot x_j)^2$$

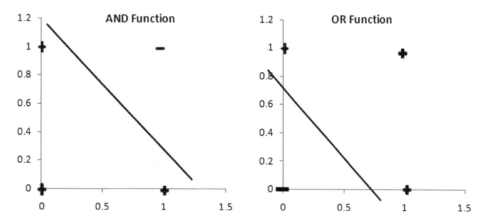

FIGURE 6.99 Linearly separable.

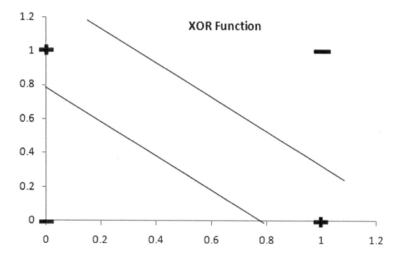

FIGURE 6.100 Nonlinearly separable.

where x_{i1} and x_{i2} are the two attributes of x_i and x_{j1} and x_{j2} are the two attributes of x_j.

$$k(x_i,x_j) = 1 + x_{i1}^2 x_{j1}^2 + 2x_{i1}x_{j1}x_{i2}x_{j2} + x_{i2}^2 x_{j2}^2 + 2x_{i1}x_{j1} + 2x_{i2}x_{j2}$$

can be rewritten as

$$k(x_i,x_j) = \left[1 \quad x_{i1}^2 \quad \sqrt{2}x_{i1}x_{i2}x_{i2}^2 \quad \sqrt{2x_{i1}} \quad \sqrt{2x_{i2}}\right] \cdot \left[1 \quad x_{j1}^2 \quad \sqrt{2}x_{j1}x_{j2}x_{j2}^2 \quad \sqrt{2x_{j1}} \quad \sqrt{2x_{j2}}\right]$$

$$= \varnothing(x_i) \cdot \varnothing(x_j)$$

where $\varnothing(x) = \left[1 \quad x_1^2 \quad \sqrt{2}x_1x_2x_2^2 \quad \sqrt{2x_1} \quad \sqrt{2x_2}\right]$. Thus, the solution of the determinant function is given as

$$g(x) = \sum_{i \in SV} \alpha_i k(x_i,x_j) + b$$

Commonly used kernel functions are the linear kernel, polynomial kernel, and Gaussian kernel.

Linear kernel is given in Equation 6.24.

$$K\left(x_i, x_j\right) = x_i \cdot x_j \tag{6.55}$$

A non-stationary kernel is also called the polynomial kernel. It is well applicable for the problems where all the training data are normalized. Polynomial of power p is given in Equation 6.25.

$$K\left(x_i, x_j\right) = (1 + x_i \cdot x_j)^p \tag{6.56}$$

where p is the polynomial power.

The polynomial kernel is a nonlinear kernel that should satisfy Mercer's theorem.

6.6.6.1 Mercer's Theorem

A kernel function can be expressed as

$$k\left(x_i, x_j\right) = \emptyset(x_i) \cdot \emptyset(x_j) \tag{6.57}$$

If and only if for any function $g(x)$ such that $\int g(x)^2 dx$ is finite, then

$$\int k(x, y) g(x) g(y) dx \, dy \geq 0$$

6.6.6.2 Radial Basis Function (RBF) Kernel

The most common kernel function is the RBF or Gaussian similarity kernel shown in Figure 6.101. This kernel results in high values near the point x, and the parameter $\sigma = 1$ is used to control over- and underfitting. The equation for the RBF kernel is given in Equation 6.27.

$$K\left(x_i, x_j\right) = e^{-\frac{\|x_i - x_j\|^2}{2\sigma^2}} \tag{6.58}$$

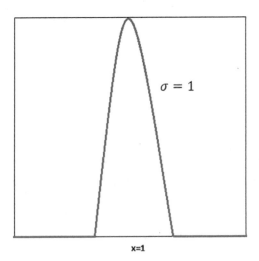

FIGURE 6.101   RBF kernel.

6.6.6.3   Other Domain-Specific Kernel

The most challenging part is choosing the right kernel function, and it is highly problem-specific.

6.6.6.4   Sigmoid Kernel

An SVM with a sigmoid kernel is equivalent to a simple two-layer neural network with no hidden layers known as a multilayer perceptron. It is also called the hyperbolic tangent kernel. It comes from neural networks, where artificial neurons often use the bipolar sigmoid mechanism as an activation function. The sigmoid kernel equation is given in Equation 6.59.

$$K\left(x_i, x_j\right) = \tanh\left(\alpha x_i \cdot x_j - \delta\right) \tag{6.59}$$

6.6.6.5   Exponential Kernel

It is closely equivalent to the Gaussian kernel and is shown below in Equation 6.60.

$$K\left(x_i, x_j\right) = e^{\left(-\frac{\|x_i - x_j\|}{2\sigma^2}\right)} \tag{6.60}$$

6.6.6.6   ANOVA Kernel

It is said to perform well in multidimensional regression problems.

$$K\left(x_i, x_j\right) = \text{sum}_{\{k=1\}}^{n} \exp\left(-\text{sigma}\left(x_i^k - x_j^k\right)^2\right)^d \tag{6.61}$$

6.6.6.7   Rational Quadratic Kernel

It is less computationally intensive than the Gaussian kernel. If the Gaussian becomes too expensive, then rational quadratic kernel can be used as an alternative.

$$k\left(x_i, x_j\right) = 1 - \frac{\|x_i - x_j\|^2}{\|x_i - x_j\|^2 + c} \tag{6.62}$$

6.6.6.8   Multiquadratic Kernel

The multiquadratic kernel can be used in the same situations as the rational quadratic kernel. As is the case with the sigmoid kernel, it is also an example of a non-positive definite kernel.

$$k\left(x_i, x_j\right) = \sqrt{\|x_i - x_j\|^2 + c^2} \tag{6.63}$$

6.6.6.9   Inverse Multiquadratic Kernel

The Gaussian kernel results in a kernel matrix with full rank and thus forms an infinite dimension feature space.

$$k\left(x_i, x_j\right) = \frac{1}{\sqrt{\|x_i - x_j\|^2 + c^2}} \tag{6.64}$$

6.6.6.10   Circular Kernel

The circular kernel is used in geostatic applications. It is an example of an isotropic stationary kernel and is positive definite in R_2.

$$k(x_i,x_j) = \frac{2}{\pi}\arccos\left(-\frac{\|x_i - x_j\|}{\sigma}\right) - \frac{2}{\pi}\frac{\|x_i - x_j\|}{\sigma} \tag{6.65}$$

6.6.6.11   Bayesian Kernel

The Bayesian kernel could be given as

$$k(x,y) = \prod_{l=1}^{N} k_l(x_l, y_l) \tag{6.66}$$

6.6.6.12   Chi-Square Kernel

It is derived from chi-square distribution and is given as follows:

$$k(x,y) = 1 - \sum_{l=1}^{n} \frac{(x_i - y_i)^2}{\frac{1}{2}(x_i + y_i)} \tag{6.67}$$

6.6.6.13   Histogram Intersection Kernel

It is widely used in image classification and is also called as min kernel.

$$k(x,y) = \sum_{l=1}^{n} \min(x_i, y_i) \tag{6.68}$$

6.6.6.14   Generalized Histogram Intersection Kernel

It is a variant of histogram intersection kernel and is widely applicable in image classification.

$$k(x,y) = \sum_{l=1}^{n} \min\left(|x_i|^\alpha, |y_i|^\beta\right) \tag{6.69}$$

6.6.7   NU SVM

In soft margin SVM, finding the parameter C is difficult. Instead of using C, Scholkopf et al. introduce nu SVM. nu is bounded between 0 and 1. The function is given as in Equation 6.70.

$$\text{minimize} \frac{1}{2}\|w\|^2 - \gamma p + \frac{1}{2}\sum_{t} \xi^t \tag{6.70}$$

Subject to

$$r^t\left(w^T x^t + w_0\right) \geq \rho - \xi^t, \ \xi^t \geq 0, \ \rho \geq 0$$

6.6.8   SVM Regression

Let us extend SVM to regression problem, given the training data $\{(X_1, y_1)\ldots(X_n, y_n)\} X_i \in R^m$, $y_i \in R$ the idea is to learn the best optimal function to predict y given X. This regression problem can be parameterized by weight vector w as shown below in Equation 6.71,

$$g(X, W) = w_1 \varnothing_1(x) + \cdots + w_{m'} \varnothing_{m'}(x) + b$$

$$= w^T \varnothing(x) + b \tag{6.71}$$

where $\varnothing_i : R^m \to R$. If we choose $\varnothing_i(X) = x_i$, then it is a linear regression model. By specifying $Z = \varnothing(X) \in R^{m'}$, we are learning a linear model in a newly transformed feature space. Kernel functions can be used instead of explicitly specifying the dot product.

Loss function L in regression problem is to minimize W and is given in Equation 6.72,

$$\sum_i L\left(y_{i,g}(X_i, W)\right) \tag{6.72}$$

A special loss function called ε insensitive loss is used, which allows us to use kernel trick in SVM regression as given in Equation 6.42.

$$L_\varepsilon\left(y_i, g(X_i, W)\right) = \begin{cases} 0 & \text{If } |y_i - g(X_i, W)| < \varepsilon \\ |y_i - g(X_i, W)| - \varepsilon & \text{Otherwise} \end{cases} \tag{6.73}$$

where ε is the parameter of the loss function, and if the prediction is within ε of true value, then there is no loss. And choose absolute error value instead of a square of the error to achieve high robustness.

Hence, empirical risk minimization under ε insensitive loss would minimize

$$\sum_{i=1}^{n} \max\left(|y_i - \varnothing(X_i)^T W - b| - \varepsilon, o\right) \tag{6.74}$$

The optimization problem for SVM regression is to find W, b, $\varepsilon_i, \varepsilon_i'$

$$\text{Minimize} \frac{1}{2} W^T W + C\left(\sum_{i=1}^{n} \varepsilon_i + \sum_{i=1}^{n} \varepsilon_i'\right) \tag{6.75}$$

$$\text{Subject to } y_i - W^T \varnothing(X_i) - b \le \varepsilon + \varepsilon_i, \ i = 1,\ldots,n$$

$$W^T \varnothing(X_i) + b - y_i \le \varepsilon + \varepsilon_i', \quad i = 1,\ldots,n$$

$$\varepsilon_i \ge 0, \quad \varepsilon_i' \ge 0, \quad i = 1,\ldots,n$$

To construct a dual problem for SVM regression, introduce non-negative multipliers α_i and α_i' as follows

$$\max_{\alpha, \alpha} \sum_{i=1}^{n} y_i(\alpha_i - \alpha_i') - \varepsilon \sum_{i=1}^{n} (\alpha_i + \alpha_i') - \frac{1}{2} \sum_{i,j} (\alpha_i - \alpha_i')(\alpha_j - \alpha_j') \varnothing(X_i)^T \varnothing(X_j)^T \tag{6.76}$$

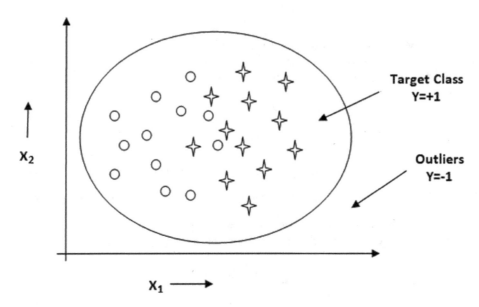

FIGURE 6.102 One-class classifier for outlier detection.

$$\text{Subject to} \sum_{i=1}^{n} (\alpha_i - \alpha_i') = 0$$

$$0 \le \alpha_i, \alpha_i' \le C,\ i = 1,\dots,n$$

6.6.9 ONE-CLASS SVM

Outlier detection is an example of one-class SVM. Outlier detection is used for anomaly detection, where one is interested in detecting abnormal or unusual observations. The training data contain outliers, which are defined as observations that are far from the others. A one-class SVM is an unsupervised learning algorithm that learns the boundaries of data points and can classify any points that lie outside the boundary as, you guessed it, outliers.

Figure 6.102 shows an example where the kitten and cub are the target classes with the label $y=+1$ and other extremes (neither kitten nor cub) are outliers $y=-1$. A one-class classifier is shown, which distinguishes kitten and cub from all other objects.

6.6.10 MULTICLASS SVM

In general, SVM is a binary classifier, but in real-time scenarios, there can be multiple classes. The multiclass classification can be achieved using one against one, one against all, and directed acyclic graph SVM methods.

6.6.10.1 One against All

In one against all, k binary SVM classifier is constructed where k is the number of classes. For example, there are three classes {1, 2, 3} as given in Figure 6.103. Initially, let us perform binary classification by assuming class 1 as positive and the remaining classes from 2 and 3 as negative. Similarly, repeat the same procedure for the other four classes.

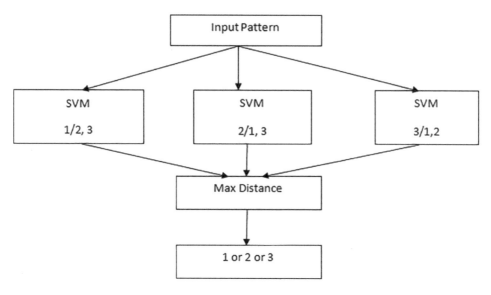

FIGURE 6.103   One against all.

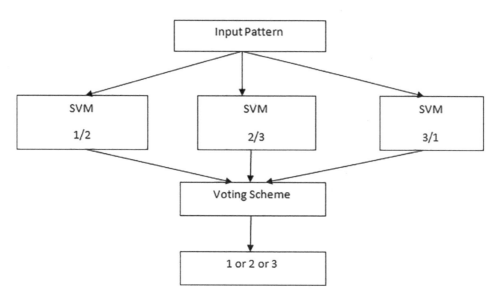

FIGURE 6.104   One against one.

6.6.10.2   One against One

In one against one method, for M classes, $M(M-1)/2$ classifiers are built. Figure 6.104 shows the architecture for three-class SVM problem using one against one method.

6.6.10.3   Directed Acyclic Graph SVM

It is a combination of one against one method and a directed acyclic graph concept. For the three-class example {1, 2, 3}, initially construct a binary classifier for classes {1 and 2} as in one against one method. The binary classifier moves to the right node if the data belong to class 1, else to the left node. Finally, the directed acyclic graph shown in Figure 6.105 is constructed to make a decision. The leaf node indicates the final class label.

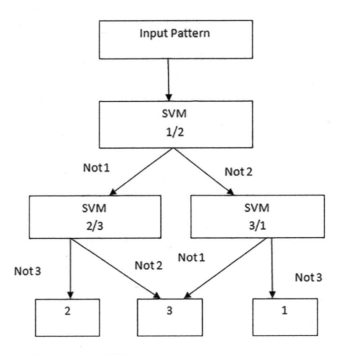

FIGURE 6.105 Directed acyclic graph SVM.

6.6.11   SVM Examples

Example 6.11

Let us see the linear SVM problem. Suppose we are given the following positively labeled data points

$$\left\{ \begin{pmatrix} 3 \\ 1 \end{pmatrix}, \begin{pmatrix} 3 \\ -1 \end{pmatrix}, \begin{pmatrix} 6 \\ 1 \end{pmatrix}, \begin{pmatrix} 6 \\ -1 \end{pmatrix} \right\}$$

and the following negatively labeled data points (see Figure 6.106):

$$\left\{ \begin{pmatrix} 1 \\ 0 \end{pmatrix}, \begin{pmatrix} 0 \\ 1 \end{pmatrix}, \begin{pmatrix} 0 \\ -1 \end{pmatrix}, \begin{pmatrix} -1 \\ 0 \end{pmatrix} \right\}$$

Let us identify a simple hyperplane that separates the positive and negative points. Linear SVM can be used because the data points are linearly separable.

Let us define a hyperplane by observing the given input data. There are three support vectors circled, as shown in Figure 6.107, which are close to the hyperplane and they are

$$\left\{ s_1 = \begin{pmatrix} 1 \\ 0 \end{pmatrix}, s_2 = \begin{pmatrix} 3 \\ 1 \end{pmatrix}, s_3 = \begin{pmatrix} 3 \\ -1 \end{pmatrix} \right\}$$

In what follows, we will use vectors augmented with 1 as a bias input

$$\left\{ \tilde{s}_1 = \begin{pmatrix} 1 \\ 0 \\ 1 \end{pmatrix}, \tilde{s}_2 = \begin{pmatrix} 3 \\ 1 \\ 1 \end{pmatrix}, \tilde{s}_3 = \begin{pmatrix} 3 \\ -1 \\ 1 \end{pmatrix} \right\}$$

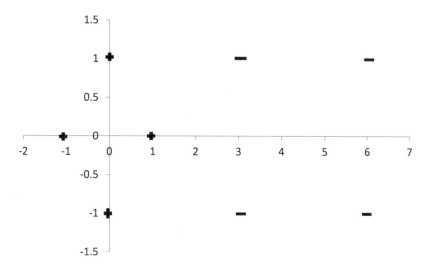

FIGURE 6.106 Linear SVM.

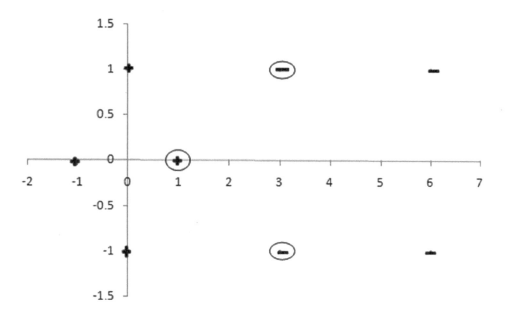

FIGURE 6.107 Linearly separable data points with support vectors.

Figure 6.108 represents the SVM architecture, and their corresponding equations 6.77 to 6.79 are given below.

$$\alpha_1 \varnothing(s_1) \cdot \varnothing(s_1) + \alpha_2 \varnothing(s_2) \cdot \varnothing(s_1) + \alpha_3 \varnothing(s_3) \cdot \varnothing(s_1) = -1 \qquad (6.77)$$

$$\alpha_1 \varnothing(s_1) \cdot \varnothing(s_2) + \alpha_2 \varnothing(s_2) \cdot \varnothing(s_2) + \alpha_3 \varnothing(s_3) \cdot \varnothing(s_2) = +1 \qquad (6.78)$$

$$\alpha_1 \varnothing(s_1) \cdot \varnothing(s_3) + \alpha_2 \varnothing(s_2) \cdot \varnothing(s_3) + \alpha_3 \varnothing(s_3) \cdot \varnothing(s_3) = +1 \qquad (6.79)$$

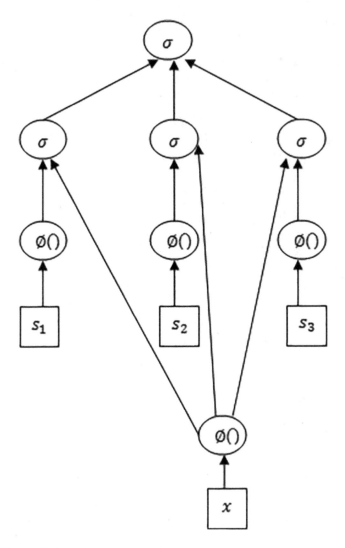

FIGURE 6.108   Linear SVM architecture.

Since, for now, we have $\varnothing() = I$, this reduces to

$$\alpha_1 \widetilde{s_1} \cdot \widetilde{s_1} + \alpha_2 \widetilde{s_2} \cdot \widetilde{s_1} + \alpha_3 \widetilde{s_3} \cdot \widetilde{s_1} = -1$$

$$\alpha_1 \widetilde{s_1} \cdot \widetilde{s_2} + \alpha_2 \widetilde{s_2} \cdot \widetilde{s_2} + \alpha_3 \widetilde{s_3} \cdot \widetilde{s_2} = +1$$

$$\alpha_1 \widetilde{s_1} \cdot \widetilde{s_3} + \alpha_2 \widetilde{s_2} \cdot \widetilde{s_3} + \alpha_3 \widetilde{s_3} \cdot \widetilde{s_3} = +1$$

Let us substitute values for $\widetilde{s_1}$, $\widetilde{s_2}$, and $\widetilde{s_3}$ in the above equations

$$\alpha_1 \begin{pmatrix} 1 \\ 0 \\ 1 \end{pmatrix} \cdot (1\ 0\ 1) + \alpha_2 \begin{pmatrix} 3 \\ 1 \\ 1 \end{pmatrix} \cdot (1\ 0\ 1) + \alpha_3 \begin{pmatrix} 3 \\ -1 \\ 1 \end{pmatrix} \cdot (1\ 0\ 1) = -1$$

$$\alpha_1 \begin{pmatrix} 1 \\ 0 \\ 1 \end{pmatrix} \cdot (3\ 1\ 1) + \alpha_2 \begin{pmatrix} 3 \\ 1 \\ 1 \end{pmatrix} \cdot (3\ 1\ 1) + \alpha_3 \begin{pmatrix} 3 \\ -1 \\ 1 \end{pmatrix} \cdot (3\ 1\ 1) = +1$$

$$\alpha_1 \begin{pmatrix} 1 \\ 0 \\ 1 \end{pmatrix} \cdot (3 \ -1 \ 1) + \alpha_2 \begin{pmatrix} 3 \\ 1 \\ 1 \end{pmatrix} \cdot (3 \ -1 \ 1) + \alpha_3 \begin{pmatrix} 3 \\ -1 \\ 1 \end{pmatrix} \cdot (3 \ -1 \ 1) = +1$$

$$2\alpha_1 + 4\alpha_2 + 4\alpha_3 = -1$$
$$4\alpha_1 + 11\alpha_2 + 9\alpha_3 = +1$$
$$4\alpha_1 + 9\alpha_2 + 11\alpha_3 = +1$$

By solving the above equations, we get $\alpha_1 = -3.5$, $\alpha_2 = 0.75$, and $\alpha_3 = 0.75$.

Now, we have the α_i. The equation of hyperplane can be written as

$$y = wx + b$$

The values of w and b are given by

$$\tilde{w} = \sum_i \alpha_i \cdot \tilde{s}_i$$

$$= -3.5 * \begin{pmatrix} 1 \\ 0 \\ 1 \end{pmatrix} + 0.75 * \begin{pmatrix} 3 \\ 1 \\ 1 \end{pmatrix} + 0.75 * \begin{pmatrix} 3 \\ -1 \\ 1 \end{pmatrix}$$

$$= \begin{pmatrix} 1 \\ 0 \\ -2 \end{pmatrix}$$

Here, $w = \begin{pmatrix} 1 \\ 0 \end{pmatrix}$ and $b = -2$. Plotting the line gives the expected decision boundary in a thick line, as shown in Figure 6.109.

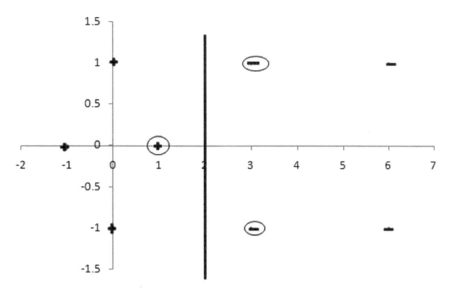

FIGURE 6.109 Linearly separable SVM with a hyperplane.

Example 6.12

Classify the given data points into two classes using SVM and find the optimal hyperplane

x	y	Label
1	1	−ve
2	1	−ve
1	−1	−ve
2	−1	−ve
4	0	+ve
5	1	+ve
5	−1	+ve
6	0	+ve

First, let us plot the data points in a graph; negative points are marked as '−', and positive points are marked as '+', as given in Figure 6.110.

There can be many possible hyperplanes, as shown in Figure 6.111, and the aim is to identify the optimal hyperplane.

There are three support vectors (Figure 6.112), namely S_1, S_2, and S_3.

$$S_1 = \begin{pmatrix} 2 \\ 1 \end{pmatrix} S_2 = \begin{pmatrix} 2 \\ -1 \end{pmatrix} S_3 = \begin{pmatrix} 4 \\ 0 \end{pmatrix}$$

Bias input is 1. So, augment the support vectors with the bias input, and then, S_1, S_2, and S_3 become $\widetilde{S_1}, \widetilde{S_2}, \widetilde{S_3}$ as shown below.

$$\widetilde{S_1} = \begin{pmatrix} 2 \\ 1 \\ 1 \end{pmatrix}, \widetilde{S_2} = \begin{pmatrix} 2 \\ -1 \\ 1 \end{pmatrix}, \widetilde{S_3} = \begin{pmatrix} 4 \\ 0 \\ 1 \end{pmatrix}$$

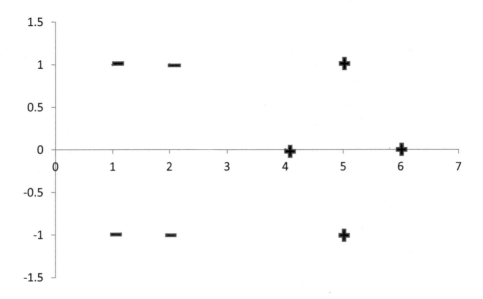

FIGURE 6.110   Representation of data points.

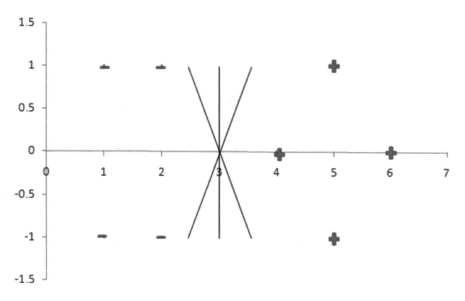

FIGURE 6.111   Possible hyperplanes.

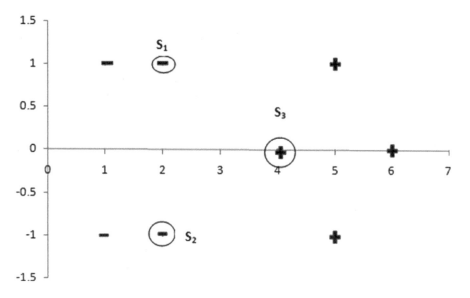

FIGURE 6.112   Support vectors representation.

We need to find the three parameters $\alpha_1, \alpha_2,$ and, α_3 based on the following three linear equations

$$\alpha_1 \widetilde{S_1} \widetilde{S_1} + \alpha_2 \widetilde{S_2} \widetilde{S_1} + \alpha_3 \widetilde{S_3} \widetilde{S_1} = -1 \left(-\text{ve class}\right)$$

$$\alpha_1 \widetilde{S_1} \widetilde{S_2} + \alpha_2 \widetilde{S_2} \widetilde{S_2} + \alpha_3 \widetilde{S_3} \widetilde{S_2} = -1 \left(-\text{ve class}\right)$$

$$\alpha_1 \widetilde{S_1} \widetilde{S_3} + \alpha_2 \widetilde{S_2} \widetilde{S_3} + \alpha_3 \widetilde{S_3} \widetilde{S_3} = +1 \left(+\text{ve class}\right)$$

Let's substitute $\widetilde{S}_1, \widetilde{S}_2, \widetilde{S}_3$ values in the above equations

$$\alpha_1 \begin{pmatrix} 2 \\ 1 \\ 1 \end{pmatrix}\begin{pmatrix} 2 \\ 1 \\ 1 \end{pmatrix} + \alpha_2 \begin{pmatrix} 2 \\ -1 \\ 1 \end{pmatrix}\begin{pmatrix} 2 \\ 1 \\ 1 \end{pmatrix} + \alpha_3 \begin{pmatrix} 4 \\ 0 \\ 1 \end{pmatrix}\begin{pmatrix} 2 \\ 1 \\ 1 \end{pmatrix} = -1$$

$$\alpha_1 \begin{pmatrix} 2 \\ 1 \\ 1 \end{pmatrix}\begin{pmatrix} 2 \\ -1 \\ 1 \end{pmatrix} + \alpha_2 \begin{pmatrix} 2 \\ -1 \\ 1 \end{pmatrix}\begin{pmatrix} 2 \\ -1 \\ 1 \end{pmatrix} + \alpha_3 \begin{pmatrix} 4 \\ 0 \\ 1 \end{pmatrix}\begin{pmatrix} 2 \\ -1 \\ 1 \end{pmatrix} = -1$$

$$\alpha_1 \begin{pmatrix} 2 \\ 1 \\ 1 \end{pmatrix}\begin{pmatrix} 4 \\ 0 \\ 1 \end{pmatrix} + \alpha_2 \begin{pmatrix} 2 \\ -1 \\ 1 \end{pmatrix}\begin{pmatrix} 4 \\ 0 \\ 1 \end{pmatrix} + \alpha_3 \begin{pmatrix} 4 \\ 0 \\ 1 \end{pmatrix}\begin{pmatrix} 4 \\ 1 \\ 1 \end{pmatrix} = +1$$

After simplification, we get

$$6\alpha_1 + 4\alpha_2 + 9\alpha_3 = -1$$

$$4\alpha_1 + 6\alpha_2 + 9\alpha_3 = -1$$

$$9\alpha_1 + 9\alpha_2 + 17\alpha_3 = 1$$

After solving the above three simultaneous equations, we get

$$\alpha_1 = \alpha_2 = -3.25 \quad \text{and} \quad \alpha_3 = 3.5$$

The hyperplane that discriminates the two classes is given by

$$\widetilde{w} = \sum_i \alpha_i S_i$$

$$\widetilde{w} = -3.25 \begin{pmatrix} 2 \\ 1 \\ 1 \end{pmatrix} - 3.25 \begin{pmatrix} 2 \\ -1 \\ 1 \end{pmatrix} + 3.5 \begin{pmatrix} 4 \\ 0 \\ 1 \end{pmatrix} = \begin{pmatrix} 1 \\ 0 \\ -3 \end{pmatrix}$$

Hence, we equate $y = wx + b$

where $w = \begin{pmatrix} 1 \\ 0 \end{pmatrix}$ and $b = -3$, and the expected hyperplane for this linear SVM is shown in Figure 6.113.

Most of the real-world data possess nonlinearity. Let's consider an example in nonlinear data in one-dimensional space as in Figure 6.114.

Convert them to higher-dimensional space by adding quadratic feature $x_2 = x_1^2$, which in turn makes the data linearly separable and is shown in Figure 6.115.

The data that are not linearly separable will not be having a single hyperplane to separate them. The data point x in the nonlinear model of feature space is mapped to the linear model of feature space $\emptyset(x)$. While mapping $x \rightarrow \emptyset(x)$, the computational cost becomes very high. We can achieve this transformation without any major hike in computational cost by using the kernel function in SVM.

Figure 6.116a is not linearly separable, but when we transform these points to appropriate high-dimensional feature space, the points may become linearly separable, as shown in Figure 6.116b.

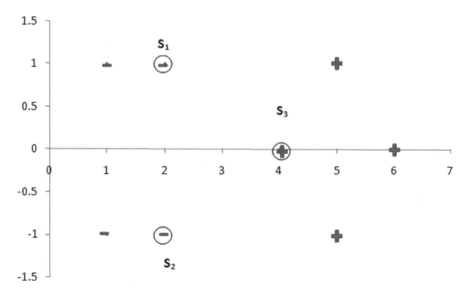

FIGURE 6.113 Optimal hyperplane.

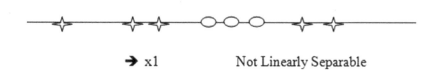

FIGURE 6.114 Nonlinearly separable data.

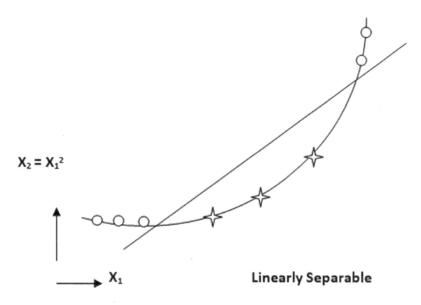

FIGURE 6.115 Linearly separable data.

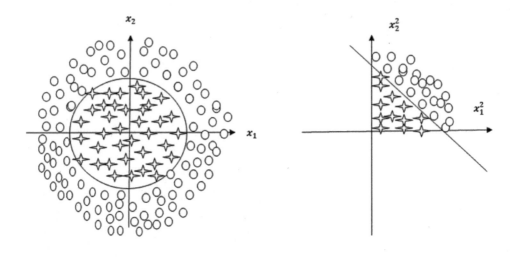

$$x \rightarrow \varphi(x)$$

FIGURE 6.116 (a) Hyperplane in the original two-dimensional space and (b) hyperplane in the transformed space.

Example 6.13

Let us see another problem to solve the nonlinear SVM case. Suppose we are given the following positively labeled (marked with '+') data points

$$\left\{ \begin{pmatrix} 2 \\ 2 \end{pmatrix}, \begin{pmatrix} 2 \\ -2 \end{pmatrix}, \begin{pmatrix} -2 \\ -2 \end{pmatrix}, \begin{pmatrix} -2 \\ 2 \end{pmatrix} \right\}$$

and the following negatively labeled (marked with '−') data points (see Figure 6.117):

$$\left\{ \begin{pmatrix} 1 \\ 1 \end{pmatrix}, \begin{pmatrix} 1 \\ -1 \end{pmatrix}, \begin{pmatrix} -1 \\ -1 \end{pmatrix}, \begin{pmatrix} -1 \\ 1 \end{pmatrix} \right\}$$

The points are nonlinearly separable, as shown in Figure 6.118. Therefore, we must use nonlinear SVM; i.e., the mapping function $\varnothing$ is a nonlinear mapping from input space into some feature space. The mapping is given as

$$\varnothing \begin{pmatrix} x_1 \\ x_2 \end{pmatrix} = \begin{cases} \begin{pmatrix} 4 - x_2 + |x_1 - x_2| \\ 4 - x_1 + |x_1 - x_2| \end{pmatrix} & \text{if } \sqrt{x_1^2 + x_2^2} > 2 \\ \begin{pmatrix} x_1 \\ x_2 \end{pmatrix} & \text{Otherwise} \end{cases}$$

The data are mapped into feature space for positive examples as

$$\left\{ \begin{pmatrix} 2 \\ 2 \end{pmatrix}, \begin{pmatrix} 6 \\ 2 \end{pmatrix}, \begin{pmatrix} 6 \\ 6 \end{pmatrix}, \begin{pmatrix} 2 \\ 6 \end{pmatrix} \right\}$$

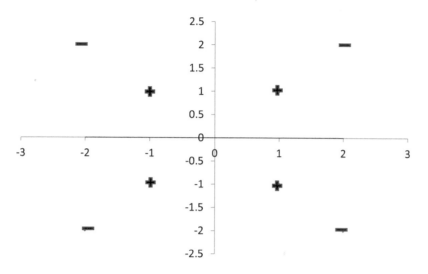

FIGURE 6.117 Nonlinear SVM.

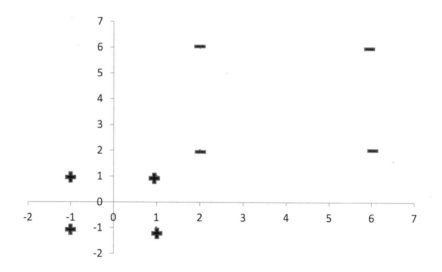

FIGURE 6.118 Nonlinearly separable data points.

and for negative examples as

$$\left\{ \begin{pmatrix} 1 \\ 1 \end{pmatrix}, \begin{pmatrix} 1 \\ -1 \end{pmatrix}, \begin{pmatrix} -1 \\ -1 \end{pmatrix}, \begin{pmatrix} -1 \\ 1 \end{pmatrix} \right\}$$

The points are plotted as shown in Figure 6.119 and support vectors (circled) are close to the hyperplane given by the coordinates.

$$\left\{ s_1 = \begin{pmatrix} 1 \\ 1 \end{pmatrix}, s_2 = \begin{pmatrix} 2 \\ 2 \end{pmatrix} \right\}$$

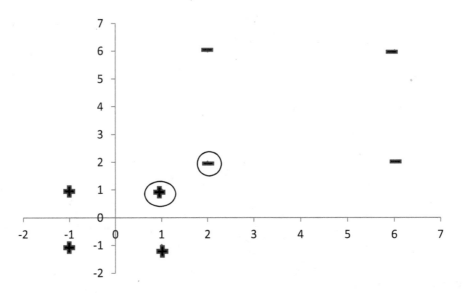

FIGURE 6.119 Nonlinear SVM with support vectors.

In what follows, we will use vectors augmented with 1 as a bias input

$$\left\{ s_1 = \begin{pmatrix} 1 \\ 1 \\ 1 \end{pmatrix}, s_2 = \begin{pmatrix} 2 \\ 2 \\ 1 \end{pmatrix} \right\}$$

The figure below represents the SVM architecture, and their corresponding equations are given below.

$$\alpha_1 \varnothing(s_1) \cdot \varnothing(s_1) + \alpha_2 \varnothing(s_2) \cdot \varnothing(s_1) = -1$$
$$\alpha_1 \varnothing(s_1) \cdot \varnothing(s_2) + \alpha_2 \varnothing(s_2) \cdot \varnothing(s_2) = +1$$

Since, for now, we have $\varnothing() = I$, this reduces to

$$\alpha_1 \widetilde{s_1} \cdot \widetilde{s_1} + \alpha_2 \widetilde{s_2} \cdot \widetilde{s_1} = -1$$
$$\alpha_1 \widetilde{s_1} \cdot \widetilde{s_2} + \alpha_2 \widetilde{s_2} \cdot \widetilde{s_2} = +1$$

Let us substitute values for $S1$, $S2$, and $S3$ in the above equations

$$\alpha_1 \begin{pmatrix} 1 \\ 1 \\ 1 \end{pmatrix} \cdot (1\ 1\ 1) + \alpha_2 \begin{pmatrix} 2 \\ 2 \\ 1 \end{pmatrix} \cdot (1\ 1\ 1) = -1$$

$$\alpha_1 \begin{pmatrix} 1 \\ 1 \\ 1 \end{pmatrix} \cdot (2\ 2\ 1) + \alpha_2 \begin{pmatrix} 2 \\ 2 \\ 1 \end{pmatrix} \cdot (2\ 2\ 1) = +1$$

$$3\alpha_1 + 5\alpha_2 = -1$$
$$5\alpha_1 + 9\alpha_2 = +1$$

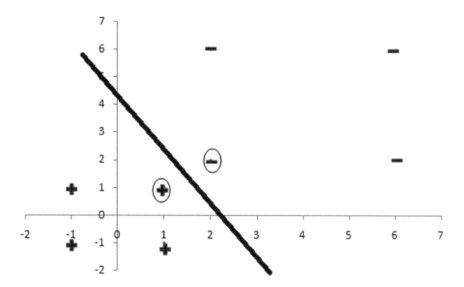

FIGURE 6.120 Nonlinear SVM with hyperplane.

By solving the above equations, we get $\alpha_1 = -7$, $\alpha_2 = 4$

Now, we have the α_i. The equation of hyperplane can be written as

$$y = wx + b$$

The values of w and b are given by

$$\tilde{w} = \sum_i \alpha_i \cdot \tilde{s}_i$$

$$= -7 \cdot \begin{pmatrix} 1 \\ 1 \\ 1 \end{pmatrix} + 4 \cdot \begin{pmatrix} 2 \\ 2 \\ 1 \end{pmatrix}$$

$$= \begin{pmatrix} 1 \\ 1 \\ -3 \end{pmatrix}$$

Here, $w = \begin{pmatrix} 1 \\ 1 \end{pmatrix}$ and $b=-3$. The expected decision boundary is the dark line shown in Figure 6.120.

Example 6.14

Given the ten instances in a table which is a nonlinearly separable case as shown in Figure 6.121. How to transform the nonlinearly separable into linearly separable using the kernel trick?

To transform the feature space from the original nonlinear space, then x_1 and x_2 are transformed to high-dimensional space z_1 and z_2 using the formula.

$$z_1 = x_1^2 \quad \text{and} \quad z_2 = x_1 \cdot x_2$$

The results are tabulated, and the output is shown in Figure 6.122.

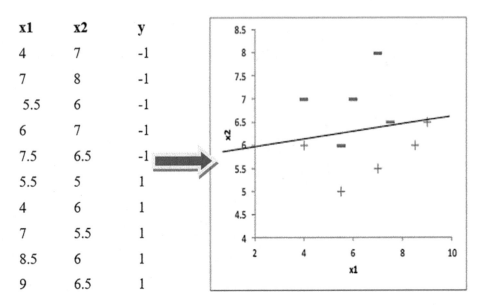

x1	x2	y
4	7	-1
7	8	-1
5.5	6	-1
6	7	-1
7.5	6.5	-1
5.5	5	1
4	6	1
7	5.5	1
8.5	6	1
9	6.5	1

FIGURE 6.121 Nonlinearly separable data points.

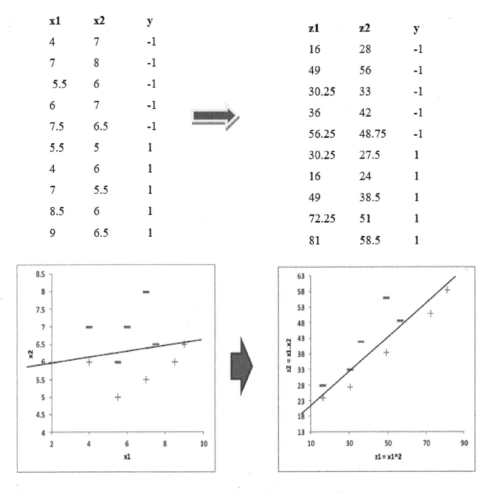

x1	x2	y
4	7	-1
7	8	-1
5.5	6	-1
6	7	-1
7.5	6.5	-1
5.5	5	1
4	6	1
7	5.5	1
8.5	6	1
9	6.5	1

z1	z2	y
16	28	-1
49	56	-1
30.25	33	-1
36	42	-1
56.25	48.75	-1
30.25	27.5	1
16	24	1
49	38.5	1
72.25	51	1
81	58.5	1

FIGURE 6.122 Transforming nonlinearly separable into linearly separable.

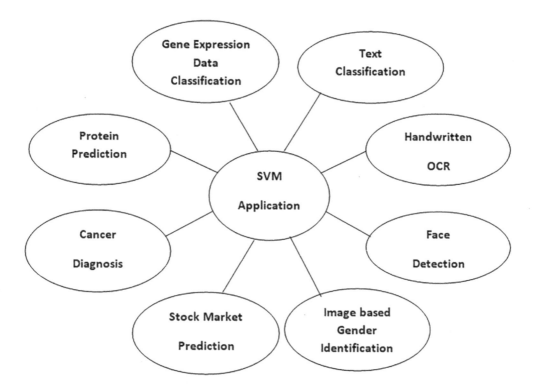

FIGURE 6.123 Applications of SVM.

6.6.12 REAL-WORLD APPLICATIONS

SVM has been used in many real-world applications such as image classification, handwritten OCR, bioinformatics, and text categorization (Figure 6.123). In addition, the bioinformatics field has been used for cancer diagnosis based on gene expression of data and protein secondary structure prediction. The advantages of SVM are that sparseness of solution to problems and overfitting can be controlled by using a soft margin approach make it used in a wide range of applications.

6.6.12.1 Classification of Cognitive Impairment

Alzheimer's disease (AD) is a degenerative brain disease and the most common cause of dementia. The symptoms of dementia include memory loss and difficulties with thinking, problem-solving, or language, which seriously affect a patient's daily life. Mild cognitive impairment (MCI) is an early stage of AD characterized by significant cognitive impairment in the absence of dementia. In the United States, there were more than 5.2 million people with AD in 2014, and it is estimated that 13.8 million Americans have AD by 2050. Thus, precise prediction and diagnosis of AD, especially at its early warning stage such as MCI, have become a crucial step to delay or even avoid dementia.

Commonly used modalities include magnetic resonance imaging (MRI), functional magnetic resonance imaging (fMRI), and positron emission tomography (PET). Owing to its easy access in clinical settings, MRI receives the most attention of researchers compared with other modalities. The structural changes in the brain associated with AD can be noninvasively assessed using MRI.

Early detection of AD at the early stage is of great importance in terms of patient management. Some of the earliest symptoms of AD, such as short-term memory loss, are often mistaken as related to aging and stress; it remains challenging to predict the disease in an early stage. The Alzheimer's Disease Neuroimaging Initiative (ADNI) dataset is used for evaluation. The design of the system is given in Figure 6.124.

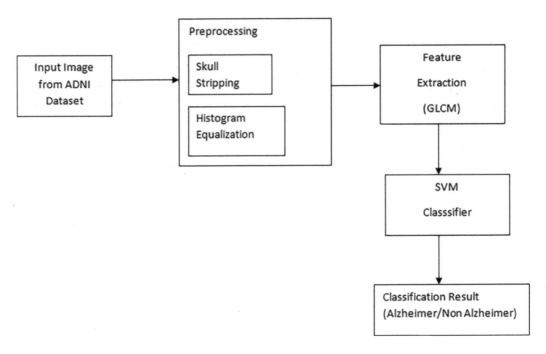

FIGURE 6.124   Design of cognitive impairment classification.

6.6.12.2 Preprocessing

A three-step preprocessing is applied to each MRI brain image. Steps in preproces-sing are as follows:

Step 1: Skull in the brain is not required for AD analysis, so skull stripping is done using a free surfer tool

Step 2: MRI image is segmented in white matter, gray matter, and CSF (cerebra spinal fluid) using free surfer tool

Step 3: Histogram equalization is done to adjust the contrast by modifying intensity distribution. Histogram equalization is preferred without loss of data; it equalizes the contrast of images.

6.6.12.3 Feature Extraction

Gray-level co-occurrence matrix (GLCM) is used to extract the 3D texture parameters of each region of interest (ROI). GLCM parameters are described in Table 6.38.

6.6.12.4 SVM Classification

SVM plots each data item as a point in n-dimensional space (where n is the number of features you have), with the value of each feature being the value of a particular coordinate. SVM maps the original features via a kernel function to construct a maximum classifier in a high-dimensional feature space. Gaussian RBF kernel with an empirical scaling factor of three differentiates the two classes very well. Finally, SVM with fivefold cross-validation is done.

6.6.12.5 Procedure

Input: ADNI dataset

Output: SVM model for AD diagnosis with accuracy for a given dataset

TABLE 6.38
GLCM Parameters

Parameter	Description
Entropy	Measures the degree of disorder among pixels in the image
Energy	Provides the sum of squared elements in the GLCM
Contrast	Measures the local variations in GLCM
Correlation	Measures the joint probability occurrence of the specified pixel pairs
Homogeneity	Measures the closeness of the distribution of elements in the GLCM to the GLCM diagonal.
Difference variance	Measures the dispersion related to the gray-level difference distribution of image
Difference entropy	Measures the disorder related to the gray-level difference distribution of image

TABLE 6.39
Evaluation of Result

Performance Metrics	Formula	Result
Accuracy	$\dfrac{TP + TN}{TP + TN + FP + FN}$	0.7500
Recall/sensitivity	$\dfrac{TP}{TP + FN}$	0.8600
Specificity	$\dfrac{TN}{TN + FP}$	0.6400
Precision	$\dfrac{TP}{TP + FP}$	0.7049
F-score	$\dfrac{2 * \text{Recall} * \text{precision}}{(\text{Recall} + \text{precision})}$	0.7748

Step 1: Get a dataset for training the model as input

Step 2: Select the features and class label for a given dataset

Step 3: Set the value for classification type (0 – C-SVC, 1 – nu SVC, 2 – one-class SVM, 3 – epsilon SVR, 4 – nu-SVR)

Step 4: Set the value for kernel type (0 – linear, 1 – polynomial, 2 – RBF, 3 – sigmoid: tanh)

Step 5: Set the value for gamma (1/number_of_attributes)

Step 6: Set the value for the cost (default cost 1).

Step 7: Train the model using the given dataset based on specified options.

Step 8: Perform cross-validation for the generated model with the number of folds as 10.

Step 9: Accuracy by class is calculated for the model by constructing a confusion matrix.

6.6.12.6 Performance Analysis

The accuracy of the algorithm is implemented by using the confusion matrix. A confusion matrix illustrates the accuracy of the solution to a classification problem. A confusion matrix contains information about actual and predicted classifications done by a classification system. The performance of such systems is commonly evaluated using the matrix data and presented in Table 6.39.

6.6.12.7 Text Categorization

As the volume of electronic information increases, there is growing interest in developing tools to help people find, filter, and manage these resources better. In real-life scenarios, we have hundreds

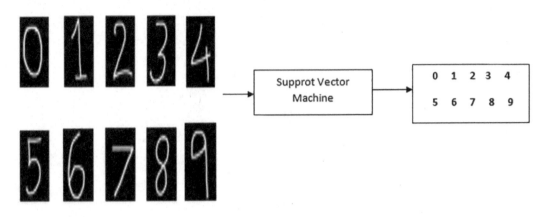

Handwritten Images   Results

FIGURE 6.125   Handwritten OCR.

of files and mails, and there is a need to organize and manage those files, since human text categorization is time-consuming with increase in data. The rule-based approach was carried out to categorize text, but it requires manual rule construction. Spam email detection and topic modeling of documents are based on text classification. For example, given mail content, the idea is to classify whether it is spam or not. Each document is represented as a vector of words. Document x can be represented by vector (doc2vec), i.e., $x \rightarrow \varnothing(x)$.

$$\varnothing_i(x) = \frac{tf_i \log\left(idf_i\right)}{k}$$

The distance between two documents, say x and y in vector space, is represented as the dot product of $\varnothing(x) \cdot \varnothing(y)$. Using the kernel function $k(x, y) = \varnothing(x) \cdot \varnothing(y)$. SVM works well for linearly separable text categorization applications. The choice of kernel and kernel parameter improves the performance of categorization. The Reuters collection is popular for text categorization research.

6.6.12.8   Handwritten Optical Character Recognition

Optical character recognition is converting handwritten digits or text into an editable document, as given in Figure 6.125. In other words, it is a process of converting scanned documents and printed documents into readable and editable forms. SVM outperforms other ML models in recognizing handwritten characters. MNIST is an open-source dataset with 60,000 handwritten digit samples. SVM achieves a good accuracy when compared to neural network models. NIST and USPS are other datasets that can be used for evaluation. The polynomial kernel gives good results with better accuracy and a low error rate.

Represent input image as a vector $x \in R$. Learn a SVM classifier $f(x)$ such that,

$$f : x \rightarrow \{0,1,2,3,4,5,6,7,8,9\}$$

6.6.12.9   Natural Language Processing

Natural language processing is a process of automatically analyzing and processing natural languages. SVM is utilized for various natural languages processing techniques such as part-of-speech (POS) tagging, word sense disambiguation, text categorization, named entity recognition,

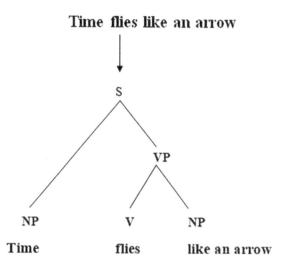

FIGURE 6.126   Parse tree.

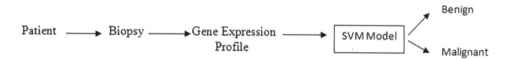

FIGURE 6.127   Cancer prediction.

information retrieval, and machine translation. The SVMTool is an open-source tool used for the effective generator of the sequential POS tagger. For a given sequence of words, the POS tagger tags the appropriate parts of speech, as shown in Figure 6.126.

SVM^{struct} is another open-source tool used for natural language processing applications. SVM^{struct} supports the task such as SVM^{cfg} (SVM used for context-free grammars), SVM^{multiclass} (used for multiclass classification problem), and SVM^{hmm} (uses the features of Markov model).

6.6.12.10   Cancer Prediction

In the last two decades, ML methods have been extensively applied to disease prediction. In particular, SVM is widely used in the bioinformatics field, such as gene classification, protein classification, and medical diagnosis.

SVM classifiers classify the tumor as either benign or malignant based on the size and gene expression (Figure 6.127). SVM can also be used in cancer recurrence and cancer prognosis prediction. The various types of data such as clinical pathology, clinical gene expression, and clinical genomic can train and test the model. A schematic representation of SVM based on the patient age and size of the tumor is represented in Figure 6.128. SVM is classified into two classes called benign (*O*) and malignant *x* by an optimal decision boundary.

6.6.12.11   Stock Market Forecasting

In the financial sector, ML methods have made a great impact. The objective of stock prediction is to decide whether the stock value in the near future is high or low, given the present stock rate. The prediction can be either short term or long term. Stock market prediction is a nonlinear time series model because prediction is uncertain and depends on various external factors. Henceforth, nonlinear SVM works well for stock market prediction (Figure 6.129). Google finance Python is an open-source data available for stock prediction.

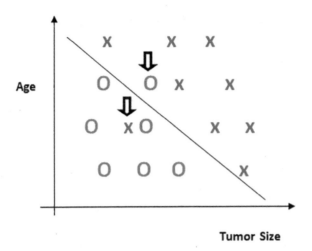

FIGURE 6.128   SVM cancer predictions.

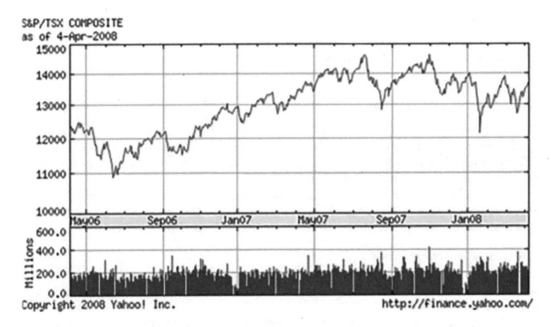

FIGURE 6.129   Stock price predictions.

6.6.12.12   Protein Structure Prediction

In bioinformatics, protein structure prediction plays a significant role in disease diagnosing and drug production. The Structural Classification of Proteins (SCOP) is the database used for protein classification, which is composed of four protein domain classes: (a) all α, (b) all β, (c) α / β, and (d) $\alpha + \beta$. SVM classifies this four-class problem optimally.

6.6.12.13   Face Detection Using SVM

Face detection is widely used in computer vision tasks. Given as input an image, which could be a photograph, the goal is to determine whether there are any human faces in the image and fit the face in the bounding box. However, face detection is a difficult task because of the significant differences in pattern (Figure 6.130).

FIGURE 6.130   Face detection using SVM.

6.6.13   ADVANTAGES AND DISADVANTAGES OF SVM

The pros of SVM are

- Ability to handle high-dimensional dataset
- Kernel tricks are used to process the nonlinear problems in an efficient manner
- Nonparametric
- Robust against the outliers
- The number of support vectors provides a good indication of the complexity of the problem to handle
- Allow flexibility in using various parameter adjustments (e.g., linear vs. nonlinear, regularization, etc.)

     The cons of SVM are

- SVM is highly sensitive in identifying the optimal values of the parameters
- Difficulty in analyzing a large dataset

6.7   SVM CLASSIFICATION IN PRACTICE USING PYTHON

A SVM is grouped under a supervised ML algorithm used for both classification and regression purposes. SVMs are more commonly utilized in classification problems, and per se, this is often what we'll concentrate on in this example code below.

SVMs have supported the thought of finding a hyperplane that best divides a dataset into two classes.

6.7.1   SUPPORT VECTORS

Support vectors are the information points nearest to the hyperplane, the points of a dataset that, if removed, would alter the position of the dividing hyperplane. Because of this, it can be considered the critical elements of an information set.

6.7.2   What Is a Hyperplane?

For a classification task with only two features, you'll consider a hyperplane as a line that linearly separates and classifies a set of information. Intuitively, the more beyond the hyperplane our data points lie, the more confident we are that they need to be correctly classified. We, therefore, want our data points to be as far off from the hyperplane as possible while still being on the right side of it. So when new testing data are added, whatever side of the hyperplane it lands will decide the category that we assign. Let's revisit the iris dataset:

```python
import numpy as np
from sklearn.model_selection import cross_val_score, train_test_split
from sklearn import datasets
from sklearn import svm

iris = datasets.load_iris()

X_train, X_test, y_train, y_test = train_test_split(iris.data, iris.
target, test_size=0.4, random_state=0)

# Build an SVC model for predicting iris classifications using training data
clf = svm.SVC(kernel='linear', C=1).fit(X_train, y_train)

# Now measure its performance with the test data
clf.score(X_test, y_test)

# The output is shown below.

0.9666666666666667
```

For K-fold cross-validation, let's use a K of 5

```python
# let us give cross_val_score a model, the entire data set and its "real"
values, and the number of folds:
scores = cross_val_score(clf, iris.data, iris.target, cv=5)

# Print the accuracy for each fold:
print(scores)

# and the mean accuracy of all 5 folds:
print(scores.mean())

# The output is shown below.

[0.96666667 1. 0.96666667 0.96666667 1. ]
0.9800000000000001
clf = svm.SVC(kernel='poly', C=1).fit(X_train, y_train)
scores = cross_val_score(clf, iris.data, iris.target, cv=5)
print(scores)
print(scores.mean())

# The output is shown below.

[1. 1. 0.9 0.93333333 1. ]
0.9666666666666666
```

SUMMARY

This chapter introduced the supervised learning algorithms applied for classification applications. Logistic regression, decision trees, RF, and SVMs were covered in detail with solved examples, real-world applications, and implementation in Python.

Some of the key points to be remembered are as follows:

- A decision tree is a tree-structured classifier. The decision node and leaf node are the two nodes in the decision tree. A test is done on the decision node. A leaf node represents the class label. The path from the root to the leaf represents the classification rule. Information gain is the amount of energy that cannot be used to do work or measure disorders in the system. $\sum_{i=1}^{c} -P\log P$.

- In the ID3 algorithm, the information gain is used for the selection of root attributes. The information gain is calculated for each attribute, and the attributes having high information gain are selected as the root node.
- In C 4.5 algorithm, the gain information is used for the calculation of root attributes. The attributes having maximum gain ratio are selected as the root node.
- The CART 4.5 algorithm uses the Gini index to identify the attributes for the root node. The attribute having a low Gini index is selected as the root node.
- Advantages of the decision tree are
  - Interpretability, used in data exploration, capture nonlinear relationship, simple rule-based approach.
- Disadvantages of the decision tree are a low bias and overfitting problem
- Overfitting is the phenomenon in which the learning process matches exactly with all the training data. The accuracy of the model is high for trained data and low for untrained data. Overfitting can be eliminated by prepruning and postpruning.
- Underfitting occurs when the training model does not capture the underlying pattern. Underfitting is destroying the accuracy of our model of ML.
- Decision trees are used for predicting library book, identification of tumor, and classification of telescope image.
- RF is a method that operates by constructing multiple decision trees during the training phase. The main advantage of the RF tree is that it has less training due to multiple trees.
- The various features of RF are high accuracy, and it runs efficiently on a large dataset, less error, handling missing data, no overfitting.
- The main drawback of RF is that it has less control on the model and does not work well for regression.
- The time complexity for creating a complete unpruned decision tree is $O\ (v * n \log\ (n))$, where n is the record number and v is the number of variables/attributes.

REVIEW QUESTIONS

1. Compare and contrast linear regression and logistic regression with examples.
2. Discuss the various types of logistic regression in detail.
3. Is it possible to use a logistic model given all the independent variables are continuous? Justify.
4. Define odds ratio.
5. Compare and contrast nominal and ordinal logistic regression with suitable examples.
6. A dependent or outcome variable, say direction with values North, South, East, and West, is a nominal or ordinal variable. Another dependent variable called symptom with values absent, mild, moderate, and severe is a nominal or ordinal variable. Justify your answer.

7. Design a suitable logistic model with a neat sketch to differentiate tumor grade into three categories such as well-differentiated, moderately differentiated, and poorly differentiated using the input variables as age (categorical), sex (categorical), and type of cancer (adenocarcinoma, adenosquamous, and others).
8. Discuss any three use cases of logistic regression in natural language processing.
9. Solve the below decision tree to identify strep throat and cold.

Throat Pain	Fever	Swollen Glands	Congestion	Head Pain	Diagnosis
Yes	Yes	Yes	Yes	Yes	Strep throat
Yes	Yes	No	Yes	No	Cold
Yes	No	Yes	No	No	Strep throat
No	Yes	No	Yes	No	Cold
No	No	Yes	No	No	Strep throat
No	Yes	No	Yes	Yes	Cold

10. Explain the method used to avoid overfitting in the decision tree.
11. Explain the various algorithms used in the decision tree.
12. Create your own decision tree for classification and regression tree.
13. Give some real-time application of the decision tree.
14. How do we combine the decision tree with SVM for the classification process?
15. Explain bias and variance in RF.
16. Give some application of RF.
17. What is the run-time complexity of RF?
18. Draw a RF for the following table.

Blood Flow	Blocked Arteries	Chest Pain	Weight	Heart Disease
Normal	Yes	Yes	195	Yes
Abnormal	No	No	130	No
Abnormal	Yes	Yes	180	Yes
Abnormal	Yes	Yes	180	Yes
Normal	No	No	100	No
Normal	Yes	No	150	Yes

19. Describe an extremely randomized tree.
20. Create a RF with your own dataset and validate your result with sample input.
21. Explain linearly separable and nonlinearly separable data with an example.
22. Explain in brief why SVM is fast and works more accurately than logistic regression.
23. Discuss hard margin and soft margin with a sketch.
24. How to use SVM for multiclass classification?
25. List out the different kernels used in SVM and justify which will best suit massive datasets.
26. Name some software available for highly optimized SVM.
27. Identify the optimal hyperplane for AND function.
28. Identify the optimal hyperplane for XOR function using kernel trick.

7 Feature Engineering

LEARNING OBJECTIVES

At the end of this chapter, the reader will be able to

- Understand the need for feature engineering in machine learning
- Appreciate the methods for feature selection
- Knowledge of factor analysis
- Understand the concepts of dimensionality reduction using PCA and LDA
- Implement Python-based examples using PCA and LDA

7.1 INTRODUCTION

Machine learning fits the types of statistics in the data for understanding or prediction. These types take features such as input. Feature representation of raw data is named as feature numbers. Features remain between data and models within the device, getting to know the machine learning pipeline. Feature engineering is the act of extracting features from raw data and converting them into formats suitable for machine learning models. It is an important step in the machine learning pipeline because proper features can reduce the issue of modeling and, therefore, allow the pipeline to produce high-quality results. Experts agree that most of the time building a machine learning pipeline is spent on feature engineering and statistics cleaning. However, as important as it is, the topic is not often discussed alone. Perhaps, this is because the relevant features can only be defined in the context of every model and data; because facts and models are so diverse, it's difficult to generalize the exercise of feature engineering in all projects.

Feature engineering is the task of improving model prediction in the database by changing its feature space. Existing strategies to change this procedure depend on flexible spatial testing of performance by experimentally guided search or the explicit enlargement of datasets with all the modified features observed by feature selection. However, such methods present higher computational expenses during operation and/or memory.

Feature engineering is the process of converting raw data into features that better represent the underlying problem in speculative models, which has led to the development of model accuracy on intangible data.

Feature engineering is the central task of preparing machine learning data. It is the practice of constructing relevant features from given features that lead to improved guesswork performance. Feature engineering involves using transformational functions such as arithmetic and integrated operators in a given new design feature. Conversion helps measure a feature or convert nonlinear relationships between an element and a target category in a line relationship, which is easy to read. Feature engineering is usually done by a data scientist who relies on the technology of his/her field and error testing and model testing. To carry out automated feature engineering, some present methods use targeted search in the feature space using heuristic feature quality measures and other contractual action steps.

A feature is a numeric illustration of raw data. There are numerous methods to convert raw data into numerical values, which is why features can end up looking like many things. Naturally, features should come from the type of data available. Less ambiguous spaces are also tied to the model; some models are more suitable for certain types of features and vice versa. Appropriate features align with the work being done and should be easy for the model to swallow. Feature engineering is the technique of building the most relevant features given data, model, and function. If there aren't

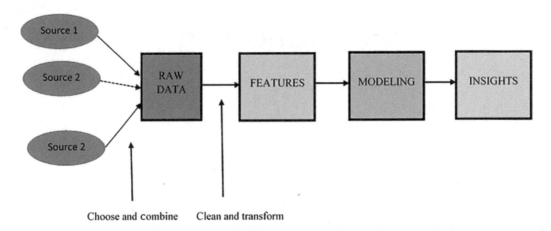

Choose and combine   Clean and transform

FIGURE 7.1   Feature engineering position in the workflow of machine learning.

enough teaching features, the model will not perform the final task. If too many features or many of them do not work, the model will be more expensive and the trick to training it. Something may be wrong with the training process affecting the performance of the model.

Features and models reside between the raw data and the desired insight, depicted in Figure 7.1. In the workflow of machine learning, the model is not only chosen but also the features. This is a double-edged coin, and one choice affects the other. Positive features make the next step of modeling easier, and the emerging model is able to complete the task you are looking for. Negative features may require a more sophisticated model to achieve the same level of performance. Throughout the book, we will talk about different features and discuss the advantages and disadvantages of different types of data and models.

Knowing where feature engineering fits into the context of the process of machine learning equipment highlights that it is not independent.

It is a repetitive process associated with data selection and model testing, over and over again, until we run out of time on our problem.

The process may look like the following:

1. **Brainstorm capabilities:** Get into the problem, see more details, learn the feature engineering of other problems and see what you can steal.
2. **Devise capabilities:** The automatic feature extraction, text feature creation, and both combinations can be used depending on the problem.
3. **Select capabilities:** Use key feature variations and feature selection methods to prepare one or more views for your working models.
4. **Examine models:** Evaluate model accuracy on invisible data using selected features.

A well-defined problem is needed to know when to stop this repetitive process and then continue to try other models, other model configurations, model combinations, and so on. A well-thought-out test device is also needed to be designed to measure the potential of a model in intangible data. It will be the only measure got from the feature engineering process.

7.2   FEATURE SELECTION

Feature selection strategies have eliminated useless features to reduce the complexity of the emerging model. The ultimate goal is a model of pride that is quick to reckon with, with little or no damage to speculation. To get to such a model, some feature selection techniques require more than one model training. In other words, the selection of features is not about reducing training time – in fact, some strategies increase the total training time – but reduce model installation time. Simply put, feature selection techniques fall into three categories: Preprocessing filtration methods to remove those that may apply to the model. For example, one can combine the knowledge of the relation or interaction between each element and the flexibility of the answer and then filter the features that fall under the threshold. Filter techniques are much cheaper than the wrapping techniques described below, but they do not consider the model used. Therefore, they may not be able to select the appropriate features of the model. Therefore, it's best to make choices before saving to avoid unnecessarily removing useful features before they get to the training step.

7.2.1 WRAPPER METHODS

Wrapper methods are expensive but try the subsets of features, which means that it can't accidentally cut out the features that are not only taught but useful when taken together. The wrap method treats the model like a black box that provides quality results of the proposed subset of features. There is a different way of over-filtering the set, which is described below.

Wrappers use a search strategy to search through the space of possible feature subsets and evaluate each subset by the performance quality on an ML algorithm. Practically, any combination of search strategy and algorithm can be used as a wrapper. It is featured as:

- use ML models to score the feature subset
- train a new model on each subset
- very computationally expensive
- usually provide the best performing subset for a given ML algorithm but probably not for another
- need an arbitrarily defined stopping criteria

The most common **search strategy** group is Sequential search, including Forward Selection, Backward Elimination, and Exhaustive Search. Randomized search is another popular choice, including Evolutionary computation algorithms such as genetic and Simulated annealing.

Another key element in wrappers is **stopping criteria**. The searching process is stopped based on three criteria:

- performance increase
- performance decrease
- the predefined number of features is reached

7.2.1.1 Forward Selection

Forward feature selection starts by evaluating all features individually and selects the one that generates the best performing algorithm, according to preset evaluation criteria. Then, the algorithm evaluates all possible combinations of the selected feature and selects the pair that produces the best performing algorithm based on the same preset criteria. This selection procedure is called greedy because it evaluates all possible single, double, triple, and feature combinations. Therefore, it is quite computationally expensive, and sometimes, if feature space is big, even unfeasible.

7.2.1.2 Backward Elimination

Backward feature selection starts by fitting a model using all features. Then, it removes one feature. Next, it will remove the one that produces the highest performing algorithm (least statistically significant) for certain evaluation criteria. The second step will remove a second feature, the one that again produces the best-performing algorithm. And it proceeds with removing feature after feature until a certain criterion is met.

7.2.1.3 Exhaustive Feature Selection

The best subset of features is selected in an exhaustive feature selection, among all possible feature subsets, by optimizing a specified performance metric for a certain machine learning algorithm. For example, if the classifier is the logistic regression and the dataset consists of **four** features, the algorithm will evaluate all feature combinations as follows:

- all possible combinations of one feature
- all possible combinations of two features
- all possible combinations of three features
- all the four features

and select the one that results in the logistic regression classifier's best performance (e.g., classification accuracy). This exhaustive search is very computationally expensive. In practice, for this computational cost, it is rarely used.

7.2.2 Featured Methods

These methods make the selection of a feature part of the model training process. For example, the decision tree naturally makes a feature selection because it selects one element of tree division in each training step. Another example is the standardizer 1, which can be added to the training purpose of any specific model. The ℓ 1 trend encourages models that use fewer features instead of many features, so it is also known as the sparsity limit on the model. The included methods include feature selection as part of the model training process. They are not as powerful as threatening methods, but they are not as expensive. Compared with filters, embedded methods select features specific to the model. In this sense, embedded methods strike a balance between computer costs and the quality of results.

The steps can be summarized to solve the problem of feature selection in a checklist:

1. Have you got any knowledge about the problem domain? If so, create an enhanced set of "ad hoc" features.
2. Is the feature appropriate? If not, normalize them.
3. Do you doubt feature interdependence? If yes, extend the feature set by formulating feature products or conjunctive features.
4. Does the input variable need to be pruned? If no, create disjunctive features or weighted sums of features.
5. Does the feature need to be accessed individually? If yes, apply a variable ranking method; otherwise, try to obtain the baseline results.
6. Have you got a predictor? If no, stop.
7. Do you doubt whether data are dirty? If yes, identify the outlier examples based on the top-ranking variables acquired from step 5 as representation; verify or reject them.
8. Have you got an idea of what to try first? If no, apply a linear predictor. Then, utilize a forward selection method with the "probe" approach as a terminating condition or apply the 0-norm embedded approach. For evaluation, as a result of the ranking of step 5, create a sequence of predictors of the same nature using increasing subsets of features. Is it possible to match or improve performance with a smaller subset? If so, use a nonlinear predictor with that subset.
9. Have you got new thoughts, time, computational resources, and enough examples? If yes, compare several feature selection methods, including your new idea, correlation coefficients, backward selection, and embedded methods. Next, apply linear and nonlinear predictors. Finally, choose the best approach with model selection.
10. Is a stable solution needed to improve performance and understanding? If so, subsample your data and redo your analysis for several "bootstraps."

7.3   FACTOR ANALYSIS

Factor analysis (FA) is a method of analyzing experimental data to search for potential influential factors or hidden variables from a set of notable variables. It helps in translating data by reducing the amount of flexibility. It subtracts a complete standard variation across all variables and sets the same points.

FA is widely used in market research, marketing, psychology, finance, and performance research. For example, market analysts utilize FA to identify price-sensitive customers, identify product features that influence consumer preferences, and help to understand the selection channels for distribution channels. FA is a straightforward mathematical model. It is used to describe the differences between visual variables and obscure a set of invisible variables called factors. Visual differences are followed as a direct combination of features and error words. Factor or latent variable is associated with multiple visual variables, which have common response patterns. Each feature describes a certain amount of variability in observed variables. It helps in translating data by reducing the amount of flexibility.

$$X_i = \beta_{i0} + \beta_{i1}F_1 + \beta_{i2}F_2 + (1)e_i$$

FA is a way of investigating whether several variables of interest, $X_1, X_2, \ldots, X_k$, are equally related to a small number of intangible factors $F_1, F_2, \ldots, F_k$.

Assumptions:

1. Outliers are not present in the data.
2. The sample size must be larger than the factor.
3. There must be no perfect multicollinearity.
4. There must be no rigidity among the variables.

7.3.1   TYPES OF FACTOR ANALYSIS

- Exploratory Factor Analysis: It is the most popular way of analyzing factors for social researchers and administrators. Its basic assumption is that any apparent flexibility is directly related to any factor.
- Confirmatory Factor Analysis (CFA): Its basic assumption is that each item is associated with a specific set of observed variables. CFA confirms basic expectations.

7.3.2   WORKING OF FACTOR ANALYSIS

The primary purpose of FA is to reduce the number of observations and detect invisible variables. These tangible variables help the market researcher to complete the research. This recognizable variation of the observed variables can be achieved in two steps:

- **Factor extraction:** In this step, the number of factors and the removal methods is chosen using variance partitioning methods like principal component analysis (PCA) and common factor analysis.
- **Factor rotation:** In this step, rotation attempts to convert factors into unrelated factors. The main purpose of this step is to improve the overall interpretation. Many rotation methods are available: Varimax rotation method, Quartimax rotation method, and Promax rotation method.

7.3.3 TERMINOLOGIES

7.3.3.1 Definition of Factor

A factor is a subtle variable that describes the correlation between the number of variables observed. The maximum number of factors is equal to the number of variables detected. Everything explains a certain variation in the visual variability. Factors with very low variability have been reduced. Factors are also known as hidden or latent variables or hypothetical variables.

7.3.3.2 Factor Loading

The loading factor is a matrix that demonstrates the relationship of each variation to an underlying factor. It expresses the coefficient correlation for the observed variable and the factor. It shows the defined differences in the observed variables.

7.3.3.3 Eigenvalues

Eigenvalues represent diversity defining each item from a complete diversity. It is also known as the root of the feature.

7.3.3.4 Communalities

Communalities are the sum of double the loading of each variable. Represents common variations. It goes from 0 to 1, and the value around 1 represents the most varied.

$$\hat{h}_i^2 = \sum_{k=1}^{n} \hat{l}_{ik}^2 \qquad (7.1)$$

7.3.3.5 Factor Rotation

Rotation is a better translation tool for FA. Rotation can be orthogonal or oblique. It also distributed the standard with a clear loading pattern.

7.3.3.6 Selecting the Number of Factors

The Kaiser method is the analytical method based on the most important part of the variance defined by the factor to be selected. The eigenvalue is a good way to determine the number of factors. Mostly, eigenvalue larger than 1 will be considered as optional factors. The graphic method represents certain eigenvalue factors, also called scree plots, as shown in Figure 7.2. This scree structure helps us determine the number of factors in which a curve forms an elbow.

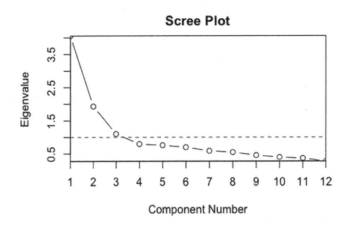

FIGURE 7.2   Scree plot.

7.4   PRINCIPAL COMPONENT ANALYSIS

With automatic data collection and feature-generating techniques, one can quickly discover a large number of features. But not all are helpful. Let's discuss feature dimensionality reduction using PCA. Often, we encounter situations where a particular outcome or decision depends not on a single indicator (forecaster) but many complex factors of the decision-making process. This is called the curse of dimensionality. It is a well-known fact that it is important to limit the number of important factors to reach the right conclusion. This process is called dimensionality reduction. In machine learning, the problem of high dimensionality is treated in two ways:

- **Feature selection**: a careful selection of key features by filtering out inconsistent features.
- **Feature extraction**: we create new and relevant features from the original features. PCA is one of the key means of extracting a feature.

Similarly, PCA converts the corresponding features of data into orthogonal components to capture all important information from the data while minimizing its size.

PCA can be used in the following means:

- Limit the number of features but cannot identify the less important ones that are ignored.
- Make sure that data features are standalone even if the features are not slightly interpreted.

7.4.1   CENTER THE DATA

Eigen decomposition produces transformation matrices where eigenvectors denote the rotational matrix, while eigenvalues denote scaling factors. Conversely, the covariance matrix has no data related to data translation. Undeniably, the translation is represented by an affine transformation required instead of a linear transformation. Consequently, before installing PCA to exchange data for obtaining unrelated axes, any existing changes need to be calculated by removing the mean data from each data point. This is just like entering the data in such a way that its scale becomes zero.

7.4.2   NORMALIZE THE DATA

Eigenvector covariance matrix points when referring to large data differences. Conversely, variance is a whole number, not a relative. This means that the difference in data measured in inches will be much greater than the same data when measured in feet. For instance, one feature denotes an object's length in meters, while the second feature denotes the object in inches. If the data is normalized, the biggest difference, and therefore the largest eigenvector, will be fully determined by the first factor. To avoid this PCA scale-based approach, it helps normalize the data by separating each feature with a standard deviation. This is particularly significant when different features are related to different metrics.

7.4.3   ESTIMATE THE EIGEN DECOMPOSITION

As details will be shown to larger eigenvectors to reduce the size, eigendecomposition must be determined. One of the most widely used methods of calculating eigendecomposition is singular value decomposition (SVD).

7.4.4   PROJECT THE DATA

To reduce the size, the data is automatically displayed to the largest eigenvectors. Let W be a matrix with its columns containing the largest eigenvectors and let O be the original data with its columns containing different observations. After that, the projected data O' is available as $O' = W^T O$. The number of residual values is selected, such as columns of W which, directly, can define the number of variations of actual data that need to be maintained while removing eigenvectors. If only N eigenvectors are stored, and $e_1,...,e_N$ denote the respective eigenvalues, the number of variants leftover after projected original d-dimensional data can be calculated as:

$$s = \frac{\sum_{i=0}^{N} e_i}{\sum_{j=0}^{d} e_j} \tag{7.2}$$

1. The original feature values of the given data are normalized by its mean and variance specified in equation 7.3, where k is the number of instances in the dataset and $X_{(i)}$ are data points.

$$\mu = \frac{1}{n} \sum_{i=1}^{n} X_{(i)} \tag{7.3}$$

2. Substitute $X_{(i)}$ with $X_{(i)} - \mu$.
3. Resize every vector $X_{j\,(i)}$ to obtain unit variance with the help of equation 7.4.

$$\sigma_j^2 = \frac{1}{n} \tag{7.4}$$

4. Substitute $X_{j\,(i)}$ with $\frac{X_{j\,(i)}}{\sigma}$.
5. Determine the covariance matrix C_M as:

$$C_M = \frac{1}{m} \left(X_{(i)}\right) \left(X_{(i)}\right)^T \tag{7.5}$$

6. Determine the eigenvectors and respective eigenvalues of C_M.
7. Decrease eigenvalues and sort the eigenvectors, and select k eigenvectors containing the largest eigenvalues to obtain V.
8. Make use of V to change the samples to a new subspace using equation (7.6)

$$y = V^T \times X \tag{7.6}$$

where X denotes $d \times 1$ dimensional vector representing one sample, y is the transformed $k \times 1$ dimensional vector sample in the new subspace. The execution of the designed PCA computational complexity depends on the number of features P that depicts each data point given by

$$O\left(P^3\right) \tag{7.7}$$

PCA's reduction ratio (RR) is defined as the relation between the number of target dimensions and several original dimensions. Thus, the efficiency of PCA is higher as the value of RR becomes low.

7.5 EIGENVALUES AND PCA

PCA uses the structure of eigendecomposition. "Eigen" is a German word meaning "own." Here, the matrix (A) is divided into:

- The diagonal matrix formed by eigenvalues of a matrix (A)
- And the matrix formed by the eigenvectors of a matrix (A)

A square matrix can have one eigenvector and as many eigenvalues as the size of the matrix. For example, a 4×4 matrix will have four eigenvalues.

7.5.1 USAGE OF EIGENDECOMPOSITION IN PCA

Suppose there is a database with a variety of "predictors." After centering the forecasters in their way, the "$n \times n$" covariance matrix is obtained. This matrix of covariance is then divided into eigenvalues and eigenvectors. The covariance matrix, also named as dispersion matrix or variance–covariance matrix, is a matrix with its feature in i, j position is the covariance among ith and jth feature of a random vector. A random vector is a random variable with a maximum size. From the covariance structures and the covariance matrix, the following aspects are defined.

- The covariance of random variables (forecasts) itself is simply a variance.
- Each item in the main diagonal of the covariance matrix demonstrates the variances of each random variance.
- The entire matrix of covariance is symmetric.

Therefore, the matrix of covariance has variances (covariance of a predictor with itself) and covariances (between predictions). Eigenvector is units that have a length or size equal to 1. It is often called the right vector, also called a column vector. Eigenvalues are coefficients used in eigenvectors that give vectors their length or magnitude.

Therefore, PCA is a way of:

- Measurement of how each variable is linked using the covariance matrix.
- Interpretation of the guidelines of the spread of the data using **eigenvectors.**
- Exposing the comparative significance of these directions using **eigenvalues.**
- The PCA method can be defined and executed using the tools of linear algebra using the numpy package in python (without using its direct implementation function from the sklearn package).

Consider the data in Table 7.1.

TABLE 7.1
Data to Implement Eigendecomposition

Age	Weight	Height
20	60	4.5
35	65	5
40	70	5.5
45	75	6

This data can be represented as a 5×3 matrix and named as *A*.

```
Matrix A:
[[20.   60.    4.5]
 [35.   65.    5. ]
 [40.   70.    5.5]
 [45.   75.    6. ]]
```

Let's center the features of this matrix to mean, determine covariance matrix, and implement eigendecomposition as depicted below.

```python
# Calculate the mean of each column

M=np.mean(A.T, axis=1)
print("\n Means of Colums n:\n",M)

#Center columns by subtracting colum means
C = A - M

print("\n Matrix after centering the column to its means\n",C)

#Calculate Covariance matrix of Centered Matrix
V=np.cov(C.T)

print("\n The Covariance Matrix :\n",V)

#Eigen decompistion of Covariance Matrix
eigen_values,eigen_vectors = LA.eig(V)

print("\n Eigen Values: \n",eigen_values)
print("\n Eigen Vectors: \n",eigen_vectors)
```

```
Means of Colums n:
[35.    67.5    5.25]

Matrix after centering the column to its means
[[-15.     -7.5    -0.75]
 [  0.     -2.5    -0.25]
 [  5.      2.5     0.25]
 [ 10.      7.5     0.75]]

The Covariance Matrix :
[[116.66666667  66.66666667   6.66666667]
 [ 66.66666667  41.66666667   4.16666667]
 [  6.66666667   4.16666667   0.41666667]]

Eigen values:
[1.56053271e+02 2.69672869e+00 7.48573384e-17]

Eigen Vectors:
[[-8.62072917e-01 -5.06784259e-01 -1.19177337e-16]
 [-5.04269186e-01  8.57794613e-01 -9.95037190e-02]
 [-5.04269186e-02  8.57794613e-02  9.95037190e-01]]
```

From the above output, it is clear that eigenvectors give PCA components, and eigenvalues give explained variances of the components. Therefore, since there are three predictors, three eigenvalues are obtained.

- Eigenvectors can now be organized by eigenvalues to reduce the supply of components or axes for the new matrix *A*.
- If there is an eigenvalue near zero, they represent disposable components.
- A total of "*n*" (here 3) or a few elements that make up the selected bottom area should be selected. Ideally, we can choose *k* (<*n*) eigenvectors, called principal components, with the largest eigenvalues.

The explained variance ratio of the first component is given as:

explained variance of 1st component/(total of all explained variances)

```
exp_ratio1=eigen_values[0] / sum(eigen_values)
print("\n The explained ratio of the first component:\n",exp_ratio1)

The explained ratio of the first component:
0.9830127326851055
```

- It can be noticed that the first component is enough to explain up to 98% of the variance in the data. So, the data can be projected into a 4×1 matrix instead of a 4×3 matrix, reducing the dimension of data, of course, with a minor loss in information.

7.6   FEATURE REDUCTION

The art of machine learning begins with the creation of appropriate data presentations. Better performance is often achieved using features taken from the original input. Creating a feature presentation can add domain information to the data and can be specified by the specific application. However, there are many ways to make common features, including clustering, basic input linear transform variables [PCA/SVD, linear discriminant analysis (LDA)], complex line variations such as spectral transformations (Fourier, Hadamard), wavelet transform, or convolutions of kernels, and apply simple functions to flexible subsets, such as monomials.

Two different objectives can be pursued by feature design: to achieve data reconstruction or be more efficient in making predictions. The first problem is an unsupervised learning problem. It is very close to data compression, and many algorithms are used in both fields. The second problem is supervised. Are there reasons to select features in an unsupervised manner when the problem is supervised? Yes, with a few possibilities. Other problems, e.g., for text processing applications, come with unlabeled data compared to labeled data. Also, the selection of unsupervised features is not usually overdone to overfitting.

Our goal is to have an algorithm-friendly dataset. What do we mean by that?

If you have a lot of features, there are a few potential problems:

- The model has a high degree of difficulty.
- It can make a lot of noise.
- If they have different scales, it reduces the performance of several algorithms that are scale-sensitive.
- More complex visualizations in n-dimensional space.

Here comes the role of PCA. It reduces the dimensionality of the dataset by extracting/eliminating the important/unimportant features.

PCA detects a change that reduces the size of the data while calculating the variance as large as possible. PCA is the oldest process in a multivariate analysis. The basic concept of PCA is a projection-based process. Here, the actual dataset $X \in R\,n$ with n columns (features) is projected into a subspace with k or lower dimensions' representation $X \in R\,K$ (fewer columns) while maintaining the total amount of original data.

The algorithm works as follows: to reduce the dimensionality of the feature from n-dimensions to k-dimensions, two stages are implemented; the preprocessing and dimensionality reduction stage. First, in the preprocessing stage (steps 1–4 in Section 7.4), the data is preprocessed to normalize its mean and variance using equations 7.3 and 7.4 in Section 7.4. Then, in the second stage (steps 5–8 in Section 7.4), which denotes the reduction phase, the covariance matrix C_M, eigenvectors and eigenvalues are calculated from equations 7.5 and 7.6 in Section 7.4.

When using PCA to reduce dimension, one has to deal with how many principal components (k) should be used. As with all hyperparameters, this number can be changed based on the quality of the emerging model. But some tests do not include expensive calculations. Therefore, another option is to select a k in the account with the desired value of the total variance. (This option is available in the scikit-learn package PCA.) The variations of projection onto the kth component are:

$$\|Xv_k\|^2 = \|u_k \; \sigma_k\|^2 \; \sigma_k^2 \qquad (7.8)$$

which is the square of the kth largest singular value of X. The ordered list of singular values of a matrix is called its spectrum. Therefore, to define how many components to use, one can perform a simple spectral analysis of the data matrix and pick the threshold that retains enough variance.

To retain enough components to cover 80% of the total variance in the data, pick k such that

$$\frac{\sum_{i=1}^{k} \sigma_i^2}{\sum_{i=1}^{d} \sigma_i^2} \geq 0.8 \qquad (7.9)$$

PCA is computationally expensive. It relies on SVD, which is an expensive process. Calculation of the full SVD of the matrix takes O-functions ($nd^2 + d^3$) by assuming $n \geq d$ where there are more data points than features. Even if we only want the principal components of k, using a reduced SVD (single k values and vectors) still takes $O((n+d)^2 k) = O(n^2 k)$ operations. This is available when there are a large number of data points or features. It is difficult to perform PCA in the form of streaming, batch updates, or a sample of full data. Streaming computation of the SVD, updating the SVD, and computing the SVD from a subsample are all difficult research problems.

Algorithms exist but at the cost of reduced accuracy. One implication is that one has to expect lower representational accuracy when capturing test data in the principal components found in the training set. In addition, as the distribution of the data changes, one needs to recompute the principal components in the current dataset.

7.6.1 Factor Analysis Vs. Principal Component Analysis

- PCA components define a high degree of variability, while FA defines covariance in data.
- PCA components are completely orthogonal to each other, while FA does not require factors to be orthogonal.
- Components of PCA are a linear combination of the observed variable, while in FA, the observed variables are a linear combination of the unobserved variables or factors.
- PCA components are not defined. In FA, key factors are sets and interpretable.
- PCA is a method of reducing the dimension, whereas FA is the latent variable method.
- PCA is a type of FA. PCA is observational, whereas FA is a modeling technique.

7.7 PCA TRANSFORMATION IN PRACTICE USING PYTHON

In this example, we consider the role of PCA in dimension reduction. A random dataset with 100 points is considered, and all the required libraries are imported as presented.

```
Import numpy as np
import matplotlib.pyplot as plt
import seaborn as sns; sns.set()
```

```
from sklearn.datasets import make_blobs
from sklearn. Pre-processing import StandardScaler
from numpy import random
from sklearn.decomposition import PCA

DATA_SET=random.randint(100, size=(100, 2))
#print(DATA_SET)
plt.plot(DATA_SET[:,0], DATA_SET[:,1], 'gx')
plt.axis('equal')
plt.show()
```

Using PCA, the relationship between the features in the data is quantified by estimating a set of *principal axes* in the data from which the dataset can be described. This is achieved in this example using the scikit-learn's PCA estimator, and the parameters, namely the "components" and "explained variance," are observed as follows:

```
pca = PCA(n_components=2)
pca.fit(DATA_SET)

print("PCA components: ", pca.components_)
print("PCA Explained Variance: ",pca.explained_variance_)
```

PCA is used for reducing the dimension, and this process involves zeroing out one or many small principal components. This results in reduced dimension data which maintains the maximal data variance. The following section of the code illustrates the dimension reduction:

```
pca = PCA(n_components=1)
pca.fit(DATA_SET)
DATA_SET_pca = pca.transform(DATA_SET)
print("original shape:   ", DATA_SET.shape)
print("transformed shape:", DATA_SET_pca.shape)
```

In this case, the n_component parameter is set to "1" to transform the data to a single dimension. To visualize the transformation, the inverse transform of the reduced data is plotted.

```
DATA_SET_new = pca.inverse_transform(DATA_SET_pca)
plt.scatter(DATA_SET[:, 0], DATA_SET[:, 1], alpha=0.2)
plt.scatter(DATA_SET_new[:, 0], DATA_SET_new[:, 1], alpha=0.5)
plt.axis('equal');
```

Observations:

The observations of PCA used for dimension reduction are as shown in Figure 7.3:

The figure shows a plot of the original data generated randomly, and the data size was 100×2. The parameter "components" and "explained variance" represent the *principal axes* of the data. This is a measure of the variance of the data when projected onto the principal axes. The projection of each data point onto the principal axes are the principal components of the data and are presented below for the random dataset chosen in this example.

```
PCA parameter components:
[[ 0.63796827 -0.77006265] [ 0.77006265  0.63796827]]
PCA parameter Explained Variance:  [931.51919577 711.44787494]
```

The original shape of the dataset was 100×2, and after reducing the dimension using PCA, we find that the dataset has been transformed to 100×1.

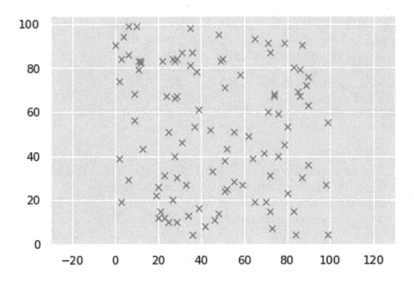

FIGURE 7.3   Plot of the original data.

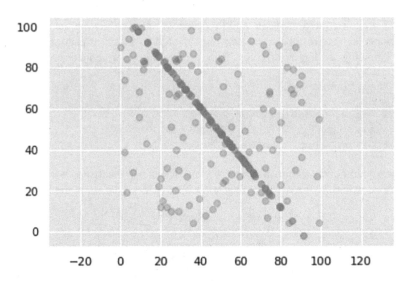

FIGURE 7.4   Plot of the transformed and reduced data.

```
Original shape of the data:       (100, 2)
Transformed shape of the data after PCA: (100, 1)
```

Figure 7.4 shows the plot of transformed data points (shown in dark shade) and the original data points (shown in lighter shade). This shows that using PCA, the data points along the least significant principal axis are removed, and the data points with the highest variance are retained.

7.8   LINEAR DISCRIMINANT ANALYSIS

Linear discriminant analysis (LDA) is a common method of dimension reduction problems as a pre-processing step for machine learning and pattern classification applications. Concurrently, it is often used as a black box, but is not well understood a few times. LDA easily manages a case where the waves within a section are uneven, and randomly generated test data assess their performance. This method increases the variance rate between class and in-class variability in any dataset, thereby ensuring high diversity. In the PCA, the structure and location of the original dataset are transformed when converted into a separate space. The LDA does not change the location but only attempts to provide additional segmentation and draw the decision area between assigned classes. This approach also benefits from getting a better understanding of the distribution of feature data. Datasets can be modified, and test vectors can be separated from the converted space in two different ways.

- **Class-dependent transformation:** This approach implicates to maximize the ratio between-class variance to within-class variance. The main objective is to maximize this ratio so that adequate class separability is obtained. The class-specific-type approach uses two optimizing criteria to transform the datasets independently.
- **Class-independent transformation:** This approach implicates to maximize the ratio of overall variance to within-class variance. This approach uses only one optimizing criterion to transform the datasets, and hence all data points irrespective of their class identity are transformed using this transform. In this type of LDA, each class is considered a separate class against all other classes.

7.8.1 MATHEMATICAL OPERATIONS IN LDA

The mathematical functions used in LDA are analyzed. To make it easier to understand, this concept is applied to the problem of two classes. Each dataset contains 100 2-D data points. The mathematical design of the classification strategy is as follows:

Step 1: Create datasets and test sets, which should be separated in the original space provided datasets and built-in test vectors, the graphical structure of datasets, and test vectors for the sample taken in the original space. For the ease of reference, let us represent datasets as a matrix containing features in the form provided below:

$$\text{set } 1 = \begin{bmatrix} a_{11} & a_{12} \\ a_{21} & a_{22} \\ \cdots & \cdots \\ \cdots & \cdots \\ a_{m1} & a_{m2} \end{bmatrix} \quad \text{set } 2 = \begin{bmatrix} b_{11} & b_{12} \\ b_{21} & b_{22} \\ \cdots & \cdots \\ \cdots & \cdots \\ b_{m1} & b_{m2} \end{bmatrix} \quad (7.10)$$

Step 2: For each dataset and entire dataset, determine the mean. Let μ_1 and μ_2 be the mean of set 1 and set 2, respectively and μ_3 represent the mean of entire data, which is achieved by merging set 1 and set 2, as given by equation 7.11.

$$\mu_3 = p_1 \times \mu_1 + p_2 \times \mu_2 \quad (7.11)$$

where p_1 and p_2 are the a priori probabilities of the classes. The probability factor is assumed to be 0.5.

Step 3: In LDA, to formulate criteria for class separability within-class and between-class scatter are used. Within-class scatter the expected covariance of each class. The scatter measures are calculated using equations 7.12 and 7.13.

$$S_w = \sum_j p_j \times \left(c_j \right) \quad (7.12)$$

Consequently, for the two-class problem, it is given as

$$S_w = 0.5 \times c_1 + 0.5 \times c_2 \qquad (7.13)$$

All the covariance matrices are symmetric. Let c_1 and c_2 be the covariance of set 1 and set 2, respectively. The covariance matrix is determined using equation 7.14

$$c_j = (x_j - \mu_j)(x_j - \mu_j)^T \qquad (7.14)$$

The between-class scatter is determined using equation 7.15

$$S_b = \sum_j (\mu_j - \mu_3) \times (\mu_j - \mu_3)^T \qquad (7.15)$$

The covariance of the dataset S_b contains the mean vectors of each class. The optimizing criterion in LDA represents the ratio of between-class scatters to the within-class scatter. The solution obtained by maximizing this criterion represents the axes of the transformed space. However, the optimizing criterion for the class-dependent transform is determined using equations 7.14 and 7.15. For L-class L, separate optimizing criteria are required for each class. The optimizing factors in the case of class-dependent type are determined as

$$Criterion_j = inv(c_j) \times S_b \qquad (7.16)$$

The optimizing criterion for the class-independent transform is determined as

$$Criterion = inv(S_w) \times S_b \qquad (7.17)$$

Step 4: The eigenvector of the transformation denotes a 1-D invariant subspace of the vector space where the transformation is applied. These eigenvector sets consisting of eigenvalues of nonzero are all linearly independent and invariant under the transformation. Therefore, any vector space could be denoted by linear combinations of the given eigenvectors. The nonredundant set of features is obtained by considering all eigenvectors, which correspond to nonzero eigenvalues, whereas eigenvalues, which correspond to zero, are ignored. Thus, the transformations of LDA are obtained as the eigenvector matrix of the distinct criterion defined in equations 7.16 and 7.17.

Step 5: In any L-class problem, there exists $L-1$ nonzero eigenvalues. In any L-class problem, there are $L-1$ nonzero eigenvalues. This is due to the problems in the mean vectors of the classes at equation 7.11. Eigenvectors corresponding to nonzero eigenvalues are the definition of change.

Now that we have the transformation matrices, we convert the datasets using a single LDA variable or the class-specific transforms. It can be observed that transforming all datasets into a single axis delivers precise parameters for classifying the data. The decision circuit in the transformed space is a solid line separating the converted datasets. Therefore, for the class-dependent LDA,

$$Transformed_{setj} = Transform_j^T \times set\_j \qquad (7.18)$$

For the class-independent LDA,

$$\text{Transformed}_{\text{set}} = \text{Transform}_{\text{spec}}^{T} \times \text{dataset}^{T} \tag{7.19}$$

Correspondingly, the Euclidean distance of the test vectors from each class mean is used to transform the test vectors and classify them.

Step 6: After the transformations are finished utilizing LDA transforms, Euclidean distance or RMS distance is used to classify data points. First, euclidean distance is determined using equation 7.20. Euclidean distances are thus obtained for each test point.

$$\text{Dist}_{n} = \left(\text{Transform}_{n_{\text{spec}}}\right)^{T} \times x - \mu_{n\text{trans}} \tag{7.20}$$

Step 7: The smallest Euclidean distance among the distances classifies the test vector as belonging to class n. Two LDA approaches, namely, the independent and dependent classes, have been described. The choice of the LDA type depends on the dataset and the purpose of the classification problem. For example, if the performance is very important, an independent class transformation is chosen. Conversely, if good discrimination is intended, the class-dependent type should be the first choice.

Algorithm 7.1: Class-Independent Linear Discriminant Analysis

1. Given a set of N samples $[x_i]_{i=1}^{N}$, where each corresponds to a row of length M (step(A)), and $X(N \times M)$ is denoted by

$$X = \begin{bmatrix} x_{11} & x_{12} & \cdots & x_{1M} \\ x_{21} & x_{22} & \cdots & x_{2M} \\ \vdots & \vdots & \vdots & \vdots \\ x_{N1} & x_{N2} & \cdots & x_{NM} \end{bmatrix} \tag{7.21}$$

2. Determine the mean of each class $\mu_i (1 \times M)$
3. Determine the total mean of all data $\mu (1 \times M)$
4. The between-class matrix $S_B (M \times M)$ is determined as

$$S_B = \sum_{i=1}^{c} n_i \left(\mu_i - \mu\right) \left(\mu_i - \mu\right)^{T} \tag{7.22}$$

5. The within-class matrix $S_w (M \times M)$ is determined as

$$S_W = \sum_{j=1}^{c} \sum_{i=1}^{nj} \left(x_{ij} - \mu_j\right) \left(x_{ij} - \mu_j\right)^{T} \tag{7.23}$$

6. From equations 7.22 and 7.23, the matrix W that maximizes Fisher's formula is determined as $W = S_W^{-1} S_B$. Determine the eigenvalues and eigenvectors of W.
7. Sort eigenvectors in decreasing order per their respective eigenvalues. The first k eigenvectors are used as a lower-dimensional space (V_k).
8. Project all original samples (X) onto the lower-dimensional space of LDA.

Algorithm 7.2: Class-Dependent Linear Discriminant Analysis

1. Given a set of N samples $[x_i]_{i=1}^N$, where each corresponds to a row of length M (step(A)), and $X(N \times M)$ is denoted by

$$X = \begin{bmatrix} x_{11} & x_{12} & \cdots & x_{1M} \\ x_{21} & x_{22} & \cdots & x_{2M} \\ \vdots & \vdots & \vdots & \vdots \\ x_{N1} & x_{N2} & \cdots & x_{NM} \end{bmatrix} \tag{7.24}$$

2. Determine the mean of each class $\mu_i (1 \times M)$
3. Determine the total mean of all data $\mu (1 \times M)$
4. The between-class matrix $S_B (M \times M)$ is determined as in equation 7.22.
5. For all class $i, i = 1, 2, \ldots, c$ do
6. The within-class matrix $S_{w_i} (M \times M)$ is determined as

$$S_{w_j} = \sum_{x_i \in \omega_j} (x_i - \mu_j)(x_i - \mu_j)^T \tag{7.25}$$

7. The transformation matrix for each class (W_i) determined as

$$W_i = S_{W_i}^{-1} S_B. \tag{7.26}$$

8. Determine the eigenvalues (λ^i) and eigenvectors (V^i) of each transformation matrix (W_i), where λ^i and V^i denote the determined eigenvalues and eigenvectors of the ith class, respectively.
9. Sort eigenvectors in decreasing order per their respective eigenvalues. The first k eigenvectors are used as a lower-dimensional space (V_k).
10. Project the samples of each class (ω_i) onto the lower-dimensional space (V_k^i) as follows:

$$\Omega_j = x_i V_k^j, \ x_i \in \omega_j \tag{7.27}$$

where Ω_j denotes the projected samples of the class ω_j.
11. End for loop

7.9   LDA TRANSFORMATION IN PRACTICE USING PYTHON

In this section, Python implementation of scattering within the class and scatter between the class is discussed on sample data.

7.9.1   IMPLEMENTATION OF SCATTER WITHIN THE CLASS (Sw)

In this example, class 1 (11×2) and class 2 (10×2) are considered to have 11 and 10 samples, respectively. The within-class matrix S_w is computed for this data according to equation 7.25, $S_{w_j} = \sum_{x_i \in \omega_j} (x_i - \mu_j)(x_i - \mu_j)^T$ where x_i is the data vector per instance per class and μ_j represents the mean vector of class j. The Python code to determine the scatter matrix within the class is as follows:

```
import numpy as np
import matplotlib.pyplot as plt
```

```
# Data creation - Here random samples in the range [0,2] are generated
for each class
class1 = np.array([[1.5,1.6,1.55,1.65,1.45,1.7,1.75,1.55,1.35,
1.8],[1.75,1, 1.5,1.65,1.45,1.22,1.75,1.5, 1.45, 1.65]])
class2 = np.array([[0.25,0.55,0.15,0.25,0.3,0.66,0.35,0.1,0.45,0.55],
[1.5,1.25,1.15,1.25,1,1,1.45,1.5,1.33,1.45]])

#Plotting the data using the plt function from matplotlib
fig = plt.figure(figsize=(10,10))
ax0 = fig.add_subplot(111)

ax0.scatter(class1[0],class1[1],marker='*',c='blue',edgecolor='blue')
ax0.scatter(class2[0],class2[1],marker='o',c='green',edgecolor='green')
plt.show()

# Calculating the mean vectors per class by creating a 2x1 vector with
means
mean_class1 = np.mean(class1,axis=1).reshape(2,1)
mean_class2 = np.mean(class2,axis=1).reshape(2,1)

# Calculaing the scatter matrices (within)
scatter_class1 = np.dot((class1-mean_class1),(class1-mean_class1).T)
scatter_class2 = np.dot((class2-mean_class2),(class2-mean_class2).T)

# Calculating the SW by adding the scatters within classes
SW = scatter_class1+scatter_class2
print(SW)
```

The resultant scatter (Figure 7.5) within the class as per the equation is computed and given as a 2×2 matrix with elements shown below:

```
Scatter within class Sw = [[ 0.49509091 -0.03355455] [-0.03355455
0.85203273]]
```

7.9.2 IMPLEMENTATION OF SCATTER BETWEEN CLASS (SB)

For the same data used in the previous section, the scatter matrix between classes is computed according to equation 7.22, $S_B = \sum_{i=1}^{c} n_i (\mu_i - \mu) (\mu_i - \mu)^T$, where μ is the overall mean and μ_i is the mean for the respective class. Here, n_i is the sample size of the respective class.

```
import numpy as np
import matplotlib.pyplot as plt

# Data creation - Here random samples in the range [0,2] are generated
for each class
class1 = np.array([[1.5,1.6,1.55,1.65,1.45,1.7,1.75,1.55,1.35, 1.8],
[1.75,1, 1.5,1.65,1.45,1.22,1.75,1.5, 1.45, 1.65]])
class2 = np.array([[0.25,0.55,0.15,0.25,0.3,0.66,0.35,0.1,0.45,0.55,0.25],
[1.5,1.25,1.15,1.25,1,1,1.45,1.5,1.33,1.45,1.15]])

# Calculating the mean vectors per class by creating a 2x1 vector with
means
mean_class1 = np.mean(class1,axis=1).reshape(2,1)
mean_class2 = np.mean(class2,axis=1).reshape(2,1)
```

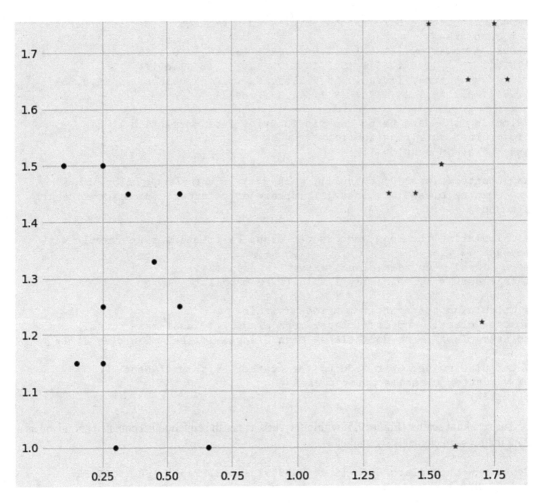

FIGURE 7.5   Plot of the data with two classes (class1 – blue stars, class 2 – green circles).

```
# Calculating the overall mean vector
ave_class = []
for i in range(len(class1)):
    row = []
    for j in range(len(class1[0])):
        row.append( ( class1[i][j] + class2[i][j] ) / 2 )
    ave_class.append(row)
print(ave_class)

overall_mean=np.mean(ave_class,axis=1).reshape(2,1)
print('overall mean=',overall_mean)

# Calculating the sample size of each class
n1=np.size(class1)
n2=np.size(class2)

Sb_class1=n1*(mean_class1 - overall_mean).
dot((mean_class1 - overall_mean).T)
Sb_class2=n2*(mean_class2 - overall_mean).
dot((mean_class2 - overall_mean).T)
```

```
# Calculate the Sb by adding the scatters between classes
Sb = Sb_class1 + Sb_class2
print('Scatter between class Sb =',Sb)
```

The output of the above code is the scatter between the matrix of size 2×2 given as follows:

```
Scatter between class Sb = [[16.13470868  2.82754909][ 2.82754909
0.49673455]]
```

SUMMARY

In this chapter, a brief analysis of feature engineering was discussed. While choosing the best features for implementing a machine learning model, it is always the best practice to ensure whether all the features computed are available for future observations. Furthermore, most of the features must have the potential to be predictive with complete domain knowledge for a detailed analysis. The chapter reviewed the basic requirements for feature selection, wrapper models, and FA. While choosing the features, it is found that dimensionality reduction plays a predominant role. This is mainly achieved by approaches, namely PCA and LDA. The implementation of these approaches regarding reducing the data dimensions is discussed in detail with relevant Python examples.

REVIEW QUESTIONS

1. What are the deterministic algorithms in machine learning? Discuss them.
2. What is the curse of dimensionality? Explain in the context of dimensionality reduction.
3. Discuss the different strategies used to reduce dimension in a dataset.
4. What happens to a dataset when collinear features are removed?
5. Develop a dimensionality reduction model using PCA and LDA on random data. Compare the performance of both approaches.
6. Are the following machine learning processes considered for feature engineering? Justify with a suitable explanation.
    a. Initial Data Collection
    b. Data Cleaning
    c. Normalization
7. How are outliers handled while extracting features? Discuss.
8. List out the machine learning models that are sensitive to outliers.
9. Compute the scatter matrices in LDA for the class-dependant and class-independent cases. Record your observations.
10. Develop a complete LDA model illustrating the concept of dimensionality reduction using the algorithms discussed in this chapter.

8 Reinforcement Engineering

LEARNING OBJECTIVES

At the end of this chapter, the reader will be able to

- Understand the goal-oriented learning based on reinforcement learning (RL)
- Appreciate the difference between RL and other ML algorithms
- Have knowledge of elements of RL such as agent, policy function, and value function
- Apprehend the Markov decision process (MDP) and dynamic programming (DP) concerning value functions, policy evaluation, and improvements
- Implement MDP and DP using Python

8.1 INTRODUCTION

When we consider the nature of learning, the idea of gaining information about dealing with our surroundings may be the first that comes to mind. A newborn does not have an unambiguous instructor when playing, swinging its fingers, or looking from side to side; instead, it is in direct contact with its senses and nature. Using this link shows a wealth of information on causes and effects, the effects of actions, and what you need to do to attain your objectives. Throughout our lives, such contact is unquestionably a rich source of information about our environment and ourselves. If we are going to learn cooking in a group, we know exactly how our place reacts to what we do, and we need to persuade what will happen with our behavior. Almost all theories of learning and knowledge acquisition support collaborative learning as a fundamental notion. In this book, we look at how to learn from interactions using a computational method. Instead of directly considering how humans or animals learn, we study the investigated settings and evaluate the efficacy of artificial intelligence researchers or engineers' numerous learning approaches. We investigate the structure of mathematical analysis and computational experimentation to design machines that effectively solve scientific or economic significance problems. The method we are testing, called reinforcement learning, is more goal-oriented learning from interaction than other machine learning (ML) methods. This chapter discusses goal-oriented learning based on reinforcement learning (RL) and how RL varies with other ML algorithms. The elements of RL such as agent, policy function, and value function are explained in detail, followed by the RL algorithms the Markov decision process (MDP) and dynamic programming (DP). The value functions, policy evaluation, and improvements are covered by implementing MDP and DP in Python.

8.2 REINFORCEMENT LEARNING

RL is the process of learning what to do – how to map situations into actions – to raise the numerical reward signal's value. The learner is not told which steps to follow; instead, he must determine which acts provide the highest reward for trying. In the most thrilling and difficult situations, actions may impact the current reward and the next situation and, as a result, all subsequent prizes. These are two most important parts of RL: trial-and-error search and delayed rewards.

RL, like other issues with names that finish in "ing," such as ML and climbing, is a problem, a category of successful solutions to the problem and a subject that studies the problem and its solutions all at the same time. It's tempting to use a single word to describe all three issues, but it's critical to keep these three issues separate in your mind. Furthermore, the distinction between problems and solutions in RL is particularly important; failing to express this distinction causes much confusion.

Therefore, we design a RL issue, including applying notions from dynamical system principles, such as complete control of Markov's completely anonymous decision-making processes.

The learning agent must sense its natural state to some extent and take actions that influence it. In addition, the agent should have a goal or set of principles in mind when it comes to the status of the environment. Markov's decision-making methods are designed to combine only these three variables – emotion, action, and purpose – in the most basic ways possible, without jeopardizing any of them. We recall that any effective strategy to solve such issues is a RL method. RL is not the same as supervised learning, which is the type of research being done in ML.

Supervised learning is based on categorized examples provided by an experienced external manager as part of a training program. Each instance represents the current condition and a specific label of the proper action that the program should perform in that situation, which is normally to assign the situation to a category. This form of training aims to get the program out or combine its responses to function best in situations that aren't covered in the training set. This is an important method of learning knowledge, but it is not sufficient in and of itself. Finding instances of the desired behavior and representing all settings under which the agent must work is frequently unproductive in cooperative problems. Instead, an agent must research from their experience in an unmarked area, where one would expect learning to be most valuable.

RL is also distinct from unsupervised learning, commonly used to uncover a structure buried in unlabeled information by machine learning researchers. Although supervised and unsupervised learning appear to be two distinct ML models, they are no longer so. Although it is tempting to think of RL as an unsupervised form of learning because it does not rely on positive behavioral models, RL aims to magnify the reward signal rather than trying to identify a hidden structure. Finding the structure of an agent's experience can be highly useful in reinforcement. Still, it does not solve the challenge of RL to increase the reward signal on its own. As a result, we consider RL to be a third ML paradigm, alongside supervised and unsupervised learning, as well as perhaps different paradigms.

The trade between exploration and exploitation is one of the challenges that arise from RL but not from other types of learning. The RL agent must choose actions that he or she has tried in the past and is proven to be effective in generating rewards to reap the most benefit. The agent must not only use his experience to win the prize, but he must also learn how to make the greatest decisions in the future. The issue is that exploration or exploitation cannot be carried out without fail. The agent must try for a broad range of acts while continuing to favor the ones that appear to be the most effective. In a stochastic challenge, each action must be repeated multiple times before an accurate estimate of the expected reward can be determined. Mathematicians have researched this problem of exploration and exploitation for decades, but it has yet to be solved. Meanwhile, we just recognize that the dilemma of balancing exploration and exploitation is no longer solvable.

Another distinguishing feature of RL is that it explicitly addresses the total difficulty of an intention-directed agent dealing with an unpredictable environment. Many ML researchers, for example, have researched supervised learning without specifying how such a capability may be valuable in the long run. Likewise, different researchers have advanced theories of planning with similar goals, but without considering the function of planning in real-time decision-making or the question of where the forecasting models needing to make plans will come from. Even though these strategies have had many positive outcomes, their focus on remote subtypes is a common problem. RL takes the opposite behavior, beginning with a whole, interactive, goal-achieving agent.

Furthermore, it is generally believed from the beginning that the agent has to function with a notwithstanding sizable uncertainty about the surroundings it faces. When planning is involved in RL, it has to address the interaction among making plans and the selection of real-time action, in addition, to knowing how the environmental model is derived and progressed. When supervised learning is involved in RL, it does so for unique reasons that determine which abilities are important and which are not.

RL starts with a full, interacting, goal-achieving agent, the polar opposite of RL. Furthermore, it is widely assumed from the start that the agent must function despite significant uncertainty about the environment in which it finds itself. When planning is used in RL, it must consider the connection between generating plans and choosing real-time action and understanding how the environmental model is created and progressed. When supervised learning is used in RL, it is done for specific reasons that help establish which skills are valuable and which are not. For example, certain RL methods' ability to study with standardized approximation addresses the classic "curse of dimensionality" in operations research and management of ideas. RL, in particular, has had a strong interaction with psychology and neuroscience, with both methods providing significant benefits. RL is the closest form of ML to study that humans and other animals conduct. Many of the primary algorithms for RL were inspired by biological studying structures.

RL has been given back through psychological models of animal learning, which matches some scientific statistics, and through influential components of the mind's reward system. The methods were classified as "weak techniques" based on general principles such as discovery or learning and as "strong techniques" if they were based on specific information. This is an odd scene in today's world. It became premature in our opinion: very little effort was expended in the search for general principles, just to discover that there was none. Modern artificial intelligence today involves research into common ideas like mastering, seeking, and making decisions. It's uncertain how far the pendulum will swing, but RL research is part of a trend toward artificial intelligence standards that are simpler and less general.

8.2.1 EXAMPLES OF REINFORCEMENT LEARNING

An amazing way to understand RL is to consider some of the examples and feasible applications that have guided its development.

- A master chess player performs a trick. An immediate, spontaneous choice informs both the importance of special positions and actions, election planning, and waiting for feasible responses and counter-responses.
- After being born, a gazelle calf fights for its feet. It is now walking at a speed of 20 miles per hour.
- A cell robotic must decide whether to enter a new room in search of additional trash to collect or to begin finding its way back to its battery recharge station. It makes decisions based on the current charge level of its battery and how quickly and easily it could locate the recharger in the past.

These examples demonstrate functions that are so basic that they are easy to overlook. All of them entail a dynamic interaction between an active selection-making agent and its environment, in which the agent strives to attain a goal despite ambiguity about its surroundings. The agent's moves can represent the future condition of the environment (for example, the next chess role, the refinery's reservoir level, the robotic's next region, and its battery's future charge level), allowing for a later time.

Because the proper goal necessitates considering indirect rather than direct implications of movements, forethought or planning may be required. At the same time, in all of these cases, the completion of activities cannot be entirely foreseen; consequently, the agent must show its environment regularly and react properly. Phil, for example, must keep an eye on the milk he puts into his cereal dish to prevent it from overflowing. Many of these examples include desires that are so unique to the experience that the agent can predict progress toward its goal only based on what it has personally experienced.

The chess participant knows whether or not he/she wins, the gazelle calf knows when it falls, and the mobile robotic knows when its batteries run out. In each of these cases, the agent can use its enthusiasm to increase its performance over time. The chess player improves his/her game by refining his/her instinct to evaluate his/her positions; the gazelle calf improves its running performance, etc.

8.3 HOW RL DIFFERS FROM OTHER ML ALGORITHMS?

8.3.1 SUPERVISED LEARNING

In supervised learning, the agent is aware of what work to do and what actions are appropriate. The data scientists train the agent in historic records on targeted data with a label. The agent receives a direct response and can predict whether there will be any changes in the target to the new data or not.

Reinforcement studying doesn't depend upon classified datasets. The agent isn't instructed which actions to take or the most desirable manner to perform a task. RL uses rewards and penalties in preference to labels related to each dataset choice to indicate whether the action performed is positive or negative. Therefore, the agent only receives comments as soon as he or she has completed the task. Thus, the delayed response and the trial-and-error process help distinguish RL from supervised studying.

> **Reinforcement Learning vs. unsupervised learning:** In unsupervised learning, the algorithm analyzes anonymous data to detect hidden connections between fact points and structures through similarities or variations. RL goals to define an excellent action version to achieve the greatest long-term reward, differentiating it from unattended learning in terms of its primary purpose.
> **Reinforcement and deep learning:** Most RL implementations use in-depth learning models. They contain the usage of deep neural networks because it is an important means of training agents. Deep learning is best suited to spotting complicated styles in snapshots, sounds, and text. In addition, neural networks permit data scientists to balance all processes into a single model without tearing down the agent structure into multiple modules.

8.4 ELEMENTS OF REINFORCEMENT LEARNING

The RL system has four basic layers – policy, reward signal, value function, and environmental model – in addition to the agency and the environment.

8.4.1 POLICY

The policy denotes the information to detect an agent's conduct over some time. The policy is a map of known regions of the surrounding areas and the steps to be taken while in those states. It goes hand in hand with what psychological research is called a set of policies or associations. In a few instances, the coverage can be an easy way to do things or a lookup table, while in others, it can contain excellent computation and search processes. A policy is a center for strengthening the acquisition of an agent's knowledge within the feel that it is only appropriate to determine the conduct. In general, the rules can be stochastic, specifying the possibilities for each agent. In general, a policy can be the behavior of the agent. It can be mapped from state to action. For instance,

$$\text{Deterministic policy, } d = \pi(p) \tag{8.1}$$

$$\text{Stochastic policy, } \pi(d|p) = \left(D_t = d \| P_t = p\right)\pi(d|p) \tag{8.2}$$

8.4.2   Reward Signal

The reward signal represents the objective of the problem of RL. In each step, the environment sends the consolidation agent to consolidate one number called reward. The agent's main goal is to maximize the total compensation he or she receives over time. The reward signal specifies the agent's positive and negative occurrences. We can think of rewards in the biological system as pleasant or sad experiences. They are succinct and descriptive descriptions of the agent's problem. The reward signal is the primary driver of policy change. If a lesser reward follows a policy-selected action, the policy can be altered in the future to select a different action. Environmental stock operations and moves are commonly used as reward signals. A pricing characteristic indicates what is beneficial in the long run, but a reward signal specifies what is desirable in the short term.

8.4.3   Value Function

The value function, in most cases, is the entire amount of reward that an agent can expect to get in the future from that point forward. Thus, the prices reflect the state's long-term goals within the natural states after evaluating the prospective provinces and the rewards accessible in those states. In contrast, the rewards indicate instantaneous desire.

For instance, the state may always offer a short and modest prize, but the price is still excessive because it is always joined by other states that offer bigger prizes. Alternatively, the inverse may be true. To use a human comparison, rewards are similar to happiness (when high), and the most sophisticated criteria determine sorrow (when low) and values.

A reward R_t is a signal response scale indicating how well an agent performs in an agent's job step to maximize aggregate reward. RL is dependent upon this reward hypothesis.

8.4.3.1   Examples of Rewards

Fly stunt flight in a helicopter
+ve reward for following your favorite route
−ve reward for colliding
Defeat the world champion at Scrabble
The ±ve reward for winning/losing a game
Manage a funding portfolio
The +ve reward for each currency in the bank
Control a power station
The +ve reward for generating electricity
The −ve reward for surpassing protection thresholds
Do a humanoid robot stroll
The +ve reward for moving forward
The −ve reward for falling over
Play many different Atari games better than humans
The ±ve reward for increasing/decreasing score

In other ways, rewards are primary, while values such as reward forecasts are secondary. There would be no values if there were no rewards because the only reason for measuring values is to get more money. Even yet, while choosing and comparing choices, it is a major source of concern. Value judgments are used to select actions. We seek behaviors that result in higher-value states, not just a bigger reward because these acts provide us with the best long-term payoff. It's far more difficult to define values than assigning rewards, to put it bluntly. In reality, reliably measuring values is the most important challenge in practically all RL systems. The crucial role of quantitative measurement is the most important lesson learned in RL over the past six decades. The value function is given by

$$\text{Value function } V_\pi(s) = \mathbb{E}_\pi \left[R_{t+1} + \gamma R_{t+2} + \gamma^2 R_{t+3} + \cdots \mid D_t = d \right] \tag{8.3}$$

8.4.4 Model of the Environment

The last aspect of elements of RL is to strengthen the environmental model. This mimics how the environment works or, more typically, allows for a hypothesis about how the environment will act. For example, based on the current state and actions of the environment, the model might predict the future state of the outcome and follow rewards. Models are used to make plans, in which we recommend any method of deciding on a course of action by contemplating potential future activities before they are experienced. Solutions for RL using modeling and planning are called model-based approaches, in contrast to simple non-model approaches that explicitly expose learners to trials and errors – which are considered almost counter-planning. Current RL encompasses a wide range from low-level, experimental, and trail-and-mistake-based learning to advanced, deliberate planning.

Environment model can be described as

$$P_{ss'}^a = \mathbb{P}\left[D_{t+1} = d' \mid D_t = d, B_t = e \right] \tag{8.4}$$

$$C_s^a = \mathbb{E}\left[C_{t+1} \mid D_t = d, B_t = e \right] \tag{8.5}$$

where P predicts the next state and C predicts the next reward.

8.4.5 The Reinforcement Learning Algorithm

The RL problem can be framed primarily based on the following key elements:

Agent(): An entity that could observe or discover the environment and use it.
Environment(): A scenario wherein an agent is presented or surrounded through. In RL, we count on the stochastic surroundings; this means that it's natural structures. It is nothing but the physical world wherein the agent works.
Action(): Actions are the moves taken using an agent inside the environment.
State(): State of affairs restored with the aid of the environment after each action is taken using the agent. It is the agent's current status.
Reward(): A feedback returned to the agent from the environment to access the agent's action. It is the response from the environment.
Policy(): Policy is an approach carried out by the agent for the next action depending upon the current state. It is an approach to map an agent's state to actions.
Value(): It is predicted that it will also meet the discount factor for the long term and infringement of the interim reward. Future reward that an agent can earn by taking action in a specific situation.
Q-value(): Very similar to a value but takes one additional parameter as the current action (a).

The algorithm is given by

At every step t the agent: Performs the action A_t recognized by observation O_t and receives scalar reward R_t
The environment: Finds action A_t, produces observation O_{t+1}, radiates scalar reward R_{t+1} at t increments.

8.4.6 METHODS TO IMPLEMENT REINFORCEMENT LEARNING IN ML

RL in ML can be implemented using three main methods.

1. **Value-based**: The value-based method determines the optimal value function, representing the maximum value at a state beneath any policy. Consequently, the agent presumes the long-term return at any state(s) beneath policy π.
2. **Policy-based**: The policy-based method determines the optimal policy for the highest rewards of the future without restoring the value function. In this method, the agent attempts to use any policy so that the action taken in every step increases future rewards.
   The policy-based method has particularly two kinds of policy:
   - **Deterministic:** At any state, the same action is produced by the policy (π).
   - **Stochastic:** The produced action is determined by probability.
3. **Model-based:** In the model-based method, the environment creates a virtual model, and the agent examines that environment to analyze it. This approach doesn't have any specific algorithm or solution because the virtual model is distinctive for every environment.

8.5 MARKOV DECISION PROCESS

In the RL framework, the decision is made by the agent from the environment as a signal function known as the environment's state. This section defines the Markov property that defines the environment's property and the state signals at a specific interest. In this section, we concentrate not on designing the state signal but on deciding the function for which the signals are available.

8.5.1 PRELIMINARIES

The state should represent the immediate sensations to the agent and be able to intimate the agent more than that. It intimates not only everything about the environment but also everything useful in making decisions. For example, if the agent is communicating on a mobile, it is expected to identify who the caller is. If the agent is playing the Baccarat game, it is expected that the agent should know what the upcoming card will be. If we analyze these examples, there is some state information hidden in the environment, which the agent knows might be useful. Still, the agent could not predict it because no such relevant sensations were received. A state signal that can retain all information is named Markov or to devise the Markov property. For instance, the position of the checkers might serve as a Markov state where it encapsulates all information about the whole sequence of positions that was played in the game. Though some sequences might be missed out, all that is needed for the future is retained. In general, we can say that it should retain the history of the signals that have been made to reach this position. Let us consider a set of finite states and reward values and an environment that respond to the action taken at time t to $t+1$. The response is dependent upon the whole thing that has occurred earlier. The dynamics are defined by stating the complete probability distribution:

$$P_r \left\{ C_{t+1} = a, D_{t+1} = d' \mid D_0, B_0, C_1, ..., D_{t-1}, B_{t-1}, C_t, D_t, B_t \right\} \tag{8.6}$$

For all r, d' and all possible values of past events, namely, $D_0, B_0, C_1, ..., D_{t-1}, B_{t-1}, C_t, D_t, B_t$. In case the state signal obtains Markov property, then the environment's response at $t+1$ be subject to the state and action representations at t, the environment's dynamics is determined by

$$p(d', a \mid d, e) = P_r \left\{ C_{t+1} = a, D_{t+1} = d' \mid D_t, B_t \right\} \tag{8.7}$$

For all a, d', D_t and B_t. It can also be stated that the state signal contains the Markov property and Markov state, iff (equation 8.7) is equal to (equation 8.6) for all r, d'. And all possible values of past events, namely, D_0, B_0, C_1,...,D_{t-1}, B_{t-1}, C_t, D_t, B_t. In this case, where the environment and complete process are said to contain the Markov property.

If the environment follows the Markov property, given the current state and action, the one-step dynamics (equation 8.6) permits forecasting the next state and anticipating the next reward. By repeating this equation, all future states can be forecasted and anticipate the rewards given the entire history until the current time. RL considers Markov property an important criterion since the decisions and values are thought to function the current state's function. So as for those to be powerful and informative, the representation of the state must be instructive.

The Markov property that is satisfied by the RL task is known as MDP. If there are a finite number of state and action spaces, then it is known as the finite Markov decision process (finite MDP). A specific finite MDP is determined by its state and action sets and the environment's one-step dynamics. In case state (d) and action (e) are provided, the probability of every feasible pair of the next state (d') and reward (a) is represented by

$$p(d', a \mid d, e) = P_r \{C_{t+1} = a, D_{t+1} = d' \mid D_t = d, B_t = e\} \tag{8.8}$$

If the dynamics represented in equation (8.8) is given, it becomes easy to compute any details about the environment, in particular for each state-action pairs the expected reward is

$$r(d,e) = \mathbb{E}[C_{t+1} \mid D_t = d, B_t = e] = \sum_{a \in C} a \sum_{d' \in D} p(d', a \mid d, e) \tag{8.9}$$

The probabilities of state transition are given by,

$$p(d' \mid d, e) = P_r \{D_{t+1} = d' \mid D_t = d, B_t = e\} = \sum_{a \in C} p(d', a \mid d, e) \tag{8.10}$$

and for state action next-state triples, the expected reward is given by,

$$r(d, e, d') = \mathbb{E}[C_{t+1} \mid D_t = d, B_t = e, D_{t+1} = d'] = \frac{\sum_{a \in C} a\, p(d', a \mid d, e)}{p(d' \mid d, e)} \tag{8.11}$$

8.5.2 VALUE FUNCTIONS

Substantially, every RL algorithms encompass measuring the state-action pairs that evaluate how well an agent can carry out a given action in a given state. The opinion of "how well" can be defined about future rewards or, more accurately, concerning the expected return. The expected reward to receive from the agent in the future is depended upon the action it takes. Consequently, value functions are defined in terms of particular policies.

A policy π is represented as a mapping from each state, $d \in D$, and action, $e \in A(d)$, to the probability $\pi(e \mid d)$ for captivating action e when in the state, d. The value of a state, d within a policy π, indicated by, is the expected return when beginning at d and under π thenceforth. $v_\pi(d)$ for MDPs is represented as

$$v_\pi(d) = \mathbb{E}_\pi[G_t \mid D_t = d] = \mathbb{E}_\pi\left[\sum_0^\infty \gamma^k C_{t+k+1} \mid D_t = d\right], \tag{8.12}$$

where given an agent who follows policy π and time step t, $\mathbb{E}_\pi[.]$ represents the expected value of a random variable and v_π represents the state value function for policy π.

Similarly, the value of captivating action e in state d within a policy π, i.e., the expected return beginning from d, represented by $q_\pi(d,e)$ the action value function for policy π is given by

$$q_\pi(d,e) = \mathbb{E}_\pi \left[G_t \,|D_t = d, B_t = e \right] = \mathbb{E}_\pi \left[\sum_0^\infty \gamma^k \, C_{t+k+1} \,\middle|\, D_t = d, B_t = e \right] \qquad (8.13)$$

The value functions v_π and q_π can be measured through expertise. For instance, for every state that is encountered, if an agent accompanies policy π and upholds an average of the actual returns for the state that has been followed, then the average shall intersect to the state's value, $v_\pi(d)$, as long as the number of times that state is confronted nears infinity.

In case for every action taken in a state, distinct averages are considered, then all these averages intersect with the value of the action, $q_\pi(d, e)$. This approach can be called the Monte Carlo approach to averaging numerous random samples of actual returns.

The consistency condition possesses among the value of d and the value of its feasible descendant states for any policy π and any state d which is represented as

$$v_\pi(d) = \mathbb{E}_\pi \left[G_t \,|D_t = d \right]$$

$$= \mathbb{E}_\pi \left[\sum_0^\infty \gamma^k \, C_{t+k+1} \,|D_t = d \right]$$

$$= \mathbb{E}_\pi \left[\sum_0^\infty \gamma^k \, C_{t+k+2} \,|D_t = d \right] \qquad (8.14)$$

$$= \sum_e \pi(e|d) \sum_{d'} \sum_r p(d', a \,|d, e) \left[r + \gamma \, \mathbb{E}_\pi \left[\sum_{k=0}^\infty \gamma^k \, C_{t+k+2} |D_{t+1} = d' \right] \right]$$

$$= \sum_e \pi(e \,|d) \sum_{d', a} p(d', a \,|d, e) \left[r + \gamma v_\pi(d') \right]$$

It is implied that from set $A(d)$, the actions, e, are interpreted from set D, the next states, d_0, and from set B, the rewards, a, are chosen. For every triple, the probability is computed, $\pi(e|d)$ $p(d_0, a|d, e)$, weight the quantity in brackets by its probability, finally find the aggregate across all possibilities to obtain the expected value. Bellman equation for v_π is given in (equation 8.14), which demonstrates a correlation among the state value of its successor states. Equation (8.14), the Bellman equation, averages all the possibilities, scaling every possibility by its occurring probability. It declares that the start state value needs to equal the expected next state value and the sum of the expected reward. The value function v_π is considered the unique solution to its Bellman equation.

8.6 DYNAMIC PROGRAMMING

DP is the collection of algorithms to find optimal policies when a perfect environment model is given as a MDP. Due to huge computational expense and the need for a perfect environment model, the utility of classical DP algorithms in RL is limited. However, still, they are considered theoretically important. Indeed, these methods are viewed as attempts to obtain a similar impact as DP but with lesser computation and no need for a perfect environment model. From hereon, we consider the environment a finite MDP. Let's assume that all the state (D), action $A(d)$, and reward sets, R for $d \in D$ is finite. Its dynamics are represented as a set of probabilities $p(d_0, a|d, e)$, for all $d \in D$, $e \in A(s)$, $a \in R$, and $d_0 \in D^+$, where $+$ denotes the terminal state if the problem is discontinuous. Even though DP can solve problems involving continuous states and action spaces, exact solutions are only attainable in a few circumstances. However, the state and action spaces must be quantized for continuous states and actions, and finite-state DP techniques must be used. Using a value function to organize and construct the search for appropriate policies is the central principle of DP and RL.

8.6.1 Policy Evaluation

Policy evaluation in DP denotes the computation of the state-value function v_π for a random policy π. This can also be referred to as a prediction problem.

$$v_\pi(s) = \mathbb{E}_\pi \left[R_{t+1} + \gamma R_{t+2} + \gamma^2 R_{t+3} + \cdots D_t = d \right]$$

$$= \mathbb{E}_\pi \left[R_{t+1} + \gamma v_\pi(S_{t+!})|S_t = s \right] \tag{8.15}$$

$$\sum_e \pi(e|d) \sum_{d',a} p(d', a|d, e)[a + \gamma v_\pi(d')] \tag{8.16}$$

where $\pi(e \mid d)$ denotes the probability of considering action, e in the state, d within the policy π, whereas the subscription of π represents the expectations that indicate the conditional policy is being followed. The v_π value is guaranteed for its existence and uniqueness until $\gamma < 1$ or if a guarantee is obtained from all states within the policy π that it has been terminated.

In case the dynamics of the environment are known completely, then equation (8.16) can be the system of $|D|$ simultaneous linear equations in $|D|$ unknowns $v_\pi(d)$, $d \in D$. Let us consider a succession of value functions $v_0, v_1, v_2, \ldots$ which are approximate, and each mapping D^+ to $\mathbb{R}$. The initial approximate value function v_0 is selected randomly, and using the Bellman equation (8.14) for v_π the update rule obtains each succession approximation

$$v_\pi(s) = \mathbb{E}_\pi \left[R_{t+1} + \gamma v_k(D_{t+1})|D_t = d \right]$$

$$= \sum_a \pi(e|d) \sum_{d'} p(d', a|d, e)[a + \gamma v_k](d') \tag{8.17}$$

For all $d \in D$. It is clear that $v_k = v_\pi$ acts as a fixed point to the update rule because the Bellman equation for v_π guarantees equality for this instance. In general, the sequence $\{v_k\}$ converges to v_π as $k \to \infty$ within the same condition that assures the presence of v_π. This procedure is known as an iterative policy evaluation and is illustrated in Figure 8.1.

To develop every succession approximation, v_{k+1} from v_k, the same operation for each state, d is applied by the iterative procedure of policy evaluation. The previous value of d is applied to the obtained new value from the previous values of the states of d. The one-step transitions available within the policy and the expected immediate reward are evaluated. This operation is known as full backup. In dependence upon the state-action pair, numerous distinct types of full backups are backed up, and the estimated values of the successive states, dependent on the precise manner, are grouped. Since the backups done in DP algorithms depend on all feasible next states instead of sample next state, we say that all DP algorithms are called full backups.

Read π, the policy that needs to be evaluated

Initialize an array $V(d) = 0$, for all $d \in D^+$

Loop

    $\Delta \leftarrow 0$

    For each $d \in D$:

    $v \leftarrow V(d)$

    $V(d) \leftarrow \sum_e \pi\,(e\,|d\,) \sum_{d',a} p(d',a\,|d,e)\,[r + \gamma V(d')]$

    $\Delta \leftarrow \max(\Delta, |v - V(d)|)$

Until $\Delta < \theta$ (*small positve integer*)

Display $V \approx v_\pi$

FIGURE 8.1 Iterative policy evaluation.

8.6.2 POLICY IMPROVEMENT

The policy's value function is computed to identify good policies. Let us consider that the value function v_π for a random deterministic policy, π is determined if we want to change it to a new policy for some state, d. One question arises whether it is good to continue with the current policy or to move on with the new policy. This question could be answered by choosing e in d and continuing with the old policy π. This can be determined by

$$q_\pi(d,e) = \mathbb{E}_\pi\left[C_{t+1} + \gamma v_\pi(D_{t+1})\,|\,D_t = d,\, B_t = e\right]$$
$$= \sum_{d',a} p(d',a|d,e)[a + \gamma v_\pi(d')] \tag{8.18}$$

The main idea is to check whether the value is greater or lesser than that $v_\pi(d)$. If the value is greater, that means it would be a good choice to choose e once in d and to follow π, which insists on following π every time. In this case, it would be better to adopt the new policy. This result is considered the policy improvement theorem. Assume π and π_0 be the deterministic policy pair such that, for all $d \in D$,

$$q_\pi(d, \pi'(d)) \geq v_\pi(d) \tag{8.19}$$

Here the policy π' has to be better or good than π. This indicates that it should acquire greater or equal expected return from all states $d \in D$.

$$v_{\pi'}(d) \geq v_\pi(d) \tag{8.20}$$

In the case at any state in equation (8.19), a strict inequality exists, then in equation (8.20) also a string inequality must exist for any state. This applies to the two policies mentioned in the original deterministic policy, π, and to the new policy, π_0. Certainly, equation (8.19) will hold for all states except d. Therefore, if $q_\pi(d, e)$ is greater than $v_\pi(d)$, then the need policy is better than the original deterministic policy, π.

Now, let us prove this policy improvement theorem. Let us start from equation (8.19), expand the q_π as well as while reapplying equation (8.19) till we obtain $v_{\pi'}(d)$ which is represented as

$$v_\pi(d) \leq q_\pi\left(d, \pi'(d)\right) \quad .$$

$$= \mathbb{E}_{\pi'}\left[C_{t+1} + \gamma v_\pi\left(D_{t+1}\right)\middle| D_t = d\right]$$

$$\leq \mathbb{E}_{\pi'}\left[C_{t+1} + \gamma q_\pi\left(D_{t+1}, \pi'(D_{t+1})\right)\middle| D_t = d\right]$$

$$= \mathbb{E}_{\pi'}\left[C_{t+1} + \gamma \mathbb{E}_{\pi'}\left[C_{t+2}, + \gamma v_\pi\left(D_{t+2}\right)\right]\middle| D_t = d\right] \tag{8.21}$$

$$= \mathbb{E}_{\pi'}\left[C_{t+1} + \gamma C_{t+2} + \gamma^2 v_\pi\left(D_{t+2}\right)\middle| D_t = d\right]$$

$$\leq \mathbb{E}_{\pi'}\left[C_{t+1} + \gamma C_{t+2} + \gamma^2 C_{t+3} + \gamma^3 v_\pi\left(D_{t+3}\right)\middle| D_t = d\right]$$

$$\leq \mathbb{E}_{\pi'}\left[C_{t+1} + \gamma C_{t+2} + \gamma^2 C_{t+3} + \gamma^3 C_{t+4}\middle| D_t = d\right]$$

$$= v_{\pi'}(d)$$

The new greedy policy, π', which is the native extension considered to change at all the states and all the feasible actions, chosen at every state in which the action seems best according to $q_\pi(D,e)$ is represented as

$$\pi'(d) = \operatorname{argmax}_a q_\pi(d,a)$$

$$= \operatorname{argmax}_a \mathbb{E}\left[C_{t+1} + \gamma v_\pi\left(D_{t+1}\right)\middle| D_t = d, B_t = e\right] \tag{8.22}$$

$$= \operatorname{argmax}_a \sum_{d',a} p\left(d',a\middle| d,e\right)\left[a + \gamma v_\pi(d')\right]$$

where argmax_a represents the maximized expression for the value of a. The greedy policy meets the conditions of the policy improvement theorem described in equation (8.19). As a result, we conclude that it is nearly as good as the original deterministic approach. As a result, policy improvement refers to the process of making a new policy better than the old one by making it greedy concerning the old policy's value function.

Assume that the new greedy policy, π_0, is well but not better than the existing policy π. Then, $v_\pi = v_{\pi_0}$ and from equation (8.22), it occurs that for all $d \in D$:

$$v_{\pi'}(d) = \max_a \mathbb{E}\left[C_{t+1} + \gamma v_{\pi'}\left(D_{t+1}\right)\middle| D_t = d, B_t = e\right]$$

$$= \max_a \sum_{s',a} p\left(d',a \middle| d,e\right)\left[a + \gamma v_{\pi'}(s')\right] \tag{8.23}$$

This equation is similar to the Bellman optimality equation, and subsequently, v_{π_0} should be v^*, as well as π and π_0 should be optimal policies. Generally, a stochastic policy π indicates probabilities, $\pi(e|d)$, for each action, e, from each state, d. In specific, the policy improvement theorem carried across the stochastic case, beneath the normal definition is given by

$$q_\pi\left(d, \pi'(d)\right) = \sum_e \pi'(e,d)q_\pi(d,e) \tag{8.24}$$

In addition, if a connection exists in policy improvement stages, as shown in equation (8.22), then there is no need to choose a single action from among them in the case of a stochastic policy. Rather, each maximizing action might be given a percentage of the chance of being chosen under the new greedy policy. Because all submaximal actions have a zero probability, the newly allocated scheme could be authorized.

1. Set the initial values
   $$V(d) \in \mathbb{R} \text{ and } \pi(d) \in B(d) \text{ randomly for all } d \in D$$
2. Policy Evaluation
   Loop
   > $\Delta \leftarrow 0$
   > For each d $\in$ D:
   >
   > $v \leftarrow V(d)$
   >
   > $V(d) \leftarrow \sum_{d',a} p(d', a \mid d, e) [r + \gamma V(d')]$
   >
   > $\Delta \leftarrow \max (\Delta, |v - V(d)|)$
   >
   > until $\Delta < \theta$ (*small positve integer*)
3. Policy Improvement

   $pol_{st} \leftarrow true$

   For each d $\in$ D:

   > $e \leftarrow \pi(d)$
   >
   > $\pi(d) \leftarrow argmax_a \sum_{d',a} p(d', a \mid d, e) [a + \gamma V(d')]$
   >
   > If $e \neq \pi(d)$, then $pol_{st} \leftarrow false$

   If pol_{st}, then stop and return V and π, else go to step 2

FIGURE 8.2   Policy iteration for v^*.

8.6.3 POLICY ITERATION

As soon as the policy, π, improves using v_π to provide a better policy, π', and $v_{\pi'}$ is computed and improved to produce even a better policy π''. Thus, a sequence of uniform improved policies and value functions are obtained by

$$\pi_0 \xrightarrow{E} v_{\pi_0} \xrightarrow{I} \pi_1 \xrightarrow{E} v_{\pi_1} \xrightarrow{I} \pi_2 \xrightarrow{E} \ldots \xrightarrow{I} \pi_* \xrightarrow{E} v_{\pi_*}$$

where $\xrightarrow{E}$ represents policy evaluation and $\xrightarrow{I}$ represents policy improvement.

Because there are only a finite number of policies in a finite MDP, this technique should focus on achieving optimal policy and the ideal value function in a finite number of repetitions. Policy iteration is the term for the process of determining the best policy. The policy iteration algorithm is depicted in Figure 8.2.

In this algorithm, if the policy constantly commutes between two or more policies that are eventually good, the algorithm will never terminate.

8.6.4 EFFICIENCY OF DYNAMIC PROGRAMMING

Although DP is not ideal for really big problems, it is relatively efficient compared to other approaches to solving MDPs. In terms of the number of states and actions, the worst-case time complexity of the DP technique to achieve an optimal policy is polynomial. Assuming that n is the number of states and m is the number of actions, the DP technique requires fewer computer operations than a polynomial function n and m. Thus, DP guarantees that the optimal policy will be found in polynomial time, even though the total number of policies required is m^n. In this aspect, DP is exponentially faster than direct search in the policy space since direct search requires a thorough investigation of each policy to offer the promise. Compared to the DP approach, the worst-case intersection guarantees for linear programming approaches, which are also employed to solve MDPs, are comparably good. However, compared to DP, the linear programming approach becomes unworkable with fewer states. However, only DP techniques are practical for the most serious situations.

Because the number of states grows exponentially with the number of state variables, the curse of dimensionality (Bellman, 1957), DP is frequently thought to be unproductive. Furthermore, DP outperforms direct search and linear programming when dealing with huge state spaces. If it starts with good initial value functions or policies, DP converges substantially faster than its theoretical worst cast difficulties.

8.6.5 Dynamic Programming in Practice using Python

```
###Importing libraries
import numpy as np
from tqdm import tqdm
import matplotlib.pyplot as plt
import seaborn as sns
sns.set_style("darkgrid")
%pylab inline
import random


####### Populating the interactive namespace from numpy and matplotlib
###Policy iteration
###Parameters
gamma = 1 # discounting rate
rewardSize = -1
gridSize = 4
terminationStates = [[0,0], [gridSize-1, gridSize-1]]
actions = [[-1, 0], [1, 0], [0, 1], [0, -1]]
numIterations = 1000

###Functions
def actionRewardFunction(initialPosition, action):
    if initialPosition in terminationStates:
        return initialPosition, 0
    reward = rewardSize
    finalPosition = np.array(initialPosition) + np.array(action)
    if -1 in finalPosition or 4 in finalPosition:
        finalPosition = initialPosition
    return finalPosition, reward
###Initialize
valueMap = np.zeros((gridSize, gridSize))
states = [[i, j] for i in range(gridSize) for j in range(gridSize)]
####Value function at step 0
valueMap

####Evaluating the Policy
deltas = []
for it in range(numIterations):
    copyValueMap = np.copy(valueMap)
    deltaState = []
    for state in states:
        weightedRewards = 0
        for action in actions:
```

```
            finalPosition, reward = actionRewardFunction(state, action)
            weightedRewards += (1/len(actions))*(reward+(gamma*valueMap[f
inalPosition[0], finalPosition[1]]))
        deltaState.append(np.abs(copyValueMap[state[0],
state[1]]-weightedRewards))
        copyValueMap[state[0], state[1]] = weightedRewards
    deltas.append(deltaState)
    valueMap = copyValueMap
    if it in [0,1,2,9, 99, numIterations-1]:
        print("Iteration {}".format(it+1))
        print(valueMap)
        print("")

###Plotting the values
plt.figure(figsize=(20, 10))
plt.plot(deltas)
```

SUMMARY

RL is a ML technique that focuses on using a cut-and-try approach to train an algorithm. After each action, the algorithm (agent) examines the current situation (state), takes action, and receives feedback (reward) from the environment. Positive feedback is a form of reward (in the sense that we understand it), whereas negative feedback is a form of punishment for making a mistake. The goal-oriented learning based on RL is discussed in this chapter and how RL differs from other ML algorithms. First, the elements of RL, such as agent, policy function, and value function, are thoroughly discussed, followed by RL techniques, such as the MDP and DP. Finally, value functions, policy assessment, enhancements, and MDP and DP implementation in Python are all delineated.

REVIEW QUESTIONS

1. List out a few real-world applications of RL. Explain concerning agent, value functions, and policy functions.
2. Compare the performance of RL compared to other ML algorithms.
3. Explain the terms: policy, reward, value function, and model of an environment.
4. Consider a football ground as an environment and a robot as an intelligent agent. Try to model the game using the Bellman equation.
5. List the differences between supervised learning and RL in terms of
   a. Dataset (labeled/unlabeled)
   b. Training
   c. Interaction with the environment
   d. Decision-making
6. What are on-policy and off-policy functions? Explain.
7 Explore the application of MDP in traffic light control for decision-making.
8. Can RL be applied to self-driving cars? Interpret the agent, reward, action, and environment for the application.

9 Case Studies for Decision Sciences Using Python

LEARNING OBJECTIVES

At the end of this chapter, the reader will be able to:

- Understand the application of phases of data analytics life cycle for machine learning (ML) problems,
- Comprehend the data for a given problem and the objective of the problem such that a suitable algorithm can be identified,
- Identify alternate ML models for the listed use cases,
- Apprehend the differences between common ML models from an application perspective, and
- Implement the use cases provided in this chapter using Python.

Machine learning is endlessly fascinating and constantly evolving. The use of ML in various industries has been gaining speed in the last few years. There are multiple uses to solve industry-related business problems, from retail to financial services to healthcare to manufacturing. This chapter discusses a few uses in different industries to solve the industry problem using deep learning. Traditional programming cannot accommodate the logic for various combinations. Using the Price Elasticity of Demand Method, use case 1, Retail Price Optimization, finds the exact price at which maximum profit is gained. The use case highlights the step-by-step implementation of understanding the data, loading the data, exploring the data, and model building. In use case 2, Market Basket Analysis (MBA), we present the application based on a customer dataset in a supermarket, thus highlighting association rule mining. The product associations are compared based on Apriori and Fpgrowth algorithms. Use case 3, Sales Prediction of a Retailer, is illustrated to build a ML model and find out the sales of each product at a particular store. The code is implemented to compare different regression models and identify Gradient Boosting as the best model. Predicting the cost of insurance claims for a Property and Causalty (P&C) Insurance Company is covered in use case 4. This case study illustrates data cleaning, data preprocessing, and handling outliers. Use case 5, E-Commerce Product Ranking and Sentiment Analysis, deals with understanding the data, data preprocessing-filtering (including gibberish, language, and profanity detection), feature extraction, pairwise review scoring, and further categorization.

9.1 USE CASE 1 – RETAIL PRICE OPTIMIZATION USING PRICE ELASTICITY OF DEMAND METHOD

9.1.1 BACKGROUND

Product pricing is a vital aspect of the rental industry, and there are several strategies to determine the optimal price of the products. As such, there are two main types of goods. First, there are several goods whose prices affect their sales. Small changes in the price of these products can therefore lead to distinctive changes in sales. On the other hand, sales of goods can be unaffected by their price. These products are generally luxury items and necessities such as certain medicines. This notebook will focus on the former type of goods, where price changes the demand for the product.

Price elasticity of demand (PED) is a key economic measure defined as the degree to which demand changes as the cost of the product changes. In general, the demand for a product decreases as cost rises. However, in some cases, the demand can drop sharply even with a small increase

DOI: 10.1201/9781003258803-9

in price, while in other cases, demand can stay approximately the same even with a sharp price increase. Therefore, the term price elasticity defines the percentage change in demand due to a change in price by 1%, given that everything else is held constant.

In mathematical terms, the PED is the percentage change in quantity demanded, q, divided by the percentage change in price, p. The formula for the price elasticity (ϱ) is $e = \%\Delta Q / \%\Delta P$. In this program, we look at the sales of the items in a cafe, including burgers, coke, lemonade, and coffee. As data scientists, our task is to figure out the optimal prices to set for these items. If the price is set too high, the sales will drop, and if the price is low, then the margins will decrease. Hence, the crucial question to get an answer for is "what is the optimal price point that will maximize the profit?"

9.1.2 UNDERSTANDING THE DATA

For this use case, we will be using three files. The first file is the time dimension, which has all the calendar dates for a year, and that also has attributes, if the date is a holiday, weekend, or school beak days. It also contains another attribute, temperature, that will dictate the outdoor dining possible (as a categorical variable). The second file is the Product master data that contains the product list, and the third file contains the sale transactions.

```
# -*- coding: utf-8 -*-
"""
Created on Thu Dec  3 17:19:01 2020

@author: Suresh Rajappa
"""



# Import the reqiured libraries
import pandas as pd
import numpy as np
import statsmodels.api as sm
from statsmodels.formula.api import ols
import matplotlib.pyplot as plt
import seaborn as sns; sns.set(style="ticks", color_codes=True)

## Get multiple outputs in the same cell
from IPython.core.interactiveshell import InteractiveShell
InteractiveShell.ast_node_interactivity = "all"

## Ignore all warnings
import warnings
warnings.filterwarnings('ignore')
warnings.filterwarnings(action='ignore', category=DeprecationWarning)

## Display all rows and columns of a dataframe instead of a truncated
version
from IPython.display import display
pd.set_option('display.max_columns', None)
pd.set_option('display.max_rows', None)


# # Load the data
sold = pd.read_csv('C:/Python Files/Usecases/Cafe Dataset - Product
Master Data.csv')
transactions = pd.read_csv('C:/Python Files/Usecases/Cafe Dataset - Sales
Transaction Data.csv')
```

```
date_info = pd.read_csv('C:/Python Files/Usecases/Cafe Dataset - Time
Dimension.csv')


# Undersatdning the Product master data
sold.head()
sold.describe()
sold.describe(include = ['O'])
sold[sold.isnull().any(axis=1)]



# SELL_ID: a categorical variable identifier of the combination of items
that are contained in the product.
# SELL_CATEGORY: "0" identifies single products; the category "2"
identifies the combo ones.

# ITEM_ID: a categorical variable identifier of the item that is
contained in the product.
# ITEM_NAME: a categorical variable, identifying the name of the item

sns.pairplot(sold) #Figure 9.1

# Understanding the Transaction data
transactions.head()
transactions.describe()
transactions.describe(include = ['O'])
transactions[transactions.isnull().any(axis=1)]



# Important: It's supposed the PRICE for that product on that day will
not vary. In details:
# CALENDAR_DATE: a date/time variable, having the time always set to
00:00 AM.
# PRICE: a numeric variable associated with the price of the product
identified by the SELL_ID.
# QUANTITY: a numeric variable associated with the quantity of the
product sold, identified by the SELL_ID.
# SELL_ID: a categorical variable identifier of the product sold.
# SELL_CATEGORY: a categorical variable, category of the product sold.
plt.hist(transactions.PRICE) #Figure 9.2

sns.pairplot(transactions) #Figure 9.3

date_info.head()
date_info.describe()
date_info.describe(include = ['O'])
date_info.dtypes
date_info[date_info.isnull().any(axis=1)]
date_info['HOLIDAY'] = date_info['HOLIDAY'].fillna("No Holiday")
date_info
sns.pairplot(date_info) #Figure 9.4

# # Further understanding the data deeper

np.unique(date_info['HOLIDAY'])
date_info['CALENDAR_DATE'].min()
date_info['CALENDAR_DATE'].max()
```

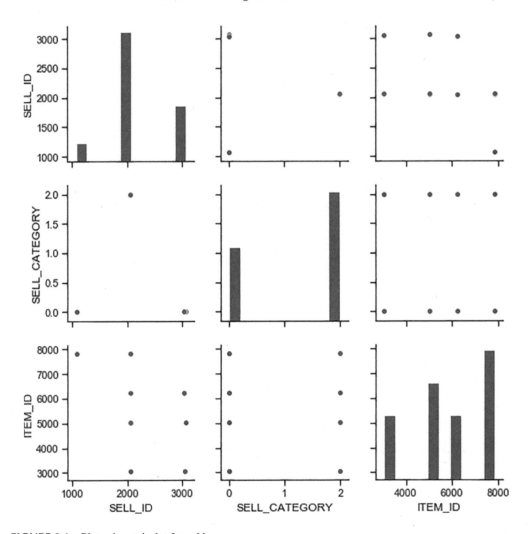

FIGURE 9.1   Plot using pairplot for sold.

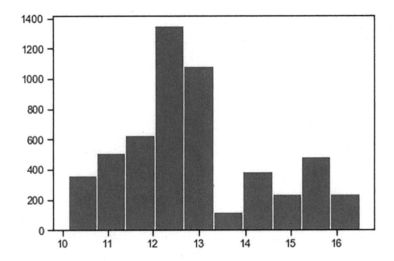

FIGURE 9.2   Plot of the histogram for price.

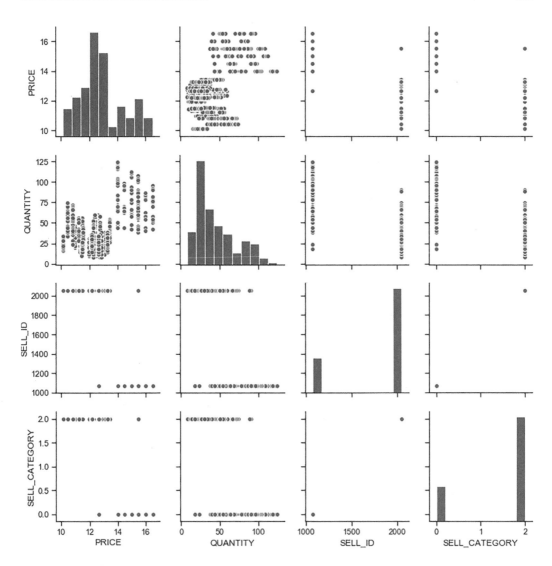

FIGURE 9.3 Plot of pairplot for transactions.

```
date_info.shape
date_info[date_info.isnull().any(axis=1)]
pd.concat([sold.SELL_ID, pd.get_dummies(sold.ITEM_NAME)], axis=1)
pd.concat([sold.SELL_ID, pd.get_dummies(sold.ITEM_NAME)], axis=1).
groupby(sold.SELL_ID).sum()


data1 = pd.merge(sold.drop(['ITEM_ID'],axis=1), transactions.drop(['SELL_
CATEGORY'], axis= 1), on =  'SELL_ID')
data1.head(20)
b = data1.groupby(['SELL_ID', 'SELL_CATEGORY', 'ITEM_NAME', 'CALENDAR_
DATE','PRICE']).QUANTITY.sum()


data1.shape
intermediate_data = b.reset_index()


data1.shape
b.shape
```

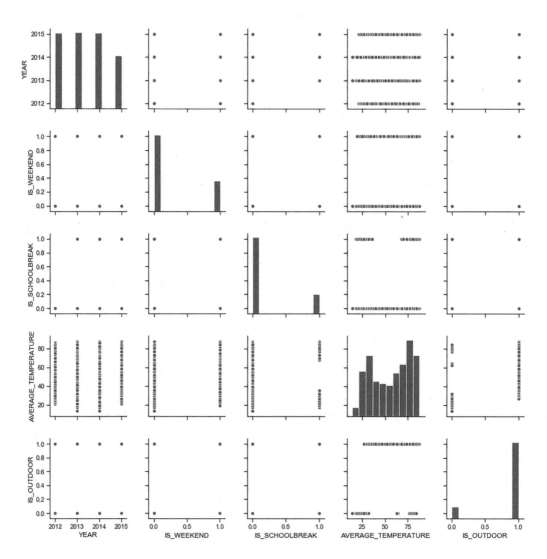

FIGURE 9.4 Plot using pairplot for dateInfo.

```
intermediate_data.head()
intermediate_data['CALENDAR_DATE'].min()
intermediate_data['CALENDAR_DATE'].max()

combined_data = pd.merge(intermediate_data, date_info, on =
'CALENDAR_DATE')
combined_data.head()
combined_data.shape
combined_data[combined_data.isnull().any(axis=1)]

np.unique(combined_data['HOLIDAY'])
np.unique(combined_data['IS_WEEKEND'])
np.unique(combined_data['IS_SCHOOLBREAK'])

bau_data = combined_data[(combined_data['HOLIDAY']=='No Holiday') &
(combined_data['IS_SCHOOLBREAK']==0) & (combined_data['IS_WEEKEND']==0)]
```

```
bau_data.head()
bau_data.shape


np.unique(bau_data['HOLIDAY'])
np.unique(bau_data['IS_WEEKEND'])
np.unique(bau_data['IS_SCHOOLBREAK'])
bau_data[bau_data['IS_WEEKEND']==1]
bau_data[bau_data['HOLIDAY']!='No Holiday']


# DATA EXPLORATION
plt.hist(bau_data.ITEM_NAME)
plt.hist(bau_data.PRICE)
plt.scatter(combined_data['PRICE'], combined_data['QUANTITY'])
plt.scatter(bau_data['PRICE'], bau_data['QUANTITY'])

sns.pairplot(combined_data[['PRICE','QUANTITY','ITEM_NAME']], hue =
'ITEM_NAME', plot_kws={'alpha':0.1})

sns.pairplot(bau_data[['PRICE','QUANTITY','ITEM_NAME']], hue = 'ITEM_
NAME', plot_kws={'alpha':0.1})

# The price density plot is bimodal. From the graph, we can see that as
the price is
#increased, quantity sold is decreased for all quantities. However, coke
is hidden in this view. We can go ahead, and #calculate the price
elasticities for this.

burger = combined_data[combined_data['ITEM_NAME'] == 'BURGER']
burger.head()
burger.shape
burger.describe()
sns.scatterplot(x = burger.PRICE, y = burger.QUANTITY )


# From the above scatter plot, it is visible that there must be different
types of burgers being sold.
#Now, let's see the same distribution when we differentiate with SELL_ID,
which indicates if the burger was
#a part of the combo and must be treated separately.


burger = combined_data[combined_data['ITEM_NAME'] == 'BURGER']
# print(burger)
# print(burger.describe())
sns.scatterplot(data = burger, x = burger.PRICE, y = burger.QUANTITY ,
hue = 'SELL_ID', legend=False, alpha = 0.1)
np.unique(combined_data.SELL_ID)
np.unique(combined_data.SELL_CATEGORY)


burger_1070 = combined_data[(combined_data['ITEM_NAME'] == 'BURGER') &
(combined_data['SELL_ID'] == 1070)]

burger_1070.head()
burger_1070.describe()
sns.scatterplot(data = burger_1070, x = burger_1070.PRICE, y =
burger_1070.QUANTITY, alpha = 0.1)
```

```
# # MODELING
# This is for the combined data
burger_model = ols("QUANTITY ~ PRICE", data=burger_1070).fit()
print(burger_model.summary())
fig = plt.figure(figsize=(12,8))
fig = sm.graphics.plot_partregress_grid(burger_model, fig=fig)


burger = bau_data[bau_data['ITEM_NAME'] == 'BURGER']
burger.head()
burger.shape
burger.describe()
sns.scatterplot(x = burger.PRICE, y = burger.QUANTITY )

burger = bau_data[bau_data['ITEM_NAME'] == 'BURGER']
# print(burger)
# print(burger.describe())
sns.scatterplot(data = burger, x = burger.PRICE, y = burger.QUANTITY ,
hue = 'SELL_ID', legend=False, alpha = 0.1)

np.unique(bau_data.SELL_ID)
np.unique(bau_data.SELL_CATEGORY)


burger_1070 = bau_data[(bau_data['ITEM_NAME'] == 'BURGER') & (bau_
data['SELL_ID'] == 1070)]
burger_1070.head()
burger_1070.describe()
sns.scatterplot(data = burger_1070, x = burger_1070.PRICE, y =
burger_1070.QUANTITY, alpha = 0.1)

# As we can see, the scatter plot is much cleaner. Although there does
seem to be 2 separate trends
burger_model = ols("QUANTITY ~ PRICE", data=burger_1070).fit()
print(burger_model.summary())
fig = plt.figure(figsize=(12,8))
fig = sm.graphics.plot_partregress_grid(burger_model, fig=fig)

# Let's look at the burger data again to see if there is anything else we
can use to refine our model further.


bau_data.head()
bau2_data = combined_data[(combined_data['HOLIDAY']=='No Holiday') &
(combined_data['IS_SCHOOLBREAK']==0) & (combined_data['IS_WEEKEND']==0) &
(combined_data['IS_OUTDOOR']==1)]

burger_1070 = bau2_data[(bau2_data['ITEM_NAME'] == 'BURGER') & (bau2_
data['SELL_ID'] == 1070)]

burger_1070.head()
burger_1070.describe()
sns.scatterplot(data = burger_1070, x = burger_1070.PRICE, y =
burger_1070.QUANTITY, alpha = 0.1)

burger_model = ols("QUANTITY ~ PRICE", data=burger_1070).fit()
print(burger_model.summary())
fig = plt.figure(figsize=(12,8))
```

```
fig = sm.graphics.plot_ccpr(burger_model, "PRICE")

fig = plt.figure(figsize=(12,8))
fig = sm.graphics.plot_regress_exog(burger_model, "PRICE", fig=fig)

burger_2051 = combined_data[(combined_data['ITEM_NAME'] == 'BURGER') &
(combined_data['SELL_ID'] == 2051)]

burger_2051.head()
burger_2051.describe()
sns.scatterplot(data = burger_2051, x = burger_2051.PRICE, y =
burger_2051.QUANTITY, alpha = 0.1)

burger_model = ols("QUANTITY ~ PRICE", data=burger_2051).fit()
print(burger_model.summary())
fig = plt.figure(figsize=(12,8))
fig = sm.graphics.plot_partregress_grid(burger_model, fig=fig)
coke = combined_data[combined_data['ITEM_NAME'] == 'COKE']
coke.head()
coke.shape
coke.describe()
sns.scatterplot(x = coke.PRICE, y = coke.QUANTITY , alpha = 0.1)

coke_model = ols("QUANTITY ~ PRICE", data=coke).fit()
print(coke_model.summary())
fig = plt.figure(figsize=(12,8))
fig = sm.graphics.plot_partregress_grid(coke_model, fig=fig)
fig = plt.figure(figsize=(12,8))
fig = sm.graphics.plot_regress_exog(coke_model, 'PRICE', fig=fig)


df = combined_data[combined_data['ITEM_NAME'] == 'COFFEE']
df.head()
df.shape
df.describe()
sns.scatterplot(x = df.PRICE, y = df.QUANTITY , alpha = 0.1)

model = ols("QUANTITY ~ PRICE", data=df).fit()
print(model.summary())
fig = plt.figure(figsize=(12,8))
fig = sm.graphics.plot_partregress_grid(model, fig=fig)
fig = plt.figure(figsize=(12,8))
fig = sm.graphics.plot_regress_exog(model, 'PRICE', fig=fig)

df = combined_data[combined_data['ITEM_NAME'] == 'LEMONADE']
df.head()
df.shape
df.describe()
sns.scatterplot(x = df.PRICE, y = df.QUANTITY , alpha = 0.1)

model = ols("QUANTITY ~ PRICE", data=df).fit()
print(model.summary())
fig = plt.figure(figsize=(12,8))
fig = sm.graphics.plot_partregress_grid(model, fig=fig)
fig = plt.figure(figsize=(12,8))
fig = sm.graphics.plot_regress_exog(model, 'PRICE', fig=fig)
elasticities = {}
```

```
def create_model_and_find_elasticity(data):
    model = ols("QUANTITY ~ PRICE", data).fit()
    price_elasticity = model.params[1]
    print("Price elasticity of the product: " + str(price_elasticity))
    print(model.summary())
    fig = plt.figure(figsize=(12,8))
    fig = sm.graphics.plot_partregress_grid(model, fig=fig)
    return price_elasticity, model

price_elasticity, model_burger_1070 =
create_model_and_find_elasticity(burger_1070)
elasticities['burger_1070'] = price_elasticity

burger2051_data = bau2_data[(bau2_data['ITEM_NAME'] == "BURGER") & (bau2_
data['SELL_ID'] == 2051)]
elasticities['burger_2051'], model_burger_2051 =
create_model_and_find_elasticity(burger2051_data)

burger2052_data = bau2_data[(bau2_data['ITEM_NAME'] == "BURGER") & (bau2_
data['SELL_ID'] == 2052)]
elasticities['burger_2052'], model_burger_2052 =
create_model_and_find_elasticity(burger2052_data)

burger2053_data = bau2_data[(bau2_data['ITEM_NAME'] == "BURGER") & (bau2_
data['SELL_ID'] == 2053)]
elasticities['burger_2053'], model_burger_2053 =
create_model_and_find_elasticity(burger2053_data)

coke_data = bau2_data[bau2_data['ITEM_NAME'] == "COKE"]
create_model_and_find_elasticity(coke_data)

# 2 coke are available in combo, while 1 is available as single. So, it
is likely that the bottom distribution belongs to single purchases of
coke. Let's verfy this
coke_data = bau2_data[(bau2_data['ITEM_NAME'] == "COKE") & (bau2_
data['SELL_ID'] == 3067)]
elasticities['coke_3067'], model_coke_3067 =
create_model_and_find_elasticity(coke_data)

coke_data
coke_data_2053 = bau2_data[(bau2_data['ITEM_NAME'] == "COKE") & (bau2_
data['SELL_ID'] == 2053)]
elasticities['coke_2053'], model_coke_2053 =
create_model_and_find_elasticity(coke_data_2053)

coke_data_2051 = bau2_data[(bau2_data['ITEM_NAME'] == "COKE") & (bau2_
data['SELL_ID'] == 2051)]
elasticities['coke_2051'], model_coke_2051 =
create_model_and_find_elasticity(coke_data_2051)

lemonade_data_2052 = bau2_data[(bau2_data['ITEM_NAME'] == "LEMONADE") &
(bau2_data['SELL_ID'] == 2052)]
elasticities['lemonade_2052'], model_lemonade_2052 =
create_model_and_find_elasticity(lemonade_data_2052)

lemonade_data_3028 = bau2_data[(bau2_data['ITEM_NAME'] == "LEMONADE") &
(bau2_data['SELL_ID'] == 3028)]
```

```
elasticities['lemonade_3028'], model_lemonade_3028 =
create_model_and_find_elasticity(lemonade_data_3028)

coffee_data_2053 = bau2_data[(bau2_data['ITEM_NAME'] == "COFFEE") &
(bau2_data['SELL_ID'] == 2053)]
elasticities['coffee_2053'], model_coffee_2053 =
create_model_and_find_elasticity(coffee_data_2053)

coffee_data_3055 = bau2_data[(bau2_data['ITEM_NAME'] == "COFFEE") &
(bau2_data['SELL_ID'] == 3055)]
elasticities['coffee_3055'], model_coffee_3055 =
create_model_and_find_elasticity(coffee_data_3055)

# ## List in a table the items and their price elasticities

elasticities

# # Find optimal price for maximum profit
# Now, let's take coke (the sell_id was 2051 for the last coke data) and
since we do not the buying price #of coke, let's assume it to be a little
less than the minimum coke price in the dataset

coke_data = coke_data_2053
coke_data.PRICE.min()
coke_data.PRICE.max()

# Let's take nine as the buying price of coke. We now want to be able to
set the price of coke to get the maximum profit. PRICE is the selling price

buying_price_coke = 9

# $$coke data.PROFIT = (coke data.PRICE - buying price coke) * coke data.
QUANTITY$$
# Let's see the profit for various price points:

start_price = 9.5
end_price = 20

test = pd.DataFrame(columns = ["PRICE", "QUANTITY"])
test['PRICE'] = np.arange(start_price, end_price,0.01)

test['QUANTITY'] = model_coke_2051.predict(test['PRICE'])

test
test['PROFIT'] = (test["PRICE"] - buying_price_coke) * test["QUANTITY"]
test

plt.plot(test['PRICE'],test['QUANTITY'])
plt.plot(test['PRICE'],test['PROFIT'])
plt.show()

# Let's find the exact price at which maximum profit is gained:
ind = np.where(test['PROFIT'] == test['PROFIT'].max())[0][0]
test.loc[[ind]]

def find_optimal_price(data, model, buying_price):
    start_price = data.PRICE.min() - 1
```

```
        end_price = data.PRICE.min() + 10
        test = pd.DataFrame(columns = ["PRICE", "QUANTITY"])
        test['PRICE'] = np.arange(start_price, end_price,0.01)
        test['QUANTITY'] = model.predict(test['PRICE'])
        test['PROFIT'] = (test["PRICE"] - buying_price) * test["QUANTITY"]
        plt.plot(test['PRICE'],test['QUANTITY'])
        plt.plot(test['PRICE'],test['PROFIT'])
        plt.show()
        ind = np.where(test['PROFIT'] == test['PROFIT'].max())[0][0]
        values_at_max_profit = test.iloc[[ind]]
        return values_at_max_profit


# ## Calculate the optimal price for all and list in table
optimal_price = {}
buying_price = 9

optimal_price['burger_1070'] = find_optimal_price(burger_1070, model_
burger_1070, buying_price)
optimal_price

optimal_price['burger_2051'] = find_optimal_price(burger2051_data, model_
burger_2051, buying_price)

optimal_price['burger_2052'] = find_optimal_price(burger2052_data, model_
burger_2052, buying_price)

optimal_price['burger_2053'] = find_optimal_price(burger2053_data, model_
burger_2053, buying_price)
optimal_price['coke_2051'] = find_optimal_price(coke_data_2051, model_
coke_2051, buying_price)
optimal_price['coke_2053'] = find_optimal_price(coke_data_2053, model_
coke_2053, buying_price)
optimal_price['lemonade_2052'] = find_optimal_price(lemonade_data_2052,
model_lemonade_2052, buying_price)
optimal_price['coffee_2053'] = find_optimal_price(coffee_data_2053,
model_coffee_2053, buying_price)
optimal_price

coke_data_2051.PRICE.describe()
```

9.1.3 Conclusion

Based on its previous sales data, this is the optimal price the cafe must set on its items to earn the highest profit. It is essential to note that this is on a normal day. On "other" days, such as a holiday or an event, it has a different impact on customer buying behaviors and patterns. Usually, an increase in consumption is seen on such days. These must be treated separately.

Similarly, it is important to remove any external effects other than price that will affect customers' purchase behaviors, including the data points when the item was on discount. Once the new prices are put up, it is important to monitor the sales and profit continuously. If this pricing method is a part of a product, a dashboard can be created to monitor these items and calculate the lift in the profit.

9.2 USE CASE 2 – MARKET BASKET ANALYSIS (MBA)

9.2.1 INTRODUCTION

Customer MBA is one of the important techniques used by large retailers to uncover combinations and links between items. This process is done by looking for combinations of items that arise together, usually within transactions. To rephrase, this allows the retailers to identify connections between the items that people buy. This proposition is based on the theory that customers who buy one item are more likely to buy another related item.

For example, people who buy women's hosiery usually buy kids' clothes too. So the marketing teams at retail chains will target those customers who buy women's and kids' clothes and provide a discount to them to buy the third item, like small jewelry (which has a high margin for the retailer). This also dictates how the stores are organized. The variation of this is called space and capacity analysis. Based on customer behavior, the store layout can be arranged to maximize the revenue of the shelf space.

So, if customers buy women's and kids' clothes and see a discount or an offer on jewelry, they will be encouraged to spend more and buy the jewelry. This is what is referred to as Basket Analysis, or Market Basket Analysis, or, in short, called MBA. This is just one example. So, if we take hundreds and thousands of items of the supermarket's data, we can get a huge number of insights. And that is why association rule mining is so critical.

9.2.2 UNDERSTATING THE DATA

For this example, we use a customer dataset that describes the customer in detail such as location, age, income, and education, and product and product class give the sufficient details of the product and their groupings, store with details of location, sqft, store type (if this is a super market, ministore, etc.), region, and time dimension. We also use the sales transaction data.

In this solution, we use Apriori and Fpgrowth algorithms. Apriori is an algorithm for frequent item set mining and association rule mining based on learning over relational databases. It progresses by identifying the recurring individual items within the dataset and increasing them to larger item sets as long as those item sets appear sufficiently often in the database. On the other hand, Fpgrowth, also known as Frequent Pattern Growth Algorithm, only generates the frequent item sets per the user's minimum support. One difference between Apriori and Fpgrowth algorithms is that the Fpgrowth algorithm doesn't scan the whole database multiple times, and the scanning time increases linearly. Hence, the Fpgrowth algorithm is much faster than the Apriori algorithm.

```
#!/usr/bin/env python
# coding: utf-8
@author: Suresh Rajappa
# # Market Basket Analysis
#

# **What is Market Basket Analysis ?**
#
# Market Basket Analysis is one of the large retailers' important
techniques to discover the relationship between items using the customer
buying patterns.
# It works by looking for combinations of items that occur together
frequently in transactions. To put it another way, it allows retailers to
identify relationships between the items that people buy
# # Market Basket Analysis (MBA) For Foodmart Store sample Dataset
# Food Mart (FM) is a chain of convenience stores in the United States.
The private company's headquarters are located in Mentor, Ohio, and there
```

are currently approximately **325 stores located in the US**. Food Mart
operates on the franchise system.

```python
# **Importing Libraries**
import pandas as pd
import numpy as np
import matplotlib.pyplot as plt

## Get multiple outputs in the same cell
from IPython.core.interactiveshell import InteractiveShell
InteractiveShell.ast_node_interactivity = "all"

## Ignore all warnings
import warnings
warnings.filterwarnings('ignore')
warnings.filterwarnings(action='ignore', category=DeprecationWarning)

## Display all rows and columns of a dataframe instead of a truncated
version
from IPython.display import display
pd.set_option('display.max_columns', None)
pd.set_option('display.max_rows', None)

# LOADING AND UNDERSTANDING THE DATAFILES
# **Loading Customers Dataset**

customer=pd.read_csv("/Python Files/Usecases/Use Case3/data/customer.
csv")
customer.head()

# **Loading Products Dataset**
product=pd.read_csv("../data/product.csv")
product.head()

# **Loading Departments Dataset**
product_class=pd.read_csv("../data/product_class.csv")
product_class.head()

# **Loading Region Dataset**
region=pd.read_csv("../data/region.csv")
region.head()

# **Loading Sales transaction Dataset**
df=pd.read_csv("../data/sales.csv")
df.head()

# **Loading Stores Dataset**
store=pd.read_csv("../data/store.csv")
store.head()

# **Loading Time by Day Dataset**
time_by_day=pd.read_csv("../data/time_by_day.csv")
time_by_day.head()

time_by_day.tail()

#DATA PREPROCESSING
```

```
# **Merging Customer Dataset in df Dataframe**
df=df.merge(customer,on='customer_id')
df.head()

# **Merging Products Dataset in df Dataframe**
df=df.merge(product,on='product_id')
df.head()

# **Merging Department Dataset in df Dataframe**
df=df.merge(product_class,on='product_class_id')
df.head()

# **Merging Stores Dataset in df Dataframe**
df=df.merge(store,on='store_id')
df.head()

# **Merging Region Dataset in df Dataframe**
df=df.merge(region,on='region_id')
df.head()

# **Merging Time by Day Dataset in df Dataframe**
df=df.merge(time_by_day,on='time_id')
df.head()


# **Converting Dataframe to Final Foodmart Offline Dataset**
df.to_csv("../data/Foodmart_dataset.csv")

# # Exploratory Data Analysis (EDA)
# **Importing Libraries**
import pandas as pd
import numpy as np
import matplotlib.pyplot as plt
import seaborn as sns
import squarify
import networkx as nx
import warnings
import matplotlib as mpl
import gapminder as gapminder

get_ipython().run_line_magic('matplotlib', 'inline')

from mlxtend.frequent_patterns import apriori
from mlxtend.frequent_patterns import association_rules

# **Loading Foodmart Offline Dataset**
df=pd.read_csv("../data/Foodmart_dataset.csv")

# **Size of Foodmart Dataset**
df.shape
df.head()

# # Data Exploration
# **Describe**

df.describe()
df.describe(include='all')
```

```
# **Missing Values**
df.isnull().sum()

# **Datatypes**
df.dtypes

# **Checking Datatypes, Mising Value, Unique Value**
temp = pd.DataFrame(index=df.columns)
temp['data_type']=df.dtypes
temp['null_count']=df.isnull().sum()
temp['unique_count']=df.nunique()

temp

# # Univariate Analysis
# **Histograms**
# **Frequency Plot Of Department Id**

fig=plt.figure(figsize=(15,10))
df['product_class_id'].plot.hist(bins = 50)
plt.xlabel('department id')

# **Frequency Plot Of Product Id**
fig=plt.figure(figsize=(15,10))
df['product_id'].plot.hist(bins = 100)
plt.xlabel('product id')

# **Frequency Plot Of Unit Sales**
fig=plt.figure(figsize=(15,10))
df['unit_sales'].plot.hist(bins = 25)
plt.xlabel('Unit Sales')

# **When do people order**
# **Year**
fig=plt.figure(figsize=(12,10))
df['the_year'].plot.hist(bins=10)
plt.xlabel('year')
plt.xticks([1996,1997,1998,1999])

# **Month**
fig=plt.figure(figsize=(15,10))
df['the_month'].plot.hist(bins=50)
plt.xlabel('Month')

# **Day Of Month**
fig=plt.figure(figsize=(15,10))
df['day_of_month'].plot.hist(bins=75)
plt.xlabel('Day of month')

# **Day Of Week**
df_day_freq=df['the_day'].value_counts()
fig=plt.figure(figsize=(15, 10))
df_day_freq.plot.bar()

# ### Top choices
# **Top 10 First Choices in Products**
df['products'] = 'Products'
products = df.truncate(before = 605, after = 615)
```

```
products = nx.from_pandas_edgelist(products, source = 'products', target
= 'product_name', edge_attr = True)
products

warnings.filterwarnings('ignore')

plt.rcParams['figure.figsize']=(20,20)
pos=nx.spring_layout(products)
color=plt.cm.Reds(np.linspace(0,15,1))
nx.draw_networkx_nodes(products,pos,node_size=15000,node_color=color)
nx.draw_networkx_edges(products, pos, width = 3, alpha = 0.6, edge_color
= 'black')
nx.draw_networkx_labels(products, pos, font_size = 20)
plt.axis('off')
plt.grid()
plt.title('Top 10 First Choices in Products', fontsize = 40)
plt.show()

# **Top 10 First Choices in Department**
df['departments'] = 'Departments'
departments = df.truncate(before = 150, after = 195)
departments = nx.from_pandas_edgelist(departments, source =
'departments', target = 'department', edge_attr = True)

warnings.filterwarnings('ignore')

plt.rcParams['figure.figsize']=(20,20)
pos=nx.spring_layout(departments)
color=plt.cm.Blues(np.linspace(0,15,1))
nx.draw_networkx_nodes(departments,pos,node_size=15000,node_color=color)
nx.draw_networkx_edges(departments, pos, width = 3, alpha = 0.6, edge_
color = 'black')
nx.draw_networkx_labels(departments, pos, font_size = 20)
plt.axis('off')
plt.grid()
plt.title('Top 10 First Choices in Departments', fontsize = 40)
plt.show()

# **Highest Ordered**
# **Most Ordered Products**
df['product_name'].value_counts()

# **Most Ordered Products in Percentage**
df['product_name'].value_counts()/len(df)*100

# **Most Visited Departments**
df['department'].value_counts()

# **Most Visited Departments in Percentage**
df['department'].value_counts()/len(df)*100

# **Most Visited Aisle**
df['subcategory'].value_counts()

# **Most Visited Aisle in Percentage**
df['subcategory'].value_counts()/len(df)*100

# **BarPlot**
```

```
# **BarPlot of Most Visied Aisle**
df_subcategory_freq=df['subcategory'].value_counts().iloc[:50]
fig=plt.figure(figsize=(15,10))
df_subcategory_freq.plot.bar()

# **BarPlot of Most Visited Department**
fig=plt.figure(figsize=(15,10))
df['department'].value_counts().plot(kind='bar')

# **BarPlot of Most Bought Product**
df_freq_products=df['product_name'].value_counts().iloc[:50]
fig=plt.figure(figsize=(15, 10))
df_freq_products.plot.bar()

# **Array of Most Bought Product**
y=df_freq_products.head(50).to_frame()
y.index

# **TreeMap for Most Bought Products**
plt.rcParams['figure.figsize']=(20,20)
color=plt.cm.cool(np.linspace(0,1,50))
squarify.plot(sizes=y.values,label=y.index,alpha=0.8,color=color)
plt.title('tree map for frequent products')
plt.axis('off')

# # Data Manipulation
df.shape

# **Drop Duplicates**
df.drop_duplicates()
df.shape

# **Missing Values**
df.isnull().sum()

# **Datatypes**
df.dtypes

# # Bivariate Analysis
# **Bar Plot**
# **Bar Plot between customers and their products per order**
data_user_orders_num=df.groupby('customer_id')['unit_sales'].count()
data_user_orders_num

source_data = {}
for i in range(10):
    source_data[str(10*i)+'~'+str(10*(i+1))]=len([x for x in list(data_
user_orders_num) if x>=i*10 and x<(i+1)*10])

source_data

font_size=10
fig_size=(8,6)
mpl.rcParams['font.size']=font_size
mpl.rcParams['figure.figsize']=fig_size
bar_width=0.3
```

```
x_axis = tuple(source_data.keys())
y_axis = tuple(source_data.values())
#assign color
plt.bar(x_axis, y_axis, color='rgb')
# descrpitions for x-axis, y-axis
plt.xlabel('Unit sales')
plt.ylabel("No. of customers")
plt.title("Orders Scatter Plot")
plt.show()

# **Transaction ID** - create transaction id which denotes a basket
df['transaction_id'] = df['customer_id'].astype(str) + df['time_id'].
astype(str)
df.head()

# **Filtering out Columns**
cols = [77,3,1,24]
order_products=df[df.columns[cols]]
order_products.head()

# **Average products bought by customers per order**
data_user_products_num1=order_products.groupby('transaction_id')
['product_id'].count()
data_user_products_num1=pd.DataFrame(data_user_products_num1)
data_user_products_num1['transaction_id']=list(data_user_products_num1.
index)

data_user_products_num1.columns=['product_num','orderid']
data_user_products_num2=pd.merge(data_user_products_num1,df[
['transaction_id','customer_id']],on='transaction_id',how='left')

data_user_products_num3=data_user_products_num2.groupby('customer_id')
['product_num'].agg(['sum','count'])
data_user_products_num3['avg']=data_user_products_num3['sum']/
data_user_products_num3['count']
data_user_products_num3.head()

# # Featured Products Department Wise
cols = [1,36,38,24]
departments=df[df.columns[cols]]
departments.head()

# **List Of Departments**
temp=['department']
for i in temp:
    print('@@@@@@Value Count in',i,'@@@@@@@@@')
    print(df[i].value_counts())

# **Produce Department**
produce=departments.loc[df['department'] == 'Produce']
produce.head()

# **Featured Products in Produce Department**
top_produce=produce['product_name'].value_counts().iloc[:10]
top_produce.head()
```

```python
# **Featured Products in Snack Foods Department**
snacks=df.loc[df['department']=='Snack Foods']
top_snacks=snacks['product_name'].value_counts().iloc[:10]
top_snacks.head()

# **Featured Products in HouseHold Department**
household=df.loc[df['department']=='Household']
top_household=household['product_name'].value_counts().iloc[:10]
print(top_household)

# **Featured Products in Frozen Foods Department**
frozen=df.loc[df['department']=='Frozen Foods']
top_frozen=frozen['product_name'].value_counts().iloc[:10]
print(top_frozen)

# **Featured Products in Baking Goods Department**
baking=df.loc[df['department']=='Baking Goods']
top_baking=baking['product_name'].value_counts().iloc[:10]
print(top_baking)

# **Featured Products in Canned Foods Department**
canned=df.loc[df['department']=='Canned Foods']
top_canned=canned['product_name'].value_counts().iloc[:10]
print(top_canned)

# **Featured Products in Dairy Department**
dairy=(df.loc[df['department'] == 'Dairy'])
top_dairy=dairy['product_name'].value_counts().iloc[:10]
print(top_dairy)

# **Featured Products in Health and Hygiene Department**
dairy=(df.loc[df['department'] == 'Health and Hygiene'])
top_dairy=dairy['product_name'].value_counts().iloc[:10]
print(top_dairy)

# **Featured Products in Beverages Department**
dairy=(df.loc[df['department'] == 'Beverages'])
top_dairy=dairy['product_name'].value_counts().iloc[:10]
print(top_dairy)

# **Featured Products in Deli Department**
dairy=(df.loc[df['department'] == 'Deli'])
top_dairy=dairy['product_name'].value_counts().iloc[:10]
print(top_dairy)

# **Featured Products in Alcoholic Beverages Department**
dairy=(df.loc[df['department'] == 'Alcoholic Beverages'])
top_dairy=dairy['product_name'].value_counts().iloc[:10]
print(top_dairy)

# **Featured Products in Starchy Foods Department**
dairy=(df.loc[df['department'] == 'Starchy Foods'])
top_dairy=dairy['product_name'].value_counts().iloc[:10]
print(top_dairy)

# **Featured Products in Eggs Department**
dairy=(df.loc[df['department'] == 'Eggs'])
```

```python
top_dairy=dairy['product_name'].value_counts().iloc[:10]
print(top_dairy)

# # Market Basket Analysis
# ![market-basket-analysis.png](attachment:market-basket-analysis.png)
# **Importing Libraries**
import pandas as pd
import numpy as np
from mlxtend.frequent_patterns import apriori
from mlxtend.frequent_patterns import association_rules
from sklearn.preprocessing import LabelEncoder
import seaborn as sns
import matplotlib.pyplot as plt

# **Filtering the Columns**
cols = [77,3,1,24,7,2]
product_name=df[df.columns[cols]]
product_name.head()

# **Counting each product** The number of transactions a product appeared
in
productCountDf = product_name.groupby("product_id",as_index = False)
['transaction_id'].count()
productCountDf.head()

# **Arranging Top Products**
productCountDf = productCountDf.sort_values("transaction_id",ascending =
False)
productCountDf.head()

# **Top 100 most frequently purchased products**
topProdFrame = productCountDf.iloc[0:100,:]
productId= topProdFrame.loc[:,["product_id"]]
topProdFrame

# **Orders containting the the most frequently purchased products**
MarketBasketdf = product_name[0:0]
for i in range(0,99):
    pId = productId.iloc[i]['product_id']
    stDf = product_name[product_name.product_id == pId ]
    MarketBasketdf = MarketBasketdf.append(stDf,ignore_index = False)

MarketBasketdf.head()

# **Putting the items into 1 transaction**
basket = MarketBasketdf.groupby(['transaction_id','product_name'])['unit_
sales'].sum().unstack().reset_index().fillna(0).
set_index('transaction_id')
basket

# # One Hot Encoding
# **Converted the units into 1 encoded value**
def encode_units(x):
    if x <= 0:
        return 0
    if x >= 1:
        return 1
```

```python
basket_sets = basket.applymap(encode_units)
basket_sets.head()

# **Size and shape of basket**
basket_sets.size
basket_sets.shape
dummy=basket_sets.head(10000)

# Model building using Apriori Algotithm
# # Apriori Algorithm
# **Importing Apriori and Association rules Libraries**
from mlxtend.frequent_patterns import apriori
from mlxtend.frequent_patterns import association_rules

# **Frequent items with support 0.01% using Apriori Algorithm**
frequent_itemsets = apriori(dummy, min_support=0.0001, use_colnames=True)
frequent_itemsets

# **Association rules using Apriori Algorithm**
apriori_rules = association_rules(frequent_itemsets, metric="lift",
min_threshold= 1)
apriori_rules

# **Filtering out co-realted products with higher Probability**
apriori_rules[ (apriori_rules['lift'] >= 50) & (apriori_
rules['confidence'] >= 0.01) ]

# # Recommendations using Apriori Algorithm
def recommendations_using_Apriori(item):
    recommend = []
    for i in range(0,2646):
        if item == apriori_rules.iloc[i,0]:
            recommend.append(apriori_rules.iloc[i,1])

    return recommend


# **5 Recommendations with Better Chicken Noodle Soup**
product_name = {'Better Chicken Noodle Soup'}
recommentations=recommendations_using_Apriori(product_name)
print(*recommentations[0:5], sep = "\n")

# **10 Recommendations with Moms Potato Salad**
product_name = {'Moms Potato Salad'}
recommentations=recommendations_using_Apriori(product_name)
print(*recommentations[0:10], sep = "\n")


# **15 Recommendations with Carrington Ice Cream Sandwich**
product_name = {'Carrington Ice Cream Sandwich'}
recommentations=recommendations_using_Apriori(product_name)
print(*recommentations[0:15], sep = "\n")

# # Fpgrowth Algorithm
# **Importing Fpgrowth Libraries**
from mlxtend.frequent_patterns import fpgrowth

# **Frequent Items with support 0.001% using Fpgrowth Algorithm**
```

```
freq_items=fpgrowth(dummy,min_support=.0001,use_colnames=True)
freq_items

# **Association Rules using Fpgrowth Algorithm**
fpgrowth_rules=association_rules(freq_items,metric="lift",min_
threshold=1)
fpgrowth_rules

# # Recommendations using Fpgrowth Algorithm
def recommendations_using_Fpgrowth(item):
    recommend = []
    for i in range(0,2646):
        if item == fpgrowth_rules.iloc[i,0]:
            recommend.append(fpgrowth_rules.iloc[i,1])

    return recommend

# **5 Recommendations with Better Chicken Noodle Soup**
product_name = {'Better Chicken Noodle Soup'}
recommentations=recommendations_using_Fpgrowth(product_name)
print(*recommentations[0:5], sep = "\n")

# **10 Recommendations with Moms Potato Salad**
product_name = {'Moms Potato Salad'}
recommentations=recommendations_using_Fpgrowth(product_name)
print(*recommentations[0:10], sep = "\n")

# **15 Recommendations with Carrington Ice Cream Sandwich**
product_name = {'Carrington Ice Cream Sandwich'}
recommentations=recommendations_using_Fpgrowth(product_name)
print(*recommentations[0:15], sep = "\n")

# # Comapring Apriori VS fpgrowth Algorithms
# **Calculating Run Time of Apriori Algorithm**
import time
l=[0.01,0.02,0.03,0.04,0.05]
t=[]
for i in l:
    t1=time.time()
    apriori(dummy,min_support=i,use_colnames=True)
    t2=time.time()
    t.append((t2-t1)*1000)

# **Calculating Run Time of Fpgrowth Algorithm**
l=[0.01,0.02,0.03,0.04,0.05]
f=[]
for i in l:
    t1=time.time()
    fpgrowth(dummy,min_support=i,use_colnames=True)
    t2=time.time()
    f.append((t2-t1)*1000)

# **Graph of Run Time between Apriori and Fpgrowth Algorithm**
sns.lineplot(x=l,y=f,label="fpgrowth")
sns.lineplot(x=l,y=t,label="apriori")
plt.xlabel("Min_support Threshold")
plt.ylabel("Run Time in ms")
```

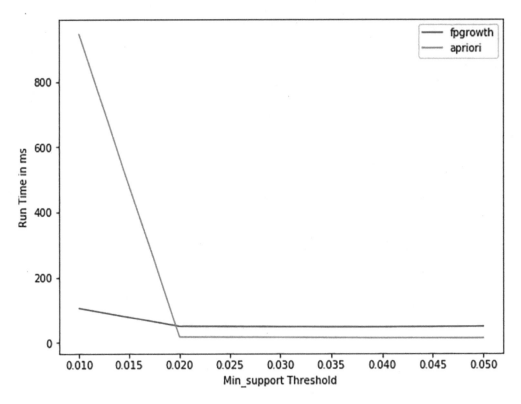

FIGURE 9.5   Time taken by Apriori and Fpgrowth algorithms.

TABLE 9.1

Differences between the Apriori and Fpgrowth algorithms

Apriori Algorithm	Fpgrowth Algorithm
More memory usage	Less memory usage
Time consuming	Quicker than Apriori
Tree-based algorithm	Array-based algorithm
Conducts multiple data scans of the database	Requires two scans of the database
Uses breadth file search	Used depth file search

9.2.3   Conclusion

We have used the two famous algorithms, Apriori and Fpgrowth, to develop product associations for the item set mining. The time taken by each algorithm is compared and evaluated. The graph in Figure 9.5 shows the time taken in milliseconds by each algorithm.

There are few subtle differences between these algorithms shown in Table 9.1.

9.3   USE CASE 3 – SALES PREDICTION OF A RETAILER

9.3.1   Background

Sales prediction or forecasting sales are a common use case of ML. Sales forecasts can identify benchmarks, determine the progressive influence of new initiatives, plan resources in response to expected demand, and project future budgets. The data scientists of a retailer have collected sales

Item_Identifier	Item_Weight	Item_Fat_Content	Item_Visibility	Item_Type	Item_MRP	Outlet_Ide	Outlet_Establishment
FDW58	20.75	Low Fat	0.007564836	Snack Foods	107.8622	OUT049	
FDW14	8.3	reg	0.038427677	Dairy	87.3198	OUT017	
NCN55	14.6	Low Fat	0.099574908	Others	241.7538	OUT010	
FDQ58	7.315	Low Fat	0.015388393	Snack Foods	155.034	OUT017	
FDY38		Regular	0.118599314	Dairy	234.23	OUT027	
FDH56	9.8	Regular	0.063817206	Fruits and Vegetables	117.1492	OUT046	
FDL48	19.35	Regular	0.082601537	Baking Goods	50.1034	OUT018	
FDC48		Low Fat	0.015782495	Baking Goods	81.0592	OUT027	

FIGURE 9.6 Sales prediction data.

data by-products across the stores in different cities. Also, various attributes of each product and store have been defined. This project aims to build a ML model and find out the sales of each product at a particular store. Using this model, the retailer will try to understand the properties of products and stores, which play a key role in increasing sales.

9.3.2 UNDERSTANDING THE DATA

The test and training dataset we use has the following format: item identifier or productId, and its features such as weight, fat content, and product category. This also contains information about the store such as, when the store was established, size of the store, location, and store type. The sample data are shown in Figure 9.6.

At a glance, we can see there are many null values in the Outlet Size column. We will examine the data using features engineering techniques to see which attributes are useful for the analysis and if there is an imbalance in the data, which is a very common data challenge as missing data.

```python
#Importing Necessary Libraries
#Matplot and seaborn for making graphs
get_ipython().run_line_magic('matplotlib', 'notebook')
from sklearn.linear_model import Ridge
from sklearn.model_selection import KFold, cross_val_score
import featuretools as ft
import numpy as np
import pandas as pd
from sklearn.model_selection import train_test_split
from sklearn.preprocessing import LabelEncoder
from scipy import stats
import matplotlib.pyplot as plt
from sklearn.model_selection import GridSearchCV
from sklearn.model_selection import RandomizedSearchCV
import seaborn as sns
get_ipython().run_line_magic('matplotlib', 'inline')
import warnings
warnings.filterwarnings('ignore')
#Imorting the datasets
train =pd.read_csv("train.csv")
test=pd.read_csv("test.csv")
print(train.shape,test.shape)
def concat(X,Y):
df= pd.concat([X,Y],ignore_index=True)
return df
df=concat(train,test)
#Undersatning the data and data preprocessing
print(df.shape)
```

```python
df.head()
#Checks number of null values for all the variables
#Item_Weight has 2439 null values
#Outlet Size has 4016 null values
df.isnull().sum()
#Checks the number of unique entries correspnding to each variable
df.apply(lambda x: len(x.unique()))
#defining a function:
#frequency of unique entries in each column with their names
def frequency_each_item(X,Y):
for i in Y:
print("frequency of each category for",i)
print(X[i].value_counts())
#frequency of unique entries in each columns with their names
category=['Item_Fat_Content','Item_Type','Outlet_Location_Type','Outlet_
Size','Outlet_Type']
frequency_each_item(df,category)
mode_Outlet_Size=df.pivot_table(values='Outlet_Size', index='Outlet_
Type',aggfunc=(lambda x: stats.mode(x)[0]))
print(mode_Outlet_Size)
bool2=df['Outlet_Size'].isnull()
df['Outlet_Size'][bool2]=df['Outlet_Type'][bool2].apply(lambda x : mode_
Outlet_Size.loc[x]).values
sum(df['Outlet_Size'].isnull())
# Correcting the mis-written datas
df['Item_Fat_Content'].replace(to_replace =['low fat','reg','LF'],
value =['Low Fat','Regular','Low Fat'],inplace=True)
df['Item_Fat_Content'].value_counts()
df.head()
avg_item_weight=df.pivot_table(values='Item_Weight', index='Item_
Identifier',aggfunc=[np.mean])
print(avg_item_weight)
bool=df['Item_Weight'].isnull()
df['Item_Weight'][bool]=df['Item_Identifier'][bool].apply(lambda x :avg_
item_weight.loc[x]).values
sum(df['Item_Weight'].isnull())
#Reducing food category to only 3 types with the help of the first 2
alphabets of the Item_Identifier column
df['Item_Type_combined']=df['Item_Identifier'].apply(lambda x : x[0:2])
df['Item_Type_combined'].replace(to_replace =['FD','DR','NC'],
value =['Food','Drinks','Non_consumable'],inplace=True)
#dropping the redundant column
df=df.drop(columns=['Item_Type'])
df.head()
#Calculating number of Item_fat_contents that are also non_consumable
bool3=df['Item_Type_combined']=='Non_consumable'
df['Item_Fat_Content'][bool3]='Non_edible'
df['Item_Fat_Content'].value_counts()
#Using feature Engineering and adding new column
df['yearsold']=2013-df['Outlet_Establishment_Year']
df=df.drop(columns=['Outlet_Establishment_Year'])
df.head()
# Converting all the zero values to mean in the visibility column
Item_Visibility_mean=df.pivot_table(index='Item_Identifier',values='Item_
Visibility',aggfunc=[np.mean])
print(Item_Visibility_mean)
```

```
bool4=df['Item_Visibility']==0
df['Item_Visibility'][bool4]=df['Item_Identifier'][bool4].apply(lambda
x:Item_Visibility_mean.loc[x]).values
df.head()
#Checks for correation between different numerical columns
df.corr()
# # Identifying outliers and fixing them
df.describe()
sns.set(style="whitegrid")
ax = sns.boxplot(x=df["Item_Outlet_Sales"])
#As we know, only Item_Outlet_Sales have outliers we can fix them, but
fixing them will increase our RMSE score
#to a large extent
# Plotting Graphs for more Analysis
#value of sales increases for the increase in MRP of the item
plt.scatter(df.Item_MRP,df.Item_Outlet_Sales,c='g')
plt.show()
sns.FacetGrid(df, col='Item_Type_combined', size=3, col_wrap=5).map(plt.
hist, 'Item_Outlet_Sales').add_legend();
# Maximum contribution to outlet sales is from Items that are food type
and least is from drinks
sns.FacetGrid(df, col='Outlet_Location_Type', size=3, col_wrap=5).
map(plt.hist, 'Item_Outlet_Sales').add_legend();
#Tier3 type of outlet location provides for the maximum sales and other
two provides the least sales
sns.FacetGrid(df, col='Outlet_Size', size=3, col_wrap=5).map(plt.hist,
'Item_Outlet_Sales').add_legend();
#Small sized Outlets are providing the maximum sales whereas large sized
outlets
# are contributing the least
sns.FacetGrid(df, col='Item_Fat_Content', size=3, col_wrap=5).map(plt.
hist, 'Item_Outlet_Sales').add_legend();
# people are prefering items with lowest fat content the most
sns.FacetGrid(df, col='Outlet_Type', size=3, col_wrap=2).map(plt.hist,
'Item_Outlet_Sales').add_legend();
#Maximum of the high sales margin is from Supermarket Type1
#Grocery store has the least sales
#Label Encoding all the columns with text entries and dropping
Item_identifier
le=LabelEncoder()
list=['Item_Fat_Content','Outlet_Location_Type','Outlet_Size','Outlet_
Type','Item_Type_combined',
'Outlet_Size']
for i in list:
le.fit(df[i])
df[i]=le.transform(df[i])
df_new=df.drop(columns='Item_Identifier')
df_new= pd.get_dummies(df_new,columns=['Outlet_Identifier'])
df_new.head()
#Separating test and train set
df_new_train=df_new.iloc[:8523,:]
df_new_test=df_new.iloc[8523:,:]
df_new_test=df_new_test.drop(columns=['Item_Outlet_Sales'])
Y_train=df_new_train['Item_Outlet_Sales']
df_train_test=df_new_train.drop(columns=['Item_Outlet_Sales'])
from sklearn.linear_model import LinearRegression
```

```
from sklearn.linear_model import Ridge
from sklearn.ensemble import RandomForestRegressor
from sklearn.ensemble import ExtraTreesRegressor
from sklearn.ensemble import BaggingRegressor
from sklearn.ensemble import GradientBoostingRegressor
from sklearn.linear_model import ElasticNet
from sklearn.neural_network import MLPRegressor
from sklearn.model_selection import KFold, cross_val_score
from xgboost import XGBRegressor
import xgboost as xgb
models = [('lr',LinearRegression()),('ridge',Ridge()),('rfr',RandomForest
Regressor()),('etr',ExtraTreesRegressor()),
('br',BaggingRegressor()),('gbr',GradientBoostingRegressor()),('en',Elast
icNet()),('mlp',MLPRegressor())]
#Making function for making best 2 models for further hyperparameter
tuning
def basic_model_selection(x,y,cross_folds,model):
scores=[]
names = []
for i, j in model:
cv_scores = cross_val_score(j, x, y, cv=cross_folds,n_jobs=5)
scores.append(cv_scores)
names.append(i)
for k in range(len(scores)):
print(names[k],scores[k].mean())
basic_model_selection(df_train_test,Y_train,4,models)
#Average score for XGBoost matrix
# define data_dmatrix
data_dmatrix = xgb.DMatrix(data=df_train_test,label=Y_train)
# import XGBRegressor
xgb1 = XGBRegressor()
cv_score = cross_val_score(xgb1, df_train_test, Y_train, cv=4,n_jobs=5)
print(cv_score.mean())
# Gradient Boost Regression and XGBoost Regression will be used for
further hyperparameter tuning
def model_parameter_tuning(x,y,model,parameters,cross_folds):
model_grid = GridSearchCV(model,
parameters,
cv = cross_folds,
n_jobs = 5,
verbose=True)
model_grid.fit(x,y)
y_predicted = model_grid.predict(x)
print(model_grid.score)
print(model_grid.best_params_)
print("The RMSE score is",np.sqrt(np.mean((y-y_predicted)**2)))
#defining function for hyperparameter tuning and using RMSE as my metric
parameters_xgb = {'nthread':[3,4],
'learning_rate':[0.02,0.03], #so called `eta` value
'max_depth': [3,2,4],
'min_child_weight':[3,4,5],
'silent': [1],
'subsample': [0.5],
'colsample_bytree': [0.7],
'n_estimators': [300,320]
}
```

```
parameters_gbr={'loss':['ls','lad'],
'learning_rate':[0.3],
'n_estimators':[300],
'min_samples_split':[3,4],
'max_depth':[3,4],
'min_samples_leaf':[3,4,2],
'max_features':['auto','log2','sqrt']
}
# Defining the useful parameters for parameter tuning
# to get the optimum output
model_parameter_tuning(df_train_test,Y_train,xgb1,parameters_xgb,4)
gbr=GradientBoostingRegressor()
model_parameter_tuning(df_train_test,Y_train,gbr,parameters_gbr,4)
from sklearn.neural_network import MLPRegressor
mlp=MLPRegressor()
parameters_mlp = {'hidden_layer_sizes':[300,400,500],
'activation':['relu','tanh'],
'learning_rate':['adaptive'],
'learning_rate_init':[0.001,0.004],
'solver':['adam'],
'max_iter':[200,300]
}
model_parameter_tuning(df_train_test,Y_train,mlp,parameters_mlp,4)
# Standardization of the model before training
from sklearn.preprocessing import StandardScaler
scaler = StandardScaler()
standardized=scaler.fit_transform(df_train_test)
column_names = df_train_test.columns
df_standardized = pd.DataFrame(data=standardized,columns=column_names)
df_standardized.head()
basic_model_selection(df_standardized,Y_train,4,models)
#Average score for XGBoost matrix
# define data_dmatrix
data_dmatrix = xgb.DMatrix(data=df_standardized,label=Y_train)
# import XGBRegressor
xgb1 = XGBRegressor()
cv_score = cross_val_score(xgb1, df_standardized, Y_train, cv=4,n_jobs=5)
print(cv_score.mean())
# The Models for hyperparameter tuning are the same XGBoost and
GradientBoostingRegression
model_parameter_tuning(df_standardized,Y_train,xgb1,parameters_xgb,4)
model_parameter_tuning(df_standardized,Y_train,gbr,parameters_gbr,4)
df_train_test.head()
# Using Robust Scaler
# My dataset having outliers make it more prone to mistakes
# Robust Scaler handles the outliers as well
# It scales according to the quartile range
from sklearn.preprocessing import RobustScaler
from sklearn.preprocessing import MinMaxScaler
normalize = MinMaxScaler()
robust = RobustScaler(quantile_range = (0.1,0.8)) #range of inerquartile
is one of the parameters
robust_stan = robust.fit_transform(df_train_test)
robust_stan_normalize = normalize.fit_transform(robust_stan)
# also normalized the dataset using MinMaxScaler i.e has bought the data
set between (0,1)
```

```
df_robust_normalize = pd.DataFrame(robust_stan_normalize,columns=
column_names)
df_robust_normalize.head()
basic_model_selection(df_robust_normalize,Y_train,4,models)
cv_score = cross_val_score(xgb1, df_robust_normalize, Y_train,
cv=4,n_jobs=5)
print(cv_score.mean())
model_parameter_tuning(df_robust_normalize,Y_train,xgb1,parameters_xgb,4)
model_parameter_tuning(df_robust_normalize,Y_train,gbr,parameters_gbr,4)
# Best Model
# Comparing all models using RMSE score
# Gradient Boosting Method is the best method when implemented using
Robust Scaler and MinMaxScaler normalization
# PARAMETERS AND RMSE RESPECTIVELY
# {'learning_rate': 0.3, 'loss': 'lad', 'max_depth': 3, 'max_features':
'auto', 'min_samples_leaf': 2, 'min_samples_split': 2, 'n_estimators':
300}
# The RMSE score is 1049.14085875651
robust_test = robust.fit_transform(df_new_test)
robust_normalize_test = normalize.fit_transform(robust_test)
df_test_robust_normalize = pd.DataFrame(robust_normalize_test,columns=
column_names)
gbr = GradientBoostingRegressor(learning_rate= 0.3, loss= 'lad',max_
depth= 3,min_samples_leaf=2,min_samples_split=3
,n_estimators= 300)
# Defining my final model that I will use for prediction
gbr.fit(df_robust_normalize,Y_train)
final_prediction=gbr.predict(df_test_robust_normalize) #Predicting the
outlet sales
#the prediction is in the form of numpy array
# Converting into Dataframe
df_final_prediction = pd.DataFrame(final_prediction,columns=
['Item_Outlet_Sales'])
df_final_prediction.head()
# Saving the final model using Joblib
import joblib
filename = 'final_model.sav' # Name of the model
joblib.dump(gbr, filename) # it is saved in your current working
directory
# This command loads the model once again
load_model = joblib.load(filename)
```

9.3.3 Conclusion

When comparing the models, we can assess that overall, the XGBoost model had the best performance, followed closely by other models. A caveat here is that all of the models above were derived in their most basic form to establish how they can be used for sales prediction. In addition, the models were only slightly tuned to minimize complexity.

To identify which model is right for the real-world use case, we must consider the following:

- The degree of model complexity vs. interpretability that we are content with.
- Models can be tuned, and features can be engineered to include combinations of attributes, etc.

- Understand how we should be using the results and how data will be coming into the model.
- Tune models using cross-validation or similar practices to avoid overfitting and underfitting data.

9.4 USE CASE 4 – PREDICTING THE COST OF INSURANCE CLAIMS FOR A PROPERTY AND CAUSALTY (P&C) INSURANCE COMPANY

9.4.1 BACKGROUND

Property and Casualty Insurance (a.k.a P&C insurance) are types of coverage that help protect the insurer and the property they own. Property insurance helps cover the thing the insurer owns, like a home or a car. On the other hand, casualty insurance refers to the policy that includes liability coverage to help protect the insurer if they are found legally responsible for an accident that causes injuries to another person or damage to their person's belongings. Property and Casualty Insurance are typically packaged together into one policy. A clear understanding of a given claim's future cost, or severity, is fundamental to an insurance company and would enable it to price its plans more effectively. Additionally, knowing the perspective of different attributes would allow the company to evaluate potential customers more efficiently.

9.4.2 UNDERSTANDING THE DATA

The given dataset contains 131 columns (Figure 9.7) of unlabeled data, as shown in the sample screenshot. We use the pickle library of python to implement binary protocols for serializing and deserializing a Python object structure ("Pickling" is the process through which a Python object hierarchy is transformed into a byte stream, and "unpickling" is the inverse operation of the pickling.).

```
# ##### Import the packages and load the training data
import pandas as pd
import numpy as np
import re
import matplotlib.pyplot as plt
from sklearn.impute import SimpleImputer
import seaborn as sns
from sklearn.feature_selection import VarianceThreshold
from sklearn.preprocessing import LabelEncoder
from sklearn.feature_selection import chi2
import math
import pickle # this module implements binary protocols for serializing
and de-serializing a Python object structure

#modify the display options to view entire dataframe
pd.options.display.max_columns = None

train_data = pd.read_csv("train.csv")

#Analyze the size of training data
#Verify the first few observations
#Check the column headers

train_data.shape
```

id	cat1	cat2	cat3	cat4	cat5	cat6	cat7	cat8	cat9	cat10	cat11	cat12	cat13	cat14	cat15	cat16	cat17	cat18	cat19	cat20	cat21	cat22	cat23	cat24	cat25	cat
4	A	B	A	A	A	A	A	A	B	B	B	A	A	A	A	A	A	A	A	A	A	A	A	A	A	A
6	A	B	A	B	B	A	B	A	B	B	A	B	B	B	A	A	A	A	A	A	A	A	B	B	A	A
9	A	B	A	B	B	A	B	A	A	A	A	B	B	B	A	A	A	A	A	A	A	A	B	A	A	A
12	A	A	A	A	B	B	A	A	A	A	A	A	A	A	A	A	A	A	A	A	A	A	A	A	A	A
15	B	A	A	A	B	B	A	A	A	A	A	A	A	A	A	A	A	A	A	A	A	A	A	A	A	A
17	A	A	A	A	B	A	A	A	A	A	A	A	A	A	A	A	A	A	A	A	A	A	A	A	A	A
21	B	A	A	A	A	B	A	A	B	A	A	A	B	A	A	A	A	A	A	A	A	A	A	A	A	A
28	B	B	A	A	A	B	A	A	B	A	A	B	A	A	A	A	A	A	A	A	A	A	A	A	A	A
32	B	B	A	A	A	A	A	A	B	B	A	A	B	A	A	A	A	A	A	A	A	A	A	A	A	A
43	A	B	A	A	A	A	A	A	B	B	B	A	A	A	A	A	A	A	A	A	A	A	A	A	A	A
46	A	A	A	A	B	B	A	A	A	A	A	A	A	A	A	A	A	A	A	A	A	A	A	A	A	A
50	A	A	A	A	B	B	A	A	A	A	A	A	A	A	A	A	A	A	A	A	A	A	A	A	A	A
54	B	A	A	A	A	B	A	A	A	A	A	A	A	A	A	A	A	A	A	A	A	A	A	A	A	A
62	B	A	A	A	A	B	A	A	A	A	A	A	A	A	A	A	A	A	A	A	A	A	A	A	A	A
70	A	A	A	A	B	B	A	A	A	A	A	A	A	A	A	A	A	A	A	A	A	A	A	A	A	A
71	A	A	A	A	A	B	A	A	A	A	A	A	A	A	A	A	A	A	A	A	A	A	A	A	A	A
75	A	A	A	B	B	B	A	A	A	A	A	A	A	A	A	A	A	A	A	A	A	A	A	A	A	A
77	A	A	A	A	A	B	A	A	A	A	A	A	A	A	A	A	A	A	A	A	A	A	A	A	A	A
81	A	A	A	A	B	A	A	A	A	A	A	A	A	A	A	A	A	A	A	A	A	A	A	A	A	A
...																										

FIGURE 9.7 Sample view of the dataset for use case 4.

```
train_data.head()

column_names = np.array(train_data.columns)
print(column_names)

# ###### Identify the categorical and numerical columns to check the data
distribution and 5 point summary
column_datatypes = train_data.dtypes
categorical_columns = list(column_datatypes[column_datatypes=="object"].
index.values)
continuous_columns = list(column_datatypes[column_datatypes=="float64"].
index.values)
continuous_columns.remove('loss')

# ##### check the distribution of categorical variables
#function to check the distribution of values in categorical columns
#Training data and Categorical columns list
def category_distribution(train_data,categorical_columns):
    categorical_column_distribution = list()
    for cat_column in categorical_columns:
        categorical_column_distribution.append(train_data[cat_column].
value_counts())
    return(categorical_column_distribution)

categorical_column_distribution =
category_distribution(train_data,categorical_columns)

categorical_column_distribution

length_categorical_columns = list(map(lambda
x:len(x),categorical_column_distribution))

#count the number of columns having the same number of unique values
distribution_dict = dict()
for val in length_categorical_columns:
    if val in distribution_dict.keys():
        count = distribution_dict[val]
        distribution_dict[val] = count+1
    else:
        distribution_dict[val]=1

distribution_dict

# ### Plot a bar-graph
#plot showing the count of columns having same number of unique values
keys = distribution_dict.keys()
values = distribution_dict.values()
plt.bar(keys, values,width=0.8)
plt.xlabel('Distinct Values in Categorical Variable', fontsize=15)
plt.ylabel('Count', fontsize=15)
plt.title('Categorical Labels with Same Unique Values',fontsize=20)
plt.rcParams['figure.figsize'] = [48/2.54, 10/2.54]
plt.show()

# ##### check the distribution of continuous variables
#filter out the continous columns and view the descriptive statistics
train_data[continuous_columns].describe()
```

```python
# #### Data cleaning and pre-processing
#Check if there is any missing value in the columuns
#value of 0 indicates no missing values
missing_values = train_data.isnull().sum()
np.max(missing_values)

#Manually insert a blank value across 5 rows
total_rows = train_data.shape[0]
columns_with_blanks_cat = np.random.randint(1,116,2)
columns_with_blanks_cont = np.random.randint(117,130,3)
columns_with_blank = np.append(columns_with_blanks_cat,
columns_with_blanks_cont)

#for every column insert 5 blanks at random locations
for col in columns_with_blank:
    rows_with_blanks = np.random.randint(1,total_rows,5)
    train_data.iloc[rows_with_blanks,col] = np.nan

#Validate the number of columns with missing values
missing_values = train_data.isnull().sum()
np.max(missing_values)

#Displaying the columns with missing values
columns_with_missing = train_data.columns[train_data.isnull().any()]
print(columns_with_missing)

# ##### Data Preprocessing class with the following functions:
#missing_value_continuous: function to handle missing values of
continuous variables
#missing_value_categorical: function to handle missing values of
categorical variables
#outlier_treatment: function to handle continuous outliers in the dataset

class Data_preprocessing:
    def __init__(self,train_data):
        self.train_data = train_data

    def
missing_value_continuous(self,column_names_with_specific_type,imputation_
type="mean"):
        if imputation_type=="mean":
            mean_imputer = SimpleImputer(missing_values=np.nan,
strategy='mean')
            mean_imputer.fit(self.train_data[column_names_with_specific_type])
            self.train_data[column_names_with_specific_type]=mean_
imputer.transform(self.train_data[column_names_with_specific_type])
        if imputation_type=="median":
            median_imputer = SimpleImputer(missing_values=np.nan,
strategy='median')
            median_imputer.fit(self.train_data[column_names_with_specific_type])
            self.train_data[column_names_with_specific_type]=median_
imputer.transform(self.train_data[column_names_with_specific_type])
        return self.train_data
```

```
    def
missing_value_categorical(self,column_names_with_specific_
type,imputation_type="most_frequent"):
        most_frequent = SimpleImputer(strategy="most_frequent")
        most_frequent.fit(self.
train_data[column_names_with_specific_type])
        self.train_data[column_names_with_specific_type] = most_frequent.
transform(train_data[column_names_with_specific_type])
        return self.train_data


    def outlier_treatment(self,Q1,Q3,IQR,columns_with_outlier,action):
        if action=="median":
            for i in range(len(columns_with_outlier)):
                column_name = columns_with_outlier[i]
                meadian_outlier = np.median(self.train_data[column_name])
                self.train_data.loc[self.train_data[((self.train_
data[column_name]<(Q1[column_name]-(1.5*IQR[column_name])))|(self.train_
data[column_name]>(Q3[column_name]+(1.5*IQR[column_name]))))].
index,column_name]=meadian_outlier
        if action=="mean":
            for i in range(len(columns_with_outlier)):
                column_name = columns_with_outlier[i]
                mean_outlier = np.mean(self.train_data[column_name])
self.train_data.loc[self.train_data[((self.train_data[column_
name]<(Q1[column_name]-(1.5*IQR[column_name])))|(self.train_data[column_
name]>(Q3[column_name]+(1.5*IQR[column_name]))))].
index,column_name]=mean_outlier
        if action=="remove":
            for i in range(len(columns_with_outlier)):
                column_name = columns_with_outlier[i]
                self.train_data = self.train_data[~((self.train_
data[column_name]<(Q1[column_name]-(1.5*IQR[column_name])))|(self.
train_data[column_name]>(Q3[column_name]+(1.5*IQR[column_name]))))]
        return self.train_data

Data_preprocessing_obj = Data_preprocessing(train_data)
train_data = Data_preprocessing_obj.
missing_value_continuous(continuous_columns,"median")
train_data = Data_preprocessing_obj.
missing_value_categorical(categorical_columns)

# ##### Section on handling outliers in the dataset
ax = sns.boxplot(data=train_data[continuous_columns], orient="h",
palette="Set2")

columns_with_outlier = ['cont7','cont9','cont10']

#compute the interquartile range for all continuous columns
Q1 = train_data[continuous_columns].quantile(0.25)
Q3 = train_data[continuous_columns].quantile(0.75)
IQR = (Q3-Q1)
train_data = Data_preprocessing_obj.
outlier_treatment(Q1,Q3,IQR,columns_with_outlier,"median")
```

```python
ax = sns.boxplot(data=train_data[continuous_columns], orient="h",
palette="Set2")

# ##### Feature elimination techniques for continuous and categorical
features
#Function for feature selection of numeric variables
#Remove variables with constant variance
#Remove variables with Quasi-Constant variance with a fixed threshold
#Remove correlated variables

def
feature_selection_numerical_variables(train_data,qthreshold,corr_
threshold,exclude_numerical_cols_list):
    num_columns = ['int16', 'int32', 'int64', 'float16', 'float32',
'float64']
    numerical_columns = list(train_data.select_dtypes(include=num_
columns).columns)
    numerical_columns = [column for column in numerical_columns if column
not in exclude_numerical_cols_list]

    #remove variables with constant variance
    constant_filter = VarianceThreshold(threshold=0)
    constant_filter.fit(train_data[numerical_columns])
    constant_columns = [column for column in train_data[numerical_
columns].columns
                        if column not in train_data[numerical_columns].
columns[constant_filter.get_support()]]
    if len(constant_columns)>0:
        train_data.drop(labels=constant_columns, axis=1, inplace=True)

    #remove deleted columns from dataframe
    numerical_columns = [column for column in numerical_columns if column
not in constant_columns]

    #remove variables with qconstant variance
    #Remove quasi-constant variables
    qconstant_filter = VarianceThreshold(threshold=qthreshold)
    qconstant_filter.fit(train_data[numerical_columns])
    qconstant_columns = [column for column in train_data[numerical_
columns].columns
                         if column not in train_data[numerical_columns].
columns[constant_filter.get_support()]]
    if len(qconstant_columns)>0:
        train_data.drop(labels=qconstant_columns, axis=1, inplace=True)

    #remove deleted columns from dataframe
    numerical_columns = [column for column in numerical_columns if column
not in qconstant_columns]

    #remove correlated variables
    correlated_features = set()
    correlation_matrix = train_data[numerical_columns].corr()
    ax = sns.heatmap(
    correlation_matrix,
    vmin=-1, vmax=1, center=0,
    cmap=sns.diverging_palette(20, 220, n=200),
```

```
        square=True)
    ax.set_xticklabels(
        ax.get_xticklabels(),
        rotation=45,
        horizontalalignment='right');
    #print(correlation_matrix)

    for i in range(len(correlation_matrix.columns)):
        for j in range(i):
            if abs(correlation_matrix.iloc[i, j]) > corr_threshold:
                colname = correlation_matrix.columns[i]
                colcompared = correlation_matrix.columns[j]
                #check if the column compared against is not in the
columns excluded list
                if colcompared not in correlated_features:
                    correlated_features.add(colname)
    train_data.drop(labels=correlated_features, axis=1, inplace=True)

    return train_data,constant_columns,qconstant_columns,correlated_features

train_data,constant_columns,qconstant_columns,correlated_features
=feature_selection_numerical_variables(train_
data,0.01,0.75,['loss','id'],)
correlated_features

# ##### Handling correlation between categorical variables
# save the encoders to disk to be fitted on test data
for cf1 in categorical_columns:
    le = LabelEncoder()
    le.fit(train_data[cf1].unique())
    filename = cf1+".sav"
    pickle.dump(le, open(filename, 'wb'))
    train_data[cf1] = le.transform(train_data[cf1])

#snippet to calculate the unique values with a categorical columns
df = pd.DataFrame(columns=["Column_Name","Count"])
for cat in categorical_columns:
    unique_value_count = len(train_data[cat].unique())
    df = df.append({'Column_Name': cat, "Count":int(unique_value_count)},
ignore_index=True)
columns_unique_value = np.array(df.Count.value_counts().index)

#snippet to identify the dependent/correlated categorical variables and
drop them
columns_to_drop_cat = set()
correlated_columns = dict()
for unique_value_count in columns_unique_value:
    if unique_value_count>1:
        categorical_columns = df.loc[df.
Count==unique_value_count,'Column_Name']
        categorical_columns = categorical_columns.reset_index(drop=True)
        columns_length=len(categorical_columns)
        for col in range(columns_length-1):
            column_to_compare = categorical_columns[col]
            columns_compare_against =
categorical_columns[(col+1):columns_length]
```

```python
            chi_scores =
chi2(train_data[columns_compare_against],train_data[column_to_compare])
            if column_to_compare not in columns_to_drop_cat:
                columns_to_be_dropped = [i for i in range(len(columns_
compare_against)) if chi_scores[1][i]<=0.05]
                columns_to_drop_array = np.array(columns_compare_against)
[columns_to_be_dropped]
                correlated_columns[column_to_compare]=columns_to_drop_array
                columns_to_drop_cat.update(columns_to_drop_array)

train_data = train_data.drop(columns_to_drop_cat,axis=1)

correlated_features = list(correlated_features)
columns_to_drop_cat = list(columns_to_drop_cat)
columns_to_drop_cat.extend(correlated_features)
columns_to_drop = columns_to_drop_cat.copy()

#output the columns_to_drop file to a csv
columns_to_drop_df=pd.DataFrame(columns_to_drop,columns=['colnames'])
columns_to_drop_df.to_csv("/model/columns_to_drop.csv",index=False)

# ##### Visualizing the Output Variable
#Visualizing the distribution of loss value
# Density Plot and Histogram of loss
sns.distplot(train_data['loss'], hist=True, kde=True,
            bins=int(180/5), color = 'darkblue',
            hist_kws={'edgecolor':'black'},
            kde_kws={'linewidth': 4})

#We will use a log transformation on the dependent variable to reduce the scale
train_data['loss'] = np.log(train_data['loss'])

# Visualizing the distribution of loss value
# Density Plot and Histogram of loss
sns.distplot(train_data['loss'], hist=True, kde=True,
            bins=int(180/5), color = 'darkblue',
            hist_kws={'edgecolor':'black'},
            kde_kws={'linewidth': 4})

#taking a anti-log to transform the variable back to its original scale
sns.distplot(np.exp(train_data['loss']), hist=True, kde=True,
            bins=int(180/5), color = 'darkblue',
            hist_kws={'edgecolor':'black'},
            kde_kws={'linewidth': 4})

# ##### Fit an ML Model
from sklearn.ensemble import RandomForestRegressor
from sklearn.datasets import make_regression
from sklearn.model_selection import train_test_split
from sklearn.metrics import mean_squared_error
from sklearn.model_selection import RandomizedSearchCV

#convert the int64 columns categorical
Column_datatypes= train_data.dtypes
Integer_columns = list(Column_datatypes.where(lambda x: x =="int64").
dropna().index.values)
```

```
train_data[Integer_columns] = train_data[Integer_columns].
astype('category',copy=False)
X,y = train_data.drop(['id','loss'],axis=1),train_data['loss']
X_train, X_test, y_train, y_test = train_test_split(X, y, test_size=0.33,
random_state=42)
# Instantiate model with 100 decision trees
rf_base = RandomForestRegressor(n_estimators = 100, random_state =
42,oob_score = True)
rf_base.fit(X_train, y_train)

#save the model output
pickle.dump(rf_base, open("basemodel_rf", 'wb'))

#load the saved model and predict on the test data
basedmodel_rf = pickle.load(open("basemodel_rf", 'rb'))

#validate the accuracy of the base model
#compare the model accuracies
Y_test_predict_base = basedmodel_rf.predict(X_test)
print("Base model accuracy:",np.sqrt(mean_squared_error(y_test,
Y_test_predict_base)))

# ###### HyperParameter Tuning Using RandomSearchCV
#number of trees
n_estimators = [100,200,300,400,500]
# Number of features to consider at every split
max_features = ['auto', 'sqrt']
# Maximum number of levels in tree
max_depth = [int(x) for x in np.linspace(10, 110, num = 11)]
# Minimum number of samples required to split a node
min_samples_split = [200,400,600]
# Minimum number of samples required at each leaf node
min_samples_leaf = [1, 2, 4]
# Method of selecting samples for training each tree
bootstrap = [True, False]

# Create the random grid
random_grid = {'n_estimators': n_estimators,
               'max_features': max_features,
               'max_depth': max_depth,
               'min_samples_split': min_samples_split,
               'min_samples_leaf': min_samples_leaf,
               'bootstrap': bootstrap}

# Use the random grid to search for the best hyperparameters
# base model to tune
rf = RandomForestRegressor()

# 5 fold cross validation,
# search across 150 different combinations, and use all available cores
rf_tuned = RandomizedSearchCV(estimator = rf, param_distributions =
random_grid, cv = 3,n_iter = 5, verbose=2, random_state=42, n_jobs = -1)

# Fit the random search model
rf_tuned.fit(X_train, y_train)
```

```
#save the model output
pickle.dump(rf_tuned, open("tunedmodel_rf", 'wb'))

#check the best params
rf_tuned.best_params_

#load the saved model and predict on the test data
tunedmodel_rf = pickle.load(open("tunedmodel_rf", 'rb'))

Y_test_predict_tuned = tunedmodel_rf.predict(X_test)
print("Tuned model accuracy:",np.sqrt(mean_squared_error(y_test,
Y_test_predict_tuned)))

# ##### fit a GBM model
from sklearn.ensemble import GradientBoostingRegressor  #GBM algorithm
gbm_base = GradientBoostingRegressor(
    max_depth=2,
    n_estimators=3,
    learning_rate=1.0)

gbm_base.fit(X_train,y_train)

#save the GBM model
pickle.dump(gbm_base, open("basemodel_GBM", 'wb'))

#load the saved model and predict on the test data
basemodel_GBM = pickle.load(open("basemodel_GBM", 'rb'))

Y_test_predict_tuned = basemodel_GBM.predict(X_test)
print("Base model GBM accuracy:",np.sqrt(mean_squared_error(y_test,
Y_test_predict_tuned)))

###############  Model loss function prediction
#############################

 #### Script to Predict the output on new observations
import pandas as pd
import pickle
import numpy as np

test_data = pd.read_csv("test_data_subset.csv")

#load the columns to drop file
columns_to_drop=pd.read_csv("columns_to_drop.csv")
columns_to_Retain = set(test_data.columns.values) - set(columns_to_drop.
colnames.values)
test_data = test_data[columns_to_Retain]

column_datatypes = test_data.dtypes
categorical_columns = list(column_datatypes[column_datatypes=="object"].
index.values)

#Transfor the categorical columns by loading the fit encodings on
training data

for cf1 in categorical_columns:
    filename = cf1+".sav"
```

```
    le = pickle.load(open(filename, 'rb'))

    #if an new classes is observed, set it to the 0 class
    le_dict = dict(zip(le.classes_, le.transform(le.classes_)))
    test_data[cf1]=test_data[cf1].apply(lambda x: le_dict.get(x, -1))

test_data_id = test_data['id']
test_data = test_data.drop('id',axis=1)

Column_datatypes= test_data.dtypes
Integer_columns = list(Column_datatypes.where(lambda x: x =="int64").
dropna().index.values)
#convert the int64 columns categorical
test_data[Integer_columns] = test_data[Integer_columns].
astype('category',copy=False)

#load the saved model and predict on the test data
tunedmodel_rf = pickle.load(open("tunedmodel_rf", 'rb'))

Y_test_predict = tunedmodel_rf.predict(test_data)
test_data['predict_loss']=Y_test_predict
test_data['id']=test_data_id
test_data = test_data[['id','predict_loss']]

test_data

############ Operationalize / Deploying to production using FLASK API
#######################

from flask import Flask, request #import main Flask Class and request
import pandas as pd
import pickle
import numpy as np
from pandas.io.json import json_normalize
app = Flask(__name__) #create the Flask app

@app.route('/load_model',methods=['POST'])
def load_model():
    req_data = request.get_json()
    test_data_subset = pd.DataFrame.from_dict(json_normalize(req_data),
orient='columns')

    #load the columns to drop file
    columns_to_drop=pd.read_csv("/model/columns_to_drop.csv")

    #select the columns to be retained
    columns_to_Retain = set(test_data_subset.columns.values) -
set(columns_to_drop.colnames.values)
    test_data_selected_columns = test_data_subset[columns_to_Retain]

    #select the categorical columns from the dataframe
    column_datatypes = test_data_selected_columns.dtypes
    categorical_columns = list(column_datatypes[column_
datatypes=="object"].index.values)

    #read the label encoders and apply the encoded values to the
categorical variables
```

```
    for cf1 in categorical_columns:
        filename = "/model/"+cf1+".sav"
        le = pickle.load(open(filename, 'rb'))

        #if an new classes is observed, set it to the 0 class
        le_dict = dict(zip(le.classes_, le.transform(le.classes_)))
        test_data_selected_columns[cf1]=test_data_selected_columns[cf1].
apply(lambda x: le_dict.get(x, -1))

    test_data_id = test_data_selected_columns['id']
    test_data_selected_columns = test_data_selected_columns.
drop('id',axis=1)

    #convert the interger columns to categories as required by the ML
model
    Column_datatypes= test_data_selected_columns.dtypes
    Integer_columns = list(Column_datatypes.where(lambda x: x =="int64").
dropna().index.values)

    #convert the int64 columns categorical
    test_data_selected_columns[Integer_columns] = test_data_selected_
columns[Integer_columns].astype('category',copy=False)

    #load the saved model and predict on the test data
    tuned_model = pickle.load(open("/model/tunedmodel_rf", 'rb'))
    Y_test_predict = tuned_model.predict(test_data_selected_columns)

    #create a new output dataframe
    output = pd.DataFrame()
    output['id']=test_data_id
    output['predict_loss']=Y_test_predict

    output=output.to_json(orient='records')
    return output
if __name__ =='__main__':
    app.run(debug=True,port=4000)#run app in debug mode on port 4000
```

9.5   USE CASE 5 – E-COMMERCE PRODUCT RANKING AND SENTIMENT ANALYSIS

9.5.1   BACKGROUND

Customers can buy a product with the extra benefit of additional recommendations in the form of reviews, which are provided through E-Commerce applications. Reviews are, without question, valuable and effective for clients who are considering purchasing those products. Customers, on the other hand, will have difficulty separating relevant feedback from the avalanche of reviews. Nonetheless, these large reviews pose a problem for users, as useful filtering evaluations become extremely difficult. In this use instance, the proportionate issue has been addressed. After that, we'll discuss how we rank reviews based on their relevance to the product and how we rate immaterial reviews.

Understating the data, data preprocessing-filtering (which includes gibberish, language, and profanity detection), feature extraction, pairwise review scoring, and further categorization were the phases of this project. The result will be a collection of reviews used to create a precise product ranking based on applicability using a pairwise ranking approach. The process is shown as a timeline graph, as shown in Figure 9.8.

9.5.2 UNDERSTANDING THE DATA

The dataset we will use has two distinct product and answer options columns, as shown below. We will use this training dataset for analysis and preprocessing of the data, including language detection. Furthermore, as shown in the preprocessing data code below, we will preprocess the data (understand the bad data) for gibberish and profanity detection.

#1. Data Preprocessing: This has four stages. The first stage is language detection. The second stage is gibberish review detection and filtering. The third stage is profanity filtering. In the last stage, spell check is performed tocorrect and improve the quality of the data. These phases are shown in Figure 9.9.

```
#!/usr/bin/env python
# coding: utf-8

%%capture
```

Product	Answer_option
Accucheck	Fast and accurate delivery
Accucheck	As usual, it is genuine
Accucheck	Behavior of delivery boy is very bad. Delivery time is long whereas other online stores are providing better facilities
Accucheck	Fwegwrqdsdvwfg
Accucheck	These strips were as per my requirement
Accucheck	Fast service was good
Accucheck	Received 10 strips and 2 packets of lancets in place of 100 strips
Accucheck	Does not fit my machine
Accucheck	Discount and quick response
Accucheck	Fast delivery with good packing

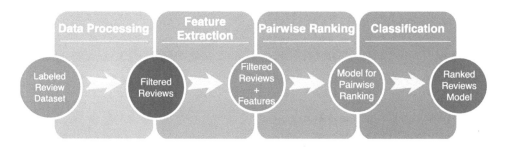

FIGURE 9.8 Phases of implementation of E-Commerce Product Ranking and Sentiment Analysis.

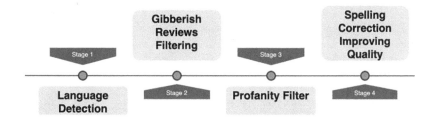

FIGURE 9.9 Data preprocessing phases.

```
!python3 -m spacy download en_core_web_sm
!python3 -m textblob.download_corpora

import pandas as pd
import numpy as np
from matplotlib import pyplot as plt
from pylab import rcParams
rcParams['figure.figsize'] = 7, 6

from copy import deepcopy
import seaborn as sns

import sys
sys.path.append('./utils')
from utils import review_feature
rf = review_feature()
%matplotlib inline

!ls data
df = pd.read_csv('data/train.csv')
df

# ## Analysis to understand per product who many informative and how many
not informative reviews are there.
label_analysis = pd.crosstab(df['product'],df['label'], margins='All')
label_analysis

analysis = label_analysis.reset_index()
analysis.columns = ['product','not info', 'info', 'All']
analysis.iloc[:-1].plot(x="product", y=["not info", "info"], kind="bar")

# ## Lets check the length quality of reviews we have?
df['review_len'] = df['answer_option'].apply(lambda x: len(x.split()))
df

checklen = []
for i in range(5,50, 5):
    checklen.append(len(df[ (df['review_len']>=i-5) &
(df['review_len']<i)]))
checklen

index = np.arange(len(checklen))
plt.bar(index, checklen)
plt.xlabel('Length of a Review', fontsize=15)
plt.ylabel('No. of Reviews', fontsize=15)
plt.xticks(index, range(5,50,5), fontsize=15, rotation=30)
plt.title('Review Survey Length Analysis')
plt.show()

# ## We have a fair amount of both details reviews (having length >=5)
and short reviews (having length <5)
# ## Data Preprocessing
# ![datapreprocessing](Photos/datapreprocessing.png)
# ## Stage1: Language Detection
bad_reviews = []
for indx in df.index:
    review = df.at[indx, 'answer_option']
```

```
    try:
        b = rf.language_detection(review)
        if b == 'hi' or b == 'mr':
            bad_reviews.append(indx)
    except:
        bad_reviews.append(indx)
        print("Language exception for:", review)
print("Number of Bad Reviews at Stage 1: ", len(bad_reviews))

df[df.index.isin(bad_reviews)]

df = df[~df.index.isin(bad_reviews)].reset_index(drop = True)

# ## Stage 2: Gibberish Reviews
# When we collect data from customers, just out of frustration, many
reviews write gibberish reviews.
# Example: svfsfg, fsdfgdfgfsgsfgdgh, ffgrthyryj, rhrhfas, kuopip
# We need to detect such reviews and filter those out.
# Working
# we could build a model of character to character transitions from a
bunch of text in English. So for example, you find out how common it is
for there to be a 'h' after a 't' (pretty common).

# If you have a bunch of query logs, you might first make a model of
general English text and then heavily weigh your queries in that model
training phase
# For background read about Markov Chains.
# Source: https://github.com/rrenaud/Gibberish-Detector
# we have trained a model for and have stored its pickle file.
bad_reviews = []
for indx in df.index:
    review = df.at[indx, 'answer_option']
    if rf.gibberish_detection(review, prefix_path = 'utils'):
        bad_reviews.append(indx)

print("Number of Bad Reviews at Stage 2: ", len(bad_reviews))

bad_reviews

df[df.index.isin(bad_reviews)]

df = df[~df.index.isin(bad_reviews)].reset_index(drop = True)

# ## Stage 3: Profanity Detection
# At times, reviewers are not happy with the delivery or service out of
frustration, they type profanity words in reviews.
# Profanity content also penalizes SEO ranking
bad_reviews = []
for indx in df.index:
    review = df.at[indx, 'answer_option']
    if rf.english_swear_check(review) or rf.hindi_swear_check(review):
        bad_reviews.append(indx)

print("Number of Bad Reviews at Stage 3: ", len(bad_reviews))

df[df.index.isin(bad_reviews)]
df = df[~df.index.isin(bad_reviews)].reset_index(drop = True)
```

```
# ## Stage 4: Spelling Correction (Optional Stage not that necessary)
# Trying to improve quality of reviews which have high confidence spell
errors. Like withut -> without
for indx in df.index:
    review = df.at[indx, 'answer_option']
    df.at[indx, 'answer_option'] = rf.spell_correct(review, 0.9)


# ## Stage 4.1: Company Tag (Optional Stage)
bad_reviews = []
for indx in df.index:
    review = df.at[indx, 'answer_option']
    if rf.competitive_brand_tag(review):
        bad_reviews.append(indx)

print("Number of Bad Reviews at Stage 4.1: ", len(bad_reviews))

df[df.index.isin(bad_reviews)]

df = df[~df.index.isin(bad_reviews)].reset_index(drop = True)

print("Total Count of Reviews after preprocessing: ", len(df))

df.to_csv('data/Preprocessed_Reviews.csv',index = False)

# # Summary :
# So far, we have done EDA (Exploratory Data Analysis) of Data.
# Preprocessing of reviews in 4 main stages.
# ### Initial Count of Reviews was: 1676
# ### Final Count of Reviews is: 1655
# We must be strict in preprocessing so that no bad content is shown on
our website.
# By preprocessing, we are reducing False positives.
# ### Note: You may feel that only 21 reviews are scrapped, but when you
will be working on a full scale, we observe that about 7-10% of total
reviews would be junk.
```

#Features Engineering:

This contains 7 step process as shown in Figure 9.10- Starting with Noun
Scoring till compound score.

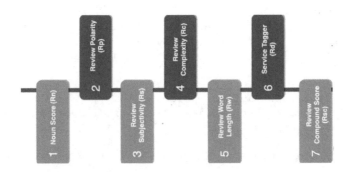

FIGURE 9.10   Seven-step feature engineering process.

```python
#!/usr/bin/env python
# coding: utf-8
import pandas as pd
import numpy as np
from copy import deepcopy
import sys
sys.path.append('./utils')
from utils import review_feature
rf = review_feature()

from pandas_profiling import ProfileReport

df = pd.read_csv('data/Preprocessed_Reviews.csv').sort_values(by =
['product'], ignore_index = True)

df
# Features extraction covers every necessary property/viewpoint, and to
# live features quantitatively may be a much-needed task. Hence, let us
# discuss all the features extracted from reviews.
# Step 1: Noun Strength (Rn): Nouns are subjects regarded as the most
# informative language section. The number of subjects shows the importance
# of review because only a noun describes the prime factors of review
# (which tells us what the review is about). We did POS Tagging to seek out
# nouns during a review and computed score as:
# Step 2: Score (Rn) = TFIDF(noun) / TFIDF(all words)
# Step 3: Review Polarity (Rp): Its value lies between -1 to +1, which
# tells whether a review has sentiment or negative sentiment.
# Step 4: Review Subjectivity (Rs): The subjectivity could measure the
# objective to subjective sentiment and goes from 0 to 1. Objective
# expressions are facts, while Subjective expressions are opinions that
# describe a person's feelings. Consider the following expression:
# Bournvita tastes excellent with milk: Subjective
# Bournvita is brown: Objective
# Step 5: Review Complexity (Rc): to gauge how good and sophisticated a
# review is in terms of unique words within and across a specific product's
# entire review corpus.
# Rc = Number of unique words during a Review / Number of unique words in
# the entire Corpus
# Step 6: Review Word Length (Rw): Word count of a Review
# Step 7: Service Tagger (Rd): the simplest review talks more about how
# the product, how it tastes, what its uses are, and therefore the one
# which talks about the effectiveness of a product. Reviews are basically
# to describe a product. So, a dictionary of words is made, which might
# mark reviews as service-based, delivery reviews, and customer support.
# Fuzzy matching each word during a review is finished with the words
# within the dictionary with Levenshtein distance. Levenshtein distance
# helps measure the difference between two sequences and tackles spell
# errors in review. For instance, rather than "My delivery was on time",
# Reviews is wrongly written as "My delivery was on time". In this case,
# Fuzzy matching would help us to match both the reviews.
# Step 8: Compound Score (Rsc): to enhance the efficiency of the system.
# We compute the compound score using VaderSentimentAnalyser. This library
# is taken from VADER (Valence Aware Dictionary and sEntiment Reasoner).
# This is a lexicon and rule-based sentiment analysis tool specifically
# tuned to figure out sentiments expressed in social media content. It has
# the power to seek out the sentiment of Slang (e.g., SUX!), Emoji (☹, ☹),
```

Emoticons (:), :D) and, therefore, the difference between capitalized word expressions(I am SAD, I'm sad are different expressions).

```
#Rsc ≥ 0.5 (Positive Sentiment)
# -0.5
(Positive Sentiment)
# -0.5<Rsc<+0.5 (Neural Sentiment)
# Rsc≤ -0.5 (Negative Sentiment)
# Miscellaneous: We purposely did not include Reviews Rating as a
feature. The inclusion of Ratings blunders the entire system because of
two reasons:
# 1. Common confusion between Rating and Reviews. For example, someone
who rates the product '1' (On a rating scale of 1-5, '1' being the
'lowest' and '5' being the 'highest') writes the review comment as 'very
good and useful medicine'.
# 2. A large portion of Reviews from customers are either five stars or
one star.
#
# TextBlob: https://textblob.readthedocs.io/en/dev/index.html
# VaderSentiment: https://github.com/cjhutto/vaderSentiment
# spaCy: https://spacy.io/


## Add Feature Columns
df['Rn'] = 0.0
df['Rp'] = 0.0
df['Rs'] = 0.0
df['Rc'] = 0.0
df['Rd'] = 0.0
df['Rsc'] = 0.0


df

product_list = df['product'].unique()
for product in product_list:
    data = df[df['product']==product]
    unique_bag = set()
    for review in data['answer_option']:
        review = review.lower()
        words = review.split()
        unique_bag = unique_bag.union(set(words))

    for indx in data.index:
        review = data.at[indx, 'answer_option']
        df.at[indx, 'Rp'] = rf.polarity_sentiment(review)
        df.at[indx, 'Rs'] = rf.subjectivity_sentiment(review)
        df.at[indx, 'Rd'] = rf.service_tag(review)
        df.at[indx, 'Rsc'] =
rf.slang_emoji_polarity_compoundscore(review)
        df.at[indx, 'Rc'] = float(len(set(review.split()))) /
float(len(unique_bag))

    df.loc[df['product']==product, 'Rn'] = rf.noun_score(data['answer_
option'].values).values


 df

#With these features, we have leached out all informative from a Review.
```

```
#One may add more features like Readability Score: SMOG Index depending
on the use case of your problem.
#Reason we are not taking Readability score as a metric is that we have
taken reviews from Tier I, Tier II, and Tier III cities. We don't want to
penalize reviews (from an underprivileged background) by adding this.
#Source- [Wikipedia](https://en.wikipedia.org/wiki/Readability)

df.to_csv('data/Features.csv',index = False)

# ## Now more insightful analysis
profile = ProfileReport(df)

profile

profile.to_file(output_file="feature_analysis.html")
# ## We have 1655 Reviews with use, let's get to the Model Training Section.

#MODEL BUILDING:
#!/usr/bin/env python
# coding: utf-8

import pandas as pd
import numpy as np
from joblib import load, dump
from copy import deepcopy
from statistics import mean

from sklearn.metrics import accuracy_score, classification_report,
confusion_matrix
from collections import Counter

df = pd.read_csv('data/Features.csv')

df


# Ranking is a canonical problem for humans. It is easy to classify
whether a review is useful (informative) or not. However, ranking reviews
based on usefulness is a complex task. Our ranking methodology is based
on this simple education.
#Pairwise ranking approach is applied to rank reviews in the semi-
supervised learning method. The pairwise ranking approach looks at a pair
of documents in a loss function and predicts a relative ordering. The
objective is not to determine the relevance score but to find which
document is more relevant. This relevance is developed to judge the
preference of one review over another.
#In this semi-supervised learning method, mapping is constructed between
input and output. This input-output pair in the training model is used to
learn the system.

#Review Segregation: We segregated two sets of reviews on which we train
our model.
#Set 0 represents reviews with label 0, i.e., ones that are not
informative. These include reviews based on delivery, customer support,
packaging, etc. These reviews do not describe the product.

#Set 1 represents reviews with label 1, i.e., reviews that are
informative and are better than all reviews of Set 0;
```

```
#How we segregated and determined labels for reviews:
#Our entire review ranking system is based on the idea that it is easier
for humans to binary classify reviews which we call Set 0 and Set 1.

#For each product 'Accucheck', 'Becadexamin', 'Evion', 'Neurobion','Seven
seascodLiverOil', 'Shelcal', 'Supradyn','shampoo', we asked 10 different
people to label reviews as a 1 (informative review) and 0 ( not
informative review). Different participants were asked to label so that
there is no bias and the model learns to its best.

data_split = pd.crosstab(df['product'],df['label'])
data_split

# ## Building the training set:
# #### We pairwise compared each review of set1 with all reviews of set0
and vice-versa
# + (Rx, Ry,1) where x∈Set1 and y∈Set0 → Rx is better than Ry
# + (Ry, Rx, 0) where x∈Set1 and y∈Set0 → Ry is worst than Rx

# #### This now becomes a classification problem, as illustrated in
Figure 9.11.

def building_training_data(df):
    A = df[df['label']==1]
    A.loc[df['label']==1,'join'] = 'j'
    B = df[df['label']==0]
    B.loc[df['label']==0,'join'] = 'j'
    trainset1 = pd.merge(A,B,how='outer',on='join')
    trainset2 = pd.merge(B,A,how='outer',on ='join')

    trainset = pd.merge(trainset1,trainset2,how='outer')
    return trainset

product_list = df['product'].unique()
data_stack = []
for product in product_list:
    temp = deepcopy(df[df['product']==product].iloc[:,2:])
    build_data = building_training_data(temp)
    print(product, len(temp), len(build_data))
```

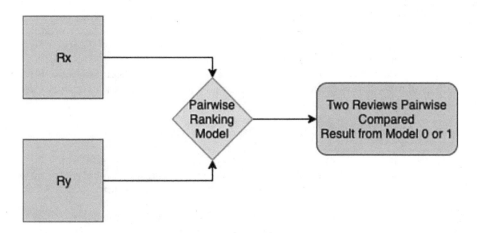

FIGURE 9.11 Pairwise ranking model.

```
    build_data.drop(columns = ['join','label_y'],inplace=True)
    data = build_data.iloc[:,1:]
    data['target'] = build_data.iloc[:,0]
    data_stack.append(data)

train = pd.concat(data_stack).reset_index(drop = True)

train

X = train.iloc[:,:-1].values
y = train.iloc[:,-1].values

from sklearn.model_selection import train_test_split
X_train,X_test, y_train, y_test = train_test_split(X,y,test_size =
0.2,shuffle = True, stratify = y)
print("Test Len:",len(X_test)," ",len(y_test))

train


# # Spot Checking-
# Linear Model
# Non-Linear Model
# Ensemble Model

# ## Linear Model: Logistic Regression

from sklearn.linear_model import LogisticRegression
classifier = LogisticRegression()
classifier.fit(X_train,y_train)
print("Training Accuracy\n", accuracy_score(y_train,classifier.
predict(X_train)))
print("Test Accuracy\n", accuracy_score(y_test,classifier.
predict(X_test)))

print('CLASSIFICATION REPORT')
print("Training\n", classification_report(y_train,classifier.
predict(X_train)))
print("Test \n", classification_report(y_test,classifier.
predict(X_test)))

# ### Accuracy: 85%
# ### F1-score: 85%

# ## Non-Linear Model: DecisionTree
# Decision Tree
from sklearn.tree import DecisionTreeClassifier
classifier = DecisionTreeClassifier()
classifier.fit(X_train,y_train)

print("Training Accuracy\n", accuracy_score(y_train,classifier.
predict(X_train)))
print("Test Accuracy\n", accuracy_score(y_test,classifier.
predict(X_test)))

print('CLASSIFICATION REPORT')
print("Training\n", classification_report(y_train,classifier.
predict(X_train)))
```

```
print("Test \n", classification_report(y_test,classifier.
predict(X_test)))


# ## Ensemble Model: RandomForest
from sklearn.ensemble import RandomForestClassifier
classifier = RandomForestClassifier(n_estimators=50, n_jobs = -1, oob_
score = True,random_state=42)
classifier.fit(X_train,y_train)

print("Training Accuracy\n", accuracy_score(y_train,classifier.
predict(X_train)))
print("Test Accuracy\n", accuracy_score(y_test,classifier.
predict(X_test)))

print('CLASSIFICATION REPORT')
print("Training\n", classification_report(y_train,classifier.
predict(X_train)))
print("Test \n", classification_report(y_test,classifier.
predict(X_test)))

print("Test\nConfusion Matrix: \n", confusion_matrix(y_test, classifier.
predict(X_test)))

## Score of the training dataset obtained using an out-of-bag estimate.
This attribute exists only when oob_score is True.

classifier.oob_score_
feature_importances = pd.DataFrame(classifier.feature_importances_,
                              index = train.iloc[:,:-1].columns,

columns=['importance']).sort_values('importance',ascending=False)
feature_importances
dump(classifier, 'randomforest.joblib', compress = 2)

# ## RandomForest Classifier Weights Saved.
# ### Accuracy: 0.98
# ### oob_score: 0.98
# Note, if in your usecase data is too small to split to train-test-split
then one can train model on entire data and measure out of bag score.

#PART 2. Model Ranking Metric
#Accuracy of Ranking Methodology
#After sorting the reviews by the review score, we wanted all reviews in
Set 1 to be above all reviews of Set 0.
#To test this hypothesis, we developed the following Ranking Metric
#Let the number of 1s in our Dataset be x.
# `Ranking Accuracy on Single Product = Number of 1s found in first x
positions / x

classifier = load('randomforest.joblib')

product_list = df['product'].unique()
df['win']=0
df['lose']=0
df['review_score'] = 0.0
df.reset_index(inplace = True, drop = True)
```

```
def score_giver(C,D):
    E = pd.merge(C,D,how='outer',on='j')
    E.drop(columns=['j'],inplace = True)
    q= classifier.predict(E.values)
    return Counter(q)

for product in product_list:
    data = df[df['product']==product]
    for indx in data.index:
        review = df.iloc[indx, 3:-3]
        review['j'] = 'jn'
        C = pd.DataFrame([review])
        D = data[data.index!=indx].iloc[:,3:-3]
        D['j'] = 'jn'
        score = score_giver(C,D)
        df.at[indx, 'win'] = 0 if score.get(1) is None else score.get(1)
        df.at[indx, 'lose'] = 0 if score.get(0) is None else score.get(0)
        df.at[indx, 'review_score'] = float(0 if score.get(1) is None
else score.get(1)) / len(data) * 1.0

df = df.sort_values(by = ['product','review_score'], ascending = False)

r_accuracy =[]
for product in product_list:
    x = data_split[data_split.index == product][1][0]
    number_of_1_in_x = Counter(df[df['product']==product].iloc[:x, ]
['label']).get(1)
    rank_accuracy = float(number_of_1_in_x*1.0 / x*1.0)
    print("Product: {} | Rank Accuracy: {}".format(product,
rank_accuracy))
    r_accuracy.append(rank_accuracy)
print("Mean Rank Accuracy: {}".format(mean(r_accuracy)))

df

df.iloc[:, [0,1,-1]].to_csv('data/train_ranked_output.csv',index = False)

!ls
t = pd.read_csv('data/test.csv')
```

SUMMARY

In this chapter, we discussed a few ML applications in various industries to solve problems where traditional programming cannot accommodate the reasoning for many combinations. The first use case, Retail Price Optimization Using the Price Elasticity of Demand Method, identifies the exact price at which the most profit may be made. Next, we present the application based on a customer dataset in a supermarket in use case 2, Market Basket Analysis, highlighting association rule mining. Next, use case 3, Retailer Sales Prediction, shows how to create a ML model and determine the sales of each product at a certain store. Finally, in use case 4, the cost of insurance claims is predicted for a Property and Casualty (P&C) Insurance Company. This case study shows how to clean data, preprocess data, and deal with outliers.

REVIEW QUESTIONS

1. Develop the phases of data analytics life cycle for MNIST Handwritten Digit Classification data.
2. Apply different supervised learning algorithms for Wine Quality Prediction using Wine Quality Dataset and compare the results in terms of model parameters.
3. Develop a ML model for Sales Forecasting using Walmart dataset starting from understanding the data, data preprocessing, exploratory data analysis, model building, and prediction of output.
4. Evaluate ML models for Sensorless Drive Diagnosis and choose the optimal model.
5. Compare supervised learning algorithms for classifying Human Body Postures and Movements. Note down your observations and identify the best algorithm for classification.
6. Implement a prediction model for BigMart Sales using unsupervised learning algorithms and compare their performance. In addition, identify the time and space complexity of the algorithms.
7. Estimate the suitable ML model for Mine Social Media Sentiment and Improve Health Care dataset.
8. Apply ML algorithms to predict Quora Question Pairs Meaning using Natural Language Processing in Python.
9. For the Human Activity Recognition using Smartphone Dataset, identify the process to choose features. How are outliers handled while extracting features?
10. Develop feature engineering model based on Principal Componant Analysis (PCA) and Linear Discrimination Analysis (LDA) for Walmart dataset.

Appendix
Python Cheat Sheet for Machine Learning

Matplotlib Cheat Sheet

from *matplotlib* **import** *pyplot* **as** *plt*

x_values
days = [0, 1, 2, 3, 4, 5, 6]
y_values1
money_spent = [10, 12, 12, 10, 14, 22, 24]
y_values2
money_spent_2 = [11, 14, 15, 15, 22, 21, 12]
assigend to one plot
plt.plot(days, money_spent)
plt.plot(days, money_spent_2)
plt.show()

\# **Create subplots**
plt.subplot(***rows, columns, index_of_subplot***)
\# **Example**
\# *First Subplot*
plt.subplot(1, 2, 1)
plt.plot(x, y, color='green')
\# *Second Subplot*
plt.subplot(1, 2, 2)
plt.plot(x, y, color='steelblue')
\# **Format Subplots**
plt.subplots_adjust(***arguements***)
left, right, top, bottom -margin
***wspace, hspace* horizontal/vertical margin between plots**

The object that contains all subplots is called *figure*
Always put specific Attributes (color, markers, ...) for a subplot
directly under *plt.plot()*

plt.plot(x, y, ***style*=" ")**
Keywords to put in for *style*:

color= *green, #AAAAAA*
linestyle= dotted: :, dashed: -- or -.
marker= *o, *, s, x, d, h*
linewidth= 1, 2, ...

alpha= 0.1 - 1

Boilerplate Styles:
plt.style.use(*"fivethirtyeight"*)
plt.style.use(*"ggplot"*)
plt.style.use(*"seaborn"*)

\# **Create Legend**
plt.legend([*"**first_line**", "**second_line**", **loc=**])
\# **loc Numbercode**
1 upper left
2 upper right
3 lower left
4 lower right
5 right
6 center left
7 center right
8 lower center
9 upper center
10 center

loc specifies the legends location (if not specified: finds "best" location)

\# **Create Figure with custom size**
plt.figure(figsize=(***width, heigth***))
plt.plot(x, y)
plt.savefig('tall_and_narrow.***png/ .svg/ .pdf***')

When we're making lots of plots, it's easy to end up with **lines that have been plotted and not displayed.** If we're not careful, these "forgotten" lines will show up in your new plots. In order to be sure that you don't have any stray lines, you can use the command **plt.close('all')** to clear all existing plots before you plot a new one.

\# **Specify subplot to modify**
ax1 = plt.subplot(***row, column, index***)
\# **Attributes**
ax1.set_xticks([***1, 2, 4***])
ax1.set_yticks([***0.1, 0.2, ...***])
ax1.set_xticklabels(["Jan", "Feb", "Apr"], **rotation=30**)
\# *rotation=degrees rotates the labels*
ax1.set_yticklabels(["10%", "20%", ...])

We have to do it this way, even if we only have one plot

443

Axis and Labels

Zoom in or out of the plot:

plt.axis(*x_min*, *x_max*, *y_min*, *y_max*)

Labeling the Axes:

plt.xlabel("*str* ")/ plt.ylabel() / plt.title()

Add Text to Graph

plt.text(x_coord, y_coord, "text");

Simple Bar Chart

plt.bar(range(len(y_values)), y_values)

We use **range(len(y_values))** to get a tick for each value we want to represent in the Bar Chart

Scatter Plot

plt.scatter(x_values, y_values)

Side-By-Side Bars

```
# We have to specifiy the location of each Dataset in the Plot
using this pattern:
n = ? # Number of specific dataset
t = ? # Number of datasets
d = ? # Number of sets of bars
w = 0.8 # Width of each bar
x_values1 = [t*element + w*n for element in range(d)]
# Get x_values in the middle of both bars
middle_x = [ (a + b) / 2.0 for a, b in zip(x_val-ues1, x_values2)]
```

Pie Chart

```
payment_names = ["Card Swipe", "Cash", "Apple Pay",
"Other"]
payment_freqs = [270, 77, 32, 11]
# Creating Pie Chart
plt.pie(payment_freqs)
plt.axis('equal')
# Two Methods for Labeling
# First Method
plt.legend(payment_names)
# Second Method (directly when creating)
plt.pie(payment_freqs, labels=payment_names)
Show percentages of total in each slice:
plt.pie(payment_freqs, labels=payment_names, auto-pct='%
0.1f%%')
# autopct takes a string formatting instruction
# %d%% -> round to decimal
plt.show()
```

Stacked Bars

```
# We use the keyword  bottom to do this
# The top bar will have  bottom set as height # First Bar
video_game_hours = [1, 2, 2, 1, 2]
plt.bar(range(len(video_game_hours)),
 video_game_hours)
# Second Bar
book_hours = [2, 3, 4, 2, 1]
plt.bar(range(len(book_hours)),

 book_hours,
 bottom=video_game_hours)
# Get each bottom for 3+ bars
sport_hours = np.add(video_game_hours, book_hours)
```

If we want to compare *"different sub-attributes from one attribute"* we can use stacked bar charts. For example:

Attribute: Entertainment hours

Sub-Attributes: Gaming, Reading, ...

Error Bars

```
# Use the keyword yerr to repersent the error range
values = [10, 13, 11, 15, 20]
yerr = [1, 3, 0.5, 2, 4] # singe value possible plt.bar(y, x, yerr
=yerr, capsize=10)
plt.show()
```

If we want to present an uncertainty Range within a Bar Chart we can use Error Bars

Fill Between (Line Plot)

```
x = range(3)
y = [10, 12, 13]
y_lower = [8, 10, 11]
y_upper = [i + 2 for i in y_values]
# Calculate a % deviation
y_lower_bound = [element - (element * error_in_-decimal) for
element in original_list_of_y_values] #this is the shaded error
plt.fill_between(x, y_lower, y_upper, alpha=0.2) #this is the line
itself
plt.plot(x, y)
plt.show()
```

Returns a shaded are around the line

Histogram

```
# Create one Histogram
plt.hist(dataset,  range=(0,100),   bins=20)
# Specifiy number of bins (default = 10)
 5.9049 pt

# Create multiple Histograms
plt.hist(a, alpha=0.5, normed=True)
plt.hist(b, histtype='step', linewidth=2 normed-=True)
```

Seaborn Cheat Sheet

Import the Seaborn Library

from matplotlib import pyplot as plt
import seaborn as sns
import numpy as np

Seaborn is a extension to **Matplotlib** with more visually appealing syntax and additional Chart Types. That's why **Matplotlib** should also be imported.

If we want to calculate **aggregates** we need to **import numpy** aswell.

Bar Plot

sns.barplot(
 data=df ,
 x="x value column" , y="y
value column",
# everything specified below is optional
 ci="sd"
estimator=np.median | len
hue="column to compare"
)
plt.show()
# ci="sd" changes the error bar to standard deviation
# estimator is used to specifiy the aggr egation and takes any argument that works on a list.(examples provided in code)
# hue adds a nested categorical variableto compare to the "y value column"

If the specified columns need to be **aggr egated** first, **Seaborn** will perform that aggregation automatically. *(mean by default)*

Seaborn will, by default, provide an **error bar** displaying the **bootstrapped confidence interval**(95%).

Aggregates (with numpy)

Median   **np.median**(df.column_name)

Boxplots

sns.boxplot(
data=df,
x='label',
y='value',

# optional
 width=0.45
)
plt.show()
# In Seaborn it's also possible to plot multiple Boxplots in one viz

The box represents the **interquartile range**
The line in the middle of the box is the **median**
The end lines are the **first** and **third quarti- les**
The diamonds show **outliers**

Violin Plots

sns.violinplot(
data=df,   x="l
abel", y="valu
e"
)

Two KDE plots that are symmetrical along the center line. (Just for visual effect)

A **white dot** represents the median.

The **thick black line** in the center of each violin represents the interquartile range.

The **lines that extend from the center** are the confidence intervals (95%)

sns.kdeplot(*dataset1*,   shade=True)
sns.kdeplot(*dataset2*,   shade=True)
...

KDE Plots show the **distribution** of an **univariate** dataset.
univariate datasets have only **one** variable.(e.g.: Temperature)

shade defines if the are under the line is shaded

Seaborn Styling (Figure Style and Scale)(cont)

'font.size': 19.2,
 'grid.linewidth': 1.6,
 'legend.fontsize': 16.0,
 'lines.linewidth': 2.8,
 'lines.markeredgewidth': 0.0, 'li
nes.markersize': 11.2,
 'patch.linewidth': 0.48,
 'xtick.labelsize': 16.0,
 'xtick.major.pad': 11.2,
 'xtick.major.width': 1.6,
 'xtick.minor.width': 0.8,
 'ytick.labelsize': 16.0,
 'ytick.major.pad': 11.2,
 'ytick.major.width': 1.6,
 'ytick.minor.width': 0.8
}

Seaborn Styling (Color)

# If you want to quickly see what a palette looks like
# Save a palette to a variable:
 palette = sns.color_palette -("bright")#
Use palplot and pass in the variable:
         sns.palplot(palette)
        # Select a palette in Seaborn:
sns.set_palette("Paired")
# Default Palettes
-> deep, muted, pastel, bright, dark, colorblind

Themes: (called prior to plot) sns.set _style("")
->darkgrid, whitegrid, dark, white, ticks
#Removes Plot Borders (called after plot) sns.despine() (default:
top=True, right=True)
-> bottom, left
#Adjust font- and label size sns.set_co ntext(context="paper", font_scale=1.4, rc ={"grid.li-newidth": 0.6})

Scikit-Learn Python Cheat Sheet

Machine Learning

Supervised Learning	Unsupervised learning
The model maps input to an output based on the previous input-output pairs	No training is given to the model and it has to discover the features of input by self-training mechanism.

Scikit learn can be used in Classification, Regression, Clustering, Dimensionality reduction, Model Selection and preprocessing by supervised and unsupervised training models.

Basic Commands

```
>>> from sklearn import neighbors,
datasets, preprocessing
>>> from sklearn.model_selection import
train_test_split
>>> from sklearn.metrics import accuracy_-
score
>>> iris = datasets.load_iris()
>>> X, y = iris.data[:, :2], iris.target
>>> X_train, X_test, y_train, y_test = train_-
test_split(X, y, random_state=33)
>>> scaler = preprocessing.StandardScale-
r().fit(X_train)
>>> X_train = scaler.transform(X_train)
>>> X_test = scaler.transform(X_test)
>>> knn = neighbors.KNeighborsClassifier-
(n_neighbors=5)
>>> knn.fit(X_train, y_train)
>>> y_pred = knn.predict(X_test)
>>> accuracy_score(y_test, y_pred)
```

Loading Data example

```
>>> import numpy as np
>>> X = np.random.random((20,2))
>>> y = np.array(['A','B','C','D','E','F','G','-
A','C','A','B'])
>>> X[X < 0.7] = 0
```

The data being loaded should be numeric and has to be stored as NumPy arrays or SciPy sparse matrices.

Processing Loaded Data

Standardi-	Normal-	Binarization
```>>> from sklearn.prep- import StandardS- caler```	```>>> from sklearn.p- sklearn.p- reproc- essing import Normalizer```	```>>> from sklearn.p- rocessing reproc- essing import Binarizer```
```>>> scaler = StandardS- caler().fit(X_t- rain)```	```>>> scaler = Normalize- r().fit(X- _train)```	```>>> binarizer = Binarizer- (threshol-```
```>>> standa- rdized_X = scaler.trans- form(X_train)```	```>>> normal- ized_X = scaler.tr- ansform(X-```	```>>> binary_X = binarizer.tr-```
```>>> standa- rdized_X_test = scaler.tr- ansform(X- _test)```	```>>> normalized_X_test = scaler.transform(X_test)```	

Training And Test Data

```
>>> from sklearn.model_selection import
train_test_split
>>> X_train, X_test, y_train, y_test = train_-
test_split(X,y,random_state=0)
```

Creating Model

Supervised Learning Estimators

Linear Regression	Support Vector Machines (SVM)	Naive Bayes
```>>> from sklearn.line- ar_model import Linear- Regression```	```>>> from sklear- n.svm import SVC```	```>>> from sklearn.naiv- e_bayes import GaussianNB```
```>>> lr = Linear- Regression(n- ormalize=True)```	```>>> svc = SVC(ke- rnel='lin```	```>>> gnb = Gaussi-```

Creating Model

Unsupervised Learning Estimators

Principal Component Analysis (PCA)	K Means
```>>> from sklear- n.decomposition import PCA```	```>>> from sklearn.c- luster import KMeans```
```>>> pca = PCA(n_compon- ents=0.95)```	```>>> k_means = KMeans(n_clusters=3, random_state=0)```

Model Fitting

Supervised Learning	Unsupervised learning
```>>> lr.fit(X, y)```	```>>> k_means.fit(X_train)```
```>>> knn.fit(X- _train, y_train)```	```>>> pca_model = pca.fi- t_transform(X_train)```
```>>> svc.fit(X_train, y_train)```	

Predicting output

Supervised Estimators	Unsupervised Estimators
>>> y_pred = svc.predict(np.ran-dom.random((2,5)))	>>> y_pred = k_means.p-redict(X_test)
>>> y_pred = lr.predict(X_test)	
>>> y_pred = knn.predict_proba(X_test))	

Classification Metrics Model Performance

Accuracy Score	Classification Report	Confusion Matrix
>>> knn.score-(X_test, y_test)	>>> from sklearn.m-etrics import classi-fication_report	>>> from sklear-n.metrics import confusion_matrix
>>> from sklear-n.metrics import accuracy_score	>>> print(classific-ation_report(y_test, y_pred)))	>>> print(confus-ion_matrix(y_test, y_pred)))
>>> accuracy_score(y_test, y_pred)		

Clustering Metrics Model Performance

Adjusted Rand Index	Homogeneity	Cross-Validation
>>> from sklear-n.metrics import adjusted_ran-d_score	>>> from sklear-n.metrics import homogeneity_-score	>>> print(cross_-val_score(knn, X_train, y_train, cv=4))
>>> adjusted_ran-d_score(y_true, y_pred))	>>> homogenei-ty_score(y_true, y_pred))	>>> print(cross_-val_score(lr, X, y, cv=2))

Bibliography

Aeberhard, S., Coomans, D., and de Vel, O. (1992a) The classification performance of RDA. Technical Report no. 92-01, Department of Computer Science and Department of Mathematics and Statistics, James Cook University of North Queensland.

Aeberhard, S., Coomans, D., and de Vel, O. (1992b) Comparison of classifiers in high dimensional settings, Technical Report no. 92-02, Department of Computer Science and Department of Mathematics and Statistics, James Cook University of North Queensland.

Ayodele, T. (2010) Types of machine learning algorithms. In: Zhang, Y. (ed.) *New Advances in Machine Learning* (pp. 19–48). InTech, London.

Bellman, R. (1958). Dynamic programming and stochastic control processes. *Information and Control* 1(3), 228–239.

Bioconductor.org. (2017) Bioconductor - BiocViews. [online] Available at: https://bioconductor.org/packages [Accessed 28 December 2017].

Bone, D., Goodwin, M., Black, M., Lee, C., Audhkhasi, K., and Narayanan, S. (2014) Applying machine learning to facilitate autism diagnostics: Pitfalls and promises. *Journal of Autism and Developmental Disorders*, 45(5), 1121–1136.

Breiman, L. (2001) Random forests. *Machine Learning*, 45(1), 5–32.

Carbonell, J., Michalski, R., and Mitchell, T. (1983) An overview of machine learning. In: *Machine Learning*, pp. 3–23. Springer, Berlin Heidelberg.

Chen, T., and Guestrin, C. (2016) XGBoost: A scalable tree boosting system. In *Proceedings of the 22nd ACM SIGKDD International Conference on Knowledge Discovery and Data Mining*, pp. 785–794, ACM, San Francisco.

Cortes, C., and Vapnik, V. (1995) Support vector networks. *Machine Learning*, 20(3), 273–297.

Criminisi, A., and Shotton, J. (2013) *Decision Forests for Computer Vision and Medical Image Analysis*. Springer, Berlin.

Data-mining-blog.com. (2017) RapidMiner at CeBIT 2010: The Enterprise Edition, Rapid-I and Cloud Mining - Data Mining - Blog.com. [online] Available at: http://www.data-mining-blog.com/cloud-mining/rapid-miner-cebit-2010/ [Accessed 20 December 2017].

De Ville, B. (2006) *Decision Trees for Business Intelligence and Data Mining: Using SAS Enterprise Miner*. SAS Institute, Cary.

Díaz-Uriarte, R., and Alvarez de Andrés, S. (2006) Gene selection and classification of microarray data using random forest. *BMC Bioinformatics*, 7, 3.

Dietterich, T.G. (2000) An experimental comparison of three methods for constructing ensembles of decision trees: Bagging, boosting, and randomization. *Machine Learning*, 40(2), 139–157.

Drucker, H., Burges, C.J., Kaufman, L., Smola, A.J., and Vapnik, V. (1997) Support vector regression machines. In *Conference on Advances in Neural Information Processing Systems*, San Diego, pp. 155–161.

Duda, R.O., Hart, P.E., and Sytork, D.G. (2001) *Pattern Classification*, 2nd ed. John Wiley & Sons, Hoboken, NJ.

Friedman, J., Hastie, T., and Tibshirani, R. (2001) *The Elements of Statistical Learning*, vol. 1. Springer Series in Statistics New York, NY.

Geladi, P., and Kowalski, B.R. (1986) Partial least-squares regression: A tutorial. *Analytica Chimica Acta*, 185, 1–17.

Hastie, T., Tibshirani, R., and Friedman, J. (2000) *The Elements of Statistical Learning*. Springer Series in Statistics, Berlin, Heidelberg.

He, Q. (1999) A review of clustering algorithms as applied to IR. Technical Report UIUCLIS– 1999/6+IRG, University of Illinois at Urbana-Champaign.

Hehn, T.M., and Hamprecht, F.A. (2018) End-to-end learning of deterministic decision trees. *In German Conference on Pattern Recognition*, Berlin, Springer, pp. 612–627.

Ho, T.K. (1995) Random decision forests. *Proceedings of the 3rd International Conference on Document Analysis and Recognition*, Montreal, QC, 14–16 August 1995, pp. 278–282.

Hyafil, L., and Rivest, R.L. (1976) Constructing optimal binary decision trees is NP-complete. *Information Processing Letters*, 5(1), 15–17.

Jain, A.K., Murthy, M.N., and Flynn, P.J. (1999) Data clustering, a review. *ACM Computing Surveys*, 31(3), 265–323.

Jordan, M.I. (1994) A statistical approach to decision tree modeling. *In Proceedings of the Seventh Annual Conference on Computational Learning Theory*, COLT'94, New York, NY, pp. 13–20.x

Karthikeyan, T., and Ravikumar, N. (2014) A survey on association rule mining. *International Journal of Advanced Research in Computer and Communication Engineering*, 3(1), 2278–1021.

Kohavi, R., and John, G. (1997) Wrappers for feature subset selection. *Artificial Intelligence*, 97(1–2), 273–324.

Kuhn, M., and Johnson, K. (2013) *Applied Predictive Modeling*, vol. 26. Springer, Berlin, Heidelberg.

Kutner, M.H., Nachtsheim, C.J., Neter, J., and Li, W. (2005) *Applied Linear Statistical Models*, 5th ed. McGraw Hill, New York.

LeCun, Y., Bengio, Y., and Hinton, G. (2015) Deep learning. *Nature*, 521(7553), 436–444.

Linde, Y., Buzo, A., and Gray, R.M. (1980) An algorithm for vector quantizer design. *IEEE Transaction Communications*, COM-28(1), 84–95.

Montillo, A., Tu, J., Shotton, J., Winn, J., Iglesias, J., Metaxas, D., and Criminisi, A. (2013) Entanglement and differentiable information gain maximization, Chapter 19. In: Criminisi, A. and Shotton, J. (eds), *Decision Forests for Computer Vision and Medical Image Analysis*, pp. 273–293). Springer, Berlin, Heidelberg.

Prinzie, A., and Van den Poel, D. (2008) Random forests for multiclass classification: Random MultiNomial Logit. *Expert Systems with Applications*, 34(3), 1721–1732.

Puterman, M.L. (2014) *Markov Decision Processes: Discrete Stochastic Dynamic Programming*. John Wiley & Sons, Hoboken, NJ.

Quinlan, J.R. (1986) Induction of decision trees. *Machine Learning*, 1(1), 81–106.

Rakhmetulayeva, S.B., Duisebekova, K.S., Mamyrbekov, A.M., Kozhamzharova, D.K., Astaubayeva, G.N., and Stamkulova, K. (2018) Application of classification algorithm based on SVM for determining the effectiveness of treatment of tuberculosis. *Procedia Computer Science*, 130, 231–238. doi: 10.1016/j.procs.2018.04.034.

Rangarajan, L., and Nagabhushan, P. (2005) Linear regression for dimensionality reduction and classification of multi dimensional data. In: Pal, S.K., Bandyopadhyay, S., and Biswas S. (eds), *Pattern Recognition and Machine Intelligence*. PReMI 2005. Lecture Notes in Computer Science, vol. 3776. Springer, Berlin, Heidelberg. doi: 10.1007/11590316_25.

Rokach, L. (2016) Decision forest: Twenty years of research. *Information Fusion*, 27, 111–125.

Shi, T., and Horvath, S. (2006) Unsupervised learning with random forest predictors. *Journal of Computational and Graphical Statistics*, 15(1), 118–138. doi: 10.1198/106186006X94072.

Skiena, S.S. (2017) Linear and Logistic Regression. In: *The Data Science Design Manual*. Texts in Computer Science. Springer, Cham. doi: 10.1007/978-3-319-55444-0_9.

Uyanık, G.K., and Güler, N. (2013) A study on multiple linear regression analysis. *Procedia - Social and Behavioral Sciences*, 106, 234–240. doi: 10.1016/j.sbspro.2013.12.027.

Vapnik, V.N. (1995) *Statistical Learning Theory*. Springer, New York.

Xu, T., Duy Le, T., Liu, L., Su, N., Wang, R., Sun, B., Colaprico, A., Bontempi, G., and Li, J. (2017) CancerSubtypes: An R/Bioconductor package for molecular cancer subtype identification, validation, and visualization. *Bioinformatics*, 33(19), 3131–3133.

Yahiaoui, O. Er, and Yumusak, N. (2017) A new method of automatic recognition for tuberculosis disease diagnosis using support vector machines. *Biomedical Research*, 28(9), 1–9.

Zhang, Y. (2012) Support vector machine classification algorithm and its application. In: Liu, C., Wang, L., and Yang, A. (eds), *Information Computing and Applications*. ICICA 2012. Communications in Computer and Information Science, vol. 308. Springer, Berlin, Heidelberg. doi: 10.1007/978-3-642-34041-3_27.

Zhang, Y., Zhu, Y., Lin, S., and Liu, X. (2011) *Application of Least Squares Support Vector Machine in Fault Diagnosis*. In: Liu, C., Chang, J., and Yang, A. (eds.) ICICA 2011, Part II. CCIS, vol. 244, pp. 192–200. Springer, Heidelberg.

datascienceschool.net.

Abdulhammed, R., Musafer, H., Alessa, A., Faezipour, M., and Abuzneid, A. (2019). Features dimensionality reduction approaches for machine learning based network intrusion detection. *Electronics*, 8(3), 322.

hirogosomewhere.com.

http://cs.uef.fi/sipu/pub/MSc_JarkkoPiiroinen.pdf.

http://www.ee.columbia.edu/~vittorio/UnsupervisedLearning.pdf.

http://www.hnhdqp.com/.

http://www.incompleteideas.net/book/RLbook2020.pdf.

https://blog.clairvoyantsoft.com/eigen-decomposition-and-pca-c50f4ca15501.

https://heartbeat.fritz.ai/understanding-the-mathematics-behind-k-means-clustering-40e1d55e2f4c.
https://ieeexplore.ieee.org/document/7837907.
https://towardsdatascience.com/selecting-the-best-machine-learning-algorithm-for-your-regression-problem-20c330bad4ef.
https://www.datacamp.com/community/tutorials/introduction-factor-analysis.
https://www.datasciencee.org/post/data-science-life-cycle.
https://www.displayr.com/what-is-hierarchical-clustering/.
https://www.ibm.com/cloud/learn/data-science-introduction#toc-data-scien-92g2jgm.
https://www.javatpoint.com/reinforcement-learning#Approaches.
https://www.jmlr.org/papers/volume3/guyon03a/guyon03a.pdf.
https://www.kaggle.com/datasets?datasetsOnly=true.
https://www.kaggle.com/datasets?tags=13302-Classification.
https://www.python-course.eu/linear_discriminant_analysis.php.
https://www.researchgate.net/publication/316994943_Linear_discriminant_analysis_A_detailed_tutorial.
https://www.visiondummy.com/2014/05/feature-extraction-using-pca.
incompleteideas.net.
jonathonbechtel.com.
machinelearningmastery.com.
medium.com.
myditto.tistory.com.

Index